Who Wrote the Bible?

by Washington Gladden

Copyright©2018 by Ashed Phoenix Library

All rights reserved.

Ashed Phoenix Library

All Rights Reserved ©2018 Ashed Phoenix.
First Printing: 2018.

The editorial arrangement, analysis, professional commentary and glossary are subject to this copyright notice. No portion of this book may be copied, retransmitted, reposted, duplicated, or otherwise used without the express written approval of the author, except by reviewers who may quote brief excerpts in connection with a review.

United States laws and regulations are public domain and not subject to copyright. Any unauthorized copying, reproduction, translation, or distribution of any part of this material without permission by the author is prohibited and against the law.

Disclaimer and Terms of Use: No information contained in this book should be considered as financial, tax, or legal advice. Your reliance upon information and content obtained by you at or through this publication is solely at your own risk. Teumessian Fox Library or the authors assume no liability or responsibility for damage or injury to you, other persons, or property arising from any use of any product, information, idea, or instruction contained in the content or services provided to you through this book. Reliance upon information contained in this material is solely at the reader's own risk. The authors have no financial interest in and receive no compensation from manufacturers of products or websites mentioned in this book.

Created in the United States of America

Who Wrote the Bible?

BY

Washington Gladden

Contents.

I. A Look Into the Hebrew Bible
II. What Did Moses Write?
III. Sources of the Pentateuch
IV. The Earlier Hebrew Histories
V. The Hebrew Prophecies
VI. The Later Hebrew Histories
VII. The Poetical Books
VIII. The Earlier New Testament Writings
IX. The Origin of the Gospels
X. New Testament History and Prophecy
XI. The Canon
XII. How the Books Were Written
XIII. How Much Is the Bible Worth?

Who Wrote the Bible?

Chapter I.

A Look Into the Hebrew Bible.

The aim of this volume is to put into compact and popular form, for the benefit of inte readers, the principal facts upon which scholars are now generally agreed concerning thi history of the Bible. The doctrines taught in the Bible will not be discussed; its clai supernatural origin will not be the principal matter of inquiry; the book will concern itse with those purely natural and human agencies which have been employed in writing, transc editing, preserving, transmitting, translating, and publishing the Bible.

The writer of this book has no difficulty in believing that the Bible contains supei

ELEMENTS. HE IS READY TO AFFIRM THAT OTHER THAN NATURAL FORCES HAVE BEEN EMPLOYED IN PROD It is to these superhuman elements in it that reference and appeal are most frequently made. But the BIBLE HAS A NATURAL HISTORY ALSO. IT IS A BOOK AMONG BOOKS. IT IS A PHENOMENON AMONG PHENO ITS ORIGIN AND GROWTH IN THIS WORLD CAN BE STUDIED AS THOSE OF ANY OTHER NATURAL OBJEC STUDIED. THE OLD APPLE-TREE GROWING IN MY GARDEN IS THE WITNESS TO ME OF SOME TRANSCENDENT THE SHRINE OF MYSTERIES THAT I CANNOT UNRAVEL. WHAT THE LIFE IS THAT WAS HIDDEN IN THE SI WHICH IT SPRANG, AND THAT HAS SHAPED ALL ITS GROWTH, COÖRDINATING THE FORCES OF NAT PRODUCING THIS INDIVIDUAL FORM AND THIS PARTICULAR VARIETY OF FRUIT,--THIS I DO NOT KNOW. TH QUESTIONS HERE THAT NO MAN OF SCIENCE CAN ANSWER. LIFE IN THE SEED OF THE APPLE AS WELL AS IN ' OF MAN IS A MYSTERY. BUT THERE ARE SOME THINGS ABOUT THE APPLE-TREE THAT MAY BE KNOWN. KNOW--IF ANY ONE HAS BEEN CURIOUS ENOUGH TO KEEP THE RECORD--WHEN THE SEED WAS PLANTED, WH SHOOT FIRST APPEARED ABOVE THE GROUND, HOW MANY BRANCHES IT HAD WHEN IT WAS FIVE YEARS OLI HIGH IT WAS WHEN IT WAS TEN YEARS OLD, WHEN THIS LIMB AND THAT TWIG WERE ADDED, WHEN TH BLOSSOM APPEARED, WHEN THAT BRANCH WAS GRAFTED AND THOSE OTHERS WERE TRIMMED OFF. A KNOWLEDGE I MAY HAVE GAINED; AND IN SETTING FORTH THESE FACTS, OR SUCH AS THESE, CONCERN NATURAL HISTORY OF THE TREE, I DO NOT ASSUME THAT I AM TELLING ALL ABOUT THE LIFE THAT IS IN MANNER WE MAY STUDY THE ORIGIN AND GROWTH OF THE BIBLE WITHOUT ATTEMPTING TO DECIDE THI questions concerning the inspiration of its writers and the meaning of the truths they reveal.

THAT THE BIBLE HAS A NATURAL AS WELL AS A SUPERNATURAL HISTORY IS EVERYWHERE ASSUMED U PAGES. IT WAS WRITTEN AS OTHER BOOKS ARE WRITTEN, AND IT WAS PRESERVED AND TRANSMITTED A BOOKS ARE PRESERVED AND TRANSMITTED. IT DID NOT COME INTO BEING IN ANY SUCH MARVELOUS WAY . IN WHICH JOSEPH SMITH'S "BOOK OF MORMON," FOR EXAMPLE, IS SAID TO HAVE BEEN PRODUCED. THE S IS, THAT AN ANGEL APPEARED TO SMITH AND TOLD HIM WHERE HE WOULD FIND THIS BOOK; THAT HE WEN SPOT DESIGNATED, AND FOUND IN A STONE BOX A VOLUME SIX INCHES THICK, COMPOSED OF THIN GOLD EIGHT INCHES BY SEVEN, HELD TOGETHER BY THREE GOLD RINGS; THAT THESE PLATES WERE COVERED WI IN THE "REFORMED EGYPTIAN" TONGUE, AND THAT WITH THIS BOOK WERE "THE URIM AND THE THUMM PAIR OF SUPERNATURAL SPECTACLES, BY MEANS OF WHICH HE WAS ABLE TO *read* *translate* THIS "REFORMED EGYPTIAN" LANGUAGE. THIS IS THE SORT OF STORY WHICH HAS BEEN BELIEVED, IN THIS NINETEENTH CEN TENS OF THOUSANDS OF MORMON VOTARIES. CONCERNING THE BOOKS OF THE BIBLE NO SUCH ASTC STORIES ARE TOLD. NEVERTHELESS SOME GOOD PEOPLE SEEM INCLINED TO THINK THAT IF SUCH STORIE TOLD, THEY MIGHT WELL BE; THEY IMAGINE THAT THE BIBLE MUST HAVE ORIGINATED IN A MANNER MIRACULOUS; AND THOUGH THEY KNOW VERY LITTLE ABOUT ITS ORIGIN, THEY CONCEIVE OF IT AS A BOOK WRITTEN IN HEAVEN IN THE ENGLISH TONGUE, DIVIDED THERE INTO CHAPTERS AND VERSES, WITH HEAD I REFERENCE MARKS, PRINTED IN SMALL PICA, BOUND IN CALF, AND SENT DOWN TO EARTH BY ANGELS IN ITS FORM. WHAT I DESIRE TO SHOW IS, THAT THE WORK OF PUTTING THE BIBLE INTO ITS PRESENT FORM DONE IN HEAVEN, BUT ON EARTH; THAT IT WAS NOT DONE BY ANGELS, BUT BY MEN; THAT IT WAS NOT DO ONCE, BUT A LITTLE AT A TIME, THE WORK OF PREPARING AND PERFECTING IT EXTENDING OVER SEVERAL AND EMPLOYING THE LABORS OF MANY MEN IN DIFFERENT LANDS AND LONG-DIVIDED GENERATIONS. A history of the Bible as a book, and of the natural and human agencies employed in producing it, will prove, I trust, of much interest to those who care to study it.

MR. HUXLEY HAS WRITTEN A DELIGHTFUL TREATISE ON "A PIECE OF CHALK," AND ANOTHER CRAYFISH;" A FRENCH WRITER HAS PRODUCED AN ENTERTAINING VOLUME ENTITLED "THE STORY OF A ST BOOKS OF THE BIBLE, CONSIDERED FROM A SCIENTIFIC OR BIBLIOGRAPHICAL POINT OF VIEW, SHOULD RE study not less richly than such simple, natural objects.

A GREAT AMOUNT OF STUDY HAS BEEN EXPENDED OF LATE ON THE SCRIPTURES, AND THE CONC REACHED BY THIS STUDY ARE OF IMMENSE IMPORTANCE. WHAT IS CALLED THE HIGHER CRITICISM HA BUSY SCANNING THESE OLD WRITINGS, AND TRYING TO FIND OUT ALL ABOUT THEM. WHAT IS THE CRITICISM? IT IS THE ATTEMPT TO LEARN FROM THE SCRIPTURES THEMSELVES THE TRUTH ABOUT THEIR CONSISTS IN A CAREFUL STUDY OF THE LANGUAGE OF THE BOOKS, OF THE MANNERS AND CUSTOMS REFER THEM, OF THE HISTORICAL FACTS MENTIONED BY THEM; IT COMPARES PART WITH PART, AND BOOK WITH BO DISCOVER AGREEMENTS, IF THEY EXIST, AND DISCREPANCIES, THAT THEY MAY BE RECONCILED. THIS CRITICISM HAS SUBJECTED THESE OLD WRITINGS TO SUCH AN ANALYSIS AND INSPECTION AS NO OTHER \

have ever undergone. Some of this work has undoubtedly been destructive. It has started (the assumption that these books are in no respect different from other sacred books; that no more a revelation from God than the Zendavesta or the Nibelungen Lied is a revelati God; and it has bent its energies to discrediting, in every way, the veracity and the authori Scriptures. But much of this criticism has been thoroughly candid and reverent, even cons in its temper and purpose. It has not been unwilling to look at the facts; but it has held to Bible a devout and sympathetic attitude; it believes it to contain, as no other book in th contains, the message of God to men; and it has only sought to learn from the Bible itself message has been conveyed. It is this conservative criticism whose leadership will be follo these studies. No conclusions respecting the history of these writings will be stated which accepted by conservative scholars. Nevertheless it must be remembered that the resi conservative scholarship have been very imperfectly reported to the laity of the churchi facts about the Bible are now known by intelligent ministers of which their congregation hear. An anxious and not unnatural feeling has prevailed that the faith of the people in would be shaken if the facts were known. The belief that the truth is the safest thing in t and that the things which cannot be shaken will remain after it is all told, has led to the p of this volume.

I have no doubt, however, that some of the statements which follow will fall upon some minds with a shock of surprise. The facts which will be brought to light will conflict very shar some of the traditional theories about the Bible. Some of my readers may be inclined to f the foundations of faith are giving way. Let me, at the outset, request all such to suspe judgment and read the book through before they come to such a conclusion. Doubtless it necessary to make some readjustment of theories; to look at the Bible less as a miraculous a as a spiritual product; to put less emphasis upon the letter and more upon the spirit; but a this is done it may appear that the Bible is worth more to us than it ever was before, beca have learned how rightly to value it.

The word "Bible" is not a biblical word. The Old Testament writings were in the hands men who wrote the books of the New Testament, but they do not call these writings the Bi name them the Scriptures, the Holy Scriptures, the Sacred Writings, or else they refer under the names that were given to specific parts of them, as the Law, the Prophets, or the Our word Bible comes from a word which began to be applied to the sacred writings as a about four hundred years after Christ. It is a Greek plural noun, meaning the books, or books. These writings were called by this plural name for about eight hundred years; it was the thirteenth century that they began to be familiarly spoken of as a single book. This fact is instructive. For though a certain spiritual unity does pervade these sacred writings, yet t collection of books, rather than one book. The early Christians, who honored and priz sufficiently, always spoke of them as "The Books," rather than as "The Book,"--and their na more accurate than ours.

The names Old and New Testament are Bible words; that is to say we find the names i English Bibles, though they are not used to describe these books. Paul calls the old dispens old covenant; and that phrase came into general use among the early Christians as contra the Christian dispensation which they called the new covenant; therefore Greek-speaking C used to talk about "the books of the old covenant," and "the books of the new covenant; and by they shortened the phrase and sometimes called the two collections simply "Old Co and "New Covenant." When the Latin-speaking Christians began to use the same terms translated the Greek word "covenant" by the word "testament" which means a will, and whi not fairly convey the sense of the Greek word. And so it was that these two collections writings began to be called The Old Testament and The New Testament. It is the former (that we are first to study.

When Jesus Christ was on the earth he often quoted in his discourses from the Scriptures, and referred to them in his conversations. His apostles and the other New Te writers also quote freely from the same Scriptures, and books of the early Christian Fathei of references to them. What were these Jewish Scriptures?

At the time when our Lord was on the earth, the sacred writings of the Jews were coll two different forms. The Palestinian collection, so called, was written in the Hebrew lang the Alexandrian collection, called the Septuagint, in the Greek. For many years a large devout and learned Jews had lived in Alexandria; and as the Greek language was spoken th had become their common speech, they translated their sacred writings into Greek. This tra soon came into general use, because there were everywhere many Jews who knew Greek enough but knew no Hebrew at all. When our Lord was on earth, the Hebrew was a dead lan it may have been the language of the temple, as Latin is now the language of the Roman C mass; but the common people did not understand it; the vernacular of the Palestinian Jews Aramaic, a language similar to the Hebrew, sometimes called the later Hebrew, and havin such relation to it as the English has to the German tongue. There is some dispute as to when the Jews lost the use of their own language and adopted the Aramaic; many of the historians hold the view that the people who came back from the captivity to Jerusalem had to use the Aramaic as their common speech, and that the Hebrew Scriptures had to be inte when they were read to them. Others think that this change in language took place a littl that it resulted in great measure from the close intercourse of the Jews with the peopl about them in Palestine, most of whom used the Aramaic. At any rate the change had tak before the coming of Christ, so that no Hebrew was then spoken familiarly in Palestine. Wh Hebrew tongue" is mentioned in the New Testament it is the Aramaic that is meant, and n ancient Hebrew. The Greek, on the other hand, was a living language; it was spoken on the and in the markets everywhere, and many Jews understood it almost as well as they di Aramaic vernacular, just as many of the people of Constantinople and the Levant now speak French more fluently than their native tongues. The Greek version of the Scriptures was, for th more freely used by the Jews even in Palestine than the Hebrew original; it was from the Se that Christ and his apostles made most of their quotations. Out of three hundred and fift in the New Testament from the Old Testament writings about three hundred appear to be from the Greek version made at Alexandria. Between these two collections of sacred writ one written in Hebrew, then a dead language, and the other in Greek,--the one used by only, and the other by the common people,--there were some important differences, not onl phraseology and in the arrangement of the books, but in the contents themselves. Of the speak more fully in the following chapters. It is to the Hebrew collection, which is the or these writings, and from which our English Old Testament was translated, that we shall our attention. What were these Hebrew Scriptures of which all the writers of the New T knew, and from which they sometimes directly quote?

The contents of this collection were substantially if not exactly the same as those o Testament, but they were arranged in very different order. Indeed they were regarded distinct groups of writings, rather than as one book, and the three groups were of differen of sacredness and authority. Two of these divisions are frequently referred to in t Testament, as The Law and The Prophets; and the threefold division is doubtfully hinted at xxiv. 44, where our Lord speaks of the predictions concerning himself which are found in t and the Prophets and in the Psalms.

The first of these holy books of the Jews was, tThe, Law contained in the first five boo of our Bible, known among us as the Pentateuch, and called by the Jews sometimes simply Law," and sometimes "The Law of Moses." This was supposed to be the oldest portion of t Scriptures, and was by them regarded as much more sacred and authoritative than any portion. To Moses, they, said, God spake face to face; to the other holy men much less dis Consequently their appeal is most often to the law of Moses.

The group of writings known as "The Prophets" is subdivided into the Earlier and the Prophets.*The Earlier Prophets* comprise Joshua, the Judges, the two books of Samuel, counte one, and the two books of the Kings, counted also as TheeL*ater Prophets* comprise Isaiah, Jeremiah, Ezekiel, and the twelve Minor Prophets, the last books in our Old Testament,-

Joel, Amos, Obadiah, Jonah, Micah, Nahum, Habakkuk, Zephaniah, Haggai, Zechariah, Malachi. These twelve *were counted as one book*; so that there were four volumes of the earlier and four of the later prophets. Why the Jews should have called Joshua, Judges, Samuel, and the books of the Prophets is not clear; perhaps because they were supposed to have been writt prophets; perhaps because prophets have a conspicuous place in their histories. This portion o Hebrew Scriptures, containing the four historical books named and the fifteen prophetic (reckoned, however, as four), was regarded by the Jews as standing next in sacredness and v the book of the Law.

The third group of their Scriptures was known among them as Kethubim, or Writings, si Sometimes, possibly, they called it The Psalms, because the book of the Psalms was the initia of the collection. It consisted of the Psalms, the Proverbs, Job, the Song of Solomo Lamentations, Ecclesiastes, Esther, Daniel, Ezra, Nehemiah, and the Chronicles. This gr writings was esteemed by the Jews as less sacred and authoritative than either of the ot groups; the authors were supposed to have had a smaller measure of inspiration. Respecting t three of these books there was also some dispute among the rabbis, as to their right to be r as sacred Scripture.

Such, then, were the Hebrew Scriptures in the days of our Lord, and such was the man their arrangement.

They had, indeed, other books of a religious character, to which reference is sometim in the books of the Bible. In Numbers xxi. 14, 15, we have a brief war song quoted from "The I of the Wars of Jehovah," a collection of which we have no other knowledge. In Joshua x. story of the sun standing still over Gibeon is said to have been quoted from "The Book of and in 2 Samuel i. 18, the beautiful "Song of the Bow," written by David on the death of Sa Jonathan, is said to be contained in the "Book of Jasher." It is evident that this must have collection of lyrics celebrating some of the great events of Hebrew history. The title seem "The Book of the Just." The exploits of the worthies of Israel probably furnished its pi theme.

In 1 Chronicles xxix. 29, we read: "Now the acts of David the king, first and last, beho are written in the History of Samuel the Seer, and in the History of Nathan the Prophet, a History of Gad the Seer." There is no reason to doubt that the first named of these is th contained in the books of Samuel in our Bible; but the other two books are lost. We have reference to the "History of Nathan," in 2 Chronicles ix. 29,--the concluding words of the King Solomon's life. "Now the rest of the acts of Solomon, first and last, are they not writ History of Nathan the Prophet, and in the Prophecy of Abijah the Shilonite, and in the Vi Iddo the Seer concerning Jeroboam the son of Nebat?" Here are two more books of which w no other knowledge; their titles quoted upon the page of this chronicle are all that is left similar reference, in the last words of the sketch of Solomon's son Rehoboam, gives us o knowledge of the "Histories of Shemaiah the Prophet."

In the Kings and in the Chronicles, reference is repeatedly made to the "Books Chronicles of the Kings of Israel," and the "Books of the Chronicles of the Kings of Juda which titles volumes that are now lost are brought to our notice. Undoubtedly much of th in the biblical books of Kings and Chronicles was derived from these ancient annals. They sources from which the writers of these books drew their materials.

We are also told in 2 Chronicles xxvi. 22, that Isaiah wrote a history of the "Acts of which is wholly lost.

Other casual references are made to historical writings of various sorts, composed by pi and seers, and thus apparently accredited by the biblical writers as authoritative utterances truth. Why were they suffered to perish? Has not Emerson certified us that

"One accent of the Holy Ghost
The heedless world has never lost"?

But this is a fond exaggeration. Mr. Emerson was certainly not himself inspired wi uttered it. Many and many an accent of the Holy Ghost has been lost by this heedless worl is not at all improbable that some of these histories of Nathan and Gad and Shemaiah hi and precious truth,--truth that the world has needed. The very fact that they are hopel raises some curious questions about the method of revelation. Is it to be supposed th Providence which suffers whole books to be lost by men would infallibly guarantee tho remain against errors in the copies, and other imperfections? As a matter of fact, we know t has not so protected any of them.

Still I doubt not that Providence has kept for us the best of this Hebrew literature. To it is the best literature that the world has produced is to say very little. It is separated wi all other sacred writings. Its constructive ideas are as far above those of the other books c as the heavens are above the earth. I pity the man who has had the Bible in his hand fro infancy, and who has learned in his maturer years something of the literature of the other but who now needs to have this statement verified. True it is that we find pure maxims, el thoughts, genuine faith, lofty morality, in many of the Bibles of the other races. True it some of them visions are vouchsafed us of the highest truths of religion, of the very subs the gospel of the Son of God. But when we take the sacred books of the other religions entirety, and compare them with the sacred writings of the Hebrews, the superiority of t their fundamental ideas, in the conceptions that dominate them, in the grand uplifting vis purposes that vitalize them, can be felt by any man who has any discernment of spiritual real is in these great ideas that the value of these writings consists, and not in any petty infal phrase, or inerrancy of statement. They are the record, as no other book in the world is a r that increasing purpose of God which runs through the ages. I hope that it will appear as th of our studies, that one may continue to reverence the Scriptures as containing a unique an revelation from God to men, and yet clearly see and frankly acknowledge the facts concer origin, and the human and fallible elements in them, which are not concealed, but lie upo very face.

Chapter II.

What Did Moses Write?

We are now to study the first five books of the Bible, known as the Pentateuch. Thi "Pentateuch" is not in the Bible; it is a Greek word signifying literally the Five-fold Wo *penta*, five, and *teuchos*, which in the later Greek means roll or volume.

The Jews in the time of our Lord always considered these five books as one connected they called the whole sometimes "Torah," or "The Law," sometimes "The Law of Mo sometimes "The Five-fifths of the Law." It was originally one book, and it is not easy to det at what time its division into five parts took place.

Later criticism is also inclined to add to the Pentateuch the Book of Joshua, and to say that the first six books of the Bible were put into their present form by the same hand. "The Hexateu Six-fold Work, has taken the place in these later discussions of the Pentateuch, or Five-fo Doubtless there is good reason for the new classification, but it will be more convenient with the traditional division and speak first of the five books reckoned by the later Jew "Torah," or the Five-fifths of the Law.

Who wrote these books? Our modern Hebrew Bibles give them the general "*Quinque*

Libri Mosis." This means "The Five Books of Moses." But Moses could never have given them title, for these are Latin words, and it is not possible that Moses should have used th language because there was no Latin language in the world until many hundreds of years a day of Moses. The Latin title was given to them, of course, by the editors who compiled the preface and the explanatory notes in these Hebrew Bibles are also written in Latin.

But over this Latin title in the Hebrew Bible is the Hebrew word "Torah." This was the by which these books were chiefly known among the Jews; it signifies simply "The Law." This gives us no information, then, concerning the authorship of these books.

When we look at our English Bibles we find no separation, as in the Hebrew Bible, of five books from the rest of the Old Testament writings, but we find over each one of them a title by which it is ascribed to Moses as its author,--"The First Book of Moses, commonly called Ge "The Second Book of Moses, commonly called Exodus;" and so on. But when I look int Hebrew Bible again no such title is there. Nothing is said about Moses in the Hebrew t Genesis.

It is certain that if Moses wrote these books he did not call them "Genesis," "Ex "Leviticus," "Numbers," "Deuteronomy;" for these words, again, come from languages th never heard. Four of them are Greek words, and one of them, Numbers, is a Latin word. names were given to the several books at a very late day. What are their names in the Hebre Each of them is called by the first word, or some of the first words in the book. The Jews w to name their books, as we name our hymns, by the initial word or words; thus they called t of these five books, "Bereshith," "In the Beginning;" the second one "Veelleh Shemoth," these are the names;" the third one "Vayikra," "And he called," and so on. The titles in our Bible are much more significant and appropriate than these original Hebrew titles; thus signifies origin, and Genesis is the Book of Origins; Exodus means departure, and the describes the departure of Israel from Egypt; Leviticus points out the fact that the book i occupied with the Levitical legislation; Numbers gives a history of the numbering of the and Deuteronomy, which means the second law, contains what seems to be a recapitulatic reënactment of the legislation of the preceding books. But these English titles, which translated and partly transferred to English from older Latin and Greek titles, tell trustworthy about the authorship of the books.

How, then, you desire to know, did these books come to be known as the books of Moses?

"They were quoted," answer some, "and thus accredited by our Lord and his apostles. They are frequently mentioned in the New Testament as inspired and authoritative books; they are to as the writings of Moses; we have the testimony of Jesus Christ and of his apostles t genuineness and authenticity." Let us see how much truth this answer contains. It confronts a very important matter which may as well be settled before we go on.

It is true, to begin with, that Jesus and the Evangelists do quote from these books, a they ascribe to Moses some of the passages which they quote. The soundest criticism c impugn the honesty or the intelligence of such quotations. There is good reason, as we shal believing that a large part of this literature was written in the time of Moses, and under t Moses, if not by his hand. In a certain important sense, which will be clearer to us as we go o literature is all Mosaic. The reference to it by the Lord and his apostles is therefore legitimate.

But this reference does by no means warrant the sweeping conclusion that the five b the law were all and entire from the pen of the Lawgiver. Our Lord nowhere says that the books of the Old Testament were all written by Moses. Much less does he teach that the co these books are all equally inspired and authoritative. Indeed he quotes from them several the express purpose of repudiating their doctrines and repealing their legislation. In the v front of his teaching stands a stern array of judgments in which undoubted commandments Mosaic law are expressly condemned and set aside, some of them because they are inadequa superficial, some of them because they are morally defective. "Ye have heard that it was them of old time" thus and thus; "but I say unto you"--and then follow words that i contradict the old legislation. After quoting two of the commandments of the Decal

GIVING THEM AN INTERPRETATION THAT WHOLLY TRANSFORMS THEM, HE PROCEEDS TO CITE SEVERAL FROM THESE MOSAIC BOOKS, IN ORDER TO SET HIS OWN WORD FIRMLY AGAINST THEM. ONE OF THESE A LAW OF THE DECALOGUE ITSELF. THERE CAN BE LITTLE DOUBT THAT THE THIRD COMMANDMENT IS QU CRITICISED BY OUR LORD, IN THIS DISCOURSE. THAT COMMANDMENT FORBIDS, NOT CHIEFLY PROFANI PERJURY; BY IMPLICATION IT PERMITS JUDICIAL OATHS. AND JESUS EXPRESSLY FORBIDS JUDICIAL OATHS. "S NOT AT ALL." I AM AWARE THAT THIS IS NOT THE USUAL INTERPRETATION OF THESE WORDS, BUT I BELIEVE THE ONLY MEANING THAT THE WORDS WILL BEAR. NOT TO INSIST UPON THIS, HOWEVER, SEVERAL OTHER I are given in the discourse concerning which there can be no question.

JESUS QUOTES THE LAW OF DIVORCE FROM DEUTERONOMY XXIV. 1,2. "WHEN A MAN TAKETH A WIF MARRIETH HER, THEN IT SHALL BE, IF SHE FIND NO FAVOUR IN HIS EYES, BECAUSE HE HATH FOUNI unseemly thing in her, that he shall write her a bill of divorcement, and give it in her hand, and send HER OUT OF HIS HOUSE. AND WHEN SHE IS DEPARTED OUT OF HIS HOUSE SHE MAY GO AND BE ANOTHER WIFE." THESE ARE THE WORDS OF A LAW WHICH MOSES IS REPRESENTED AS UTTERING BY THE AUTHO JEHOVAH. THIS LAW, AS THUS EXPRESSED, JESUS CHRIST UNQUALIFIEDLY REPEALS. "I SAY UNTO YOU THAT ONE THAT PUTTETH AWAY HIS WIFE, SAVING FOR THE CAUSE OF FORNICATION, MAKETH HER AN ADULTEI whosoever shall marry her when she is put away committeth adultery."

THE LAW OF REVENGE IS TREATED IN THE SAME WAY. "YE HAVE HEARD THAT IT WAS SAID, AN EYE EYE AND A TOOTH FOR A TOOTH." WHO SAID THIS? WAS IT SOME RABBIN OF THE OLDEN TIME? IT WAS NAY, THE OLD RECORD SAYS THAT THIS IS THE WORD OF THE LORD BY MOSES: "THE LORD SPAKE UNTO SAYING [AMONG OTHER THINGS], IF A MAN CAUSE A BLEMISH IN HIS NEIGHBOR, AS HE HATH DONE SO SHAI DONE TO HIM; BREACH FOR BREACH, EYE FOR EYE, TOOTH FOR TOOTH; AS HE HATH CAUSED A BLEMISH IN SO SHALL IT BE RENDERED UNTO HIM." (LEV. XXIV. 19,20.) SO IN EXODUS XXI. 24, "THOU SHALT GIVE LI LIFE, EYE FOR EYE, TOOTH FOR TOOTH, HAND FOR HAND, BURNING FOR BURNING, WOUND FOR WOUND, S STRIPE." IT IS SOMETIMES SAID THAT THESE RETALIATIONS WERE SIMPLY PERMITTED UNDER THE MOSAIC I THIS IS A GREAT ERROR; THEY WERE ENJOINED: "THINE EYE SHALL NOT PITY," IT IS SAID IN ANOTHER PLAC XIX. 21); "LIFE SHALL GO FOR LIFE, EYE FOR EYE, TOOTH FOR TOOTH, HAND FOR HAND, FOOT FOR FOOT." RETALIATION IS AN INTEGRAL PART OF THE MORAL LEGISLATION OF THE PENTATEUCH. IT IS NO PA CEREMONIAL LAW; IT IS AN ETHICAL RULE. IT IS CLEARLY ASCRIBED TO MOSES; IT IS DISTINCTLY SAID TO I ENACTED BY COMMAND OF GOD. BUT CHRIST IN THE MOST UNHESITATING MANNER CONDEMNS countermands it.

"YE HAVE HEARD," HE CONTINUES, "THAT IT WAS SAID, THOU SHALT LOVE THY NEIGHBOR AND HAT ENEMY; BUT I SAY UNTO YOU, LOVE YOUR ENEMIES, AND PRAY FOR THEM THAT PERSECUTE YOU." "BUT TH IS OBJECTED, "IS NOT A QUOTATION FROM THE OLD TESTAMENT. THESE WORDS DO NOT OCCUR IN T LEGISLATION." AT ANY RATE JESUS INTRODUCES THEM WITH THE VERY SAME FORMULA WHICH HE HAS A BEEN APPLYING TO THE WORDS WHICH HE HAS QUOTED FROM THE MOSAIC LAW. IT IS EVIDENT THAT HE M GIVE THE IMPRESSION THAT THEY ARE PART OF THAT LAW. HE IS NOT CAREFUL IN ANY OF THESE CASES THE EXACT WORDS OF THE LAW, BUT HE DOES GIVE THE MEANING OF IT. HE GIVES THE EXACT MEANII HERE. THE MOSAIC LAW COMMANDED JEWS TO LOVE THEIR NEIGHBORS, MEMBERS OF THEIR OWN TRIBE, I HATE THE PEOPLE OF SURROUNDING TRIBES: "AN AMMONITE OR A MOABITE SHALL NOT ENTER IN ASSEMBLY OF THE LORD; EVEN TO THE TENTH GENERATION SHALL NONE BELONGING TO THEM ENTE ASSEMBLY OF THE LORD FOR EVER.... THOU SHALT NOT SEEK THEIR PEACE NOR THEIR PROSPERITY ALL THY ever." (Deut. xxiii. 3-6.)

"WHEN THE LORD THY GOD SHALL BRING THEE INTO THE LAND WHITHER THOU GOEST TO POSSE SHALT CAST OUT MANY NATIONS BEFORE THEE, ... THEN THOU SHALT UTTERLY DESTROY THEM; THOU SHAI COVENANT WITH THEM, NOR SHOW MERCY UNTO THEM." (DEUT. VII. 1,2.) THIS IS THE SPIRIT OF MUCH O ANCIENT LEGISLATION; AND THESE LAWS WERE, IF THE RECORD IS TRUE, LITERALLY EXECUTED, IN AFTE JOSHUA AND SAMUEL, UPON THE PEOPLE OF CANAAN. AND THESE BLOODY COMMANDS, ALBEIT THEY H "THUS SAID THE LORD" BEHIND EVERY ONE OF THEM, JESUS, IN THE GREAT DISCOURSE WHICH IS THE CHA his kingdom, distinctly repeals.

SUCH IS THE METHOD BY WHICH OUR LORD SOMETIMES DEALS WITH THE OLD TESTAMENT. IT IS MEANS TRUE THAT HE ASSUMES THIS ATTITUDE TOWARD ALL PARTS OF IT. SOMETIMES HE QUOTES LAWGI PROPHETS IN CONFIRMATION OF HIS OWN WORDS; OFTEN HE REFERS TO THESE ANCIENT SCRIPTURES AS PI

THE WAY FOR HIS KINGDOM AND FORESHADOWING HIS PERSON AND HIS WORK. NAY, HE EVEN SAYS OF TH WHICH WE ARE NOW STUDYING THAT NOT ONE JOT OR TITTLE SHALL IN ANY WISE PASS FROM IT TILL ALL ACCOMPLISHED. WHAT HE MEANS BY THAT WE SHALL BE ABLE BY AND BY TO DISCOVER. BUT THESE PA: WHICH I HAVE CITED MAKE IT CLEAR THAT JESUS CHRIST CANNOT BE APPEALED TO IN SUPPORT (traditional view of the nature of these old writings.

THE COMMON ARGUMENT BY WHICH CHRIST IS MADE A WITNESS TO THE AUTHENTICITY AND INF authority of the Old Testament runs as follows:

CHRIST QUOTES MOSES AS THE AUTHOR OF THIS LEGISLATION; THEREFORE MOSES MUST HAVE WRI whole Pentateuch.

Moses was an inspired prophet; therefore all the teaching of the Pentateuch must be infallible.

THE FACTS ARE, THAT JESUS NOWHERE TESTIFIES THAT MOSES WROTE THE WHOLE OF THE PENTATI THAT HE NOWHERE GUARANTEES THE INFALLIBILITY EITHER OF MOSES OR OF THE BOOK. ON THE CONTR/ aside as inadequate or morally defective certain laws which in this book are ascribed to Moses.

IT IS NEEDFUL, THUS, ON THE THRESHOLD OF OUR ARGUMENT, TO HAVE A CLEAR UNDERSTANDING R THE NATURE OF THE TESTIMONY BORNE BY OUR LORD AND HIS APOSTLES TO THIS ANCIENT LITERATURE. THIS THAT THE ADVOCATES OF THE TRADITIONAL VIEW OF THE OLD TESTAMENT WHOLLY RELY. "(AUTHORITY," THEY SAY; "THE NEW TESTAMENT WRITERS WERE INSPIRED; YOU ALL ADMIT THIS; NOW CHR THE NEW TESTAMENT WRITERS CONSTANTLY QUOTE THE SCRIPTURES OF THE OLD TESTAMENT AS INSPIRI AUTHORITATIVE. THEREFORE THEY MUST BE THE INFALLIBLE WORD OF GOD." TO THIS IT IS SUFFICIENT CHRIST AND THE APOSTLES DO QUOTE THE OLD TESTAMENT SCRIPTURES; THEY FIND A GREAT TRI INSPIRED AND INSPIRING TRUTH IN THEM, AND SO CAN WE; THEY RECOGNIZE THE FACT THAT THEY ARE OF RELATED TO THAT KINGDOM WHICH CHRIST CAME TO FOUND, AND THAT THEY RECORD THE EARLIER STA GREAT COURSE OF REVELATION WHICH CULMINATES IN CHRIST; BUT THEY NOWHERE PRONOUNCE ANY WRITINGS FREE FROM ERROR; THERE IS NOT A HINT OR SUGGESTION ANYWHERE IN THE NEW TESTAMENT OF THE WRITINGS OF THE OLD TESTAMENT ARE INFALLIBLE; AND CHRIST HIMSELF, AS WE HAVE SEEN WARNS HIS DISCIPLES THAT THEY DO NOT EVEN FURNISH A SAFE RULE OF MORAL CONDUCT. AFTER ATTEMPT TO PROVE THE INERRANCY OF THE OLD TESTAMENT BY SUMMONING AS WITNESSES THE WRITER New Testament may as well be abandoned.

BUT DID NOT JESUS SAY, "SEARCH THE SCRIPTURES, FOR IN THEM YE THINK YE HAVE ETERNAL LIFE, / ARE THEY THAT TESTIFY OF ME?" WELL, IF HE HAD SAID THAT, IT WOULD NOT PROVE THAT THE SCRIP SEARCHED WERE ERRORLESS. THE INJUNCTION WOULD HAVE ALL THE FORCE TO-DAY THAT IT EVER HAD. VERY PROFITABLY STUDY DOCUMENTS WHICH ARE FAR FROM INFALLIBLE. THIS WAS NOT, HOWEVER, WH LORD SAID. IF YOU WILL LOOK INTO YOUR REVISED VERSION YOU WILL SEE THAT HIS WORDS, ADDRESSEI JEWS, ARE NOT A COMMAND BUT AN ASSERTION: "YE SEARCH THE SCRIPTURES, FOR IN THEM YE THINK Y ETERNAL LIFE" (JOHN V. 39); IF YOU SEARCHED THEM CAREFULLY YOU WOULD FIND SOME TESTIMON CONCERNING ME. IT IS NOT AN INJUNCTION TO SEARCH THE SCRIPTURES; IT IS SIMPLY THE STATEMENT OF THAT THE JEWS TO WHOM HE WAS SPEAKING DID SEARCH THE SCRIPTURES, AND SEARCHED THEM AS people in our own time do, to very little purpose.

BUT DOES NOT PAUL SAY, IN HIS LETTER TO TIMOTHY, THAT "ALL SCRIPTURE IS GIVEN BY INSPIR/ GOD?" NO, PAUL DOES NOT SAY THAT. LOOK AGAIN AT YOUR REVISED VERSION (2 TIM. III. 16): "E SCRIPTURE INSPIRED OF GOD IS ALSO PROFITABLE FOR TEACHING, FOR REPROOF, FOR CORRECTION, FOR IN WHICH IS IN RIGHTEOUSNESS." EVERY WRITING INSPIRED OF GOD IS PROFITABLE READING. THAT IS THE statement.

BUT PAUL SAYS IN THE VERSES PRECEDING, THAT TIMOTHY HAD KNOWN FROM A CHILD THE ! WRITINGS WHICH WERE ABLE TO MAKE HIM WISE UNTO SALVATION THROUGH FAITH IN JESUS CHRIST. WA NOT, THEN, IN HIS HANDS, A VOLUME OR COLLECTION OF BOOKS, KNOWN AS THE SACRED WRITINGS, DEFINITE TABLE OF CONTENTS; AND DID NOT PAUL REFER TO THIS COLLECTION, AND IMPLY THAT ALL TH were inspired of God and profitable for the uses specified?

NO, THIS IS NOT THE PRECISE STATE OF THE CASE. THESE SACRED WRITINGS HAD NOT AT THIS TI GATHERED INTO A VOLUME BY THEMSELVES, WITH A FIXED TABLE OF CONTENTS. WHAT IS CALLED THE (THE OLD TESTAMENT HAD NOT YET BEEN FINALLY DETERMINED.[FOOTNOTE: SEE CHAPTER XI] THI INDEED, AS WE SAW IN THE LAST CHAPTER, TWO COLLECTIONS OF SACRED WRITINGS, ONE IN HEBREW /

OTHER IN GREEK. THE HEBREW COLLECTION WAS NOT AT THIS TIME DEFINITELY CLOSED; THERE W. DISPUTE AMONG THE PALESTINIAN JEWS AS TO WHETHER TWO OR THREE OF THE BOOKS WHICH IT NOW C SHOULD GO INTO IT; THAT DISPUTE WAS NOT CONCLUDED UNTIL HALF A CENTURY AFTER THE DEATH OF THE OTHER COLLECTION, AS I HAVE SAID, WAS IN THE GREEK LANGUAGE, AND IT INCLUDED, NOT ONLY TESTAMENT BOOKS, BUT THE BOOKS NOW KNOWN AS THE OLD TESTAMENT APOCRYPHA. THIS WAS COLLECTION, REMEMBER, MOST USED BY OUR LORD AND HIS APOSTLES. WHICH OF THESE COLLECTIONS THE HANDS OF TIMOTHY WE DO NOT CERTAINLY KNOW. BUT THE FATHER OF TIMOTHY WAS A GREEK, TH(MOTHER WAS A JEWESS; AND IT IS ALTOGETHER PROBABLE THAT HE HAD STUDIED FROM HIS CHILDH(GREEK VERSION OF THE OLD TESTAMENT WRITINGS. SHALL WE UNDERSTAND PAUL, THEN, AS CERTII AUTHENTICITY AND INFALLIBILITY OF THIS WHOLE COLLECTION? DOES HE MEAN TO SAY THAT THE SUSANNA" AND "BEL AND THE DRAGON," AND ALL THE REST OF THESE FABLES AND TALES, ARE PROF. TEACHING AND INSTRUCTION IN RIGHTEOUSNESS? THIS TEXT, SO INTERPRETED, EVIDENTLY PROVES TC DOUBTLESS PAUL DID MEAN TO COMMEND TO TIMOTHY THE OLD TESTAMENT SCRIPTURES AS CONT PRECIOUS AND SAVING TRUTH. BUT WE MUST NOT FORCE HIS LANGUAGE INTO ANY WHOLESALE INDORSE every letter and word, or even of every chapter and book of these old writings.

SO FAR, THEREFORE, AS OUR LORD HIMSELF AND HIS APOSTLES ARE CONCERNED, WE HAVE NO D JUDGMENT EITHER AS TO THE AUTHORSHIP OF THESE OLD WRITINGS OR AS TO THEIR ABSOLUTE FREED ERROR. THEY HANDLED THESE SCRIPTURES, QUOTED FROM THEM, FOUND INSPIRED TEACHING IN THEM; SCRIPTURES WHICH THEY CHIEFLY HANDLED, FROM WHICH THEY GENERALLY QUOTED, IN WHICH THEY FO inspired teaching, contained, as we know, worthless matter. It is not to be assumed that they did not KNOW THIS MATTER TO BE WORTHLESS; AND IF THEY KNEW THIS, IT IS NOT TO BE ASSERTED THAT THEY IN place upon the whole of it the stamp of their approval.

WE HAVE WANDERED SOMEWHAT FROM THE PATH OF OUR DISCUSSION, BUT IT WAS NECESSARY IN ORD DETERMINE THE SIGNIFICANCE OF THOSE REFERENCES TO THE OLD TESTAMENT WITH WHICH THE NEW T ABOUNDS. THE QUESTION BEFORE US IS, WHY DO WE BELIEVE THAT MOSES WROTE THE FIVE BOOKS WHIC HIS NAME IN OUR BIBLES? WE HAVE SEEN THAT THE NEW TESTAMENT WRITERS GIVE US NO DECISIVE TEST on this point. On what testimony is the belief founded?

DOUBTLESS IT RESTS WHOLLY ON THE TRADITIONS OF THE JEWS. SUCH WAS THE TRADITION PI AMONG THEM IN THE TIME OF OUR LORD. THEY BELIEVED THAT MOSES WROTE EVERY WORD OF THESE THAT GOD DICTATED THE SYLLABLES TO HIM AND THAT HE RECORDED THEM. BUT THE TRADITIONS OF T NOT, IN OTHER MATTERS, HIGHLY REGARDED BY CHRISTIANS. OUR LORD HIMSELF SPEAKS MORE THAN STERN CENSURE OF THESE TRADITIONS BY WHICH, AS HE CHARGES, THEIR MORAL SENSE WAS BLUNTED AND OF GOD WAS MADE OF NONE EFFECT. MANY OF THESE OLD TALES OF THEIRS WERE EXTREMELY CHILD TRADITION ASCRIBES, AS WE HAVE SEEN, TO MOSES THE AUTHORSHIP OF THE WHOLE PENTATEUCH; DECLARES THAT WHEN, DURING AN INVASION OF THE CHALDEANS, ALL THE BOOKS OF THE SCRIPTU DESTROYED BY FIRE, EZRA WROTE THEM ALL OUT FROM MEMORY, IN AN INCREDIBLY SHORT SPACE O ANOTHER TRADITION RELATES HOW THE SAME EZRA ONE DAY HEARD A DIVINE VOICE BIDDING HIM RET THE FIELD WITH FIVE SWIFT AMANUENSES,--"HOW HE THEN RECEIVED A FULL CUP, FULL AS IT WERE OF WA THE COLOR OF IT WAS LIKE FIRE, ... AND WHEN HE HAD DRANK OF IT, HIS HEART UTTERED UNDERSTAN WISDOM GREW IN HIS BREAST, FOR HIS SPIRIT STRENGTHENED HIS MEMORY, ... AND HIS MOUTH WAS OP AND SHUT NO MORE AND FOR FORTY DAYS AND NIGHTS HE DICTATED WITHOUT STOPPING TILL TWO HUN FOUR BOOKS WERE WRITTEN DOWN." [FOOTNOTE: 2 ESDRAS XIV. SEE, ALSO, STANLEY'S *Jewish Church*, III, 151.] THESE FABLES HAD WIDE CURRENCY AMONG THE JEWS; THEY WERE BELIEVED BY IRENÆUS, TERT AUGUSTINE, AND OTHERS OF THE GREAT FATHERS OF THE CHRISTIAN CHURCH; BUT THEY ARE NOT C THESE DAYS. IT IS EVIDENT THAT JEWISH TRADITION IS NOT ALWAYS TO BE TRUSTED. WE SHALL NEED SOM reason than this for believing that Moses was the author of the Pentateuch.

I DO NOT KNOW WHERE ELSE WE CAN GO FOR INFORMATION EXCEPT TO THE BOOKS THEMSELVES. A EXAMINATION OF THEM MAY THROW SOME LIGHT UPON THE QUESTION OF THEIR ORIGIN. A GREAT MULT scholars have been before us in their examination; what is their verdict?

FIRST WE HAVE THE VERDICT OF THE TRADITIONALISTS,--THOSE, I MEAN, WHO ACCEPT THE JEWISH TF AND BELIEVE WITH THE RABBINS THAT MOSES WROTE THE WHOLE OF THE FIRST FIVE BOOKS OF THE BIB WHO HOLD THIS THEORY ARE READY TO ADMIT THAT THERE MAY BE A FEW VERSES HERE AND THERE INT

INTO THE RECORD BY LATER SCRIBES; BUT THEY MAINTAIN THAT THE BOOKS IN THEIR SUBSTANCE ANI CAME IN THEIR PRESENT FORM FROM THE HANDS OF MOSES. THIS IS THE THEORY WHICH HAS BEEN GE received by the Christian church. It is held to-day by very few eminent Christian scholars.

OVER AGAINST THIS TRADITIONAL THEORY IS THE THEORY OF THE RADICAL AND DESTRUCTIVE C MOSES WROTE NOTHING AT ALL; THAT PERHAPS THE TEN COMMANDMENTS WERE GIVEN BY HIM, BUT ANYTHING MORE; THAT THESE BOOKS WERE NOT EVEN WRITTEN IN THE TIME OF MOSES, BUT HUNDREDS AFTER HIS DEATH. MOSES IS SUPPOSED TO HAVE LIVED ABOUT 1B00C.; THESE WRITINGS, SAY THE DESTRUCT CRITICS, WERE FIRST PRODUCED IN PART ABOUT B.C.., BUT WERE MAINLY WRITTEN AFTER THE EXILE (AI 444 B.C..), ALMOST A THOUSAND YEARS AFTER THE DEATH OF MOSES. "STRICT AND IMPARTIAL INVESTIGA SHOWN," SAYS DR. KNAPPERT, "THAT ... NOTHING IN THE WHOLE LAW REALLY COMES FROM MOSES H EXCEPT THE TEN COMMANDMENTS. AND EVEN THESE WERE NOT DELIVERED BY HIM IN THE SAME FORM FIND THEM NOW." [FOOTNOTE: *The Religion of Israel*, P. 9.] THIS IS, TO MY MIND, AN ASTOUNDING STATEMEN IT ILLUSTRATES THE LENGTHS TO WHICH DESTRUCTIVE CRITICISM CAN GO. AND I DARE SAY THAT WE SH OUR STUDY OF THESE BOOKS REASON FOR BELIEVING THAT SUCH VIEWS AS THESE ARE AS FAR ASTRAY ON side as those of the traditionalists are on the other.

Let us test these two theories by interrogating the books themselves.

FIRST, THEN, WE FIND UPON THE FACE OF THE RECORD SEVERAL REASONS FOR BELIEVING THAT TI cannot have come, in their present form, from the hand of Moses.

MOSES DIED IN THE WILDERNESS, BEFORE THE ISRAELITES REACHED THE PROMISED LAND, BEF Canaanites were driven out, and the land was divided among the tribes.

IT IS NOT LIKELY THAT HE WROTE THE ACCOUNT OF HIS OWN DEATH AND BURIAL WHICH WE FIND IN CHAPTER OF DEUTERONOMY. THERE ARE THOSE, IT IS TRUE, WHO ASSERT THAT MOSES WAS INSPIRED T THIS ACCOUNT OF HIS OWN FUNERAL; BUT THIS IS GOING A LITTLE FARTHER THAN THE RABBINS; THEY DI THIS CHAPTER WAS ADDED BY JOSHUA. IT IS CONCEIVABLE THAT MOSES MIGHT HAVE LEFT ON RE PREDICTION THAT HE WOULD DIE AND BE BURIED IN THIS WAY; BUT THE SPIRIT OF THE LORD COULI INSPIRE A MAN TO PUT IN THE PAST TENSE A PLAIN NARRATIVE OF AN EVENT WHICH IS YET IN THE FUTU statement when written would be false, and God is not the author of falsehood.

IT IS NOT LIKELY EITHER THAT MOSES WROTE THE WORDS IN EXODUS XI. 3: "MOREOVER THE MAN WAS VERY GREAT IN THE LAND OF EGYPT, IN THE SIGHT OF ALL THE PEOPLE;" NOR THOSE IN NUMBEI "NOW THE MAN MOSES WAS VERY MEEK ABOVE ALL THE MEN WHICH WERE ON THE FACE OF THE EARTH." BEEN SAID, INDEED, THAT MOSES WAS DIRECTED BY INSPIRATION TO SAY SUCH THINGS ABOUT HIMSELF; BU not believe that egotism is a supernatural product; men take that in the natural way.

OTHER PASSAGES SHOW UPON THE FACE OF THEM THAT THEY MUST HAVE BEEN ADDED TO THESE AFTER THE TIME OF MOSES. IT IS STATED IN EXODUS XVI. 35, THAT THE ISRAELITES CONTINUED TO E UNTIL THEY CAME TO THE BORDERS OF THE LAND OF CANAAN. BUT MOSES WAS NOT LIVING WHEN THEY that land.

IN GENESIS XII. 6, IN CONNECTION WITH THE STORY OF ABRAHAM'S ENTRANCE INTO PALESTI HISTORICAL EXPLANATION IS THROWN IN: "AND THE CANAANITE WAS THEN IN THE LAND." IT WOULD SE THIS MUST HAVE BEEN WRITTEN AT A DAY WHEN THE CANAANITE WAS NO LONGER IN THE LAND,--AI OCCUPATION OF THE LAND AND THE EXPULSION OF THE CANAANITES. IN NUMBERS XV. 32, AN INCII RELATED WHICH IS PREFACED BY THE WORDS, "WHILE THE CHILDREN OF ISRAEL WERE IN THE WILDERNES NOT THIS LOOK BACK TO A PAST TIME? CAN WE IMAGINE THAT THIS WAS WRITTEN BY MOSES? AGA DEUTERONOMY III. 11, WE HAVE A DESCRIPTION OF THE BEDSTEAD OF OG, ONE OF THE GIANTS CAPTUR KILLED BY THE ISRAELITES, JUST BEFORE THE DEATH OF MOSES; AND THIS BEDSTEAD IS REFERRED TO AS AN ANTIQUE CURIOSITY; THE VILLAGE IS MENTIONED IN WHICH IT IS KEPT. IN GENESIS XXXVI. WE GENEALOGY OF THE KINGS OF MOAB, RUNNING THROUGH SEVERAL GENERATIONS, PREFACED WITH TH "THESE ARE THE KINGS THAT REIGNED IN THE LAND OF EDOM BEFORE THERE REIGNED ANY KING CHILDREN OF ISRAEL." THIS IS LOOKING BACKWARD FROM A DAY WHEN KINGS WERE REIGNING OVER THE C OF ISRAEL. HOW COULD IT HAVE BEEN WRITTEN FIVE HUNDRED YEARS BEFORE THERE EVER WAS A KING IN IN GENESIS XIV. 14, WE READ OF THE CITY OF DAN; BUT IN JUDGES XVIII. 29, WE ARE TOLD THAT THIS C NOT RECEIVE ITS NAME UNTIL HUNDREDS OF YEARS LATER, LONG AFTER THE TIME OF MOSES. SIMI ACCOUNT OF THE NAMING OF THE VILLAGES OF JAIR, WHICH WE FIND IN DEUTERONOMY III. 14, IS

INCONSISTENT WITH ANOTHER ACCOUNT IN JUDGES X. 3, 4. ONE OF THEM MUST BE ERRONEOUS, AN probable that the passage in Deuteronomy is an anachronism.

MOST OF THESE PASSAGES COULD BE EXPLAINED BY THE ADMISSION THAT THE SCRIBES IN LATE ADDED SENTENCES HERE AND THERE BY WAY OF INTERPRETATION. BUT THAT ADMISSION WOULD OF DISCREDIT THE INFALLIBILITY OF THE BOOKS. OTHER DIFFICULTIES, HOWEVER, OF A MUCH MORE SERIC present themselves.

IN THE FIRST VERSE OF THE TWENTIETH CHAPTER OF NUMBERS WE READ THAT THE PEOPLE CAME TO IN THE FIRST MONTH. THE FIRST MONTH OF WHAT YEAR? WE LOOK BACK, AND THE FIRST NOTE OF TIME TO THIS IS THE SECOND MONTH OF THE SECOND YEAR OF THE WANDERING IN THE WILDERNESS. THEIR KADESH DESCRIBED IN THE TWENTIETH CHAPTER WOULD SEEM, THEN, TO HAVE BEEN IN THE FIRST MONT THIRD YEAR. IN THE TWENTY-SECOND VERSE OF THIS CHAPTER THE CAMP MOVES ON TO MOUNT HOR, ANI DIES THERE. THERE IS NO NOTE OF ANY INTERVAL OF TIME WHATEVER; YET WE ARE TOLD IN THE TH CHAPTER OF THIS BOOK THAT AARON DIED IN THE FORTIETH YEAR OF THE WANDERING. HERE IS A SKIP EIGHT YEARS IN THE HISTORY, WITHOUT AN INDICATION OF ANYTHING HAVING HAPPENED MEANTIME. SUPPOSITION THAT THIS IS A CONTINUOUS HISTORY WRITTEN BY THE MAN WHO WAS A CHIEF ACTOR IN IT, GAP IS INEXPLICABLE. THERE IS A REASONABLE WAY OF ACCOUNTING FOR IT, AS WE SHALL SEE, BUT IT CA accounted for on the theory that the book in its present form came from the hand of Moses.

SOME OF THE LAWS ALSO BEAR INTERNAL EVIDENCE OF HAVING ORIGINATED AT A LATER DAY THA MOSES. THE LAW FORBIDDING THE REMOVAL OF LANDMARKS PRESUPPOSES A LONG OCCUPATION OF THE AND THE LAW REGULATING MILITARY ENLISTMENTS IS MORE NATURALLY EXPLAINED ON THE THEORY T FRAMED IN THE SETTLED PERIOD OF THE HEBREW HISTORY, AND NOT DURING THE WANDERINGS. T indeed, have been anticipatory legislation, but the explanation is not probable.

VARIOUS REPETITIONS OF LAWS OCCUR WHICH ARE INEXPLICABLE ON THE SUPPOSITION THAT THE WERE ALL WRITTEN BY THE HAND OF ONE PERSON. THUS IN EXODUS XXXIV. 17-26, THERE IS A COLLEC LEGAL ENACTMENTS, ALL OF WHICH CAN BE FOUND, IN THE SAME ORDER AND ALMOST THE SAME WORD TWENTY-THIRD CHAPTER OF THE SAME BOOK. THUS, TO QUOTE THE SUMMARY OF BLEEK, WE FIND I PLACES, (*a*) THAT ALL THE MALES SHALL APPEAR BEFORE JEHOVAH THREE TIMES IN EVERY YEAR; (*b*) THAT NO LEAVENED BREAD SHALL BE USED AT THE KILLING OF THE PASCHAL LAMB, AND THAT THE FAT SHALL BE UNTIL THE NEXT MORNING; (*c*) THAT THE FIRST OF THE FRUITS OF THE FIELD SHALL BE BROUGHT INTO THE the Lord; (*d*) THAT THE YOUNG KID SHALL NOT BE SEETHED IN ITS MOTHER'S MILK.[Footnote: *Introduction to the Old Testament*, i. 240.]

WE CANNOT IMAGINE THAT ONE MAN, WITH A FAIRLY GOOD MEMORY, MUCH LESS AN INFALLIBLY IN MAN, SHOULD HAVE WRITTEN THESE LAWS TWICE OVER, IN THE SAME WORDS, WITHIN SO SMALL A SPACE, I SAME LEGAL DOCUMENT. IN LEVITICUS WE HAVE A SIMILAR INSTANCE. IF ANY ONE WILL TAKE THAT BO CAREFULLY COMPARE THE EIGHTEENTH WITH THE TWENTIETH CHAPTER, HE WILL SEE SOME REASON FOR THAT BOTH CHAPTERS COULD HAVE BEEN INSERTED BY ONE HAND IN THIS COLLECTION OF STATUTES. ' PROBABLE," AS BLEEK HAS SAID, "THAT MOSES WOULD HAVE WRITTEN THE TWO CHAPTERS ONE AFTER TH AND WOULD SO SHORTLY AFTER HAVE REPEATED THE SAME PRECEPTS WHICH HE HAD BEFORE GIVEN, ONL well arranged the second time." [Footnote: *Introduction to the Old Testament*, i. 240.]

THERE ARE ALSO QUITE A NUMBER OF INCONSISTENCIES AND CONTRADICTIONS IN THE LEGISLATIC WHICH MAY BE EASILY EXPLAINED, BUT NOT ON THE THEORY THAT THE LAWS ALL CAME FROM THE PEN INFALLIBLY INSPIRED LAWGIVER. WE FIND ALSO SEVERAL HISTORICAL REPETITIONS AND HISTORICAL DISCI ALL OF WHICH MAKE AGAINST THE THEORY THAT MOSES IS THE AUTHOR OF ALL THIS PENTATEUCHAL LI SINGLE AUTHOR, IF HE WERE A MAN OF FAIR INTELLIGENCE, GOOD COMMON SENSE, AND REASONAB MEMORY, COULD NOT HAVE WRITTEN IT. AND UNLESS TAUTOLOGY, ANACHRONISMS, AND CONTRADICTIO PROOF OF INSPIRATION, MUCH LESS COULD IT HAVE BEEN WRITTEN BY A SINGLE INSPIRED WRITEI TRADITIONAL THEORY CANNOT THEREFORE HE TRUE. WE HAVE APPEALED TO THE BOOKS THEMSELVES, bear swift witness against it.

NOW LET US LOOK AT THE OTHER THEORY OF THE DESTRUCTIVE CRITICS WHICH NOT ONLY DENIES T WROTE ANY PORTION OF THE PENTATEUCH, BUT ALLEGES THAT IT WAS WRITTEN IN PALESTINE, NONE OF I six or seven hundred years after he was dead and buried.

IN THE FIRST PLACE THE BOOK EXPRESSLY DECLARES THAT MOSES WROTE CERTAIN PORTIONS OF mentioned several times as having written certain historical records and certain words of t] Exodus xxiv., we are told that Moses not only rehearsed to the people the Covenant which the Lord had made with them, but that he wrote all the words of the Covenant in a book, and that the book of the Covenant and read it in the audience of all the people. After the idola' people Moses was again commanded to write these words, "and" it is added, "he wrote upo] tables the words of the Covenant, the ten commandments." In Exodus xvii. 14, we are to] Moses wrote the narrative of the defeat of Amalek in a book; and again in Numbers xxxiii. read that Moses recorded the various marches and halts of the Israelites in the wilderness. also in the Book of Deuteronomy (xxxi. 24-26) a statement that Moses wrote "the words of ' in a book, and put it in the ark of the covenant for preservation. Precisely how much of the statement is meant to cover is not clear. Some have interpreted it to cover the whole Pe] but that interpretation, as we have seen, is inadmissible. We may concede that it does ref body or code of laws,--probably that body or code on which the legislation of Deutero] based.

These are all the statements made in the writings themselves concerning their oric prove, if they are credible, that portions of these books were written by Moses; they do n(that the whole of them came from his hand.

I see no reason whatever to doubt that this is the essential fact. The theory of the di critics that this literature and this legislation was all produced in Palestine, about the eig] before Christ, and palmed off upon the Jews as a pious fraud, does not bear investigation. I] portions of these laws we are constantly meeting with legal provisions and historical allu: take us directly back to the time of the wandering in the wilderness, and cannot be explaine other theory. "When," says Bleek, "we meet with laws which refer in their whole tenor to a things utterly unknown in the period subsequent to Moses, and to circumstances existin(Mosaic age, and in that only, it is in the highest degree likely that these laws not onl essential purport proceeded from Moses, but also that they were written down by Moses or in the Mosaic age. Of these laws which appear to carry with them such clear and exact trace Mosaic age, there are many occurring, especially in Leviticus, and also in Numbers and E which laws relate to situations and surrounding circumstances only existing whilst the p] was the case in Moses' time, wandered in the wilderness and were dwellers in the close confi of camps and tents." [Footnote: Vol. i. p. 212.] It is not necessary to draw out this evide length; I will only refer to a few out of scores of instances. The first seven chapters of containing laws regulating the burnt offerings and meat offerings, constantly assume that the people are in the camp and in the wilderness. The refuse of the beasts offered in sacrifice was to be out of the camp to the public ash heap, and burned. The law of the Great Day of Atonemen xvi.) is also full of allusions to the fact that the people were in camp; the scapegoat was to b into the wilderness, and the man who drove it out was to wash his clothes and bathe, and af come into the camp; the bullock and the goat, slain for the sacrifice, were to be carri without the camp; he who bears them forth must also wash himself before he returns to th] Large parts of the legislation concerning leprosy are full of the same incidental references to the fact that the people were dwelling in camp.

There are also laws requiring that all the animals killed for food should be slaughte] the door of the Tabernacle. There was a reason for this law; it was intended to guard a debasing superstition; but how would it have been possible to obey it when the people scattered all over the land of Palestine? It was adapted only to the time when they were d a camp in the wilderness.

Besides, it must not be overlooked that in all this legislation "the priests are not at a] to in general, but by name, as Aaron and his sons, or the sons of Aaron the priests."

All the legislation respecting the construction of the tabernacle, the disposition o camp, the transportation of it from place to place in the wilderness, the order of the m summoning of the people when camp was to be broken, with all its minute and circumsta directions, would be destitute of meaning if it had been written while the people were l

PALESTINE, SCATTERED ALL OVER THE LAND, DWELLING IN THEIR OWN HOUSES, AND ENGAGED IN AG pursuits.

THE SIMPLE, UNFORCED, NATURAL INTERPRETATION OF THESE LAWS TAKES US BACK, I SAY, TO THE MOSES, TO THE YEARS OF THE WANDERING IN THE WILDERNESS. THE INCIDENTAL REFERENCES TO THE C OF THE WILDERNESS LIFE ARE FAR MORE CONVINCING THAN ANY EXPLICIT STATEMENT WOULD HAVE BEEN. ONE CONCEIVE THAT A WRITER OF LAWS, LIVING IN PALESTINE HUNDREDS OF YEARS AFTERWARDS, CO FABRICATED THESE ALLUSIONS TO THE CAMP LIFE AND THE TENT LIFE OF THE PEOPLE? SUCH A NOVELIS EXIST AMONG THEM; AND I QUESTION WHETHER PROFESSOR KUENEN AND PROFESSOR WELLHAUSEN, ' THEIR WEALTH OF IMAGINATION, COULD HAVE DONE ANY SUCH THING. MANY OF THESE LAWS WERE C WRITTEN IN THE TIME OF MOSES; AND I DO NOT BELIEVE THAT ANY MAN WAS LIVING IN THE TIME OF MO: WAS MORE COMPETENT TO WRITE SUCH LAWS THAN WAS MOSES HIMSELF. THE CONCLUSION OF BLEEK THEREFORE TO ME ALTOGETHER REASONABLE: "ALTHOUGH THE PENTATEUCH IN ITS PRESENT STATE AND NOT HAVE BEEN COMPOSED BY MOSES, AND ALSO MANY OF THE SINGLE LAWS THEREIN MAY BE THE PROD A LATER AGE, STILL THE LEGISLATION CONTAINED IN IT IS GENUINELY MOSAIC IN ITS ENTIRE SPIRIT AND [Footnote: Vol. i. p. 221.] We are brought, therefore, in our study, to these inevitable conclusions:

1. The Pentateuch could never have been written by any one man, inspired or otherwise.

2. IT IS A COMPOSITE WORK, IN WHICH MANY HANDS HAVE BEEN ENGAGED. THE PRODUCTION (extends over many centuries.

3. IT CONTAINS WRITINGS WHICH ARE AS OLD AS THE TIME OF MOSES, AND SOME THAT ARE MUCH O IS IMPOSSIBLE TO TELL HOW MUCH OF IT CAME FROM THE HAND OF MOSES, BUT THERE ARE CONSIE PORTIONS OF IT WHICH, ALTHOUGH THEY MAY HAVE BEEN SOMEWHAT MODIFIED BY LATER EDITO: substantially as he left them.

I HAVE SAID THAT THE PENTATEUCH IS A COMPOSITE WORK. IN THE NEXT CHAPTER WE SHALL FIN CURIOUS FACTS CONCERNING ITS COMPONENT PARTS, AND THE WAY IN WHICH THEY HAVE BEEN PUT TO(AND ALTHOUGH IT DID NOT COME INTO BEING IN THE WAY IN WHICH WE HAVE BEEN TAUGHT BY THE TR/ OF THE RABBINS, YET WE SHALL SEE THAT IT CONTAINS SOME WONDERFUL EVIDENCE OF THE SUPERINTENI OF GOD,--OF THAT CONTINUOUS AND GROWING MANIFESTATION OF HIS TRUTH AND HIS LOVE TO THE F Israel, which is what we mean by revelation.

REVELATION, WE SHALL BE ABLE TO UNDERSTAND, IS NOT THE DICTATION BY GOD OF WORDS TO M THEY MAY BE WRITTEN DOWN IN BOOKS; IT IS RATHER THE DISCLOSURE OF THE TRUTH AND LOVE OF GOI IN THE PROCESSES OF HISTORY, IN THE DEVELOPMENT OF THE MORAL ORDER OF THE WORLD. IT IS THE L LIGHTETH EVERY MAN, SHINING IN THE PATHS THAT LEAD TO RIGHTEOUSNESS AND LIFE. THERE IS LEADERSHIP OF GOD IN HISTORY; REVELATION IS THE RECORD OF THAT LEADERSHIP. IT IS BY NO MEANS (TO WORDS; ITS MOST IMPRESSIVE DISCLOSURES ARE IN THE FIELD OF ACTION. "Thus did THE LORD," AS DR BRUCE HAS SAID, IS A MORE PERFECT FORMULA OF REVELATION THAN "THUS SAID THE LORD." IT IS IN TH historical movement of which the Bible is the record that we find the revelation of God to men.

CHAPTER III.

SOURCES OF THE PENTATEUCH.

IN THE LAST CHAPTER WE FOUND EVIDENCE THAT THE PENTATEUCH AS IT STANDS COULD NOT HAVE WORK OF MOSES, THOUGH IT CONTAINS MUCH MATERIAL WHICH MUST HAVE ORIGINATED IN THE TIME OF AND IS MORE LIKELY TO HAVE BEEN DICTATED BY HIM THAN BY ANY ONE ELSE; THAT LARGE PORTION MOSAIC LAW WERE OF MOSAIC AUTHORSHIP; THAT THE ENTIRE SYSTEM OF LEVITICAL LEGISLATION GREW THIS MOSAIC GERM, THOUGH MUCH OF IT APPEARED IN LATER GENERATIONS; AND THAT, THEREFORE, TH

the Jews of calling it all the law of Moses is easily understood. We thus discovered in this s
the Pentateuch is a composite book.

The Christian Church in all the ages has been inclined to pin its faith to what the rabi
about the origin of this book, and this is not altogether surprising; but in these day
testimony is sifted by criticism we find that the traditions of the rabbins are not at all tru
and when we go to the Book itself, and ask it to tell us what it can of the secret of its orig
that it has a very different story to tell from that with which the rabbins have beguiled us.
study of the Book makes it perfectly certain that it is not the production of any one m
growth that has been going on for many centuries; that it embodies the work of many ha
together in an artless way by various editors and compilers. The framework is Mosaic, b
details of the work were added by reverent disciples of Moses, the last of whom must have lived and written many hundred years after Moses' day.

Some of the evidences of composite structure which lie upon the very face of the narrative will
now come under our notice. It is plain that the whole of this literature could not have bee
by any one man without some kind of assistance. All the books, except the first, are indeed
of events which occurred mainly during the lifetime of Moses, and of most of which he mig
had personal knowledge. But the story of Genesis goes back to a remote antiquity. The la
related in that book occurred four hundred years before Moses was born; it was as distant f
as the discovery of America by Columbus is from us; and other portions of the narrative, s
the story of the Flood and the Creation, stretch back into the shadows of the age which
history. Neither Moses nor any one living in his day could have given us these reports from
knowledge. Whoever wrote this must have obtained his materials in one of three ways.

1. They might have been given to him by direct revelation from God.

2. He might have gathered them up from oral tradition, from stories, folk-lore, tra
from mouth to mouth, and so preserved from generation to generation.

3. He might have found them in written documents existing at the time of his writing.

The first of these conjectures embodies the rabbinical theory. The later form of th
declared, however, that God did not even dictate while Moses wrote, but simply handed th
written and punctuated, out of heaven to Moses; the only question with these rabbins was
he handed it down all at once, or one volume at a time. It is certain that this is not th
theory. The repetitions, the discrepancies, the anachronisms, and the errors which the
certainly contains prove that it could not have been dictated, word for word, by the Om
One. Those who maintain such a theory as this should beware how they ascribe to Go
imperfections of men. It seems to me that the advocacy of the verbal theory of inspiratio
perilously near to the sin against the Holy Ghost.

The second conjecture, that the writer of these books might have gathered up oral t
of the earlier generations and incorporated them into his writings, is more plausible; yet
examination of the writings themselves does not confirm this theory. The form of this l
shows that it must have had another origin.

The only remaining conjecture, that the books are compilations of written docume
been established beyond controversy by the most patient study of the writings themselves
Book of Genesis the evidence of the combination of two documents is so obvious that he wh
may read. These two documents are distinguished from each other, partly by the style of
and partly by the different names which they apply to the Supreme Being. One of these old
called the Deity Elohim, the other called him Yahveh, or Jehovah. These documents are
therefore, as the Elohistic and the Jehovistic narratives. Sometimes it is a little difficult to
the line runs which separates these narratives, but usually it is distinct. Readers of Gen
many passages in which the name given to the Deity is "God," and others in which "Lord," in
small capitals. The first of these names represents the Hebrew Elohim, the second the
Yahveh or Jehovah. In one important section, beginning with the fourth verse of the
chapter, and continuing through the chapter, the two names are combined, and we ha
Supreme Being spoken of as "The Lord God," Jehovah-Elohim. It is evident to every observi

reader that we have in the beginning of Genesis two distinct accounts of the Creation, occupying the first chapter and three verses of the second, the other occupying the remaini second chapter with the whole of the third. The difference between these accounts is quite The style of the writing, particularly in the Hebrew, is strongly contrasted; and the det story are not entirely harmonious. In the first narrative the order of creation is, first thi its vegetation, then the lower animals, then man, male and female, made in God's image. second narrative the order is, first the earth and its vegetation, then man, then the lowei animals, then woman. In the first story plant life springs into existence at the direct com God; in the second it results from a mist which rose from the earth and watered the wholi the ground. These striking differences would be hard to explain if we had not before our clear evidence of two old documents joined together.

I spoke in the last chapter of certain historical discrepancies which are not explicabli supposition that this is the work of a single writer. Such are the two accounts of the orig name of Beersheba, the one in the twenty-first and the other in the twenty-sixth chapter o The first account says that it was named by Abraham, and gives the reason why he called th by this name. The second account says that it received its name from Isaac, about ninety yeai and gives a wholly different explanation of the reason why he called it by this name. When that in the first of these stories God is called Elohim, [Footnote: In the last verse of thi the word Jehovah is used, but this is probably an interpolation.] and in the second Jehovah, readily explain this discrepancy. The compiler took one of these narratives from one of t documents, and the other from the other, and was not careful to reconcile the two.

A similar duplication of the narrative is found in chapters xx. and xxvi., with respect incident of Abimelech; in the first of these narratives a serious complication is described as between Abimelech King of Gerar on the one hand and Abraham and Sarah on the other second Abimelech is represented as interfering, in precisely the same way and with the same in the domestic felicity of Isaac and Rebekah. The harmonizers have done their work, of upon these two passages; they have said that there were two Abimelechs, and that Isaac repeated the blunder of his father; but it is a little singular, if this were so, that no reference is made in narrative to the former. It is altogether probable that we have the same story ascribed to actors; and when we find that the one narrative is Elohistic and the other Jehovistic, the pi solved.

More curious than any other of these combinations is the account of the Flood, in wh compiler has taken the narratives of these two old writers and pieced them together like pa Refer to your Bibles and note this piece of literary joiner-work. At the fifth verse of chapter of Genesis this story begins; from this verse to the end of the eighth verse the J document is used. The name of the Deity is Jehovah, translLord. From the ninth verse to th end of the chapter the Elohistic document is used. The word applied to God is Elohim, tra God. With the seventh chapter begins again the quotation from the other document, " Lord [Jehovah] said unto Noah." This extends only to the sixth verse; then the Elohistic n begins again, and continues to the nineteenth verse of the eighth chapter, including it; Jehovistic narrative begins again, and continues through the chapter; then the Elohist tak tale for the first seventeen verses of the ninth chapter; then the Jehovist goes on to t seventh verse, and the Elohist closes the chapter. It is true that we have in the midst of these Elohistic passages a verse or two of the other document inserted by the compiler; outlines of the different documents are marked as I have told you. If you take this story an out of it the portions which I have ascribed to the Elohist and put them together, you wil clear, complete, consecutive story of the Flood; the portions of the Jehovistic narrative rather tend to confusion. "The consideration of the context here," says Bleek, "quite apart changes in the naming of God, shows that the Jehovistic passages of the narrative did not o belong to it. It cannot fail to be observed that the connection is often interrupted by the passages, and that by cutting them out a more valuable and clearer continuity of the nai almost always obtained. For instance, in the existing narrative certain repetitions keep on o

ONE OF THESE, ESPECIALLY, IS CONNECTED WITH A DIFFERENCE IN THE MATTERS OF FACT RELATED, INTRC slight difficulty and obscurity." [Footnote: Vol. i. p. 273.]

HEAR THE JEHOVIST: "AND JEHOVAH SAW THAT THE WICKEDNESS OF MAN WAS GREAT IN THE EART VI. 5). NOW HEAR THE ELOHIST (VI. 11): "AND THE EARTH WAS CORRUPT BEFORE ELOHIM, AND THE EAR FILLED WITH VIOLENCE." THE JEHOVIST SAYS (VI. 7): "AND JEHOVAH SAID, I WILL DESTROY MAN WHOM I CREATED FROM THE FACE OF THE GROUND." THE ELOHIST SAYS (VI. 13): "THE EARTH IS FILLED WITH THROUGH THEM, AND BEHOLD I WILL DESTROY THEM WITH THE EARTH." IN THE NINTH VERSE OF CHAPTER WE READ: "NOAH WAS A RIGHTEOUS MAN AND PERFECT IN HIS GENERATIONS; NOAH WALKEI ELOHIM." IN THE FIRST VERSE OF THE SEVENTH CHAPTER, WE READ, "AND JEHOVAH SAID UNTO NOAH, THOU AND ALL THY HOUSE INTO THE ARK; FOR THEE HAVE I SEEN RIGHTEOUS BEFORE ME IN THIS GEN THESE REPETITIONS SHOW HOW THE SAME STORY IS TWICE TOLD. BUT THE CONTRADICTIONS ARI SIGNIFICANT. HERE THE ONE NARRATIVE REPRESENTS ELOHIM AS SAYING (VI. 19): "AND OF EVERY LIVIN OF ALL FLESH, TWO OF EVERY KIND SHALT THOU BRING INTO THE ARK TO KEEP THEM ALIVE WITH THEE; BE MALE AND FEMALE. OF THE FOWL AFTER THEIR KIND AND OF THE CATTLE AFTER THEIR KIND, OF EVEI THING OF THE EARTH AFTER ITS KIND, TWO OF EVERY SORT SHALL COME UNTO THEE TO KEEP THEM ALIVI OTHER NARRATIVE REPRESENTS JEHOVAH AS SAYING, "OF EVERY CLEAN BEAST THOU SHALT TAKE TO THEE SEVEN, THE MALE AND THE FEMALE; AND OF THE BEASTS THAT ARE NOT CLEAN, TWO, THE MALE AND THE THE FOWL ALSO OF THE AIR SEVEN AND SEVEN, MALE AND FEMALE, TO KEEP SEED ALIVE UPON THE FACE C EARTH." THE ONE STORY SAYS THAT OF EVERY KIND OF LIVING CREATURE ONE PAIR SHOULD BE TAKEN INT THE OTHER SAYS THAT *clean* BEASTS, SEVEN PAIRS OF EACH SPECIES SHOULD BE RECEIVED, AND OF UNCI BEASTS ONLY ONE PAIR. THE HARMONISTS HAVE WRESTLED WITH THIS PASSAGE ALSO; SOME OF THEM SA PERHAPS THE FIRST PASSAGE ONLY MEANT THAT THEY SHOULD *walk in* TWO AND TWO; OTHERS SAY THAT A GC MANY YEARS HAD ELAPSED BETWEEN THE GIVING OF THE TWO COMMANDS (OF WHICH THERE IS NOT A PAR EVIDENCE), AND WE ARE LEFT TO INFER THAT IN THE MEAN TIME THE ALMIGHTY EITHER FORGOT HIS FI OR ELSE CHANGED HIS MIND. IT IS A PITIFUL INSTANCE OF AN ATTEMPT TO EVADE A DIFFICULTY THAT C EVADED. ONE OF THE VERY CONSERVATIVE COMMENTATORS, DR. PEROWNE, IN SMITH'S "BIBLE DICTIO CONCLUDES TO FACE IT: "MAY WE NOT SUPPOSE," HE TIMIDLY ASKS, "THAT WE HAVE HERE TRACES OF A SI DOCUMENT, INTERWOVEN BY A LATER WRITER, WITH THE FORMER HISTORY? THE PASSAGE HAS NOT, INDEI INCORPORATED INTACT, BUT THERE IS A COLORING ABOUT IT WHICH SEEMS TO INDICATE THAT MOSES, OR PUT THE BOOK OF GENESIS INTO ITS PRESENT SHAPE, HAD HERE CONSULTED A DIFFERENT NARRATIVE. THI USE OF THE DIVINE NAMES IN THE SAME PHRASE (VI. 22; VII. 5), IN THE FORMER ELOHIM, IN THE I JEHOVAH, SUGGESTS THAT THIS MAY HAVE BEEN THE CASE." [FOOTNOTE: ART. "NOAH," III. 2179, AMI Edition.]

"MAY WE NOT SUPPOSE," THE GOOD DOCTOR ASKS, THAT WE HAVE TRACES OF TWO DOCUMENTS CERTAINLY, YOUR REVERENCE. IT IS JUST AS SAFE TO SUPPOSE IT, AS IT IS TO SUPPOSE, WHEN YOU SEE A NO A MAN'S FACE, THAT IT IS A NOSE. THERE IS NO MORE DOUBT ABOUT IT THAN THERE IS ABOUT ANY PALPABLE FACT. THE TRUTH IS, THAT THE COMPOSITE CHARACTER OF GENESIS IS NO LONGER, IN SCHOLARI AN OPEN QUESTION. THE MOST CAUTIOUS, THE MOST CONSERVATIVE OF SCHOLARS CONCEDE THE POINT PRESIDENT BARTLETT, OF DARTMOUTH COLLEGE, A HEBRAIST OF SOME EMINENCE, AND AS STURDY A DEI OLD-FASHIONED ORTHODOXY AS THIS COUNTRY HOLDS, MADE THIS ADMISSION MORE THAN TWENTY YE "WE MAY ACCEPT THE TRACES OF EARLIER NARRATIVES AS HAVING BEEN EMPLOYED AND AUTHENTICATED [MOSES]; AND WE MAY ADMIT THE MARKS OF LATER DATE AS INDICATIONS OF A SURFACE REVISION OF AUTI PERSONS NOT LATER THAN EZRA AND NEHEMIAH." AND DR. PEROWNE, THE CONSERVATIVE SCHOLAR quoted, in the article on the "Pentateuch" in "Smith's Bible Dictionary," sums up as follows:--

> "1. THE BOOK OF GENESIS RESTS CHIEFLY ON DOCUMENTS MUCH EARLIER THAN THE TIME OF MOSES, THOUGH IT WAS PROBABLY BROUGHT TO VERY NEARLY PRESENT SHAPE EITHER BY MOSES himself, or by one of the elders who acted under him.
>
> "2. THE BOOKS OF EXODUS, LEVITICUS, AND NUMBERS ARE TO A GREAT EXTENT Mosaic. BESIDES THOSE PORTIONS WHICH ARE EXPRESSLY DECLARED TO HAVE BEEN WRITTEN BY HIM, OTHER PORTIONS, AND ESPECIALLY THE LEGAL SECTIONS, WERE, IF NOT ACTUALLY WRITTEN, IN ALL PROBABILI

dictated by him.

"3. DEUTERONOMY, EXCEPTING THE CONCLUDING PART, IS ENTIRELY THE WORK OF MOSES, AS IT professes to be.

. . . .

"5. THE FIRST *composition* OF THE PENTATEUCH AS A WHOLE COULD NOT HAVE TAKEN PLACE TILL after the Israelites entered Canaan.

"6. THE WHOLE WORK DID NOT FINALLY ASSUME ITS PRESENT SHAPE TILL ITS REVISION WAS undertaken by Ezra after the return from the Babylonish captivity."

THE VOLUME FROM WHICH I HAVE QUOTED THESE WORDS BEARS THE DATE OF 1870. TWENTY YE. VERY BUSY WORK HAVE BEEN EXPENDED UPON THE PENTATEUCH SINCE DR. PEROWNE WROTE THESE WO HE WERE TO WRITE TO-DAY HE WOULD BE MUCH LESS CONFIDENT THAT MOSES WROTE THE WH DEUTERONOMY, AND HE WOULD PROBABLY MODIFY HIS STATEMENTS IN OTHER RESPECTS; BUT HE WOULD none of these admissions respecting the composite character of these five books.

THE SAME FACT OF A COMBINATION OF DIFFERENT DOCUMENTS CAN EASILY BE SHOWN IN ALL TH MIDDLE BOOKS OF THE PENTATEUCH, AS WELL AS IN GENESIS. THIS IS THE FACT WHICH EXPLAINS REPETITIONS OF LAWS, AND THOSE SINGULAR BREAKS IN THE HISTORY, TO WHICH I CALLED YOUR ATTENT LAST CHAPTER. THERE IS, AS I BELIEVE, A LARGE ELEMENT OF PURELY MOSAIC LEGISLATION IN THESE BOC OF THESE LAWS WERE WRITTEN EITHER BY THE HAND OF MOSES OR UNDER HIS EYE; AND THE RES CONFORMED TO THE SPIRIT WHICH HE IMPRESSED UPON THE HEBREW JURISPRUDENCE THAT THEY MAY BE CALLED MOSAIC; BUT MANY OF THEM, ON THE OTHER HAND, WERE WRITTEN LONG AFTER HIS DAY, AND T Pentateuch did not reach its present form until after the exile, in the days of Ezra and Nehemiah.

THE UPHOLDERS OF THE TRADITIONAL THEORY--THAT MOSES WROTE THE PENTATEUCH, JUST AS B WROTE HIS COMMENTARIES--ARE WONT TO MAKE MUCH ACCOUNT OF THE DISAGREEMENTS OF THOSE CRIT HAVE UNDERTAKEN TO ANALYZE IT INTO ITS COMPONENT PARTS. "THESE CRITICS," THEY SAY, "ARI LOGGERHEADS; THEY DO NOT AGREE WITH ONE ANOTHER; NONE OF THEM EVEN AGREES WITH HIMSELF \ MOST OF THEM HAVE SEVERAL TIMES REVISED THEIR THEORIES, AND THERE SEEMS TO BE NEITHER CERTA COHERENCY IN THEIR SPECULATIONS." BUT THIS IS NOT QUITE TRUE. WITH RESPECT TO SOME SUBC QUESTIONS THEY ARE NOT AGREED, AND PROBABLY NEVER WILL BE; BUT WITH RESPECT TO THE FACT TI BOOKS ARE COMPOSITE IN THEIR ORIGIN THEY ARE PERFECTLY AGREED, AND THEY ARE ALSO REI UNANIMOUS IN THEIR JUDGMENTS AS TO WHERE THE LINES OF CLEAVAGE RUN BETWEEN THESE COMPONEN THE CONSENSUS OF CRITICAL OPINION NOW IS THAT THERE ARE AT LEAST FOUR GREAT DOCUMENTS WH BEEN COMBINED IN THE PENTATEUCH; AND THE CRITICS AGREE IN THE MAIN FEATURES OF THE ANALYSIS THEY DO NOT ALL CALL THESE SEPARATED PARTS BY THE SAME NAMES, NOR DO THEY ALL THINK ALIKE C THE RELATIVE ANTIQUITY OF THESE PORTIONS. SOME THINK THAT ONE OF THESE DOCUMENTS IS THE OI SOME GIVE THAT DISTINCTION TO ANOTHER; NOR DO THEY AGREE AS TO HOW OLD THE OLDEST IS, SOME THE EARLIEST COMPOSITION DOWN TO A RECENT PERIOD; BUT ON THE MAIN QUESTION THAT THE LITE COMPOSITE THEY ARE AT ONE. THE CLOSENESS OF THEIR AGREEMENT IS SHOWN BY PROFESSOR LADD IN OF TABLES [FOOTNOTE: *The Doctrine of Sacred Scripture*, PART II. CHAP. VII.] IN WHICH HE DISPLAYS TO THE E THE RESULTS OF THE ANALYSIS OF FOUR INDEPENDENT INVESTIGATORS, KNOBEL, SCHRADER, DILLM WELLHAUSEN. HE GOES THROUGH THE WHOLE OF THE PENTATEUCH AND THE BOOK OF JOSHUA,--THE HI AS IT IS NOW CALLED,--AND PICKS OUT OF EVERY CHAPTER THOSE VERSES ASSIGNED BY THESE SEVERAL AUT TO THAT ANCIENT WRITING WHICH WE HAVE BEEN CALLING THE ELOHISTIC NARRATIVE, AND ARRANGE PARALLEL COLUMNS. YOU CAN SEE AT A GLANCE WHEN THEY AGREE IN THIS ANALYSIS, AND WHEN THEY DI THINK THAT YOU WOULD BE ASTONISHED TO FIND THAT THE AGREEMENTS ARE SO MANY AND THE DISAG SO FEW. SO MUCH UNITY OF JUDGMENT WOULD BE IMPOSSIBLE IF THE LINES OF CLEAVAGE BETWEEN THE DOCUMENTS WERE NOT MARKED WITH CONSIDERABLE DISTINCTNESS. "THE ONLY SATISFACTORY EXPLA SAYS PROFESSOR LADD, "OF THE POSSIBILITY OF ACCOMPLISHING SUCH A WORK OF ANALYSIS IS THE FACT T analysis is substantially correct." [Footnote: *What is the Bible?* p. 311.]

PROFESSOR C. A. BRIGGS, OF THE UNION (PRESBYTERIAN) THEOLOGICAL SEMINARY IN NEW YORI THIS TESTIMONY THREE YEARS AGO IN THE "PRESBYTERIAN REVIEW:" "THE CRITICAL ANALYSIS OF THE H IS THE RESULT OF MORE THAN A CENTURY OF PROFOUND STUDY OF THE DOCUMENTS BY THE GREATEST THE AGE. THERE HAS BEEN A STEADY ADVANCE UNTIL THE PRESENT POSITION OF AGREEMENT HAS BEEN I IN WHICH JEW AND CHRISTIAN, ROMAN CATHOLIC AND PROTESTANT, RATIONALISTIC AND EVANGELICAL : REFORMED AND LUTHERAN, PRESBYTERIAN AND EPISCOPAL, UNITARIAN, METHODIST, AND BAPTIST ALL THE ANALYSIS OR THE HEXATEUCH INTO SEVERAL DISTINCT ORIGINAL DOCUMENTS IS A PURELY LITERARY IN WHICH NO ARTICLE OF FAITH IS INVOLVED. WHOEVER IN THESE TIMES, IN THE DISCUSSION OF THE PHENOMENA OF THE HEXATEUCH, APPEALS TO THE IGNORANCE AND PREJUDICES OF THE MULTITUDE AS WERE ANY PERIL TO FAITH IN THESE PROCESSES OF THE HIGHER CRITICISM, RISKS HIS REPUTATI SCHOLARSHIP BY SO DOING. THERE ARE NO HEBREW PROFESSORS ON THE CONTINENT OF EUROPE, SO I KNOW, WHO WOULD DENY THE LITERARY ANALYSIS OF THE PENTATEUCH INTO THE FOUR GREAT DOCUM PROFESSORS OF HEBREW IN THE UNIVERSITIES OF OXFORD, CAMBRIDGE, AND EDINBURGH, AND TUTO LARGE NUMBER OF THEOLOGICAL COLLEGES, HOLD TO THE SAME OPINION. A VERY CONSIDERABLE NUMBI HEBREW PROFESSORS OF AMERICA ARE IN ACCORD WITH THEM. THERE ARE, INDEED, A FEW PROFES SCHOLARS WHO HOLD TO THE TRADITIONAL OPINION, BUT THESE ARE IN A HOPELESS MINORITY. I DOUBT THERE IS ANY QUESTION OF SCHOLARSHIP WHATEVER IN WHICH THERE IS GREATER AGREEMENT AMONG than in this question of the literary analysis of the Hexateuch."

I HAVE BUT ONE MORE WITNESS TO INTRODUCE, AND IT SHALL BE THE DISTINGUISHED GERMAN PR(DELITZSCH, WHO HAS LONG BEEN REGARDED AS THE BULWARK OF EVANGELICAL ORTHODOXY IN GERMA NAME," SAYS PROFESSOR LADD, "HAS FOR MANY YEARS BEEN CONNECTED WITH THE CONCEPTION OF A CHRISTIAN SCHOLARSHIP USED IN THE DEFENSE OF THE FAITH AGAINST ATTACKS UPON THE SUPEI CHARACTER OF THE OLD TESTAMENT RELIGION AND OF THE WRITINGS WHICH RECORD ITS DEVELOPMF PREFACE TO HIS COMMENTARY ON ISAIAH PUBLISHED SINCE HIS RECENT DEATH, HE SPEAKS WITH GREAT H OF THE WORK THAT HE HAS DONE, ADDING, "OF ONE THING ONLY DO I THINK I MAY BE CONFIDENT,-- SPIRIT BY WHICH IT IS ANIMATED COMES FROM THE GOOD SPIRIT THAT GUIDES ALONG THE EVERLASTIN THE OPINION OF SUCH A SCHOLAR OUGHT TO HAVE WEIGHT WITH ALL SERIOUS-MINDED CHRISTIANS. \ GIVE YOU HIS LATEST WORD ON THIS QUESTION, YOU WILL RECOGNIZE THAT YOU HAVE ALL THAT THE R most devout scholarship can claim. Let me quote, then, Professor Ladd's abstract of his verdict:--

"IN THE OPINION OF PROFESSOR DELITZSCH ONLY THE BASIS OF THE SEVERAL CODES... INCORPORATI PENTATEUCH IS MOSAIC; THE FORM IN WHICH THESE CODES... ARE PRESENTED IN THE PENTATEUCH I ORIGIN MUCH LATER THAN THE TIME OF MOSES. THE DECALOGUE AND THE LAWS FORMING THE BOO COVENANT ARE THE MOST ANCIENT PORTIONS; THEY PRESERVE THE MOSAIC TYPE IN ITS RELATIVELY OI PUREST FORM. OF THIS TYPE DEUTERONOMY *is a development.* THE STATEMENT THAT MOSES 'WROTE' DEUTERONOMIC LAW (DEUT. XXXI. 9, 24) *does not refer to the present Book of Deuteronomy, but to the code of laws which underlies it.*

"THE PRIEST'S CODE, WHICH EMBODIES THE MORE DISTINCTIVELY RITUALISTIC AND CEREN LEGISLATION, IS THE RESULT OF A LONG AND PROGRESSIVE DEVELOPMENT. CERTAIN OF ITS PRINCIPLES O WITH MOSES, BUT ITS FORM, WHICH IS UTTERLY UNLIKE THAT OF THE OTHER PARTS OF THE PENTATI RECEIVED AT THE HANDS OF THE PRIESTS OF THE NATION. PROBABLY SOME PARTICULAR PRIEST, AT A MU DATE, INDEED, THAN THE TIME OF MOSES, BUT PRIOR TO THE COMPOSITION OF DEUTERONOMY, WAS ESF INFLUENTIAL IN SHAPING IT. BUT THE LAST STAGES OF ITS DEVELOPMENT MAY BELONG TO THE PERIOD Exile.

"THE HISTORICAL TRADITIONS WHICH ARE INCORPORATED INTO THE HEXATEUCH WERE COMMI WRITING AT DIFFERENT TIMES AND BY DIFFERENT HANDS. THE NARRATIVES OF THEM ARE SUPERIMPOSI WERE, STRATUM UPON STRATUM, IN THE PENTATEUCH AND THE BOOK OF JOSHUA. FOR THE BOOK OF J(CONNECTED INTIMATELY WITH THE PENTATEUCH, AND WHEN ANALYZED SHOWS THE SAME COMPOSITE ST THE DIFFERENCES WHICH THE SEVERAL CODES EXHIBIT ARE DUE TO MODIFICATIONS WHICH THEY RECEIVI COURSE OF HISTORY AS THEY WERE VARIOUSLY COLLECTED, REVISED, AND PASSED FROM GENERA' GENERATION.... THE PENTATEUCH, LIKE ALL THE OTHER HISTORICAL BOOKS OF THE BIBLE, IS COM DOCUMENTARY SOURCES, DIFFERING ALIKE IN CHARACTER AND AGE, WHICH CRITICAL ANALYSIS MAY STILI

WITH GREATER OR LESS CERTAINTY, TO DISTINGUISH AND SEPARATE FROM ONE ANOTHER." [Footnote: *What is the Bible?* pp. 489-491.]

THAT SUCH IS THE FACT WITH RESPECT TO THE STRUCTURE OF THESE ANCIENT WRITINGS IS NOW QUESTION. AND OUR THEORY OF INSPIRATION MUST BE ADJUSTED TO THIS FACT. EVIDENTLY NEITHER TH OF VERBAL INSPIRATION, NOR THE THEORY OF PLENARY INSPIRATION CAN BE MADE TO FIT THE FACTS careful study of the writings themselves bring before us. These writings are not inspired in the sense WHICH WE HAVE COMMONLY GIVEN TO THAT WORD. THE VERBAL THEORY OF INSPIRATION WAS ONLY T WHILE THEY WERE SUPPOSED TO BE THE WORK OF A SINGLE AUTHOR. TO SUCH A COMPOSITE LITERATURE I THEORY WILL APPLY. "TO MAKE THIS CLAIM," SAYS PROFESSOR LADD, "AND YET ACCEPT THE BEST ASCE RESULTS OF CRITICISM, WOULD COMPEL US TO TAKE SUCH POSITIONS AS THE FOLLOWING: THE ORIGINAL OF EACH ONE OF THE WRITINGS WHICH ENTER INTO THE COMPOSITE STRUCTURE WERE INFALLIBLY INSPIR ONE WHO MADE ANY CHANGES IN ANY ONE OF THESE FUNDAMENTAL WRITINGS WAS INFALLIBLY INSPIRED COMPILER WHO PUT TOGETHER TWO OR MORE OF THESE WRITINGS WAS INFALLIBLY INSPIRED, BOTH AS SELECTIONS AND TRANSMISSIONS [OMISSIONS?], AND AS TO ANY CONNECTING OR EXPLANATORY WORDS WI MIGHT HIMSELF WRITE; EVERY REDACTOR WAS INFALLIBLY INSPIRED TO CORRECT AND SUPPLEMENT AND O WHICH WAS THE PRODUCT OF PREVIOUS INFALLIBLE INSPIRATIONS. OR PERHAPS IT MIGHT SEEM CONVENIENT TO ATTACH THE CLAIM OF A PLENARY INSPIRATION TO THE LAST REDACTOR OF ALL; BUT THEN PROBABLY HAVE SELECTED OF ALL OTHERS THE ONE LEAST ABLE TO BEAR THE WEIGHT OF SUCH A CLAIM. MAKING THE CLAIM FOR A PLENARY INSPIRATION OF THE PENTATEUCH IN ITS PRESENT FORM ON THE GI THE INFALLIBILITY OF THAT ONE OF THE SCRIBES WHO GAVE IT ITS LAST TOUCHES SOME TIME SUBSEQUE date of Ezra!" [Footnote: *The Doctrine of Sacred Scripture*, i. 499]

AND YET THIS DOES NOT SIGNIFY THAT THESE BOOKS ARE VALUELESS. WHEN IT WAS DISCOVERED HOMERIC WRITINGS WERE NOT ALL THE WORK OF HOMER, THE VALUE OF THE HOMERIC WRITINGS AFFECTED. AS PICTURES OF THE LIFE OF THAT REMOTE ANTIQUITY THEY HAD NOT LOST THEIR SIGNIFI VALUE OF THESE MOSAIC BOOKS IS OF A VERY DIFFERENT SORT FROM THAT OF THE HOMERIC WRITINGS, DISCOVERIES OF THE HIGHER CRITICISM AFFECT THEM NO MORE SERIOUSLY. EVEN THEIR HISTORICAL CHA BY NO MEANS OVERTHROWN. YOU CAN FIND IN HERODOTUS AND IN LIVY DISCREPANCIES AND CONTRADI BUT THIS DOES NOT LEAD YOU TO REGARD THEIR WRITINGS AS WORTHLESS. THERE ARE NO INFALLIBLE HIS THAT IS NO REASON WHY YOU SHOULD NOT STUDY HISTORY, OR WHY YOU SHOULD READ ALL HISTORY INCLINATION TO REJECT EVERY STATEMENT WHICH IS NOT FORCED ON YOUR ACCEPTANCE BY EVIDENCE WI cannot gainsay.

THESE BOOKS OF MOSES ARE THE TREASURY, INDEED, OF NO LITTLE VALUABLE HISTORY. THEY INFALLIBLE, BUT THEY CONTAIN A GREAT DEAL OF TRUTH WHICH WE FIND NOWHERE ELSE, AND WHI WONDERFULLY CORROBORATED BY ALL THAT WE DO KNOW. EWALD DECLARES THAT IN THE FOURTEENTH GENESIS ABRAHAM IS BROUGHT BEFORE US "IN THE CLEAR LIGHT OF HISTORY." FROM MONUMENTS AND SOURCES THE SUBSTANTIAL ACCURACY OF THIS NARRATIVE IS CONFIRMED; AND THE ACCOUNT OF THE ABRAHAM TO EGYPT CONFORMS, IN ALL ITS MINUTE INCIDENTS, TO THE LIFE OF EGYPT AT THAT TIME. T PHARAOH IS THE RIGHT NAME FOR THE KINGS REIGNING THEN; THE BEHAVIOR OF THE SERVANTS OF PH PERFECTLY IN KEEPING WITH THE POPULAR IDEAS AND PRACTICES AS THE MONUMENTS REVEAL THEM. TH OF JOSEPH HAS BEEN CONFIRMED, AS TO ITS ESSENTIAL ACCURACY, AS TO THE VERISIMILITUDE OF ITS PIC EGYPTIAN LIFE, BY EVERY RECENT DISCOVERY. GEORG EBERS DECLARES THAT "THIS NARRATIVE CONTAIN WHICH DOES NOT ACCURATELY CORRESPOND TO A COURT OF PHARAOH IN THE BEST TIMES OF THE KI MANY FEATURES OF THIS NARRATIVE WHICH A RASH SKEPTICISM HAS ASSAILED HAVE BEEN VERIFIED B discoveries.

WE ARE TOLD IN THE EXODUS THAT THE ISRAELITES WERE IMPRESSED BY PHARAOH INTO BUILDING TWO STORE-CITIES ("TREASURE CITIES," THE OLD VERSION CALLS THEM), NAMED PITHOM AND RAMESES, IN THIS WORK THEY WERE MADE TO "SERVE WITH RIGOR;" THAT THEIR LIVES WERE EMBITTERED "WI SERVICE IN MORTAR AND BRICK AND ALL MANNER OF HARD SERVICE IN THE FIELD;" THAT THEY WERE SC FORCED TO MAKE BRICK WITHOUT STRAW. THE WHEREABOUTS OF THESE STORE-CITIES, AND THE PRECISE OF THE TERM APPLIED TO THEM, HAS BEEN A MATTER OF MUCH CONJECTURE, AND THE STORY HAS SO BEEN SET ASIDE AS A MYTH. TO PITHOM THERE IS NO CLEAR HISTORICAL REFERENCE IN ANY OTHER BOO EXODUS. ONLY FOUR OR FIVE YEARS AGO A GENOVESE EXPLORER UNEARTHED, NEAR THE ROUTE OF

Canal, this very city; found several ruined monuments with the name of the city plainly insc[r] them, "Pi Tum," and excavating still further uncovered a ruin of which the following Rawlinson's description: "The town is altogether a square, inclosed by a brick wall twenty-t thick, and measuring six hundred and fifty feet along each side. Nearly the whole of th occupied by solidly built, square chambers, divided one from another by brick walls, from ei ten feet thick, which are unpierced by window or door or opening of any kind. About ten fe the bottom the walls show a row of recesses for beams, in some of which decayed wood remains, indicating that the buildings were two-storied, having a lower room which could entered by a trap-door, used probably as a store-house, or magazine, and an upper one in whi keeper of the store may have had his abode. Therefore this discovery is simply that of a 'sto built partly by Rameses II.; but it further appears from several short inscriptions, that the the city was Pa Tum, or Pithom; and thus there is no reasonable doubt that one of the tw built by the Israelites has been laid bare, and answers completely to the description give [Footnote: Quoted by Robinson in *The Pharaohs of the Bondage*, p. 97.]

The walls of Egypt were not all laid with mortar, but the record speaks of mortar in t and here it is: the several courses of these buildings were usually "laid with mortar in regu More striking still is the fact that in some of these buildings, while the lower tiers are co bricks having straw in them, the upper tiers consist of a poorer quality of bricks without Photographs may be seen in this country of some of these brick granaries of this old stor Pithom, with the line of division plainly showing between the two kinds of bricks; and thus w before our eyes a most striking confirmation of the truth of this story of the bondag Israelites in Egypt. Quite a number of such testimonies to the substantial historical verity Old Testament records have been discovered in recent years as old mounds have been ope Egypt and in Chaldea, and the monuments of buried centuries have told their story wondering world. The books are not infallible, but he who sets them all aside as a colle myths or fables exposes his ignorance in a lamentable way.

But what is far more to the purpose, the ideas running all through the old litera constructive truths of science, of ethics, of religion, are pure and lofty and full of savi Even science, I say, owes much to Genesis. The story of the Creation in the first chapter of (must not indeed be taken for veritable history; but it is a solemn hymn in which some grea of the world's origin are sublimely set forth. It gives us the distinct idea of the unity of G sweeping away, at one mighty stroke, the whole system of naturalistic polytheism, which science impossible, when it declares that "In the beginning God created the heavens and th In the same words it sets forth the truth by whose light science alone walks safely, that the source of all things is a spiritual cause. The God from whose power all things proceed is not a for concourse of atoms, but a spiritual intelligence. From this living God came forth matter forces, life with its organisms, mind with its freedom. And although it may not be possible t the words of this ancient hymn into scientific statements of the order of creation, it is m that it implies a continuous process, a law of development, in the generations of the heaven earth. This is not a scientific treatise of creation, but the alphabet of science is here, as Dr. Smyth has said; and it is correct. The guiding lights of scientific study are in these great principles.

Similarly the ethical elements and tendencies of these old writings are sound and have shown you how defective many of the Mosaic laws are when judged by Christian stan but all this legislation contains formative ideas and principles by which it tends to puri Human sacrifices were common among the surrounding nations; the story of Abraham and banishes that horror forever from Hebrew history. Slavery was universal, but the law of th Year made an end of domestic slavery in Israel. The family was foundationless; the wife's rested wholly on the caprice of her husband; but that law of divorce which I quoted to which our Lord repealed, set some bounds to this caprice, for the husband was compelled through certain formalities before he could turn his wife out of doors. The law of blood v though in terms it authorized murder, yet in effect powerfully restrained the violence of age, and gave a chance for the development of that idea of the sacredness of life which t

MORAL COMMONPLACE, BUT WHICH HAD SCARCELY DAWNED UPON THE MINDS OF THOSE OLD HEBREWS. THE HISTORY SHOWS A PEOPLE MOVING STEADILY FORWARD UNDER MORAL LEADERSHIP, OUT OF BARBARIS HIGHER CIVILIZATION, AND WE CAN TRACE THE VERY PROCESS BY WHICH THE MORAL MAXIMS WHICH TO ALMOST AXIOMS HAVE BEEN CLEARED OF THE CRUDITIES OF PASSION AND ANIMALISM, AND STAMPED UPO consciousness of men. Is not God in all this history?

THOSE FIRST PRINCIPLES WHICH I HAVE CALLED THE GUIDING LIGHTS OF SCIENCE ARE ALSO THE ELE PURE RELIGION. SCIENCE AND RELIGION SPELL OUT DIFFERENT MESSAGES TO MEN, BUT THEY START WITH ALPHABET. AND THE RELIGIOUS PURITY OF THAT HYMN OF THE CREATION IS NOT LESS WONDERFUL SCIENTIFIC VERITY. COMPARE IT WITH THE OTHER TRADITIONAL STORIES OF THE ORIGIN OF THINGS; C WITH THE MYTHOLOGIES OF EGYPT, OF CHALDEA, OF GREECE AND ROME, AND SEE HOW FAR ABOVE T STANDS IN SPIRITUAL DIGNITY, IN MORAL BEAUTY. "WE COULD MORE EASILY, INDEED," SAYS DR. NE SMYTH, "COMPUTE HOW MUCH A PURE SPRING WELLING UP AT THE SOURCE OF A BROOK THAT WIDENS I RIVER, HAS DONE FOR MEADOW AND GRASS AND FLOWERS AND OVERHANGING TREES, FOR THOUSANDS (THAN ESTIMATE THE INFLUENCE OF THIS PUREST OF ALL ANCIENT TRADITIONS OF THE CREATION, AS IT F into the lives and revived the consciences of men; as it has purified countries of idolatries and swept AWAY SUPERSTITION; AND HAS FLOWED ON AND ON WITH THE INCREASING TRUTH OF HISTORY, AND KEPT FI FRUITFUL, FROM GENERATION TO GENERATION, FAITH IN THE ONE GOD AND THE COMMON PARENTAGE [Footnote: *Old Faiths in New Light*, p. 73.]

Above all, we find in all this literature the planting and the first germination of that great hope WHICH TURNED THE THOUGHT OF THIS PEOPLE FROM THE EARLIEST GENERATIONS TOWARD THE FUTURE, THEM TRUST AND PRAY AND WAIT, IN DARKEST TIMES, FOR BETTER DAYS TO COME. "SPEAK UNTO THE CHII ISRAEL THAT THEY GO FORWARD!" THIS IS THE VOICE THAT IS ALWAYS SOUNDING FROM THE HEIGHTS ABO WHETHER THEY HALT BY THE SHORE OF THE SEA, OR BIVOUAC IN THE WILDERNESS. THEY DO NOT ALWAYS (VOICE, BUT IT NEVER FAILS TO ROUSE AND SUMMON THEM. NO PEOPLE OF ALL HISTORY HAS LIVED IN THE AS ISRAEL DID. "BY FAITH" THEY WORSHIPED AND TRUSTED AND WROUGHT AND FOUGHT, THE WORTHIE OLD RELIGION; TOWARDS LANDS THAT THEY HAD NOT SEEN THEY SET THEIR FACES; CONCERNING THINC THEY WERE ALWAYS PROPHESYING; AND IT IS THIS GREAT HOPE THAT FORMS THE GERM OF THE MI EXPECTATION BY WHICH THEY REACH FORTH TO THE GLORIES OF THE LATTER DAY. THIS ATTITUDE OF IS THE GENERATIONS, IS THE ONE STRIKING FEATURE OF THIS HISTORY. NO SOULLESS SPHINX FACING A DESERT WITH BLIND EYES--NO IMPASSIVE BUDDHA ENSPHERED IN PLACID SILENCE--IS THE GENIUS OI PEOPLE, BUT SOME STRONG ANGEL POISED ON MIGHTY PINION ABOVE THE HIGHEST PEAK OF PISGAH SCANNING WITH SWIFT GLANCES THE BEAUTY OF THE PROMISED LAND. NOW ANY PEOPLE OF WHICH THIS MUST BE, IN A LARGE SENSE OF THE WORD, AN INSPIRED PEOPLE; AND THEIR LITERATURE, WITH ALL THE IMPERFECTION WHICH MUST APPEAR IN IT, ON ACCOUNT OF THE MEDIUM THROUGH WHICH IT COMES, WIL proof of the divine ideas and forces that are working themselves out in their history.

IT IS IN THIS LARGE WAY OF LOOKING AT THE HEBREW LITERATURE THAT WE DISCOVER ITS REAL PRE(AND WHEN WE GET THIS LARGE CONCEPTION, THEN PETTY QUESTIONS ABOUT THE ABSOLUTE ACCURACY AND DATES NO LONGER TROUBLE US. "HE WHO HAS ONCE GAINED THIS BROADER VIEW OF THE BIBLE," S NEWMAN SMYTH, "AS THE DEVELOPMENT OF A COURSE OF HISTORY ITSELF GUIDED AND INSPIRED BY JE WILL NOT BE DISCONCERTED BY THE CONFUSED NOISES OF THE CRITIC. HIS FAITH IN THE WORD OF (DEEPER THAN ANY DIFFICULTIES OR FLAWS UPON THE SURFACE OF THE BIBLE. HE WILL NOT BE DISTU SEEING ANY THEORY OF ITS MECHANICAL FORMATION, OR SCHOOL-BOOK INFALLIBILITY BROKEN TO F UNDER THE REPEATED BLOWS OF MODERN INVESTIGATION; THE WATER OF LIFE WILL FLOW FROM THE RO THE SCHOLAR STRIKES WITH HIS ROD. HE CAN WAIT, WITHOUT FEAR, FOR A CANDID AND THOROUGH STUDY SACRED WRITINGS TO DETERMINE, IF POSSIBLE, WHAT PARTS ARE GENUINE, AND WHAT NARRATIVES, IF UNHISTORICAL. HIS BELIEF IN THE WORD OF GOD, FROM GENERATION TO GENERATION, DOES NOT DEPE THE MINOR INCIDENTS OF THE BIBLICAL STORIES; IT WOULD NOT BE DESTROYED OR WEAKENED, EVEN HUMAN TRADITIONS COULD BE SHOWN TO HAVE OVERGROWN SOME PARTS OF THIS SACRED HISTORY, AS T CREEPING UP THE WALL OF THE CHURCH, DOES NOT LOOSEN ITS ANCIENT STONES." [FOOTNOTE: *Old Faiths in New Light*, p. 59.]

Chapter IV.

The Ealier Hebrew Histories.

We found reasons, in previous chapters, for believing that considerable portions Levitical legislation came from the hands of Moses, although the narratives of the Penta many of its laws were put into their present form long after the time of Moses. The co character of all this old literature has been demonstrated. The fact that its materials wer from several sources, by a process extending through many centuries, and that the v redaction was not completed until the people returned from the exile about five centuri Christ, and almost a thousand years after the death of Moses, are facts now as well estab any other results of scholarly research.

Nevertheless, we have maintained that the Israelites possessed, when they entered C considerable body of legislation framed under the eye of Moses and bearing his name. Thr the Book of Joshua this legislation is frequently referred to. If the Book of Joshua was, as assumed, originally connected with the first five books, constituting what is now ca Hexateuch, if these six books were put into their present form by the same writers, we expect that the Mosaic legislation would be clearly traced through all these books.

But when we go forward in this history we come at once upon a remarkable fact. The Book of Judges, the Book of Ruth, and the two books of Samuel cover a period of Jewish history est in our common chronology at more than four hundred years, and in these four books the mention whatever of that Mosaic legislation which constituted, as we have supposed, the the Pentateuch. The name of Moses is mentioned only six times in these four books; twice early chapters of the Judges in connection with the settlement of the kindred of his wife once in a reference to an order given by Moses that Hebron should be given to Caleb; tw single passage in I Samuel xii., where Moses and Aaron are referred to as leaders of the pe of Egyptian bondage, and once in Judges iii. 4, where it is said that certain of the native ra left in Canaan, "to prove Israel by them, whether they would hearken to the commandmen Lord which he commanded their fathers by the hand of Moses." This last is the only plac these books where there is the faintest allusion to any legislation left to the Israelites by this reference does not make it clear whether the "commandments" referred to were writte The word "law" is not found in these four books. There is nothing in any of these books to that the children of Israel possessed any written laws. There are, indeed, in Ruth and in th frequent accounts of observances that are enjoined in the Pentateuch; and in Samuel we re tabernacle and the ark and the offering of sacrifices; the history tells us that some of commanded in the Mosaic law were observed during this period; but when we look in these for any reference or appeal to the sacred writings of Moses, or to any other sacred writi any laws or statutes or written ordinances for the government of the people, we look Samuel the Prophet anointed Saul and afterward David as Kings of Israel; but if, on these occasions, he said anything about the writings of Moses or the law of Moses, the fact mentioned. The records afford us no ground for affirming that either Samuel or Saul was the existence of such sacred writings.

This is a notable fact. That the written law of Moses should, for four centuries of history, have disappeared so completely from notice that the historian did not find it nec make any allusion to it, is a circumstance that needs explanation.

It is true, as I have said, that during this period certain observances required by the la kept more or less regularly. But it is also true that many of the most specific and requirements of the law were neglected or violated during all these years by the holiest Mosaic law utterly forbids the offering of sacrifices at any other place than the central sa

TABERNACLE OR THE TEMPLE; BUT THE NARRATIVE OF THESE EARLY HISTORICAL BOOKS SHOWS ALL THE HEROES OF THE EARLIER HISTORY BUILDING ALTARS, AND OFFERING SACRIFICES FREELY IN MANY PLACES APPARENT CONSCIOUSNESS OF TRANSGRESSION,--NAY, WITH THE STRONGEST ASSURANCE OF THE DIVINE A "SAMUEL," SAYS PROFESSOR ROBERTSON SMITH, "SACRIFICES ON MANY HIGH PLACES, SAUL BUILDS A DAVID AND HIS SON SOLOMON PERMIT THE WORSHIP AT THE HIGH PLACES TO CONTINUE, AND THE HIS RECOGNIZES THIS AS LEGITIMATE BECAUSE THE TEMPLE WAS NOT YET BUILT (I KINGS III. 2-4). IN NO ISRAEL THIS STATE OF THINGS WAS NEVER CHANGED. THE HIGH PLACES WERE AN ESTABLISHED FEATUI KINGDOM OF EPHRAIM, AND ELIJAH HIMSELF DECLARES THAT THE DESTRUCTION OF THE ALTARS OF JEH ILLEGITIMATE ACCORDING TO THE PENTATEUCH--IS A BREACH OF JEHOVAH'S COVENANT." [FOOTNOTE: *The Old Testament in the Jewish Church*, pp. 220, 221.]

ACCORDING TO THE LEVITICAL LAW IT WAS POSITIVELY UNLAWFUL FOR ANY PERSON BUT THE HIG EVER TO GO INTO THE INNERMOST SANCTUARY, THE HOLY OF HOLIES, WHERE THE ARK OF GOD WAS KEPT HIGH PRIEST COULD GO INTO THAT AWFUL PLACE BUT ONCE A YEAR. BUT WE FIND THE BOY SAMUEL . SLEEPING "IN THE TEMPLE OF THE LORD WHERE THE ARK OF THE LORD WAS." THE OLD VERSION CONC FACT BY A MISTRANSLATION. THESE ARE ONLY A FEW OF MANY VIOLATIONS OF THE PENTATEUCHAL LI which we find recorded in these books.

FROM THE SILENCE OF THESE EARLIER HISTORIES CONCERNING THE LAW OF MOSES, AND FROM THI TRANSGRESSIONS, BY THE HOLIEST MEN, OF THE POSITIVE REQUIREMENTS OF THE PENTATEUCHAL LEGISL CONCLUSION HAS BEEN DRAWN BY RECENT CRITICS THAT THE PENTATEUCHAL LEGISLATION COULD NOT HA EXISTENCE DURING THIS PERIOD OF HISTORY; THAT IT MUST HAVE BEEN PRODUCED AT A LATER DAY. IT admitted that they make out a strong case. For reasons presented in the second chapter, I am unable TO ACCEPT THEIR THEORY. IT IS PROBABLE, HOWEVER, THAT THE CODE OF LAWS IN EXISTENCE AT THIS TI LIMITED AND SIMPLE CODE--NO SUCH ELABORATE RITUAL AS THAT WHICH WE NOW FIND IN THE PENTATEU THAT THOSE PARTICULAR REQUIREMENTS WITH RESPECT TO WHICH THE EARLIER JUDGES AND SAMUEL AN appear to behave themselves so disorderly, had not then been enacted.

MOREOVER, IT SEEMS TO BE NECESSARY TO ADMIT THAT THERE WAS A SURPRISING AMOUNT OF PO IGNORANCE RESPECTING EVEN THOSE PORTIONS OF THE LAW WHICH WERE THEN IN EXISTENCE. THIS ASTONISHING PHENOMENON. ATTEMPTS ARE MADE TO ILLUSTRATE IT BY THE IGNORANCE OF THE BIBI PREVAILED AMONG OUR OWN ANCESTORS BEFORE THE INVENTION OF PRINTING; BUT NO PARALLEL CAN BI AS I BELIEVE, IN THE MEDIÆVAL HISTORY OF EUROPE. IT IS TRUE THAT MANY OF THE COMMON PEOPLI ALTOGETHER UNFAMILIAR WITH THE BIBLE IN MEDIÆVAL TIMES; BUT WE CANNOT CONCEIVE OF SUCH A T THAT THE PRIESTS, THE LEARNED MEN, AND THE LEADERS OF THE CHURCH AT THAT TIME, SHOULD I unaware of the existence of such a book.

ON HIS DEATH-BED DAVID IS SAID TO HAVE ADMONISHED SOLOMON (I KINGS II. 3), THAT HE SH KEEP THE STATUTES AND COMMANDMENTS OF THE LORD, "ACCORDING TO THAT WHICH IS WRITTEN IN TH Moses." This is the first reference to the Mosaic law which we find in connection with the history of DAVID; THE FIRST MENTION OF A WRITTEN LAW SINCE THE DEATH OF JOSHUA, FOUR CENTURIES BEFORE. A THERE ARE THREE OTHER CASUAL ALLUSIONS TO THE LAW OF MOSES IN THE FIRST BOOK OF KINGS, AND F SECOND BOOK. THE BOOKS OF CHRONICLES, WHICH FOLLOW THE KINGS, CONTAIN FREQUENT ALLUSION LAW; BUT THESE BOOKS, AS WE SHALL SEE BY AND BY, WERE WRITTEN LONG AFTERWARD; AND THE TRADITIO THEY EMBODY CANNOT BE SO SAFE A GUIDE AS THAT OF THE EARLIER HISTORIES. IT IS IN CHRONICLES LEARN OF THE ATTEMPT WHICH WAS MADE BY ONE OF THE GOOD KINGS OF JUDAH, JEHOSHAPHAT, T CERTAIN PRINCES, PRIESTS, AND LEVITES APPOINTED TO TEACH THE LAW; THEY WENT ABOUT THE LAND, I TEACHING THE PEOPLE, "AND HAD THE BOOK OF THE LAW OF JEHOVAH WITH THEM." I THINK THAT TH FIRST INTIMATION, AFTER THE DEATH OF MOSES, THAT THE LAW DELIVERED BY HIM HAD BEEN PUBLICLY EVEN READ IN CONNECTION WITH THE ORDINANCES OF WORSHIP. THE EARLIER NARRATIVE OF JEHOS reign, which we find in the Book of the Kings, makes no allusion to this circumstance.

NEARLY THREE HUNDRED YEARS AFTER JEHOSHAPHAT, AND NEARLY FIVE HUNDRED YEARS AFTER I YOUNG KING JOSIAH WAS REIGNING IN JERUSALEM. THE TEMPLE HAD FALLEN INTO RUIN, AND THE GOO DETERMINED TO HAVE IT REPAIRED. HILKIAH, THE HIGH PRIEST, WHO WAS RUMMAGING AMONG THE RUBB THE DILAPIDATED SANCTUARY, FOUND THERE THE BOOK OF THE LAW OF THE LORD. THE SURPRISE W MANIFESTS AT THIS DISCOVERY, THE TREPIDATION OF SHAPHAN THE SCRIBE, WHO HASTENS TO TELL THE KI

IT, AND THE CONSTERNATION OF THE KING WHEN HE LISTENS FOR THE FIRST TIME IN HIS LIFE TO THE THE BOOK, AND DISCOVERS HOW GRIEVOUSLY ITS COMMANDMENTS HAVE BEEN DISOBEYED, FORM ONE C MOST STRIKING SCENES OF THE OLD HISTORY. "HOW ARE WE TO EXPLAIN," ASKS DR. PEROWNE, "THIS SI AND ALARM IN THE MIND OF JOSIAH, BETRAYING, AS IT DOES, SUCH UTTER IGNORANCE OF THE BOOK OF AND THE SEVERITY OF ITS THREATENINGS,--EXCEPT ON THE SUPPOSITION THAT AS A WRITTEN DOCUMEI WELL-NIGH PERISHED?" [FOOTNOTE: SMITBible *Bible Dictionary*, ART. "PENTATEUCH."] UNDOUBTEDLY "THE B OF THE LAW" THUS DISCOVERED WAS THAT BODY OF LEGISLATION WHICH LIES AT THE HEART DEUTERONOMIC CODE; AND THIS WAS NEVER AGAIN LOST SIGHT OF BY THE JEWISH PEOPLE. IT WAS LES FIFTY YEARS AFTER THIS THAT NEBUCHADNEZZAR DESTROYED THE CITY AND THE TEMPLE AND CARRIED AWAY INTO CAPTIVITY. AND IT WAS NOT UNTIL THEIR RETURN FROM THE CAPTIVITY, SEVENTY YEARS L THESE SACRED WRITINGS BEGAN TO ASSUME THAT PLACE OF EMINENCE IN THE RELIGIOUS SYSTEM OF T WHICH THEY HAVE HELD IN LATER TIMES. THE MAN BY WHOM THE JEWS WERE TAUGHT TO CHERISH ANI THESE WRITINGS WAS EZRA, ONE OF THE RETURNING EXILES. THIS EZRA, THE RECORD SAYS, "WAS A READ IN THE LAW OF MOSES WHICH THE LORD GOD OF ISRAEL HAD GIVEN," AND "HE HAD PREPARED HIS HI SEEK THE LAW OF THE LORD, AND TO DO IT AND TO TEACH IN ISRAEL STATUTES AND JUDGMENTS." HE I DOUBT, WHO GAVE TO THESE LAWS THEIR LAST REVISION, AND WHO PUT THE PENTATEUCH SUBSTANTIALLY SHAPE IN WHICH WE HAVE IT NOW. DOUBTLESS MUCH WAS ADDED AT THIS TIME; RITUAL RULES WHICH HAD HANDED DOWN ORALLY WERE WRITTEN OUT AND MADE PART OF THE CODE; THE PENTATEUCH, AFTER WAS A MORE ELABORATE LAW BOOK THAN THAT WHICH HILKIAH FOUND IN THE OLD TEMPLE. UNI PRESIDENCY OF EZRA IN JERUSALEM, AND IN THE DAYS WHICH FOLLOWED, THE BOOK OF THE LAW WAS E IT WAS THE STANDARD OF AUTHORITY; IT WAS READ IN THE TEMPLE AND EXPLAINED IN THE SYNAGO writings were woven into all the thought and life of the people of Israel; there never has been a time SINCE THAT DAY WHEN THE HISTORY OF THE REIGN OF ANY KING COULD HAVE BEEN WRITTEN MENTIONING THE LAW OF MOSES; THERE NEVER HAS BEEN A DECADE WHEN ANY ADEQUATE ACCOUNT OF of the Jewish people could have been given which would not bring this book constantly into view.

THIS BOOK OF THE LAW, AS FINALLY COMPLETED BY EZRA AND HIS CO-LABORERS, WAS THE FOUNDA THE HEBREW SCRIPTURES; IT POSSESSED A SACREDNESS IN THE EYES OF THE JEWS FAR HIGHER TH PERTAINING TO ANY OTHER PART OF THEIR WRITINGS. NEXT TO THIS IN AGE AND IMPORTANCE WAS T division of their Scriptures known by them as *"The Prophets."*

AFTER THE BOOK OF THE LAW WAS GIVEN TO THE PEOPLE WITH GREAT SOLEMNITY, IN THE DAYS C AND THE PUBLIC READING AND EXPLANATION OF IT BECAME A PRINCIPAL PART OF THE WORSHIP OF THE BEGAN TO BE NOISED ABROAD THAT THERE WERE CERTAIN OTHER SACRED WRITINGS WORTHY TO BE KN TREASURED. THE ONLY INFORMATION WE HAVE CONCERNING THE BEGINNING OF THIS SECOND COLL FOUND IN ONE OF THE APOCRYPHAL BOOKS, THE SECOND OF MACCABEES (II. 14), IN WHICH WE ARE TOI NEEMIAS (NEHEMIAH), IN "FOUNDING A LIBRARY, GATHERED TOGETHER THE ACTS OF THE KINGS, WRITINGS OF] THE PROPHETS, AND OF DAVID, AND THE EPISTLES OF THE KINGS CONCERNING THE HOI THESE LAST NAMED DOCUMENTS ARE NOT NOW IN EXISTENCE. THEY APPEAR TO HAVE BEEN THE LETT COMMISSIONS OF BABYLONIAN AND PERSIAN KINGS RESPECTING THE RETURN OF THE PEOPLE TO JERUSAI THE REBUILDING OF THE TEMPLE. THE OTHER WRITINGS MENTIONED ARE, HOWEVER, ALL KNOWN TO US, INCLUDED IN OUR COLLECTION. IT IS NOT CERTAIN THAT NEHEMIAH BEGAN THIS COLLECTION; IT MAY I initiated before his day, and the "founding" of the library may have been only the work of providing FOR THE PRESERVATION AND ARRANGEMENT OF BOOKS ALREADY IN HIS POSSESSION. THIS SECOND COLLE SACRED WRITINGS, CALLED THE PROPHETS, WAS DIVIDED, AS I HAVE BEFORE STATED, INTO THE EARLIER LATER PROPHETS; THE FORMER SUBDIVISION CONTAINING THE BOOKS OF JOSHUA, [FOOTNOTE: JOSHUA, AI ORIGINALLY A PORTION OF THE PENTATEUCHAL LITERATURE, WAS, ABOUT THE TIME OF THE EXILE, SEPAR THE FIRST FIVE BOOKS, AND PUT INTO THIS LATER COLLECTION.] JUDGES, SAMUEL, AND KINGS; THE L BOOKS WHICH WE NOW REGARD AND CLASS AS THE PROPHECIES. RUTH WAS AT FIRST CONSIDERED AS A F THE JUDGES, AND WAS INCLUDED AMONG THE "EARLIER PROPHETS," AND LAMENTATIONS WAS APPENI JEREMIAH, AND INCLUDED AMONG THE "LATER PROPHETS." THESE TWO BOOKS WERE AFTERWARD RE FROM THIS COLLECTION, FOR LITURGICAL REASONS, AND PLACED IN THE THIRD GROUP OF WRITINGS, OF shall speak farther on.

IT IS PROBABLE THAT THE PROPHETIC WRITINGS PROPER WERE FIRST COLLECTED; BUT IT WILL I

convenient to speak first of the books known to the Jews as the "Earlier Prophets," and to t
Old Testament Histories,--Judges, Ruth, Samuel, and the Kings.

These books take up the history of Israel at the death of Joshua, and continue it to th
the Captivity, a period of more than eight centuries. Some of the critics are inclined to
them all together as successive volumes of one great history; but there is not much found
this judgment, and it is better to treat them separately.

The Book of Judges contains the annals of the Israelites after the death of Joshua, and
period of three or four centuries. It was a period of disorder and turbulence,--the "Dark A
Jewish history; when every man, as the record often says, "did that which was right in his own
There is frequent mention of the keeping of various observances enjoined in the laws of Mos
there is no express mention of these laws in the book. The story is chiefly occupied wi
northern tribes; no mention is made of Judah after the third chapter; and it is largely a rec
various wars of deliverance and defense waged by these northern Hebrews against the surro
peoples, under certain leaders who arose, in a providential way, to take command of them.

The questions, Who wrote it? and When was it written? are not easily answered. It
appear that portions of it must have been written after the time of Saul, for the phrase, fr
repeated, "there was then no king in the land," looks back from a period when there was a king in
the land. And it would appear that the first chapter must have been written before the m
the reign of King David; for it tells us that the Jebusites had not yet been driven out of J
that they still held that stronghold; while in 2 Samuel v. 6, 7, we are told of the expulsi
Jebusites by David, who made the place his capital from that time. The tradition that Samuel
the book rests on no adequate foundation.

The evidence that this book also was compiled, by some later writer, from various w
documents, is abundant and convincing. There are two distinct introductions, one of
comprises the first chapter and five verses of the second, and the other of which occu
remainder of the second chapter. The first of these begins thus: "And it came to pass after t
of Joshua that the children of Israel asked of the Lord, saying, Who shall go up for us ag
Canaanites, to fight against them?" The second of these introductions begins by telling ho
sent the people away, after his farewell address, and goes on (ii. 8) to say, "And Joshua the
Nun the servant of the Lord died, being an hundred and ten years old." After recounting a
of events which happened, as it tells us, after the death of Joshua, the narrative goes on to
naively as possible an account of Joshua's death. If this were a consecutive narrative from t
of one writer, inspired or otherwise, such an arrangement would be inexplicable; but if w
here a combination of two or more independent documents, the explanation is not difficul
little puzzling, too, to find the circumstances of the death of Joshua repeated here, in a
same words as those which we find in the Book of Joshua (xxiv. 29-31). It would seem either
the writer of Joshua must have copied from Judges, or the writer of Judges from Joshua, o
that both copied from some older document this account of Joshua's death.

Another still more striking illustration of the manner in which these old bo
constructed is found in the account given in the first chapter of the capture of Debir, by
11-15). Here it is expressly said that this capture took place after the death of Joshu
consequence of the leadership assigned by Jehovah to the tribe of Judah in this war agai
Canaanites. But the same narrative, in the same words, is found in the Book of Joshua (xv.
and here we are told no less explicitly that the incident happened during the lifetime o
There is no doubt that the incident happened; it is a simple and natural story, and carries th
of credibility upon its face; but if it happened after the death of Joshua it did not happen be
death; one of these narrators borrowed the story from the other, or else both borrowed
common source; and one of them, certainly, put it in the wrong place,--one of them must hav
mistaken as to the time when it occurred. Such a mistake is of no consequence at all to o
holds a rational theory of inspiration; he expects to find in these old documents just suc
and misplacements; they do not in the least affect the true value of the book; but it must be
to any one that instances of this nature cannot be reconciled with the theory of an infal

which has been generally regarded as the only true theory.

The book is of the utmost value as showing us the state of morals and manners in that time, and letting us see with what crude material the great ideas committed to Israel--the spirituality and righteousness of God--were compelled to work themselves out.

The Book of Ruth, which was formerly, in the Jewish collections, regarded as a part Book of Judges, is a beautiful pastoral idyl of the same period. Its scene is laid in Judea, serves to show us that in the midst of all those turbulent ages there were quiet homes an lives. No sweeter story can be found in any literature; maternal tenderness, filial affectio chivalry, find in the book their typical representatives. The first sentence of the book giv approximate date of the incidents recorded: it was "in the days when the judges judged concluding verses give us the genealogy of King David, showing that Ruth was his grandmother; it must, therefore, have been written as late as the reign of David,--probabl later; for it describes, as if they belonged to a remote antiquity, certain usages of the Je must needs have shaped themselves after the occupation of Canaan. Yet it could scarcely ha written so late as the Captivity, for the marriage of Ruth, who is a Moabitess, to Boaz, is me as if it were a matter of course, with no hint of censure. In the latter days of Israel such a of a Jew with a foreigner would have been regarded as highly reprehensible. Inde Deuteronomic law most stringently forbids all social relations with that particular tribe Ruth belonged. "An Ammonite or a Moabite shall not enter into the assembly of the Lord; the tenth generation shall none belonging to them enter into the assembly of the Lord Thou shalt not seek their peace nor their prosperity all thy days for ever." (Deut. xxiii. 3, Ruth, the Moabitess, becomes the wife of one of the chief men of Bethlehem, with the appl all the Bethlehemites, and the highest approval of the author of this narrative; nay, she be the fourth generation, the ancestress of the greatest of all the kings of Israel. This cert that the people of Bethlehem did not know of the Deuteronomic law, for they were a God and a law-abiding people; and it also makes it probable that the incident occurred, and t book which describes the incident was written, before this part of the Deuteronomic code existence. It is therefore valuable, not only as throwing light on the life of the people at period, but also as illustrating the growth of the pentateuchal literature.

The two Books of Samuel and the two Books of Kings appear in the Septuagint and Latin Vulgate as one work in four volumes,--they are called the Four Books of Kings. In th Hebrew Bibles they are divided, however, as in our Bible, and bear the same names. constitute, it is true, a continuous history; but the supposition that they were all written at and by one author is scarcely credible. The standpoint of the writer of the Kings is cons shifted from that occupied by the writer of Samuel; we find ourselves in a new circle of ide we pass from the one book to the other.

The Books of Samuel are generally ascribed to Samuel as their author. This is a fair sa that lazy traditionalism which Christian opinion has been constrained to follow. There is slightest reason for believing that the Books of Samuel were written by Samuel any more the Odyssey was written by Ulysses, or the Æneid by Æneas, or Bruce's Address by Bruc Paracelsus by Paracelsus, or St. Simeon Stylites by Simeon himself. Even in Bible books we d hold that the Book of Esther was written by Esther, or the Book of Ruth by Ruth, or the Job by Job, or the Books of Timothy by Timothy. The fact that Samuel's name is given to the proves nothing as to its authorship. It may have been called Samuel because it begins with th of Samuel. The Hebrews were apt to name their books by some word or fact at the beginn them, as we have seen in their naming of the books of the Pentateuch.

It is true that certain facts are mentioned in this book of which Samuel would have knowledge than any one else; and he is said to have made a record of certain events, (I Sam But his death is related in the first verse of the twenty-fifth chapter of First Samuel; and it is certain, therefore, that considerably more than half of the document ascribed to him must ha written by some one else.

As to the name of the writer we are wholly ignorant, and it is not easy to determine th which he wrote. If we regarded this as a continuous history from the hand of one writer, wi be compelled to ascribe it to a date somewhat later than the separation of the two kingdon I Sam. xxvii. 6, we read of the present made by the king of Gath to David of the city of Zi the time when David was hiding from Saul; "wherefore," it is added, "Ziklag pertaineth un kings of Judah even unto this day." Now there were no "kings of Judah" until after the te seceded; Rehoboam was the first of the kings of Judah, therefore this must have been writt the time of Rehoboam. Doubtless this sentence was written after that time; and in all pro the books of Samuel did not receive their present form until some time after the secessio ten tribes. The materials from which the writer composed the book are hinted at here and is almost certain that here, as in the other books, old documents are combined by the aut not always with the best editorial care. Several old songs are quoted: the "Song of Hannah, exquisite lament over Saul and Jonathan, which is known as "The Bow;" David's "Son Deliverance," after he had escaped from Saul, which we find in the Psalter as the Eighteent and "The Last Words of David." The books contain a vivid narrative of the times of Eli and Samuel and Saul, and of the splendid reign of King David. No portion of the Old Testament h more diligently studied, and the moral teaching of the books is clear and luminous. Thi thoroughness of these writings when compared with almost any literature of equal ant always remarkable. Take, as an example, the treatment which David receives at the hands writer. He is a great hero, the one grand figure of Hebrew history; but there is nothin demigod in this picture of him; his faults and crimes are exposed and denounced, and he gai respect only by his hearty contrition and amendment. Verily the God of Israel whom th reveals is a God who loveth righteousness and hateth iniquity.

The Books of the Kings were originally one book, and ought to have remained on manuscript was torn in two by some scribe or copyist long ago, in the middle of the story reign of King Ahaziah; the first word of Second Kings goes on without so much as taking from the last word of First Kings. There is no excuse for this bisection of the narrative; it due to some accident, or to the arbitrary and unintelligent act of some person who attention to the meaning of the document. As the Books of Samuel carry the history from of Samuel down to the end of David's reign, so the Books of the Kings take up the story in days of David and carry it on to the time of the Exile, a period of four hundred and fifty y name of the author is concealed from us; there is a tradition, not altogether improbable, t written by the Prophet Jeremiah. If you will compare the last chapter of Second Kings with chapter of Jeremiah, you will discover that they are almost verbally the same. Here, Jeremiah was not the author, either writer may have copied the passage from the other, or bo have taken it from some older book. But this passage gives us a note of time. It tells us th Merodach, king of Babylon, in the first year of his reign, released the captive king o Jehoiachin, from his long confinement, and gave him a seat at his own table. The book mus been written, then, after the beginning of the reign of Evil-Merodach; and there is plenty to show that his reign began 5B1C.. And inasmuch as the book gives no hint of the return o Jews from their captivity, which began in 5B8C.., we may fairly conclude that the book written some time between those dates. Let us suppose that Jeremiah wrote it; even he, as p of the Lord, certainly used the materials of history which had accumulated in the archiv two nations.

It is evident that, after the establishment of the kingdom, considerable attention wa the preservation of the records of important national events. The kings kept chroniclers only preserved and edited old documents, but who wrote the annals of their own times. In xi. 41, at the conclusion of the narrative of Solomon's reign, we read, "Now the rest of th Solomon, and all that he did, and his wisdom, are they not written in the Book of the Solomon?" For his history of Jeroboam the writer refers in the same way to "The Book Chronicles of the Kings of Israel," and for his history of Rehoboam to "The Book Chronicles of the Kings of Judah." The same is true of the reigns of other kings. These wer course, our Books of Chronicles, for these were not written for two hundred years after of Kings was finished. It is thus evident, as one modern writer has said, "that the author lab employed the materials within his reach, very much as a modern historian might do, and f that he was as much puzzled by chronological difficulties as a modern historian freque [Footnote: Horton *Inspiration and the Bible*, p. 182.] Prophet or not, he took the materials at hands, and put them together in this history.

The splendid but corrupt reign of the son of David; the secession of the ten tribes Jeroboam; the hostile relations of the two kingdoms of Israel and Judah for two hundred years, by which both were weakened, and through unholy alliances corrupted, and the r which was the final destruction of both, are described in this book in a spirited and ev veracious manner. The two great prophets, Elijah and Elisha, are grand figures in this na much of the story revolves around them. As witnesses for the righteous Jehovah they stan warning, rebuking, counseling kings and people; the moral leadership by which Israel is cha and corrected and led in the way of righteousness expresses itself largely through thei The words of Lord Arthur Hervey, in Smith's "Bible Dictionary," none too strongly con historian's sense of the value of this part of the Old Testament:--

"Considering the conciseness of the narrative and the simplicity of the style, the amou knowledge which these books convey of the characters, conduct, and manners of kings and during so long a period is truly wonderful. The insight which they give us into the aspect (and Jerusalem, both natural and artificial, with the religious, military, and civil institutic people, their arts and manufactures, the state of education and learning among the resources, commerce, exploits, alliances, the causes of their decadence, and finally of thei most clear, interesting, and instructive. In a few brief sentences we acquire more a knowledge of the affairs of Egypt, Tyre, Syria, Assyria, Babylon, and other neighboring nati had been preserved to us in all the other remains of antiquity up to the recent disco hieroglyphical and cuneiform monuments." [Footnote: Vol. iii. p. 1561, American Edition.]

The substantial historical veracity of these books has been confirmed in many ways by very monuments to which Lord Hervey refers. And yet this substantial historical accuracy i as in other histories of the olden time, in the midst of many minor errors and discrepan would seem as if Providence had taken the utmost pains to show us that the essential truth moral and religious value of this history could not be identified with any theory of verba plenary inspiration.

Take, for example, some of the chronological items of this record. Mr. Horton statement will bring a few of them before us:--

"The author seems to have been content, in dealing with an Israelite king, to give t reckoned by the year of the reigning king in Judah just as he found it stated in the chronicles, and then to do the same in dealing with the dates of the reigning kings of Isra did not consider whether the two chronicles harmonized. We may take some illustrations f latter part of the work. Hoshea began to reign in Israel (2 Kings xv. 30) in the twentiet Jotham the king of Judah. So far writes our author, following the records of the N Kingdom. For his next paragraph he turns to his records of the Southern Kingdom, and tells us that Jotham never reached a twentieth year, but only reigned sixteen years (xv. 33); this is not the end of the difficulty; in chapter xvii. he goes back to the Northern Kingdom us that Hoshea began to reign, not in Jotham's reign at all, but in the reign of Ahaz, successor; and if now he had said, 'in the fourth year of Ahaz,' we might see our way throu perplexity, for the fourth year of Ahaz would, at any rate, be twenty years from the beg Jotham's reign, though Jotham himself had died after reigning sixteen years; but he says, nc fourth, but 'in the twelfth year of Ahaz king of Judah.' We may give it up, and exclaim w Speaker's commentator, 'The chronological confusion of the history, as it stands, is striki then perhaps we may exclaim at the Speaker's commentator, that he and the like of him havi us so little account of these unmistakable phenomena, and the cause of them, in the history.

"One other illustration may suffice. King Ahaz, according to one authority, lived twe and then came to the throne and reigned for sixteen years. (2 Kings xvi. 2.) At his death, t

AHAZ WAS THIRTY-SIX YEARS OF AGE. IN THAT YEAR HE WAS SUCCEEDED BY HIS SON HEZEKIAH, WH TWENTY-FIVE YEARS OF AGE. THIS WOULD MEAN THAT KING AHAZ WAS MARRIED AT THE AGE OF TEN, MAKING ALL ALLOWANCE FOR THE EARLIER PUBERTY OF EASTERN BOYS, DOES NOT SEEM PROBABLE; . EXPLANATION IS MUCH MORE LIKELY TO BE FOUND IN THE CHRONOLOGICAL INACCURACIES OF OUR AU WHICH, IF WE HAVE BEEN OBSERVANTLY READING HIS BOOK THROUGH, WE SHALL BY THIS TIME HAVE BI quite accustomed." [Footnote: Inspiration and the Bible, pp. 189-191.]

OBSERVE THAT WE ARE NOT GOING TO ANY HOSTILE OR FOREIGN SOURCES FOR THESE EVIDI INACCURACY; WE ARE SIMPLY LETTING THE BOOK TELL ITS OWN STORY. SUCH PHENOMENA AS THESE THROUGHOUT THIS HISTORY. THEY LIE UPON THE VERY FACE OF THE NARRATIVE. PROBABLY FEW OF THE F THESE PAGES HAVE NOTED THEM. FOR MYSELF, I MUST CONFESS THAT I READ THE BIBLE THROUGH, FRO TO COVER, SEVERAL TIMES BEFORE I WAS THIRTY YEARS OLD, BUT I HAD NEVER OBSERVED THESE INACC THE COMMENTATORS, FOR THE MOST PART,--THE ORTHODOX COMMENTATORS,--CAREFULLY KEEP THESE OF SIGHT. SOMETIMES THEY ATTEMPT, INDEED, TO EXPLAIN OR RECONCILE THEM, BUT SUCH EXPLA GENERALLY INCREASE THE INCREDIBILITY OF THE NARRATIVE. THE LATEST VERDICT OF ULTRA-CONSERVA THESE DATES AND CHRONOLOGICAL NOTES ARE INTERPOLATED BY SOME LATER HAND; BUT THIS, TOO, IS OF THE QUESTION. THE ONLY TRUE ACCOUNT OF THE MATTER IS, THAT THE AUTHOR TOOK THESE RECORD CHRONICLES OF THE KINGS OF JUDAH AND THE CHRONICLES OF THE KINGS OF ISRAEL, AND PIECI TOGETHER WITHOUT NOTICING OR CARING WHETHER THEY AGREED. HIS MIND WAS NOT FIXED UPON S ACCURACY OF DATES. HE WAS THINKING ONLY OF THE GREAT ETHICAL AND SPIRITUAL PROBLEMS THEMSELVES OUT IN THIS HISTORY,--OF THE QUESTION WHETHER OR NOT THESE KINGS "DID THAT WHICH IN THE SIGHT OF THE LORD," AND OF THE EFFECTS OF THEIR RIGHT DOING AND THEIR EVIL DOING UPO OF THE PEOPLE. WHAT DIFFERENCE, INDEED, DOES IT MAKE TO YOU AND ME WHETHER JOTHAM REIGNED YEARS OR TWENTY YEARS? IT SEEMS TO ME THAT THESE INACCURACIES ARE SUFFERED TO LIE UPON THE FA NARRATIVE THAT OUR THOUGHTS MAY BE TURNED AWAY FROM THESE DETAILS OF THE RECORD TO principles of morality and religion whose development it reveals to us.

THESE ERRORS WHICH APPEAR UPON THE SURFACE ARE OBVIOUS ENOUGH TO ANY CAREFUL READI OTHER FACTS, MOST IMPORTANT AND SUGGESTIVE, ARE BROUGHT TO LIGHT WHEN WE COMPARE THESE N OF SAMUEL AND KINGS AS WE FIND THEM IN THE HEBREW TEXT WITH THE SAME NARRATIVE IN THE GRE the Septuagint. The Old Testament, as we have seen, was translated into the Greek language, for the BENEFIT OF THOSE JEWS WHO SPOKE ONLY GREEK, EARLY IN THE THIRD CENTURY BEFORE CHRIST. UND IT WAS A PRETTY FAITHFUL TRANSLATION AT THE TIME WHEN IT WAS MADE. BUT A CAREFUL COMPARISO TWO TEXTS AS THEY EXIST AT THE PRESENT TIME SHOWS THAT CONSIDERABLE ADDITIONS HAVE BEEN BOTH OF THEM; AND THAT SOME CHANGES AND MISPLACEMENTS HAVE OCCURRED IN BOTH OF THEM. SOM IT IS EVIDENT THAT THE HEBREW IS THE MORE CORRECT, BECAUSE THE STORY IS MORE ORDERLY AND CC AND SOMETIMES IT IS EQUALLY EVIDENT THAT THE GREEK VERSION, WHICH, AS YOU REMEMBER, WAS COM USED BY OUR LORD AND HIS APOSTLES, IS THE BETTER. THIS COMPARISON GIVES US A VIVID AND CONVI ILLUSTRATION OF THE FREEDOM WITH WHICH THE TEXT WAS HANDLED BY SCRIBES AND COPYISTS; HOW NARRATIVE--MOST COMMONLY LEGENDS AND POPULAR TALES CONCERNING THE HEROES OF THE NATI THRUST INTO THE TEXT, SOMETIMES QUITE BREAKING ITS CONTINUITY; THEY MAKE IT PLAIN T preternatural supervision of it, for the prevention of error, which we have frequently heard about, is ITSELF A MYTH. IT IS IN THESE BOOKS OF SAMUEL AND THE KINGS THAT THESE VARIATIONS OF THE SE from the Hebrew text are most frequent and most instructive.

IN THE STORY OF DAVID'S INTRODUCTION TO SAUL, FOR EXAMPLE, OUR VERSION, FOLLOWING THE TELLS US (I SAM. XVI. 14-23), THAT WHEN DAVID WAS FIRST MADE KNOWN TO SAUL HE WAS "A MIGHTY MA VALOR, AND A MAN OF WAR, AND PRUDENT IN SPEECH, AND A COMELY PERSON." HE COMES INTO S HOUSEHOLD; SAUL LOVES HIM GREATLY, AND MAKES HIM HIS ARMOR-BEARER. IN THE NEXT CHAPTER D REPRESENTED AS A MERE LAD, AND IT APPEARS THAT SAUL HAD NEVER SEEN OR HEARD OF HIM. INDEED, HIS GENERAL, ABNER, WHO THIS STRIPLING IS. THE CONTRADICTION IN THESE NARRATIVES IS PALPA IRRECONCILABLE. WHEN WE TURN NOW TO THE SEPTUAGINT, WE FIND THAT IT OMITS FROM THE SEVE CHAPTER VERSES 12-31 INCLUSIVE; ALSO FROM THE 55TH VERSE TO THE END OF THE CHAPTER AND THE VERSES OF THE NEXT CHAPTER. TAKING OUT THESE PASSAGES, THE MAIN DIFFICULTIES OF THE NARRATI ONCE REMOVED. IT APPEARS PROBABLE THAT THESE PASSAGES WERE NOT IN THE NARRATIVE WHEN translated into Greek, but that they embodied a current and a very beautiful tradition ab which some later Hebrew transcriber ventured to incorporate into the text.

In the Books of the Kings the variations between these two versions are also ex suggestive. You can see distinctly, as if it were done before your eyes, how supplementary has been inserted into the one text or the other, since the Greek translation was made. In chapter of First Kings, the Septuagint omits verses 11-14, which is an exhortation to So injected into the specifications respecting the temple building. Omit these verses, a description goes on smoothly. Similarly in the ninth chapter of the same book the Septuagi verses 15-25. This passage breaks the connection; the narrative of Solomon's dealings with H consecutively told in the Greek version; in the Hebrew it is interrupted by this extraneou You can readily see which is the original form of the writing.

Now what does all this signify? Of course it signifies most distinctly that this history be judged by the canons of modern historical criticism. Mr. Horton quotes some str advocate of the traditional theory of the Bible as maintaining that "when God writes hist be at least as accurate as Bishop Stubbs or Mr. Gardiner; and if we are to admit errors historical work, then why not in his plan of salvation and doctrine of atonement?" It is th reasoning that drives intelligent men into infidelity. For the errors are here; they themselves; nothing but a mole-eyed dogmatism can evade them; and if we link the great d of the Bible with this dogma of the historical inerrancy of the Scriptures, they will all together.

But what, after all, do these errors amount to? What is the meaning and purport history? What are these writers trying to do? "It seems," says Mr. Horton, "as if their purp not so much to tell us what happened as to emphasize for us the lesson of what happene *applied* history, rather than history pure and simple; and on this ground we can underst tendency to irritation which critical historians sometimes betray in approaching it.... The pr historian would never dream, like a modern historian, of writing interminable monographs disputed name or a doubtful date; he might even take a story which rested on very d authority, finding in it more that would suit his purpose than the bare and accurate statement of the fact which could be authenticated. The standpoint of the prophetic historian and of the historian are wholly different; they cannot be judged by the same canons of criticism. prophetic eye the significance of all events seems to be in their relation to the will of prophet may not always discern what the will of God is; he may interpret events in a inadequate manner. But his predominant thought makes itself felt; and consequently the these histories leaves us in a widely different frame of mind from that which Thucydides Freeman would produce. We do not feel to know, perhaps, so accurately about the wars b Israel and Judah as we know about the wars between Athens and Sparta; we do not feel to perhaps, so much about the monarchy of Israel as we know about the Anglo-Norman mon but, on the other hand, we seem to be more aware of God, we seem to recognize his controlling the wavering affairs of states, we seem to comprehend that obedience to his more importance than any political consideration, and that in the long course of disobedience to his will means national distress and national ruin. The study of scientific has its advantages; but it is not quite certain that these advantages are greater than those study of prophetic history yields. Perhaps, after all, the one fact of history is God's work which case the scientific histories, with all their learning, with all their toil, will look rat the side of these imperfect compositions which at least saw vividly and recognized fa*the one*li *fact*."

Chapter V.

The Hebrew Prophecies

In the last chapter the opinion was expressed that the first books collected by Nehemiah, when he made up his "library," a century after the Exile, were the writings of the prophets. We the historical books first, because they stand first in the Hebrew Bible, and are there na "Earlier Prophets;" but the probabilities are that the prophetical writings proper, called by the "Later Prophets," were first gathered.

When was this collection made? If it was made by Nehemiah (and there is nothing to dis the statement of the author of 2 Maccabees that he was the collector), then it was not until one hundred years after the Exile, or only about four hundred and twenty years befo Most of the prophets had written before or during the Exile. Joel, Hosea, and Amos had fl three or four hundred years before this collection was made; Isaiah, the greatest of the been in his grave almost three centuries; Micah, nearly as long; Nahum, Habakkuk, and Zep had been silent from one to two hundred years; Jeremiah, who was alive when the sevent captivity began, and Ezekiel, who prophesied and perished among the captives on the banks Euphrates, were more remote from Nehemiah than Samuel Johnson and Jonathan Edwar from us; even Haggai and Zechariah, who came back with the returning exiles and helped t the second temple, had passed away from fifty to one hundred years before the time of Ne Malachi alone,--"The Messenger,"--and the last of the prophets, may have been alive wh compilation of the prophetic writings was made.

It may be safely conjectured that the Jews, although they had never possessed any coll the books of the prophets, had known something of their contents. Several of the proph foretold the desolation and the captivity, and there had been abundant time during the recall the words they had spoken and to wish that their fathers had heeded them remembered words of the prophets, passing from lip to lip, would thus have acquired pec sacredness. It seems clear, also, that copies of these books must have been kept,--perhaps i schools of the prophets; for the later prophets quote, verbally, from the earlier ones therefore, have been in response to a popular wish that this collection of their writi undertaken. Words so momentous as these ought to be sacredly treasured. Furthermore, th reasons to apprehend that the holy flame of prophecy was dying out. Malachi may have speaking still, but there was not much promise that he would have a successor, and the expe of prophetic voices was growing dim among the people.

The Levitical ritual, now so elaborate and cumbersome, had supplanted the prophetic The ritualist is never a prophet; and out of such a formal cult no words of inspiration ar flow. With all the greater carefulness, therefore, would the people treasure the message come to them from the past. Accordingly these prophetic writings, which had existe fragmentary and scattered form, were gathered into a collection by themselves.

It must be admitted that when we try to tell how these writings had been preserv transmitted through all these centuries, we have but little solid ground of fact to go Scriptures themselves are entirely silent with respect to the manner of their preserva traditions of the Jews are wholly worthless. We must not imagine that these books of Is Jeremiah and Hosea were written and published as our books are written and published; the no book trade then through which literature could be marketed, and no subscription hawking books from door to door. You must not imagine that every family in Judea had a c Isaiah's Works,--nor even that a copy could be found in every village; it is possible that the not, when the people were carried into captivity, more than a few dozen copies of these pro in existence, and these were in the hands of some of the prophets or literary dignitarie nation, or in the archives of some of the prophetical schools. The notion that these wo distributed among the people for study and devotional reading is not to be entertained. general use of the prophetical writings was ever conceived of by the Jews before the Captivity.

Indeed, many of these prophecies, as we call them, were not, primarily, literature at a

WERE SERMONS OR ADDRESSES, DELIVERED ORALLY TO THE INDIVIDUALS CONCERNED, OR TO ASSEMBLIE people. You can see the evidence, in many cases, that they must have been thus delivered.

WE SPEAK OF THE "PROPHECY" OF ISAIAH, OR THE "PROPHECY" OF JEREMIAH; BUT THE BOOKS BE THEIR NAMES ARE MADE UP OF A NUMBER OF "PROPHECIES," UTTERED ON VARIOUS OCCASIONS. THE DIV between these separate prophecies is generally indicated by the language; in all Paragraph Bibles it is MARKED BY BLANK LINES. IN EACH OF THESE EARLIER PROPHETICAL BOOKS WE THUS HAVE, IN ALL PROBAI SUCCESSION OF DELIVERANCES, EXTENDING THROUGH LONG PERIODS OF TIME AND PREPARED FOR occasions.

AFTER THE ORACLE WAS SPOKEN TO THOSE FOR WHOM IT WAS DESIGNED, IT WAS WRITTEN DOWN PROPHET OR BY HIS FRIENDS AND DISCIPLES, AND THUS PRESERVED. THIS SUPPOSITION SEEMS, AT ANY MORE PLAUSIBLE THAN ANY OTHER THAT I HAVE FOUND. MANIFESTLY MANY OF THESE PROPHECIE ORIGINALLY SERMONS OR PUBLIC ADDRESSES; IT IS NATURAL TO SUPPOSE THAT THEY WERE FIRST DELIVE then, for substance, reduced to writing, that a record might be made of the utterance.

IT IS SOMETIMES ALLEGED THAT THESE PROPHECIES, AS SOON AS THEY WERE PRODUCED, WERE A ADDED TO A COLLECTION OF SACRED SCRIPTURES WHICH WAS PRESERVED IN THE SANCTUARY. THERE "BOOK" OR "SCRIPTURE," IT IS SAID, "WHICH FROM THE TIME OF MOSES WAS KEPT OPEN, AND IN WHICI WRITINGS OF THE PROPHETS MAY HAVE BEEN RECORDED AS THEY WERE PRODUCED." [FOOTNOTE: ALEXAN Isaiah, i. 7.]

THE LEARNED DIVINE WHO VENTURES THIS CONJECTURE ADMITS THAT IT WOULD BE AS HARD TO PRO TO DISPROVE IT. MY OWN OPINION IS THAT IT WOULD BE MUCH HARDER. IF THERE HAD BEEN ANY SUCH C RECEPTACLE OF SACRED WRITINGS, THE PROPHETS WERE NOT GENERALLY IN A POSITION TO SECURE THE A OF THEIR DOCUMENTS INTO IT. THEY WERE OFTEN IN OPEN CONTROVERSY WITH THE PEOPLE WHO K SANCTUARY; THE POLITICAL AND THE RELIGIOUS AUTHORITIES OF THE NATION WERE THE OBJECTS OF THE DENUNCIATIONS; IT IS NOT LIKELY THAT THE PRIESTS WOULD MAKE HASTE TO TRANSCRIBE AND PRESER SANCTUARY THE SERMONS AND LECTURES OF THE MEN WHO WERE SCOURGING THEM WITH CENSUR NATIONAL *bibliotheca sacra* IN WHICH THE WRITINGS OF THE PROPHETS WERE DEPOSITED AS SOON AS THEY COMPOSED IS THE PRODUCT OF PURE FICTION. IT WAS NOT THUS THAT THE PROPHETICAL UTTERANC PRESERVED; RATHER IS IT TO BE SUPPOSED THAT THE PUPILS AND FRIENDS OF THE PROPHET FAITHFULLY MANUSCRIPTS AFTER HE WAS GONE; THAT OCCASIONAL COPIES WERE MADE OF THEM BY THOSE WHO WISI study them, and that thus they were handed down from generation to generation.

WHEN NEHEMIAH MADE HIS COLLECTION HE FOUND THESE MANUSCRIPTS, IN WHOSE HANDS WE I NOT, AND BROUGHT THEM TOGETHER IN ONE PLACE. WE MAY PRESUME THAT THE WRITINGS OF EACH I WERE COPIED UPON A SEPARATE ROLL, AND THAT THE ROLLS WERE KEPT TOGETHER IN SOME RECEPTAC TEMPLE. MOST OF THESE PROPHETS HAD NOW BEEN DEAD SOME HUNDREDS OF YEARS; THE TRUTH C MESSAGES WAS NO LONGER DISPUTED EVEN BY THE PRIESTS AND THE SCRIBES; THEIR HERESY WAS NO SOUNDEST ORTHODOXY; THE CUSTODIANS OF ORTHODOXY WOULD OF COURSE NOW MAKE A PLACE FC WRITINGS IN THE NATIONAL ARCHIVES. THE PRIESTS HAVE ALWAYS BEEN READY TO BUILD SEPULCHRES prophets after they were dead, and to pay them plenty of *post mortem* reverence.

THE BOOKS OF THE PROPHETS STAND IN THE LATER HEBREW BIBLES IN THE SAME ORDER AS THAT IN THEY ARE PLACED IN OUR OWN; THEY OCCUPY A DIFFERENT PLACE IN THE WHOLE COLLECTION: THEY A MIDDLE OF THE HEBREW BIBLE, AND THEY ARE AT THE END OF OURS; BUT THEIR RELATION TO ONE ANOT SAME IN BOTH BIBLES. THIS ORDER IS NOT CHRONOLOGICAL; IN PART, AT LEAST, IT SEEMS TO REPRESENT V SUPPOSED TO BE THE RELATIVE IMPORTANCE OF THE BOOKS. ISAIAH, JEREMIAH, AND EZEKIEL ARE PLACE PERHAPS BECAUSE THEY ARE LONGEST, ALTHOUGH SEVERAL OF THE MINOR PROPHETS ARE OF EARLIER D THEY. "DANIEL" IS NOT AMONG THE PROPHETS IN THE HEBREW BIBLE; THE BOOK WHICH BEARS THIS N ONE OF THE BOOKS OF THE THIRD COLLECTION,--THE HAGIOGRAPHA,--OF WHICH WE SHALL SPEAK AT time.

"WHEN WE FOLLOW FURTHER THE SAME COLLECTION," SAYS PROFESSOR MURRAY, "WE FIND IMMEDIATELY FOLLOWING EZEKIEL [ALTHOUGH HOSEA LIVED MORE THAN TWO CENTURIES BEFORE EZEI in turn followed by Joel and Amos, mainly on the principle of comparative bulk. Haggai, Zechariah, AND MALACHI WERE PLACED AT THE END FOR REASONS PURELY CHRONOLOGICAL, AFTER THE REST OF THE HAD BEEN MADE UP. WE CANNOT SEE ANY CLEAR OR CONSISTENT REASON FOR THE POSITION OF O

JONAH, MICAH, NAHUM, HABAKKUK, AND ZEPHANIAH, WHICH STAND TOGETHER IN THE MIDDLE C collection."

AN EXAMINATION OF THE CHRONOLOGICAL NOTES ON THE MARGIN OF OUR ENGLISH BIBLES (WI NOT ALWAYS CORRECT THOUGH THEY ARE APPROXIMATELY SO) WILL SHOW THAT THESE PROPHETICAL BOOK ARRANGED IN THE ORDER OF TIME. IT WOULD BE A GREAT IMPROVEMENT TO HAVE THEM SO ARRANGED. F THE SUNDAY-SCHOOLS WHO ATTEMPTED A FEW YEARS AGO TO FOLLOW THE "INTERNATIONAL" LESSONS THESE PROPHECIES*seriatim*, FOUND THEMSELVES SKIPPING BACK AND FORWARD OVER THE CENTURIES HISTORY-DEFYING DANCE WHICH WAS QUITE BEWILDERING TO ALL BUT THE CLEAREST HEADS. W UNDERSTAND THESE PROPHECIES MUCH BETTER IF THEY WERE ARRANGED IN THE ORDER OF THEIR DATE NO ONE SUPPOSES THAT THE PRESENT ARRANGEMENT, MADE BY JEWISH SCRIBES, IS IN ANY WISE INSPIRED, SEEMS TO BE NO GOOD REASON WHY THE LATE REVISERS MIGHT NOT HAVE ALTERED IT, AND SET THESE BC historical and intelligible order.

WHO WERE THESE PROPHETS AND WHAT WAS THEIR FUNCTION? TO GIVE ANY ADEQUATE ANSWER INQUIRY WOULD REQUIRE A TREATISE; IT IS ONLY IN THE MOST CURSORY MANNER THAT WE CAN DEAL W THIS PLACE.THE PROPHET IS THE MAN WHO SPEAKS FOR GOD. HE IS THE INTERPRETER OF THE DIVINE W SOME MEANS HE HAS COME TO UNDERSTAND GOD'S PURPOSE, AND HIS FUNCTION IS TO DECLARE IT. TI EXODUS IV. 16, JEHOVAH SAYS TO MOSES, "AARON THY BROTHER ... SHALL BE THY SPOKESMAN UNT PEOPLE, AND IT SHALL COME TO PASS THAT HE SHALL BE TO THEE A MOUTH AND THOU SHALT BE TO HIM A AND AGAIN (VII. I), "SEE, I HAVE MADE THEE A GOD TO PHARAOH, AND AARON THY BROTHER SHALL PROPHET." THESE PASSAGES INDICATE THE BIBLICAL MEANING OF THE WORD. THE PROPHET IS THE SPOK OR INTERPRETER OF SOME SUPERIOR AUTHORITY. IN CLASSIC GREEK, ALSO, APOLLO IS CALLED THE PR JUPITER, AND THE PYTHIA IS THE PROPHETESS OF APOLLO. ALMOST UNIVERSALLY, IN THE OLD TESTAM word is used to signify an expounder or interpreter of the divine will.

"THE ENGLISH WORDS 'PROPHET, PROPHECY, PROPHESYING,'" SAYS DEAN STANLEY, "ORIGINALLY TOLERABLY CLOSE TO THE BIBLICAL USE OF THE WORD. THE CELEBRATED DISPUTE ABOUT 'PROPHESYINC SENSE OF 'PREACHINGS' IN THE REIGN OF ELIZABETH, AND THE TREATISE OF JEREMY TAYLOR ON 'THE L PROPHESYING,'*i.e.*, THE LIBERTY OF PREACHING, SHOW THAT EVEN DOWN TO THE SEVENTEENTH CENT WORD WAS STILL USED AS IN THE BIBLE, FOR PREACHING OR SPEAKING ACCORDING TO THE WILL OF GOI SEVENTEENTH CENTURY, HOWEVER, THE LIMITATION OF THE WORD TO THE SENSE OF PREDICTION HAD BEGUN TO APPEAR. THIS SECONDARY MEANING OF THE WORD HAD BY THE TIME OF DR. JOHNSON SO EI SUPERSEDED THE ORIGINAL SCRIPTURAL SIGNIFICATION THAT HE GIVES NO OTHER SPECIAL DEFINITION 'TO PREDICT, TO FORETELL, TO PROGNOSTICATE,' 'A PREDICTER, A FORETELLER,' 'FORESEEING OR FORETI EVENTS;' AND IN THIS SENSE IT HAS BEEN USED ALMOST DOWN TO OUR OWN DAY, WHEN THE REVIVAL OF B CRITICISM HAS RESUSCITATED, IN SOME MEASURE, THE BIBLICAL USE OF THE WORD." [FOOT*History of the Jewish Church*, I. 459, 460.] THE PREDICTIVE FUNCTION OF THE PROPHET IS NOT, THEN, THE ONLY, NO PROMINENT FEATURE OF HIS WORK. BY FAR THE LARGER PORTION OF THE PROPHETIC UTTERANCES WERE C with the present, and made no reference to the future.

THE PROPHET EXERCISED HIS OFFICE IN MANY WAYS. MOSES WAS A PROPHET, THE FIRST AND GREAT THE PROPHETS; BUT WE HAVE FROM HIM FEW PREDICTIONS; HE INTERPRETED THE WILL OF GOD ENACTMENT OF LAWS. SAMUEL WAS A GREAT PROPHET; BUT SAMUEL WAS NOT EMPLOYED IN FORETELLING EVENTS; HE SOUGHT TO KNOW THE WILL OF GOD, THAT HE MIGHT ADMINISTER THE AFFAIRS OF TH COMMONWEALTH IN ACCORDANCE WITH IT. ELIJAH AND ELISHA WERE GREAT PROPHETS, BUT THEY WE PROGNOSTICATORS; THEY WERE PREACHERS OF RIGHTEOUSNESS TO KINGS AND PEOPLE, AND THEY DELIVE MESSAGE IN A WAY TO MAKE THE EARS OF THOSE WHO HEARD THEM TO TINGLE. AND THIS, FOR ALL THE WHO SUCCEEDED THEM, WAS THE ONE GREAT BUSINESS. THE ETHICAL FUNCTION OF THESE MEN OF GO more and more distinctly into view.

WHEN PAUL ADMONISHED TIMOTHY (2 TIM. IV. 2) TO "PREACH THE WORD; BE INSTANT IN SEASON OF SEASON; REPROVE, REBUKE, EXHORT WITH ALL LONG-SUFFERING AND TEACHING," HE WAS CALLING ON H A FOLLOWER OF THE PROPHETS. WHEN KINGS BECAME PROFLIGATE AND FAITHLESS, WHEN PRIESTS GREW AND GREEDY, WHEN THE RICH WAXED EXTORTIONATE AND TYRANNICAL, THESE MEN OF GOD AROSE TO THE TRANSGRESSORS AND THREATEN THEM WITH THE DIVINE VENGEANCE. THEY MIGHT ARISE IN ANY FROM ANY CLASS. THEY WERE CONFINED TO NO TRIBE, TO NO LOCALITY, TO NO CALLING. NEI

MONOPOLIZED THIS GIFT. MIRIAM, DEBORAH, HULDAH WERE SHINING NAMES UPON THEIR ROLL OF HON NO ECCLESIASTICISM OR OFFICIALISM DID THEY OWE THEIR AUTHORITY; NO MAN'S HANDS HAD BEEN LAI THEM IN ORDINATION; THEY WERE JEHOVAH'S MESSENGERS; FROM HIM ALONE THEY RECEIVED THEIR ME to him alone they held themselves responsible.

NO SUCH PREACHERS OF POLITICS EVER EXISTED AS THESE HEBREW PROPHETS; WITH ALL THE AFI STATE THEY CONSTANTLY INTERMEDDLED; BAD LAWS AND UNHOLY POLICIES FOUND IN THEM SH UNSPARING CRITICS; THE ENTANGLING ALLIANCES OF ISRAEL WITH THE SURROUNDING NATIONS WERE DEN THEM IN SEASON AND OUT OF SEASON. THE PEOPLE OF THEIR OWN TIME OFTEN STIGMATIZED TH UNPATRIOTIC; BECAUSE THEY WOULD NOT APPROVE POPULAR INIQUITIES, OR REFRAIN THEIR LIPS FROM RE EVEN "FAVORITE SONS," OR THE IDOLS OF THE POPULACE, THEY OFTEN FOUND THEMSELVES UNDER THI PUBLIC OPINION; THEY LIVED LONELY LIVES; NOT A FEW OF THEM DIED VIOLENT DEATHS. "WHICH PROPHETS DID NOT YOUR FATHERS PERSECUTE?" DEMANDED STEPHEN, "AND THEY KILLED THEM WHICH S BEFORE OF THE COMING OF THE RIGHTEOUS ONE; OF WHOM YE HAVE NOW BECOME BETRAYERS murderers." [Footnote: Acts vii. 52.]

THE RELATION OF THE PROPHETS TO THE POLITICAL LIFE OF THE JEWISH PEOPLE IS BROUGHT STRIKING WAY BY JOHN STUART MILL IN HIS BOOK ON "REPRESENTATIVE GOVERNMENT." IN THAT CHA WHICH HE DISCUSSES THE CRITERION OF A GOOD GOVERNMENT, HE SHOWS HOW THE EGYPTIAN HIERARC THE CHINESE PATERNAL DESPOTISM DESTROYED THOSE COUNTRIES BY STEREOTYPING THEIR INSTITUTIO he goes on:--

"IN CONTRAST WITH THESE NATIONS LET US CONSIDER THE EXAMPLE OF AN OPPOSITE CHARACTER, BY ANOTHER AND A COMPARATIVELY INSIGNIFICANT ORIENTAL PEOPLE, THE JEWS. THEY, TOO, HAD AN MONARCHY AND A HIERARCHY, AND THEIR ORGANIZED INSTITUTIONS WERE AS OBVIOUSLY OF SACERDOTAL THOSE OF THE HINDOOS. THESE DID FOR THEM WHAT WAS DONE FOR OTHER ORIENTAL RACES I INSTITUTIONS, SUBDUED THEM TO INDUSTRY AND ORDER, AND GAVE THEM A NATIONAL LIFE. BUT NEITI KINGS NOR THEIR PRIESTS EVER OBTAINED, AS IN THOSE OTHER COUNTRIES, THE EXCLUSIVE MOULDING CHARACTER. THEIR RELIGION, WHICH ENABLED PERSONS OF GENIUS AND A HIGH RELIGIOUS TONE TO BE AND TO REGARD THEMSELVES AS INSPIRED FROM HEAVEN, GAVE EXISTENCE TO AN INESTIMABLY PR UNORGANIZED INSTITUTION,--THE ORDER (IF IT MAY BE SO TERMED) OF PROPHETS. UNDER THE PRO GENERALLY THOUGH NOT ALWAYS EFFECTUAL, OF THEIR SACRED CHARACTER, THE PROPHETS WERE A POV NATION, OFTEN MORE THAN A MATCH FOR KINGS AND PRIESTS, AND KEPT UP IN THAT LITTLE CORNER OF THE ANTAGONISM OF INFLUENCES WHICH IS THE ONLY REAL SECURITY FOR CONTINUED PROGRESS. CONSEQUENTLY, WAS NOT THEN WHAT IT HAS BEEN IN SO MANY OTHER PLACES, A CONSECRATION OF ALL once established, and a barrier against further improvement. The remark of a distinguished Hebrew, M. SALVADOR, THAT THE PROPHETS WERE IN CHURCH AND STATE THE EQUIVALENT OF THE MODERN LIBE PRESS, GIVES A JUST BUT NOT AN ADEQUATE CONCEPTION OF THE PART FULFILLED IN NATIONAL AND HISTORY BY THIS GREAT ELEMENT OF JEWISH LIFE; BY MEANS OF WHICH, THE CANON OF INSPIRATION NEVI COMPLETE, THE PERSONS MOST EMINENT IN GENIUS AND MORAL FEELING COULD NOT ONLY DENOUN REPROBATE, WITH THE DIRECT AUTHORITY OF THE ALMIGHTY, WHATEVER APPEARED TO THEM DESERVING TREATMENT, BUT COULD GIVE FORTH BETTER AND HIGHER INTERPRETATIONS OF THE NATIONAL RELIC THENCEFORTH BECAME PART OF THE RELIGION. ACCORDINGLY, WHOEVER CAN DIVEST HIMSELF OF THE READING THE BIBLE AS IF IT WAS ONE BOOK, WHICH UNTIL LATELY WAS EQUALLY INVETERATE IN CHRIST UNBELIEVERS, SEES WITH ADMIRATION THE VAST INTERVAL BETWEEN THE MORALITY AND RELIGION PENTATEUCH, OR EVEN OF THE HISTORICAL BOOKS (THE UNMISTAKABLE WORK OF HEBREW CONSERVATIVE SACERDOTAL ORDER), AND THE MORALITY AND RELIGION OF THE PROPHECIES. CONDITIONS MORE FAVO PROGRESS COULD NOT EASILY EXIST; ACCORDINGLY, THE JEWS, INSTEAD OF BEING STATIONARY LIKE OTHE WERE, NEXT TO THE GREEKS, THE MOST PROGRESSIVE PEOPLE OF ANTIQUITY, AND, JOINT WITH THEM, HA THE STARTING-POINT AND MAIN PROPELLING AGENCY OF MODERN CIVILIZATION." [Footnote: *Considerations on Representative Government,* pp. 51-53, American Edition.]

NOT ONLY IN THE SPHERE OF POLITICS, BUT IN THAT OF RELIGION ALSO, WERE THEY CONSTANTLY AS CRITICS AND CENSORS. THE TENDENCY OF RELIGION TO BECOME MERELY RITUAL, TO DIVORCE ITS RIGHTEOUSNESS, IS INVETERATE. AGAINST THIS TENDENCY THE PROPHETS WERE THE CONSTANT WITNE RELIGIOUS "MACHINE" IS ALWAYS IN THE SAME DANGER OF BECOMING CORRUPT AND MISCHIEVOUS AS I

POLITICAL "MACHINE;" THE MAN WITH THE SLEDGE-HAMMER WHO WILL SMASH IT AND FLING IT INTO TH PILE HAS A WORK TO DO IN EVERY GENERATION. THIS WAS THE WORK OF THE HEBREW PROPHETS. "I D MERCY, AND NOT SACRIFICE," CRIES HOSEA, SPEAKING FOR JEHOVAH. "I HATE, I DESPISE YOUR FEAST DAYS AMOS, "AND I WILL NOT SMELL IN YOUR SOLEMN ASSEMBLIES,...BUT LET JUDGMENT RUN DOWN AS WATER RIGHTEOUSNESS AS A MIGHTY STREAM." "YOUR NEW MOONS AND YOUR APPOINTED FEASTS MY SOUL HA PROCLAIMS ISAIAH; "THEY ARE A TROUBLE UNTO ME; I AM WEARY TO BEAR THEM. WASH YE, MAKE YOU CEASE TO DO EVIL; LEARN TO DO WELL. IS NOT THIS THE FAST THAT I HAVE CHOSEN, TO LOOSE THE wickedness, to undo the heavy burden, and to let the oppressed go free?"

THIS IS, THEN, THE CHIEF FUNCTION OF THE HEBREW PROPHET; HE IS THE EXPOUNDER OF THE RI WILL OF GOD, NOT MAINLY WITH RESPECT TO FUTURE EVENTS, BUT WITH RESPECT TO PRESENT TRANSGRES PRESENT OBLIGATIONS OF KINGS AND PRIESTS AND PEOPLE. AND YET IT WOULD BE AN ERROR TO OVER DISPARAGE HIS DEALINGS WITH THE FUTURE. AS A TEACHER OF RIGHTEOUSNESS HE SAW THAT DISOBEDIENCE WOULD BRING FUTURE RETRIBUTION, AND HE POINTED IT OUT WITH THE UTMOST FIDEL MAN WHO CAREFULLY STUDIES THE LAWS OF GOD CAN MAKE SOME PREDICTIONS WITH GREAT CONFIDE KNOWS THAT CERTAIN COURSES OF CONDUCT WILL BE FOLLOWED BY CERTAIN CONSEQUENCES. SOME PREDICTIONS OF THE HEBREW PROPHETS WERE OF THIS NATURE. YET PREDICTIONS OF THIS NATURE WER CONDITIONAL. THE CONDITION WAS NOT ALWAYS EXPRESSED, BUT IT WAS ALWAYS UNDERSTOOD. THE THRE OF DESTRUCTION TO THE DISOBEDIENT WAS WITHDRAWN WHEN THE DISOBEDIENT TURNED FROM THEIR E THE PREDICTIONS OF THE PROPHETS WERE NOT ALWAYS FULFILLED FOR THIS GOOD REASON. THE RULE IS LAID DOWN BY THE PROPHET JEREMIAH: "AT WHAT INSTANT I SHALL SPEAK CONCERNING A NATION...TO IT; IF THAT NATION...TURN FROM THEIR EVIL, I WILL REPENT OF THE EVIL THAT I THOUGHT TO DO UNTO AT WHAT INSTANT I SHALL SPEAK CONCERNING A NATION...TO BUILD AND TO PLANT IT; IF IT DO EVIL IN THAT IT OBEY NOT MY VOICE, THEN I WILL REPENT OF THE GOOD WHEREWITH I SAID I WOULD BENEFI [Footnote: Jeremiah xviii. 7-9.]

AND THERE IS SOMETHING MORE THAN THIS. INSTANCES ARE HERE RECORDED OF SPECIFIC PREDIC FUTURE EVENTS, WHICH CAME TO PASS AS THEY WERE PREDICTED,--PREDICTIONS WHICH CANNOT BE EXP ON NATURALISTIC PRINCIPLES. "OF THIS SORT," SAYS BLEEK, "ARE THE PROPHECIES OF ISAIAH AS TO TH IMPENDING DESTRUCTION OF THE KINGDOMS OF ISRAEL AND SYRIA, WHICH HE PREDICTED WITH CONFIDENCE AT A TIME WHEN THE TWO KINGDOMS APPEARED PARTICULARLY STRONG BY THEIR TREATY W OTHER,...BESIDES THE REPEATED PREDICTIONS AS TO THE DESTRUCTION OF THE MIGHTY HOSTS OF SEN KING OF ASSYRIA, WHICH BESIEGED JERUSALEM, AND THE DELIVERANCE OF THE STATE FROM THE DISTRESS. AMONG THESE PREDICTIONS, THOSE IN ISAIAH XXIX. 1-8, APPEAR TO ME PARTICULARLY NOTEW WHERE HE FORETELLS THAT A LONG TIME HENCE JERUSALEM SHOULD BE BESIEGED BY A FOREIGN F PRESSED VERY HARD, BUT THAT THE LATTER, JUST AS THEY BELIEVED THEY WERE GETTING POSSESSION O SHOULD BE SCATTERED AND ANNIHILATED; FOR THIS PREDICTION, FROM ITS WHOLE CHARACTER, APPEARS BEEN UTTERED BEFORE ANY DANGER SHOWED ITSELF FROM THIS QUARTER." [Footnote: *Introduction to the Old Testament*, ii. 27.]

BEYOND AND ABOVE ALL THIS IS THE GRADUAL RISE IN ISRAEL OF THAT GREAT MESSIANIC HOPE, O THE PROPHETS WERE THE INSPIRED AND INSPIRING WITNESSES. WE FIND, AT A VERY EARLY DAY, AN EXPE OF A FUTURE REVELATION OF THE GLORY OF GOD, DAWNING UPON THE CONSCIOUSNESS OF THE NAT EXPRESSING ITSELF BY THE WORDS OF ITS MOST DEVOUT SPIRITS. EVEN IN PROSPEROUS DAYS THERE WAS OUTREACHING AFTER SOMETHING BETTER; IN TIMES OF DISASTER AND OVERTHROW THIS HOPE WAS KIND PASSIONATE LONGING. OF THIS MESSIANIC HOPE, ITS NATURE AND ITS FULFILLMENT, NO WORDS OF MINE so eloquently as these words of Dean Stanley:--

"IT WAS THE DISTINGUISHING MARK OF THE JEWISH PEOPLE THAT THEIR GOLDEN AGE WAS NOT IN T BUT IN THE FUTURE; THAT THEIR GREATEST HERO (AS THEY DEEMED HIM TO BE) WAS NOT THEIR FOUN THEIR FOUNDER'S LATEST DESCENDANT. THEIR TRADITIONS, THEIR FANCIES, THEIR GLORIES, GATHERED HEAD, NOT OF A CHIEF OR WARRIOR OR SAGE THAT HAD BEEN, BUT OF A KING, A DELIVERER, A PROPHET TO COME. OF THIS SINGULAR EXPECTATION THE PROPHETS WERE, IF NOT THE CHIEF AUTHORS, AT LEAST EXPONENTS. SOMETIMES HE IS NAMED, SOMETIMES HE IS UNNAMED; SOMETIMES HE IS ALMOST IDENTI WITH SOME ACTUAL PRINCE OF THE PRESENT OR THE COMING GENERATION, SOMETIMES HE RECEDES I DISTANT AGES. BUT AGAIN AND AGAIN, AT LEAST IN THE LATE PROPHETIC WRITINGS, THE VISTA IS CLOSE person, his character, his reign. And almost everywhere the Prophetic spirit in the delineati(coming remains true to itself. He is to be a King, a Conqueror, yet not by the common weaf earthly warfare, but by those only weapons which the Prophetic order recognized; by justice truth, and goodness; by suffering, by endurance, by identification of himself with the j sufferings of his nation; by opening a wider sympathy to the whole human race than had evi offered before. That this expectation, however explained, existed in a greater or less degrei the Prophets is not doubted by any theologians of any school whatever. It is no m/ controversy. It is a simply and universally recognized fact that, filled with these Propheti the whole Jewish nation--nay, at last, the whole Eastern world--did look forward with expectation to the coming of this future Conqueror. Was this unparalleled expectation And here again I speak only of facts which are acknowledged by Germans and Frenchmen n than by Englishmen, by critics and by skeptics even more than by theologians and eccle: There did arise out of this nation a Character as unparalleled as the expectation which had preceded him. Jesus of Nazareth was, on the most superficial no less than on the deepest view of his c(the greatest name, the most extraordinary power that has ever crossed the stage of Hist this greatness consisted not in outward power, but precisely in those qualities in which from last the Prophetic order had laid the utmost stress,--justice and love, goodness anc [Footnote: *History of the Jewish Church*, i. 519, 520.]

This is the great fact from which the student of the Old Testament must never rem attention. That this wonderful hope and expectation did suffuse all the utterances of the i not to be gainsaid by any candid man. That the expectation assumed, as the ages passed, a mo: more definite and personal form is equally certain. Isaiah was perhaps the first to give distinct shape to this prophetic hope. Ewald thus summarizes the Messianic idea in the writings of Isaiah:--

"There must come some one who should perfectly satisfy all the demands of the true f so as to become the centre from which all its truth and force should operate. His soul mus] a marvelous and surpassing nobleness and divine power, because it is his function perfec] realize in life the ancient religion, the requirements of which no one has yet satisfied, and with that spiritual glorification which the great prophets had announced. Unless there fi some one who shall transfigure this religion into its purest form, it will never be perfecte] kingdom will never come. But he will and must come, for otherwise the religion which di him would be false; he is the first true King of the community of the true God, and as noti be conceived of as supplanting him, he will reign forever in irresistible power; he is the] human King, whose coming had been due ever since the true community had set up a hu monarchy in its midst, but who had never come. He is to be looked for, to be longed for prayed for; and how blessed it is simply to expect him devoutly, and to trace out every featui likeness. To sketch the nobleness of his soul is to pursue in detail the possibility of perfe(religion; and to believe in the necessity of his coming is to believe in the perfecting of a agency on earth." [Footnote: *The History of Israel*, iv. 203, 204.]

It is precisely here that we get at the heart of the Old Testament; this wonderful foi toward the Messianic manifestations of God upon the earth, which kindled the hearts of th and found clearest utterance by the lips of its most inspired men, which binds this litera together, histories, songs, precepts, allegories. This it is which reveals the true inspiration old writings, and which makes them, to every Christian heart, precious beyond all price.

Such being the character of these prophetic books, let us glance for a moment at a them, merely for the purpose of locating the prophecy in the history, and of discerning, w possible, the providential causes which called it forth.

It is difficult to tell which of these fifteen prophets, whose utterances are treasuri collection, first appeared upon the scene. The probability seems to be that the earliest of t Joel. Opinions differ widely; I cannot discuss them nor even cite them; but the old theory t lived and preached about eight hundred and seventy-five years before Christ does not seei to be invalidated by modern criticism. He was a native of the Southern Kingdom; and at th we have named, the King of Judea was Joash, whose dramatic elevation to the throne in his s]

YEAR, BY JEHOIADA THE PRIEST, IS NARRATED IN THE BOOK OF KINGS. IT WAS A TIME OF DISTURBAN DISASTER IN JUDAH AND JERUSALEM; THE BOY-KING WAS BUT A NOMINAL RULER; THE REGENT WAS JEHOIA INCURSIONS OF THE SURROUNDING TRIBES, WHO CARRIED AWAY THE PEOPLE AND SOLD THEM AS SLAVES, K LAND IN A CONSTANT STATE OF ALARM. WORSE THAN THIS WAS THE VISITATION OF LOCUSTS, CONTINU WOULD SEEM, FOR SEVERAL YEARS, BY WHICH THE COUNTRY WAS STRIPPED AND DEVASTATED. THIS VISI FURNISHES THE THEME OF THE SHORT DISCOURSE WHICH IS HERE REPORTED. THE DESCRIPTION OF THE M THE LOCUSTS OVER THE LAND IS FULL OF POETIC BEAUTY; AND THE PEOPLE ARE ADMONISHED TO ACCEPT DIVINE CHASTISEMENT FOR THEIR SINS, AND TO DO THE WORKS MEET FOR REPENTANCE. THEN CO PROMISE OF THE DIVINE FORGIVENESS, AND OF THAT GREAT GIFT OF THE SPIRIT, WHOSE FULFILLME CLAIMED ON THE DAY OF PENTECOST: "IN THE MIDST OF THE DEEPEST WOES WHICH THEN AFFLIC KINGDOM," SAYS EWALD, "HIS GREAT SOUL GRASPED ALL THE MORE POWERFULLY THE ETERNAL HOPE OF COMMUNITY, AND IMPRESSED IT ALL THE MORE INDELIBLY UPON HIS PEOPLE, ALIKE BY THE FIERY GLOW CLEAR INSIGHT AND THE ENTRANCING BEAUTY OF HIS PASSIONATE UTTERANCE." [FOOTNOTE: *The History of Israel* iv. 139.]

THE NEXT PROPHET IN THE ORDER OF TIME IS UNDOUBTEDLY AMOS. HE TELLS US THAT HE LIVE DAYS OF UZZIAH, KING OF JUDAH, ABOUT SEVENTY YEARS AFTER JOEL. HE WAS A HERDSMAN OF TEKOA, A CITY OF JUDAH, TWELVE MILES SOUTH OF JERUSALEM. IN THESE DAYS THE NORTHERN KINGDOM WAS FA PROSPEROUS AND POWERFUL THAN THE SOUTHERN; UNDER JEROBOAM II. ISRAEL HAD BECOME RIC LUXURIOUS; AND THE PROPHET WAS SUMMONED, AS HE DECLARES, BY THE CALL OF JEHOVAH HIMSELF TO HIS HERDS UPON THE JUDEAN HILLS, AND BETAKE HIMSELF TO THE NORTHERN KINGDOM, THERE TO BEA AGAINST THE PRIDE AND OPPRESSION OF ITS PEOPLE. THIS MESSENGER AND INTERPRETER OF JEHOVAH PEOPLE IS A POOR MAN, A LABORING MAN; BUT HE KNOWS WHOSE COMMISSION HE BEARS, AND HE IS AFRAID. STERN AND TERRIBLE ARE THE WOES THAT FALL FROM HIS LIPS: THE WORDS VIBRATE YET WITH T of his righteous wrath.

"YE THAT PUT FAR AWAY THE EVIL DAY, AND CAUSE THE SEAT OF VIOLENCE TO COME NEAR; THAT L BEDS OF IVORY, AND STRETCH THEMSELVES UPON THEIR COUCHES, AND EAT THE LAMBS OUT OF THE FL THE CALVES OUT OF THE MIDST OF THE STALL; THAT SING IDLE SONGS TO THE SOUND OF THE VIOL; THA THEMSELVES INSTRUMENTS OF MUSIC, LIKE DAVID; THAT DRINK WINE IN BOWLS, AND ANOINT THEMSELVE the chief ointments; but they are not grieved for the affliction of Joseph."

SUCH LUXURY ALWAYS GOES HAND IN HAND WITH CONTEMPT OF THE LOWLY AND OPPRESSION OF THE IT IS SO TO-DAY; IT WAS SO IN THAT FAR-OFF TIME; AND THIS PROPHET POURS UPON IT THE VIALS OF THE W God:--

"FORASMUCH THEREFORE AS YE TRAMPLE UPON THE POOR, AND TAKE EXACTIONS FROM HIM OF WH HAVE BUILT HOUSES OF HEWN STONE, BUT YE SHALL NOT DWELL IN THEM; YE HAVE PLANTED PLEASANT VI BUT YE SHALL NOT DRINK THE WINE THEREOF. FOR I KNOW HOW MANIFOLD ARE YOUR TRANSGRESSIONS A MIGHTY ARE YOUR SINS; YE THAT AFFLICT THE JUST, THAT TAKE A BRIBE, AND THAT TURN ASIDE THE NE gate from their right."

IT IS NO WONDER THAT AMAZIAH, THE PRIEST OF BETHEL, WRITHED UNDER THE SCOURGE OF THE H PROPHET, AND WANTED TO BE RID OF HIM: "O THOU SEER," HE CRIED, "GO, FLEE THEE AWAY INTO THE JUDAH, AND THERE EAT BREAD, AND PROPHESY THERE: BUT PROPHESY NOT AGAIN ANY MORE IN BETHE THE PROPHET STOOD HIS GROUND AND DELIVERED HIS MESSAGE, AND IT STILL RESOUNDS AS THE VERY GOD THROUGH EVERY LAND WHERE THE GREED OF GOLD MAKES MEN UNJUST, AND THE LOVE OF banishes compassion from human hearts.

THE NEAREST SUCCESSOR OF AMOS, IN THIS COLLECTION, SEEMS TO HAVE BEEN HOSEA, WHO TELL THE OPENING OF HIS PROPHECY THAT THE WORD OF THE LORD CAME UNTO HIM IN THE DAYS OF U JOTHAM, AHAZ, AND HEZEKIAH, KINGS OF JUDAH, AND IN THE DAYS OF JEROBOAM, SON OF JOASH, KI ISRAEL. THERE IS SOME DOUBT ABOUT THE GENUINENESS OF THIS SUPERSCRIPTION; BUT IT WAS ABOUT TH UNDOUBTEDLY, THAT HOSEA FLOURISHED. TO WHICH KINGDOM HE BELONGED IT IS NOT KNOWN; PR HOWEVER, TO ISRAEL, WITH WHOSE AFFAIRS HIS TEACHING IS CHIEFLY CONCERNED. HE MUST HAVE FO CLOSE UPON THE HERDSMAN OF TEKOA; POSSIBLY THEY WERE CONTEMPORARIES. HIS PROPHECY, TOO, IS A FROM THE TRUMPET OF THE LORD OUR RIGHTEOUSNESS. SUCH AN INDICTMENT OF A PEOPLE HAS NO been heard.

"Hear the word of the Lord, ye children of Israel: for the Lord hath a controversy inhabitants of the land, because there is no truth, nor mercy, nor knowledge of God in t There is nought but swearing and breaking faith, and killing, and stealing, and committing they break out, and blood toucheth blood."

Especially severe is the prophet in his denunciation of the priesthood.

"They feed on the sin of my people, and set their heart on their iniquity. And it shall people, like priest: and I will punish them for their ways, and will reward them their doings."

These prophecies of Hosea are instinct with a severe morality; the ethical thoroughn which he chastises the national sins is unflinching; but it is not all threatening; now and hear the word of tenderness, the promise of the divine forgiveness:--

"I will heal their backsliding. I will love them freely; for mine anger is turned away fro will be as the dew unto Israel; he shall blossom as the lily, and cast forth his roots as Lebanon."

Micah follows Hosea, at an interval of perhaps fifty years. He lived in a little village west of Jerusalem, and exercised his ministry in both kingdoms, testifying impartially agai wickedness of Jerusalem and Samaria, though the weight of his censure seems to rest up Judean capital. His strain is an echo of the outcry of Amos and Hosea; it is the same i indignation against the violence and rapacity of the rich, against corrupt judges, false i rascally traders, treacherous friends. For all these sins condign punishment is threatened after these retributive woes are past, there is promise of a better day. The great Messianic h begins to find clear utterance; the former prophets have seen in their visions only the resto the people of Israel; to Micah there comes the anticipation of an individual Leader and Deliverer.

"But thou, Bethlehem Ephratah, which art little to be among the thousands of Judah thee shall one come forth that is to be ruler in Israel, whose goings forth are from everlasting.... And he shall stand and shall feed his flock in the strength of the Lord, in t of the name of the Lord his God; and they shall abide; for now shall he be great unto thi the earth."

Thus slowly broadens the dawn of the Messianic hope.

The first part of the fourth chapter of Micah, which is a prediction of the glory that sh to Zion in the latter day, is verbally identical with the first part of the second chapter of I of the prophets must have quoted from the other or else, as Dr. Geikie suggests, both copie some older prophet.

After Micah comes the greatest of the prophets, Isaiah. He appeared upon the scene native city of Jerusalem about the middle of the eighth century before Christ. His work wa done during the reigns of Ahaz, "the Grasper," one of the vilest and most ungodly of th monarchs, and of Hezekiah, the good king, about a century and a half before the destru Jerusalem.

About this time Judea was constantly exposed to the rapacity of the great Assyrian before whose armies she finally fell; sometimes her rulers entered into coalitions w surrounding nations to resist the Assyrian; sometimes they submitted and paid heavy tribute. Egypt, on the south, was also a mighty empire at this time, constantly at war with Assyria; and the Judah sometimes sought alliances with one of these great powers, as a means of protection the other. They proved to be the upper and nether millstones between which the Jewish nat was ground to powder. It was in the midst of these alarming signs of national destructi Isaiah arose. Of the prophetic discourses which he delivered in Jerusalem we have about thir words are the words of a patriot, a statesman, a servant and messenger of Jehovah. He warn kings against these entangling alliances with foreign powers; he admonished them to stan their allegiance to Jehovah, and obey his laws; yet he saw that they would not heed his wo that swift and sure destruction was coming upon the nation. And his expectation was not l of the other prophets, that the nation as a whole would be saved out of these judgments; t was made plain that only a remnant would survive; but that from that remnant should s noble race, with a purer faith, in whom all the nations of the earth should be blessed. Messianic hope as it finds expression in these words of Isaiah I have already spoken.

This Book of Isaiah contains thirty-one prophetic discourses, some of them mere frag There is reason for doubt as to whether they were all spoken by Isaiah; when they were gath two hundred years later, some utterances of other prophets may have been mingled wit Indeed it is now regarded as well-nigh certain that the last twenty-seven chapters are the later prophet,--of one who wrote during the Captivity. Professor Delitzsch, in the last edit commentary on Isaiah, finally concedes that this is probable. The Book of Isaiah, he is repo saying, "may have been an anthology of prophetic discourses by different authors; that is, have been composed partly and directly by Isaiah, and partly by other later prophets utterances constitute a really homogeneous and simultaneous continuation of Isaian p These later prophets so closely resemble Isaiah in prophetic vision that posterity might, account, well identify them with him,--his name being the correct common denominator f collection of prophecies."

These words of the most distinguished and devout of the Old Testament critics throw of light on the structure not only of Isaiah, but of other Old Testament writings; they unlike our own were the primitive ideas of authorship; and how the Pentateuch, for example, from many sources and revised by many editors, could be called the law of Moses*his* name may have been the "common denominator" of all that collection of laws.

I have shown, perhaps, in these hasty notices, something of the nature and purpose of these prophetic books. Of the rest I must speak but a single word, for the time fails me to Zephaniah, who in the time of good King Josiah, denounced the idolatry of the peop injustice of its princes and judges, and the corruption of its prophets and priests, threate rebellious with extermination, and promised to the remnant an enduring peace; of Jeremia about the same time first lifted up his voice, and continued speaking until after the destru Jerusalem,--from whose writings we may derive a more complete and intelligible account period preceding the Exile than from any other source; of Nahum, who, just before the Jerusalem, uttered his oracle against Nineveh; of Obadiah, who, after the fall of the launched his thunderbolts against the perfidious Edomites because of their rejoicing over of Jerusalem; of Ezekiel, the prophet of the Exile, who wrote among the captives by the r Babylon; of Haggai and Zechariah, who came back with the returning exiles, and whose cour voices cheered the laborers who wrought to restore the city and the temple; of Malac pungent reproofs of the people for their lack of consecration followed the erection of t temple, and closed the collection of the Hebrew prophets.

The limits of this small volume forbid us to enter upon several interesting critical respecting the component parts of Isaiah and Zechariah, and especially the matter of the v of the Septuagint from the Hebrew text in the Book of Jeremiah. In this last named book the same phenomena that we encountered in our study of Samuel and The Kings: the version differs considerably from the Hebrew; a comparison of the two illustrates, as noth can do, the processes through which the text of these old documents has passed, and the with which they have been handled by scribes and copyists. The Hebrew text, from whic English version was made, is generally better than the Greek; but there are several cases the Greek is manifestly more accurate.

There is one book, reckoned among these minor prophets, of which I have not spoken, a which I ought to make some reference. That is the book of Jonah.

It is found among the minor prophets, but it is not in any sense prophetical; it is nei sermon nor a prediction; it is a narrative. Probably it was placed by the Jews among prophetical books because Jonah was a prophet. But this book was not written by Jonah; th not a word in the book which warrants the belief that he was its author. It is a story abou told by somebody else long after Jonah's day. Jonah, the son of Amittai, was a prophet Northern Kingdom in the days of Jeroboam II., far back in the ninth century. The only refe him contained in the Old Testament is found in 2 Kings xiv. 25. But this book was almost ce written long after the destruction of Nineveh, which took place two hundred years l reason for this belief is in the fact that the writer of the book feels it necessary to explain of a city Nineveh was. He stops in the midst of his story to say: "Now Nineveh was an excei great city of three days' journey." That explanation would have been superfluous anywhere in the days of Jeroboam II., and the past tense indicates that it was written by one who was l back to a city no longer in existence. "Nineveh was." The character of the Hebrew also fav theory of a later date for the book. We have, therefore, a tale that was told about Jonah three or four hundred years after his day.

Is it a true tale, or is it a work of didactic fiction? I believe that it is the latter. It suggestive apologue, full of moral beauty and spiritual power, designed to convey several im lessons to the minds of the Jewish people. I cannot regard it as the actual experience of a prophet of God, because I can hardly imagine that such a prophet could have supposed, a Jonah of this tale is said to have supposed, that by getting out of the bounds of the King Israel, he would get out of the sight of Jehovah. This is precisely what this Jonah of t undertook to do. When he was bidden to go to Nineveh and cry against it, "he rose up to fi Tarshish *from the presence of the Lord;* and he went down to Joppa, and found a ship going to Tarsh so he paid the fare thereof, and went down into it, to go with them unto T*from the presence of the Lord"* (ch. i. 3). Is this actual history? Is this the belief of a genuine prophet of the Lord sort of a prophet is he who holds ideas as crude as this concerning the Being with whom h constant communication and from whom he receives his messages? If Jonah did entertai belief, then it is not likely that he can teach us anything about God which it is importan should know.

Thus, without touching the miraculous features of the story, we have sound reasc believing that this cannot be the actual experience of any veritable prophet of God; that history, but fiction. Why not? Can any one who has read the parable of the Prodigal Son Good Samaritan doubt that fiction may be used in Sacred Scripture for the highest purpose?

But it is argued that the references to this story which are found in the words c authenticate the story. Our Lord, in Matt. xii, 39-42, refers to this book. He speaks repentance of the Ninevites under the preaching of Jonah as a rebuke to the Jews who ha the word of life from him and had not repented; and he uses these words: "An evil and adu generation seeketh a sign; and there shall no sign be given to it but the sign of Jonah the for as Jonah was three days and three nights in the belly of the whale; so shall the Son c three days and three nights in the heart of the earth."

This confirms, say the orthodox commentators, the historical accuracy of the story o "If," says Canon Liddon, "he would put his finger on a fact in past Jewish history which, i admitted reality, would warrant belief in his own resurrection, he points to Jonah's being th and three nights in the belly of the whale." This use of the incident by our Lord authenticates the incident as an actual historical fact. So say the conservative theologian say also the men who labor to destroy the authority of Christ. Mr. Huxley perfectly ag Canon Liddon. He praises the Canon's penetration and consistency; he agrees that there ca other possible interpretation of Christ's words. The ultra-conservative and the anti-Christi are at one in insisting that Christ stands committed to the literal truth of the narrativ The inference of the ultra-conservative is that the narrative is historically true; the infer anti-Christian critic is that Jesus is unworthy our confidence as a religious teacher; that fully indorsed such a preposterous tale cannot be divine. It is instructive to observe th conservative critics thus playing steadily into the hands of the anti-Christian critics, furnish with ammunition with which to assail the very citadel of the Christian faith. It is a kind of in which, I am sorry to say, they have been diligently engaged for a good while.

Now I, for my part, utterly deny the proposition which these allied forces of skeptici traditionalism are enlisted in supporting. I deny that Jesus Christ can be fairly quo authenticating this narrative. I maintain that he used it allegorically for purposes of il without intending to express any opinion as to the historical verity of the narrative. It was literary way, and not in a dogmatic way. Our Lord speaks always after the manner of men,-- the common speech of the people, takes up the phrases and even the fables that he finds upo lips, and uses them for his own purposes. He does not stop to criticise all their stories, or them right in all their scientific errors; that would have been utterly aside from his main and would certainly have confused them and led them astray. He speaks always of the rising setting of the sun, using the phrases that were current at that time, and never hinting at underneath them. He knew what these people meant by these phrases. If he knew that these conveyed an erroneous meaning, why did he not correct them? So, too, he quotes from the the Creation in Genesis, and never intimates that the six days there mentioned are not literal days of twenty-four hours each. He knew that those to whom he was speaking entertained this bel put this interpretation upon these words. Why does he not set it aside?

These questions may admit of more than one answer; but, taking the very highest v Christ's person, it is certainly enough to say that any such discussion of scientific question have been, as even we can see, palpably unwise. There was no preparation in the human mind that day for the reception and verification of such a scientific revelation. It could not received. It would not have been preserved. It would only have confused and puzzled the mi his hearers, and would have shut their minds at once against that moral and spiritual truth came to impart. And what we have said about scientific questions applies with equal for questions of Old Testament criticism. To have entered upon the discussion of these questio the Jews would have thwarted his highest purpose. In the largest sense of the word these Sc were true. Their substantial historical accuracy he wished to confirm. Their great converg of light united in him. He constantly claimed their fulfillment in his person and his kingdo then, should he enter upon a kind of discussion which would have tended to confuse and c the main truths which he came to teach? If, then, he refers to these Scriptures, he uses them own ethical and spiritual purposes,--not to indorse their scientific errors; not to conf methods of interpretation in use among the Jews.

But Mr. Huxley insists, and all the ultra-conservative commentators join him in insistin Christ could not, if he had been an honest man, have spoken thus of Jonah if the story of Jo not been historically accurate. This is the way he puts it: "If Jonah's three days' residence whale is not an 'admitted fact,' how could it 'warrant belief' in the 'coming resurre [Footnote: *The Nineteenth Century*, July, 1890.] Mr. Huxley is using Canon Liddon's phrases here; he is using them to confute those for whom, as he knows very well, Canon Liddon does not Those who say that the story of Jonah is an "admitted reality" may, perhaps, be able to see "warrants belief" in the "coming resurrection." To my own mind, even this is by no means cl do not see how the one event, even if it were an "admitted reality," could "warrant belie other. No past event can warrant belief in any future event, unless the two events are subs identical. The growth of an acorn into an oak in the last century "warrants the belief" tha will grow into an oak in the present century; but it does not "warrant the belief" that a ci on an eligible site will grow to be a great metropolis. The one event might illustrate the no conclusions of logic can be carried from the one to the other. It is precisely so with t events. There is a certain analogy between the experience of Jonah, as told in the book, an our Lord; but it is ridiculous to say that the one event, if an "admitted reality," "warrants the other,--whether it is said by Mr. Huxley or Canon Liddon. Our Lord's words convey n meaning. In truth, if we are here dealing with scientific comparisons, the one event, if tak "admitted reality," *warrants disbelief* in the other. What are our Lord's precise words? "Jonah was three days and three nights in the whale's belly, so shall the Son of man be three days and th nights in the heart of the earth." We are told by Mr. Huxley and his orthodox allies tha take this as a literal historical parallel, or not at all; that if we treat it in any other way, we accuse our Lord of dishonesty. What, then, was the condition of Jonah during these three days and Was he dead or alive? He was certainly alive, if the tale is history--very thoroughly alive faculties. He was praying part of the time, and part of the time he was writing poetry. We long and beautiful poem which he is said to have composed during that enforced retiremen active life. It would appear that his release took place immediately after the poem was finis now, these events are bound together with the links of logic, if the one event is the

COUNTERPART OF THE OTHER, THE SON OF MAN, DURING THE THREE DAYS OF HIS SOJOURN IN THE HEA EARTH, WAS NOT DEAD AT ALL! HE WAS ONLY HIDDEN FOR A LITTLE SPACE FROM THE SIGHT OF MEN. HE all the while, *and there was no resurrection!* IT IS TO THIS THAT YOU COME WHEN YOU BEGIN TO APPLY TO T PARABLES AND ALLEGORIES OF THE BIBLE THE METHODS OF SCIENTIFIC EXPOSITION. THIS MAY BE SATIS enough to Mr. Huxley. I should like to know how it suits his orthodox allies.

THE FACT IS, THAT YOU ARE NOT DEALING HERE WITH EQUIVALENTS, BUT WITH ANALOGIES; NOT WITI EVIDENCE, BUT WITH FIGURES OF RHETORIC: AND IT IS ABSURD TO SAY THAT ONE MEMBER OF AN "WARRANTS BELIEF" IN THE EXISTENCE OF THE OTHER. THERE IS NO SUCH LOGICAL NEXUS. THE LEAVI MEAL DOES NOT "WARRANT BELIEF" IN THE SPREAD OF CHRISTIANITY, BUT IT SERVES TO ILLUSTRATE IT. OF THE PRODIGAL SON DOES NOT "WARRANT BELIEF" IN THE FATHERLY LOVE OF GOD, BUT IT HEI UNDERSTAND SOMETHING OF THAT LOVE, AND IT HELPS US PRECISELY AS MUCH AS IF IT HAD BEEN A VI history, instead of being, as it is, a pure work of fiction.

"WHAT SORT OF VALUE," ASKS MR. HUXLEY, "AS AN ILLUSTRATION OF GOD'S METHODS OF DEALI SIN, HAS AN ACCOUNT OF AN EVENT THAT NEVER HAPPENED?" SUCH AN ADMONITION, HE SAYS, IS "M ABOUT ON A LEVEL WITH TELLING A NAUGHTY CHILD THAT A BOGY IS COMING TO FETCH IT AWAY." LET this maxim to some of Mr. Huxley's homilies:--

"SURELY," HE SAYS IN ONE OF HIS "LAY SERMONS," "OUR INNOCENT PLEASURES ARE NOT SO ABUND THIS LIFE THAT WE CAN AFFORD TO DESPISE THIS OR ANY OTHER SOURCE OF THEM. WE SHOULD FE BANISHED FOR OUR NEGLECT *to that limbo where the great Florentine tells us are those who during this life wept when they might be joyful*." [FOOTNOTE: *Lay Sermons and Addresses*, P. 92.] THIS LIMBO OF DANTE'S IS NOT, DARE SAY, AN "ADMITTED REALITY" IN MR. HUXLEY'S PHYSICAL GEOGRAPHY. "WHAT SORT OF VALUE," TH HAS HIS REFERENCE TO IT? IS HE MERELY RAISING THE CRY OF BOGY? HE CERTAINLY DOES INTEND WHAT I A DISSUASIVE FROM A CERTAIN COURSE OF ERRONEOUS CONDUCT. I VENTURE TO INSIST THAT HE HA MEANING, AND THAT, ALTHOUGH THE LIMBO IS A MYTH, THE CONDITION WHICH HE INTENDS TO ILLUSTRA allusion to it is a reality.

ONCE MORE: "I DO NOT SUPPOSE THAT THE DEAD SOUL OF PETER BELL, OF WHOM THE GREAT nature says,--

> 'A primrose by the river's brim
> A yellow primrose was to him,
> And it was nothing more,'

WOULD HAVE BEEN A WHIT ROUSED FROM ITS APATHY BY THE INFORMATION THAT THE PRIMROS DICOTYLEDONOUS EXOGEN, WITH A MONOPETALOUS COROLLA AND A CENTRAL PLACENTATION." [FOOTNOTE: *Ibid.* p. 91.]

DOES MR. HUXLEY BELIEVE THAT PETER BELL WAS A HISTORICAL PERSON? IF HE WAS NOT, HOW, NAME OF BIOLOGICAL THEOLOGY, COULD HIS DEAD SOUL HAVE BEEN ROUSED BY ANY INFORMATION WH YET THESE SENTENCES OF HIS HAVE A REAL AND VALUABLE MEANING. IT IS EVIDENT THAT MR. HUXL UNDERSTAND THE USES OF ALLEGORY AND FABLE FOR PURPOSES OF ILLUSTRATION; THAT HE CAN EMPLOY AND SITUATIONS WHICH ARE NOT HISTORICAL, BUT PURELY IMAGINARY, TO ILLUSTRATE THE REALITIES WI TRYING TO PRESENT,--SPEAKING OF THEM ALL THE WHILE JUST AS IF THEY WERE HISTORICAL PERSONS AND TRUSTING HIS READERS TO INTERPRET HIM ARIGHT. SUCH A USE OF LANGUAGE IS COMMON IN ALL LI TO AFFIRM THAT OUR LORD COULD NOT RESORT TO IT WITHOUT DISHONESTY IS TO DENY TO HIM THE instruments of speech.

"WE MAY CONCLUDE, THEN," WITH PROFESSOR LADD, "THAT THE REFERENCE TO JONAH DOES NO THE QUESTION WHETHER THE PROPHET'S ALLEGED SOJOURN IN THE SEA MONSTER IS AN HISTORICAL VE THAT IT IS NO LESS UNCRITICAL THAN INVIDIOUS TO MAKE THE HOLDING OF ANY PARTICULAR THEORY OF OF JONAH A TEST OF ALLEGIANCE TO THE TEACHINGS OF THE MASTER." [FOOTNOTE: *The Doctrine of Sacred Scripture*, i. 67.]

IT IS EVIDENT ENOUGH, AS PROFESSOR CHEYNE HAS SAID, THAT THE SYMBOLIC MEANING OF THE BO THE MOST IMPORTANT PART OF IT IN THE NEW TESTAMENT TIMES. BUT OTHER AND MORE OBVIOUS ME ARE CONVEYED BY THE NARRATIVE. INDEED, THERE IS SCARCELY ANOTHER BOOK IN THE OLD TESTAME meaning is so clear, whose message is so divine. Apologue though it is, it is full of the very t God. There is not one of the minor prophecies that has more of the real gospel in it. To thi who first received it, how full of admonition and reproof it must have been! That gri Nineveh--a city which was, in its day, as Dr. Geikie says, "as intensely abhorred by the Je Carthage was by Rome, or France under the elder Napoleon was by Germany"--was a city d God! He had sent his own prophet to warn it of its danger; and his prophet, instead of being or torn asunder, as the prophets of God had often been by their own people, had been hea his message heeded. The Ninevites had turned to God, and God had forgiven them! God v less ready to forgive and save Nineveh than Jerusalem. What a wonderful disclosure of thi the universal Father! What a telling blow, even in those old days, at the "middle wall of p by which the Jew fenced out the Gentile from his sympathy!

And then the gentle rebuke of Jonah's petulant narrowness! How true is the tou describes Jonah as angry because God had forgiven the Ninevites! His credit as a prophet was I suppose that he was afraid also, like many theologians of more modern times, that if thr penalty were remitted solely on the ground of the repentance of the sinners, the foundati divine government would be undermined. How marvelously does the infinite pity and cleme God shine out through all this story, as contrasted with the petty consistency and the compassion of man; and how clearly do we hear in this beautiful narrative the very message gospel: "Let the wicked forsake his way, and the unrighteous man his thoughts: and let him to the Lord, and he will have mercy upon him; and to our God, for he will abundantly pard my thoughts are not your thoughts, neither are your ways my ways, saith the Lord."

May I say, in closing, that the treatment which the Book of Jonah has received, ali skeptics and from defenders of the faith, illustrates, in a striking way, the kind of controve is raised by the attempt to maintain the infallibility of the Bible. The all the critics, orthod and heterodox, is the story about the fish. The orthodox have assumed that the narrative the miracle was meaningless, and the heterodox have taken them at their word. In their dispute over the question whether Jonah did really compose that psalm in the belly of the fish, with festooned with seaweed, they have almost wholly overlooked the great lessons of fidelity t the universal divine fatherhood, and the universal human brotherhood, which the s beautifully enforces. How easy it is for saints as well as scoffers, in their dealing with the of God to men, to tithe the mint, anise, and cummin of the literal sense, and neglect the matters of judgment, mercy, and truth which they are intended to convey!

Chapter VI.

The Later Hebrew Histories

After the Book of the Law had been revised by Ezra, and the Book of the Prophets ha compiled by Nehemiah, there still remained a body of sacred writings, not Mosaic in their and not from the hands of any recognized prophet, but still of value in the eyes of the J cannot tell the time at which the work of collecting these Scriptures was begun; possibl going on while the Books of the Prophets were being compiled. This third collection wa from the first by the Jews, "Ketubim," meaning simply writings; the Greeks afterward called name which has been anglicized, and which has become the common designation of these wr among us, "The Hagiographa," or the Holy Writings. The adjective holy was not a part Jewish title; it would have overstated, somewhat, their first estimate of this part of their B while the degree of sacredness attached to these books gradually increased, they were alwa quite inferior to the other two groups of Scriptures. For convenience the list of book collection may be here repeated:--

The Psalms.
The Proverbs.
Job.
The Song of Solomon.
Ruth.
Lamentations.
Ecclesiastes.
Esther.
Daniel.
Ezra.
Nehemiah.
1 Chronicles.
2 Chronicles.

The arrangement is topical; first, three poetical books, The Psalms, The Proverbs, an then five so-called Megilloth, or Rolls, read in the later synagogues on certain great feas Song of Songs at the Passover, Ruth at Pentecost, Lamentations on the anniversary of the of the temple, Ecclesiastes at the Feast of Tabernacles, and Esther at the Feast of Purim; l historical and quasi-historical books, Daniel, Ezra, Nehemiah, and the Chronicles.

Of Ruth I have already spoken in its proper historical connection, taking it with the I Judges.

In treating of the remaining books I shall not follow the order of the Hebrew Bible have given above, but shall rather reverse it, treating first of the historical books, Ezra, N and the Chronicles, also of Esther and Daniel; then, in a subsequent chapter, of the poetic the Lamentations, the books attributed to Solomon,--Proverbs, Ecclesiastes, and Solomon's and finally of Job and the Psalms.

The histories which, under the title of the "Earlier Prophets," are contained in th group of the Hebrew Scriptures, have been studied in a former chapter. In this later gr writings we find certain other historical works which cover the same ground. In the word Horton:--

"Taking historical excerpts from the first six books of the Bible, and then going continuous narrative from the beginning of Judges to the end of the Second Book of K have a story--true, a story with many gaps in it, still a connected story--from the earliest tim captivity of Judah. Then, starting from the First Book of Chronicles and reading on to th Nehemiah, we have, in a very compressed form, though enlarged in some parts, a complete r from Adam to the return from the Captivity; at the end of this long sweep of narrative c Book of Esther, which is a brief appendix containing a historical episode of the Captivity. these two distinct histories, we have two lines of narrative, an older and a later, which run up to the Captivity; the older, though covering a shorter time, is much the larger and f later, very thin in most parts, becomes very full in its account of the Temple-worship and T kingship at Jerusalem, and then continues the story alone up to the end of the Captivity, reëstablishment of the Temple-worship after the return." [Footnote: *Inspiration and the Bible*, pp. 159, 160.]

The older history, contained in Samuel and Kings, breaks off abruptly in the time Captivity; we know that it must have been written during the Exile, and could not hav written earlier than about 550 B.C. The later history, in Chronicles and Ezra-Nehemiah, be with Adam, and goes on, by one or two genealogical tables, for almost two centuries a Captivity. In 1 Chronicles iii. 19, the genealogy of Zerubbabel, who came back with the capt

CARRIED ON FOR AT LEAST SIX GENERATIONS. COUNTING THIRTY YEARS FOR A GENERATION, THE TABLE TIME OF THE WRITING OF THIS RECORD TO AT LEAST ONE HUNDRED AND EIGHTY YEARS AFTER THE RE EXILES. THIS OCCURRED IN 53B.C.., AND THE BOOK MUST THEREFORE HAVE BEEN WRITTEN AS LATE A B.C.., or very nearly two centuries after the earlier history was finished.

THERE ARE CONCLUSIVE REASONS FOR BELIEVING THAT THE FOUR BOOKS NOW UNDER CONSIDERAT TWO BOOKS OF CHRONICLES, EZRA, AND NEHEMIAH, WERE ORIGINALLY BUT ONE BOOK. IN THE HEBREW THE CHRONICLES IS NOW BUT ONE BOOK; AND IN THE OLD HEBREW COLLECTIONS EZRA AND NEHEMIA BUT ONE BOOK. IT WAS IN THE SEPTUAGINT THAT THEY WERE FIRST SEPARATED. THUS WE HAVE TH CERTAINLY REDUCED TO TWO. AND IT IS NOT DIFFICULT, ON AN INSPECTION OF THE DOCUMENTS, TO RI TWO TO ONE. IF YOU WILL OPEN YOUR BIBLE AT THE LAST VERSES OF SECOND CHRONICLES, BEGINNING TWENTY-SECOND VERSE OF THE LAST CHAPTER, AND, FIXING YOUR EYES ON THIS PASSAGE, WILL ASK SOMI READ TO YOU THE FIRST THREE VERSES OF THE BOOK OF EZRA, YOU WILL SEE HOW THESE TWO BOC FORMERLY ONE; AND HOW THE MANUSCRIPT WAS TORN IN TWO IN THE WRONG PLACE; SO THAT THE E CHRONICLES ACTUALLY ENDS IN THE MIDDLE OF A SENTENCE. THE PERIOD AT THE END OF THIS BOOK OU expunged.

THE EXPLANATFON OF THIS CURIOUS PHENOMENON IS NOT DIFFICULT. THE LAST GROUP OF WRITINGS, WHAT THE JEWS CALL THE KETUBIM, WAS KEPT OPEN FOR ADDITIONS TO A VERY LATE DAY. AF HISTORY WAS WRITTEN (CHRONICLES-EZRA-NEHEMIAH) THE QUESTION AROSE WHETHER IT SHOULD BE A INTO THE CANON. THE FIRST ANSWER TO THIS QUESTION EVIDENTLY WAS: "WE DO NOT NEED THE FIRS THE HISTORY,--THE BOOK OF CHRONICLES,--FOR WE HAVE THE SUBSTANCE OF IT ALREADY IN THE E SAMUEL AND KINGS AND IN THE EARLIER WRITINGS; BUT WE DO NEED THE LAST PART OF IT, 'EZRA-NEI FOR THIS CARRIES THE HISTORY ON BEYOND THE CAPTIVITY, AND GIVES THE ACCOUNT OF THE RETURN OF AND THE REBUILDING OF THE CITY AND THE TEMPLE." SO THEY TORE THE BOOK IN TWO, AND PUT THE LA IT INTO THE GROWING COLLECTION OF "KETUBIM," OR "WRITINGS." THE CARELESS DIVISION OF THE MAN NOT AT THE BEGINNING OF A PARAGRAPH, BUT IN THE MIDDLE OF A SENTENCE, MADE IT NECESSARY, OF FOR THE SCRIBE TO COPY AT THE BEGINNING OF THE EZRA-ROLL THE WORDS BELONGING TO IT WHICH TORN OFF; BUT THEY WERE NOT ERASED FROM THE FIRST PART, AND HAVE BEEN LEFT THERE, AS THE OLD say, "unto this day."

BY AND BY THERE WERE REQUESTS THAT THIS FIRST PART--THE CHRONICLES--BE ADMITTED TO THE THE PRIESTS AND THE LEVITES OF THE TEMPLE WOULD BE SURE TO URGE THIS REQUEST, FOR THE CHRC THE ONE BOOK OF THE OLD TESTAMENT IN WHICH THEIR ORDER IS GLORIFIED; AND AT LENGTH THE RE GRANTED; THE CHRONICLES WERE ADDED TO THE COLLECTION, AND AS THEY WENT IN LAST THEY FO NEHEMIAH, ALTHOUGH THEY BELONG, CHRONOLOGICALLY, BEFORE IT. THEY STAND TO-DAY AT THE E HEBREW BIBLE, AND THUS TESTIFY, BY THEIR POSITION, RESPECTING THE LATENESS OF THE DATE AT WH were admitted to the canon. Thus the Hebrew Bible ends with an incomplete sentence.

WHAT THIS LATER HISTORY MAY HAVE BEEN CALLED BEFORE IT WAS TORN IN TWO WE HAVE NO ME KNOWING; BUT THE JEWS CALLED THE LAST PART OF IT (WHICH STANDS FIRST IN THEIR COLLECTION) BY TH EZRA, AND THE FIRST PART OF IT (WHICH IS LAST IN THEIR CANON) THEY NAMED, "EVENTS OF THE TI "ANNALS." IN THE SEPTUAGINT THIS BOOK OF THE CHRONICLES WAS CALLED "PARALEIPOMENA," "LEA "THINGS LEFT OVER," "SUPPLEMENTS." JEROME FIRST GAVE IT THE NAME OF "CHRONICLES," BY WHIC know it.

THE NAME OF THE AUTHOR OF THIS BOOK IS UNKNOWN. THE STRONG PROBABILITIES ARE THAT HI LEVITE, CONNECTED WITH THE TEMPLE SERVICE IN JERUSALEM. THE LEVITES HAD CHARGE OF THE RELIGIOUS SERVICES OF THE TEMPLE, ESPECIALLY OF ITS MUSIC; AND THE FULLNESS WITH WHICH THIS EXPATIATES UPON ALL THIS PART OF THE RITUAL SHOWS THAT IT WAS VERY DEAR TO HIS HEART. [FOOTNO CHRON. VI. 31-48; XV. 16-24; XVI 4-42; XXV.2 CHRON. V. 12, 13; VII. 6; VIII. 14; XX. 19-21; XXIII. 13; XXI 25-30; XXXI 2; ZXXIV. 12; XXXV. 15.] EVERYTHING RELATING TO THE LEVITICAL PRIESTHOOD AND ITS SEF DWELT UPON IN THIS BOOK WITH EMPHASIS AND ELABORATION; AS THE HISTORIES OF SAMUEL AND THE ARE WRITTEN FROM THE PROPHETICAL STANDPOINT, THIS IS MOST EVIDENTLY WRITTEN FROM THE PRIESTL view.

IN THESE BOOKS OF THE CHRONICLES THE AUTHOR CONSTANTLY POINTS OUT THE SOURCES INFORMATION. HE TELLS US THAT HE QUOTES FROM THE "BOOK OF THE KINGS OF JUDAH AND ISRAEL,"

"Acts of the Kings of Israel," and from "The Story of the Book of the Kings." The identity
books is a disputed question. It is supposed by some critics that he refers to the Books of Ki
our Bible; others maintain that he draws from another and much larger book of a simil/
which has been lost. The latter theory is generally maintained by the more conservative cr
it is easier to vindicate the author's trustworthiness on this supposition; yet even so tl
serious difficulties in the case; for it is hard to believe that he could have written the
without having had before him the earlier record, and between the two are many discrepanc
main facts of the history are substantially the same in the two narratives; but in minor ma
disagreements and contradictions are numerous. It is part of the purpose of this study
difficulties of this kind fairly in the face; it is treason to the spirit of all truth to refuse t(
us examine, then, a few of these discrepancies between the earlier and later history.

In 2 Samuel viii. 4, we are told that in David's victory over Hadadezer king of Zobah, hi
from the latter "a thousand and seven hundred horsemen." In 1 Chronicles xviii. 4, he is
have taken "a thousand chariots and seven thousand horsemen." In 2 Samuel xxiv. 9, David's census
is said to have returned 800,000 warriors for Israel, and 500,000 for Judah. In 1 Chronicles
the number is stated as 1,100,000 for Israel, and 470,000 for Judah. In 2 Samuel xxiv. 24, Da
said to have paid Araunah for his threshing-floor fifty shekels of silver, estimated at abc
dollars of our money; in 1 Chronicles xxi. 25, he is said to have given him "six hundred she
gold by weight," amounting to a little more than thirty-four hundred dollars. In 2 Chron
we read that Asa reigned in the stead of his father Abijah, and that in his days the land w
ten years. Again in the 10th and the 19th verses of the following chapter we learn that
fifteenth to the thirty-fifth year of Asa there was no war in the land. In 1 Kings xv. 3
explicitly told that "there was war between Asa and Baasha king of Israel all their da
Chronicles xx. the story of the taking of Rabbah seems to be abridged from 2 Samuel xi., x
the abridgment is curiously done, so that the part taken by David in the siege and captur
city is not brought out; and the whole narrative of David's relation to Uriah and Bathsh
the rebuke of Nathan and the death of David's child, is not alluded to. The relation o
narratives at this point is significant; it deserves careful study. One more curious difference
in the two accounts of the numbering of Israel. In 2 Samuel xxiv. 1, we read, "And the ange
Lord was kindled against Israel, and he moved David against them, saying, Go, number Isra
Judah." In 1 Chronicles xxi., we read, "And Satan stood up against Israel and moved Da
number Israel." The numbering in both narratives is assumed to be a grievous sin; and the p
of this sin, which was David's, was visited upon the people in the form of a pestilence, which
seventy thousand of them. I observe that the commentators try to reconcile these state
saying that Go*permitted* Satan to tempt David. I wonder if that explanation affords to any n
shade of relief. But the older record utterly forbids such a gloss. "The anger of the Lo
Israel" prompted the Lord to "move David against them," and the Lord said, "Go, number J
and Israel!" It was not a permission; it was a direct instigation. Then because David did wh
Lord moved him to do, "the Lord sent a pestilence upon Israel," which destroyed seventy th
men. We are not concerned to reconcile these two accounts, for neither of them can be tru
not suppose that we can be required, by any theory of inspiration, to blaspheme God by ac(
him of any such monstrous iniquity. Let no man open his mouth in this day to declare th
Judge of all the earth instigated David to do a presumptuous deed, and then slew seventy t
of David's subjects for the sin of their ruler. Such a view of God might have been held w
censure three thousand years ago; it cannot be held without sin by men who have th
Testament in their hands. This narrative belongs to that class of crude and defective
which Jesus, in the Sermon on the Mount, points out and sets aside. We may, nay we must app
the morality of this transaction the principle of judgment which Jesus gives us in that di
and say: "Ye have heard that it hath been said by them of old time that God sometimes inst
ruler to do wrong, and then punishes his people for the wrong done by the ruler which he
has instigated; but I say unto you that 'God cannot be tempted with evil, neither tempteth
man;' moreover the ruler shall not bear the sin of the subject, nor the subject the sin of

for every man shall give account of himself unto God." It is by the higher standard that C given us in the New Testament that we must judge all these narratives of the Old Testam when we find in these old writings statements which represent God as perfidious and unjust, not to try to "harmonize" them with other statements; we are simply to set them aside as t of a dark age.

Such blurred and distorted ideas about God and his truth we do certainly find here a in these old writings; the treasure which they have preserved for us is in earthen vessels; th element, which is a necessary part of a written revelation, all the while displays itself. It is i err; and the men who wrote the Bible were human. We may have a theory that God mus guarded them from every form of error, but the Bible itself has no such theory; and we mu make our theories of inspiration fit the facts of the Bible as we find them lying upon its pages.

The second portion of this history, the Book of Ezra-Nehemiah, presents fewer o difficulties than the Book of Chronicles. It is a fragmentary, but to all appearance a v record of the events which took place after the first return of the exiles to Jerusalem caravan returned in the first year of King Cyrus; and the history extends to the last part o of Artaxerxes Longimanus,--covering a period of more than a hundred years. The docume which it is based were largely official; and there is no doubt that considerable portions o book came from the pen of Ezra himself, and that the second book was made up in part writings left by Nehemiah. The language of the second book is Hebrew; that of the first Hebrew and partly Chaldee or Aramaic. We read in the fourth chapter of Ezra that a cert was written to King Artaxerxes, and it is said that "the writing of the letter was writt Syrian character." The margin of the revised version says "Aramaic." We find this letter Hebrew Bibles in the Aramaic language. And the writer, after copying the letter in Aram right on with the history in Aramaic; from the twelfth verse of the fourth chapter to the verse of the sixth chapter the language is all Aramaic; then the historian drops back into again, and goes on to the twelfth verse of the seventh chapter, when he returns to A record the letter of Artaxerxes, which extends to the twenty-seventh verse. The rest of Hebrew. With the exception of some short sections of the Book of Daniel, this is the only of our Old Testament that was not written originally in the Hebrew tongue.

The contents of these two books may be briefly summarized. The first book tells us h Persian king Cyrus, in the first year of his reign, issued a proclamation to the Jews dwellin kingdom, permitting and encouraging them to return to their own country and to reb temple in Jerusalem. The conquest of the Babylonians by the Persians had placed the capti in vastly improved circumstances. Between the faith of the Persians and that of the Jews th close affinity. The Persians were monotheists; and "Cyrus," as Rawlinson says, "evidently id Jehovah with Ormazd, and, accepting as a divine command the prophecy of Isaiah, underto rebuild their temple for a people who, like his own, allowed no image of God to def sanctuary.... The foundation was then laid for that friendly intimacy between the two pe which we have abundant evidence in the books of Ezra, Nehemiah, and Esther." The words o decree of Cyrus, with which the Book of Ezra opens, show how he regarded the God of th "Whosoever there is among you of all his people, his God be with him, and let him go Jerusalem, which is in Judah, and build the house of the Lord, the God of Israel, (he is God,) is in Jerusalem." The parenthetical clause is a clear confession of the faith of Cyrus that was only another name for Ormazd; that there is but one God.

In consequence of this decree, a caravan of nearly fifty thousand persons, led by Zer carrying with them liberal free-will offerings of those who remained in Babylon for the bu the temple, went back to Jerusalem, and in the second year began the erection of the secon With this pious design certain Samaritans interfered, finally procuring an injunction f successor of Cyrus by which the building of the temple was interrupted for several years. accession of Darius, the prophets Haggai and Zechariah stirred up the people to resume th and at length succeeded in getting from the great king complete authority to proceed wit sixth year of his reign the second temple was completed, and dedicated with great rejoic

CLOSES THE FIRST SECTION OF THE BOOK OF EZRA. THE REST OF THE BOOK IS OCCUPIED WITH THE STOR' himself, who is said to have been "a ready scribe in the law of Moses," and who, "in the seventh year OF ARTAXERXES, KING OF PERSIA," LED A SECOND CARAVAN OF EXILES HOME TO JERUSALEM, WITH GREAT SILVER AND GOLD AND WHEAT AND WINE AND OIL FOR THE RESUMPTION OF THE RITUAL WORSHIP OF TH HOUSE. THE STORY OF THIS RETURN OF THE EXILES IS MINUTELY TOLD; AND THE REMAINDER OF THI: DEVOTED TO A RECITAL OF THE MATTER OF THE MIXED MARRIAGES BETWEEN THE JEWISH MEN AND THI OF THE SURROUNDING TRIBES, WHICH CAUSED EZRA GREAT DISTRESS, AND WHICH HE SUCCEEDED IN AN: SO THAT THESE "STRANGE WOMEN," AS THEY ARE CALLED, WERE ALL PUT AWAY. TO OUR EYES THIS SEEMS OF DOUBTFUL MORALITY, BUT WE MUST CONSIDER THE CHANGED STANDARDS OF OUR TIME, AND REMEMI THESE MEN MIGHT HAVE DONE WITH THE PUREST CONSCIENTIOUSNESS SOME THINGS WHICH WE COULD N at all.

THE BOOK OF NEHEMIAH IS IN PART A RECITAL BY NEHEMIAH HIMSELF OF THE CIRCUMSTANCES COMING TO JERUSALEM, WHICH SEEMS TO HAVE TAKEN PLACE ABOUT THIRTEEN YEARS AFTER THE CO! EZRA. HE WAS THE CUPBEARER OF ARTAXERXES THE KING; HE HAD HEARD OF THE DISTRESS AND POVERT PEOPLE AT JERUSALEM, AND IN THE FERVID PATRIOTISM OF HIS NATURE HE BEGGED THE PRIVILEGE OF G TO JERUSALEM TO REBUILD ITS WALLS. PERMISSION WAS GAINED, AND THE FIRST PART OF THE BOOK CO! STIRRING ACCOUNT OF THE EXPERIENCES OF NEHEMIAH IN BUILDING THE WALLS OF JERUSALEM. AFTER T WAS FINISHED, NEHEMIAH UNDERTOOK A CENSUS OF THE RESTORED CITY, BUT HE FOUND, AS HE SAYS, "TH OF THE GENEALOGY OF THEM THAT CAME UP AT THE FIRST,"--THE LIST OF FAMILIES WHICH APPEARS IN E: THIS HE COPIES. IT MAY BE INSTRUCTIVE TO TAKE THESE TWO LISTS--THE ONE IN EZRA II. AND THE NEHEMIAH VII.--AND COMPARE THEM. AFTER THIS WE HAVE AN ACCOUNT OF A GREAT CONGREGATION ASSEMBLED "IN THE BROAD PLACE THAT WAS BEFORE THE WATER GATE," WHEN EZRA THE SCRIBE STOOD U PULPIT OF WOOD" FROM EARLY MORNING UNTIL MIDDAY, AND READ TO THE ASSEMBLED MULTITUDE FR BOOK OF THE LAW. "AND EZRA OPENED THE BOOK IN THE SIGHT OF ALL THE PEOPLE (FOR HE WAS ABOVE PEOPLE); AND WHEN HE OPENED IT ALL THE PEOPLE STOOD UP, AND EZRA BLESSED JEHOVAH THE GREA' AND ALL THE PEOPLE ANSWERED, AMEN, AMEN, WITH THE LIFTING UP OF THEIR HANDS; AND THEY BOWE HEADS, AND WORSHIPED JEHOVAH, WITH THEIR FACES TO THE GROUND." OTHER SCRIBES STOOD BY, APPA TO TAKE TURNS IN THE READING; AND IT IS SAID THAT "THEY READ IN THE BOOK, IN THE LAW OF ' DISTINCTLY [OR, 'WITH AN INTERPRETATION,' MARG.], AND THEY GAVE THE SENSE, SO THAT THEY UNDER READING." FROM THIS IT HAS BEEN INFERRED THAT THE PEOPLE HAD ALREADY BECOME, IN THEIR SOJOUR EAST, MORE FAMILIAR WITH ARAMAIC THAN WITH THEIR OWN TONGUE, AND THAT THEY WERE UN UNDERSTAND THE HEBREW WITHOUT SOME WORDS OF INTERPRETATION. IT IS DOUBTFUL, HOWEVER, WHE THIS MEANING CAN BE READ INTO THIS PASSAGE. AT ANY RATE, WE HAVE HERE, UNDOUBTEDLY, THE HIS THE INAUGURATION OF THE READING OF THE LAW AS ONE OF THE REGULAR ACTS OF PUBLIC WORSHIP. . must have been about 440 B.C.

THE NARRATIVE OF THE FIRST COMPLETE AND FORMAL OBSERVANCE OF THE FEAST OF TABERNACI THE DAYS OF JOSHUA; THE NARRATIVE OF THE SOLEMN LEAGUE AND COVENANT BY WHICH THE PEOPLE THEMSELVES TO KEEP THE LAW; THE NARRATIVE OF THE DEDICATION OF THE WALL OF THE CITY, AND THE VARIOUS REFORMS WHICH NEHEMIAH PROSECUTED, WITH CERTAIN LISTS OF PRIESTS AND LEVITES, FILL remainder of the book.

TAKING IT ALL IN ALL IT IS A VERY VALUABLE RECORD; NO HISTORICAL BOOK OF THE OLD TESTAM GREATER EVIDENCE OF VERACITY; NONE EXCELS IT IN HUMAN INTEREST. THE PATHETIC TALE OF THE RETI PEOPLE FROM THEIR LONG EXILE, OF THE REBUILDING OF THEIR CITY AND THEIR TEMPLE, AND OF THE H SELF-DENYING LABORS OF ZERUBBABEL AND NEHEMIAH, THE GOVERNORS, AND HAGGAI AND ZECHAR PROPHETS, AND EZRA THE SCRIBE, WITH ALL THEIR COADJUTORS, IS FULL OF SIGNIFICANCE TO ALL THOSE IN THE HISTORY OF THE PEOPLE OF ISRAEL, MORE CLEARLY THAN ANYWHERE ELSE, THE INCREASING PU God which runs through all the ages.

THAT PORTIONS OF THE FIRST BOOK WERE WRITTEN BY EZRA, AND OF THE SECOND BOOK BY NEHEI NOT DOUBTED; BUT BOTH BOOKS WERE REVISED SOMEWHAT BY LATER HANDS; ADDITIONS WERE UNDOU MADE AFTER THE DEATH OF NEHEMIAH; FOR ONE, AT LEAST, OF THE GENEALOGIES SHOWS US A CERTAIN HIGH PRIEST, AND TELLS US THAT HE WAS THE GREAT GRANDSON OF THE MAN WHO WAS HIGH PRIES NEHEMIAH CAME TO JERUSALEM. IT IS NOT PROBABLE THAT NEHEMIAH LIVED TO SEE THIS JADDUA IN TH priest's office. It is probable that the last revision of the Bible was made some time after 400 B.C..

I HAVE NOW TO SPEAK, IN THE CONCLUSION OF THIS CHAPTER, OF TWO OTHER BOOKS OF THIS LAST CONCERNING WHICH THERE HAS ALWAYS BEEN MUCH MISCONCEPTION, THE BOOK OF ESTHER AND THE B DANIEL. ESTHER STANDS IN OUR BIBLES IMMEDIATELY AFTER EZRA-NEHEMIAH, WHILE DANIEL IS IN AMONG THE PROPHETS. BUT IN THE HEBREW BIBLES BOTH BOOKS ARE FOUND IN THE GROUP WHICH WA collected and least valued.

I HAVE STYLED THESE HISTORICAL BOOKS; ARE THEY TRULY HISTORICAL? THAT THEY ARE FOUNDED U DO NOT DOUBT; BUT IT IS, PERHAPS, SAFER TO REGARD THEM BOTH RATHER AS HISTORICAL FICTIONS veritable histories. The reason for this judgment may appear as we go on with the study.

THE BOOK OF ESTHER MAY BE BRIEFLY SUMMARIZED. THE SCENE IS LAID IN SHUSHAN THE PALACE, I KNOWN AS SUSA, ONE OF THE ROYAL RESIDENCES OF THE KINGS OF PERSIA. THE STORY OPENS WITH A GRE LASTING ONE HUNDRED AND EIGHTY DAYS, GIVEN BY THE KING AHASUERUS TO ALL THE NABOBS OF THE IS ASSUMED THAT THIS KING WAS XERXES THE GREAT, BUT THE IDENTIFICATION IS BY NO MEANS CONCLU THE CLOSE OF THIS MONUMENTAL DEBAUCH, THE KING, IN HIS DRUNKEN PRIDE, CALLS IN HIS QUEEN VA SHOW HER BEAUTY TO THE INEBRIATED COURTIERS. SHE REFUSES, AND THE REFUSAL OUGHT TO BE REMEM HER HONOR; BUT THIS BOOK DOES NOT SO REGARD IT. THE SYMPATHY OF THE BOOK IS WITH THE BI MONARCH, AND NOT WITH HIS CHASTE AND MODEST SPOUSE. THE KING IS VERY WROTH, AND AFTER TAKIN LEARNED ADVICE FROM HIS COUNSELORS, PUTS AWAY HIS QUEEN FOR THIS ACT OF INSUBORDINATIO PROCEEDS TO LOOK FOR ANOTHER. HIS CHOICE FALLS UPON A JEWISH MAIDEN, A DAUGHTER OF THE EXI HAS BEEN BROUGHT UP BY HER COUSIN MORDECAI. ESTHER, AT MORDECAI'S COMMAND, AT FIRST CONCE JEWISH DESCENT FROM THE KING. AN OPPORTUNITY SOON COMES FOR MORDECAI TO REVEAL TO ESTHE against the king's life; and the circumstance is recorded in the chronicles of the realm.

SOON AFTER THIS A CERTAIN HAMAN IS MADE GRAND VIZIER OF THE KINGDOM, AND MORDECAI T REFUSES TO DO OBEISANCE TO HIM; IN CONSEQUENCE OF WHICH HAMAN SECURES FROM THE KING AN ORDERING THE ASSASSINATION OF ALL THE JEWS IN THE KINGDOM. HIS WRATH AGAINST MORDECAI BE FURTHER INFLAMED, HE ERECTS A GALLOWS FIFTY CUBITS HIGH, WITH THE PURPOSE OF HANGING THEREON ISRAELITE. THE INTERVENTION OF ESTHER PUTS AN END TO THESE MALICIOUS SCHEMES. AT THE RISK OF SHE PRESENTS HERSELF BEFORE THE KING, AND GAINS HIS FAVOR; THEN, WHILE HAMAN'S PURPOSE HAI KING IS REMINDED, WHEN THE ANNALS OF HIS KINGDOM ARE READ TO HIM ON A WAKEFUL NIGHT, FRUSTRATION OF THE PLOT AGAINST HIS PERSON BY MORDECAI, AND LEARNING THAT NO RECOMPENSE MADE TO HIM, SUDDENLY DETERMINES TO ELEVATE AND HONOR HIM; AND THE CONSEQUENCE IS, THAT HIMSELF, HIS PURPOSES BEING DISCLOSED BY THE QUEEN, IS HANGED ON THE GALLOWS THAT HE HAD PR FOR MORDECAI, AND MORDECAI IS ELEVATED TO HAINAN'S PLACE. THE DECREE OF AN EASTERN KING CA ANNULLED, AND THE MASSACRE OF THE JEWS STILL REMAINS A LEGAL REQUIREMENT; YET ESTHER AND ARE PERMITTED TO SEND ROYAL ORDERS TO ALL PARTS OF THE REALM AUTHORIZING THE JEWS UPON THE I APPOINTED MASSACRE TO STAND FOR THEIR LIVES, AND TO KILL AS MANY AS THEY CAN OF THEIR ENEMI ENCOURAGED, AND SUPPORTED ALSO BY THE KING'S OFFICIALS IN EVERY PROVINCE, WHO ARE NOW THE CR OF MORDECAI, THE JEWS TURN UPON THEIR ENEMIES, AND SLAY IN ONE DAY SEVENTY-FIVE THOUSAND OF FIVE HUNDRED IN THE PALACE OF SHUSHAN,--AMONG WHOM ARE THE TEN SONS OF HAMAN. ON THE E OF THIS BLOODY DAY, THE KING SAYS TO ESTHER THE QUEEN: "THE JEWS HAVE SLAIN FIVE HUNDRED SHUSHAN THE PALACE, AND THE TEN SONS OF HAMAN; WHAT THEN HAVE THEY DONE IN THE REST OF TH PROVINCES? [FROM THIS SAMPLE OF THEIR FEROCITY YOU CAN JUDGE HOW MUCH BLOOD MUST HAVE BEEN THROUGHOUT THE KINGDOM.] NOW WHAT IS THY PETITION? AND IT SHALL BE GRANTED THEE; OR WH REQUEST FURTHER? AND IT SHALL BE DONE." IT MIGHT BE SUPPOSED THAT THIS FAIR JEWISH PRINCESS WO SATISFIED WITH THIS BANQUET OF BLOOD, BUT SHE IS NOT; SHE WANTS MORE. "THEN SAID ESTHER, IF IT THE KING, LET IT BE GRANTED TO THE JEWS WHICH ARE IN SHUSHAN TO DO TO-MORROW ALSO, ACCORD THIS DAY'S DECREE, AND LET HAMAN'S TEN SONS BE HANGED UPON THE GALLOWS." THE REQUEST IS GRAN NEXT DAY THREE HUNDRED MORE PERSIANS ARE BUTCHERED IN SHUSHAN THE PALACE; AND THE DEAD BO the ten sons of Haman, weltering in their gore, are lifted up and hanged upon the gallows, and all to PLEASE QUEEN ESTHER! IF A SINGLE JEW LOSES HIS LIFE IN THIS OUTBREAK, THE WRITER FORGETS TO MI IT IS IDLE TO SAY THAT THIS IS REPRESENTED AS A DEFENSIVE ACT ON THE PART OF THE JEWS; THE IMPRI GIVEN THAT THE PERSIANS, BY THE MENACING ACTION OF THEIR OWN OFFICIALS UNDER MORDECAI'S AU were completely cowed, and were simply slaughtered in their tracks by the infuriated Jews.

As a memorial of this feast of blood, the Jewish festival of Purim was instituted, which to this day; and the Book of Esther is read at this feast, in dramatic fashion, with pas responses by the congregation.

Is this history? There is every reason to hope that it is not. That some deliverance of t from their enemies in Persia may be commemorated by the feast of Purim is possible; that pre such a fiendish outbreak of fanatical cruelty as this ever occurred, we may safely and cl doubt. The fact that the story was told, and that it gained great popularity among the Jew some of those in later ages came to be regarded as one of the most sacred books of their c however, a revelation to us of the extent to which the most baleful and horrible passions cherished in the name of religion. It is precisely for this purpose, perhaps, that the book h preserved in our canon. If any one wishes to see the perfect antithesis of the precepts and t of the gospel of Christ, let him read the Book of Esther. Frederick Bleek is entirely justif statement that "a spirit of revenge and persecution prevails in the book, and that no other the Old Testament is so far removed as this is from the spirit of the gospel." [Foc Introduction to the Old Testament, i. 450.] For it is not merely true that these atrocitie recited; they are clearly indorsed. There is not a word said in deprecation of the beastlin king or the vindictiveness of the hero and the heroine. It is clear, as Bleek says, "that th finds a peculiar satisfaction in the characters and mode of acting of his Jewish compatriots, and Mordecai; and that the disposition shown by them appears to him as the right one, an worthy of their nation." "Esther the beautiful queen," whose praises have been sung by many poets, possesses, indeed, some admirable qualities; her courage is illustrious; her patriot beautiful; but her bloodthirstiness is terrible.

As to the time when this book was written, or who wrote it, I am not curious. Probably written long after the Exile, but by some one who was somewhat familiar with the mann Oriental courts. The name of God is not once mentioned in the book; and it seems like bla to intimate that the Spirit of God could have had anything to do with its compositic absolutely sickening to read the commentaries, which assume that it was dictated by th Ghost, and which labor to justify and palliate its frightful narrative. One learns, with a relief, that the Jews themselves long disputed its admission to their canon; that the s Schammai would not accept it, and that several of the wisest and best of the early fathe Christian church, Athanasius and Melito of Sardis among the rest, denied it a place in Scripture. Dr. Martin Luther is orthodox enough for me, and he, more than once, expres hearty wish that the book had perished. That, indeed, we need not desire; let it remain a background on which the Christian morality may stand forth resplendent; as a striking ex the kind of ideas which Christians ought not to entertain, and of the kind of feelings w ought not to cherish.

The Book of Daniel brings us into a very different atmosphere. Esther is absolutely ba religious ideas or suggestions; Daniel is full of the spirit of faith and prayer. Whether the of Daniel, as here presented, is a sketch from life or a work of the imagination, it is . personality. The self-control, the fidelity to conscience, the heroic purposes which . attributed to him, make up a picture which has always attracted the admiration of generous hearts.

"As in the story of the Three Children," says Dean Stanley, "so in that of the Den of Lions, the element which has lived on with immortal vigor is that which tells how, 'when Daniel knew t writing was signed, he kneeled upon his knees three times a day and prayed and gave thanks to God, as he did aforetime.' How often have these words confirmed the solitary protest, not onl Flavian amphitheatre, but in the ordinary yet not more easy task of maintaining the r conscience against arbitrary power or invidious insult! How many an independent patri unpopular reformer has been nerved by them to resist the unreasonable commands of k priest! How many a little boy at school has been strengthened by them for the effort, whe knelt down by his bedside for the first time to say his prayers in the presence of indiffe scoffing companions.... Shadrach, Meshach, and Abednego in the court of Nebuchadnezzar,]

IN THE COURT OF DARIUS, ARE THE LIKENESSES OF 'THE SMALL TRANSFIGURED BAND WHOM THE WORL TAME,' WHO, BY FAITH IN THE UNSEEN, HAVE IN EVERY AGE 'STOPPED THE MOUTHS OF LIONS, AND QUE THE VIOLENCE OF FIRE.' THIS WAS THE EXAMPLE TO THOSE ON WHOM, IN ALL AGES, IN SPIRIT IF NOT IN 'THE FIRE HAD NO POWER, NOR WAS AN HAIR OF THEIR HEAD SINGED, NEITHER WERE THEIR COATS CHAN THE SMELL OF FIRE PASSED UPON THEM;' BUT IT WAS 'AS IT WERE A MOIST, WHISTLING WIND, AND THE FC THE FOURTH, WHO WALKED WITH THEM IN THE MIDST OF THE FIRE, WAS LIKE A SON OF GOD.'" [Fo *History of the Jewish Church*, pp. 41, 42.]

WAS DANIEL A HISTORICAL PERSON? THE QUESTION HAS BEEN MUCH DISPUTED, BUT I THINK TH MAY SAFELY ANSWER IT IN THE AFFIRMATIVE. IT IS TRUE THAT IN ALL THESE WRITINGS OF THE LATER PERIC DANIEL IS MENTIONED BUT TWICE, BOTH TIMES IN THE BOOK OF EZEKIEL (XIV. 14; XXVIII. 3). THE FI THESE ALLUSIONS IS A DECLARATION THAT A FEW RIGHTEOUS MEN CANNOT SAVE A WICKED CITY, WHEN TH OF DESTRUCTION AGAINST IT HAS BEEN ISSUED; "THOUGH THESE THREE MEN, NOAH, DANIEL, AND JOB WE THEY SHOULD DELIVER BUT THEIR OWN SOULS BY THEIR RIGHTEOUSNESS, SAITH THE LORD GOD." THE OT A PROPHECY AGAINST THE KING OF TYRE, IN WHICH HE IS REPRESENTED AS SAYING TO HIMSELF THAT HE THAN DANIEL; THAT THERE IS NO SECRET THAT CAN BE HIDDEN FROM HIM. WHETHER THESE CASUAL US NAME OF DANIEL FOR PURPOSES OF ILLUSTRATION CAN BE REGARDED AS ESTABLISHING HIS HISTORICAL (MAY BE QUESTIONED. AND IT IS A SINGULAR FACT THAT WE HAVE NOT IN EZRA, OR NEHEMIAH, OR HAG ZECHARIAH, OR MALACHI, ANY REFERENCE TO THE EXISTENCE OF DANIEL. NEVERTHELESS, IT IS HAR SUPPOSED THAT SUCH A CHARACTER WAS WHOLLY FICTITIOUS; WE MAY WELL SUPPOSE THAT HE EXISTED, AI the narratives of his great fidelity and piety are at any rate founded upon fact.

THE FIRST SIX CHAPTERS OF THE BOOK ARE NOT ASCRIBED TO DANIEL AS THEIR AUTHOR; HE IS SPOK THE THIRD PERSON, AND SOMETIMES IN A WAY THAT A GOOD MAN WOULD NOT BE LIKELY TO SPEAK HIMSELF. THE REMAINDER OF THE BOOK CLAIMS TO BE WRITTEN BY HIM. THE QUESTION IS WHETHER THI IS TO BE TAKEN AS AN ASSERTION OF HISTORICAL FACT, OR AS A DEVICE OF LITERARY WORKMANSHIP. ECC WAS UNDOUBTEDLY WRITTEN LONG AFTER THE EXILE, YET IT PURPORTS TO HAVE BEEN COMPOSED B SOLOMON. THE AUTHOR PUTS HIS WORDS INTO THE MOUTH OF SOLOMON, TO GAIN ATTENTION FOR TH not fair to call this a fraud; it was a perfectly legitimate literary device. It is entirely possible that this MAY BE THE CASE WITH THE AUTHOR OF THIS BOOK. DANIEL WAS A PERSON WHOSE NAME WAS WELL-K AMONG HIS CONTEMPORARIES, AND THE AUTHOR MAKES HIM HIS MOUTHPIECE. THERE MAY HAVE BEI SPECIAL REASON WHY THE AUTHOR SHOULD HAVE DESIRED TO SEND OUT THESE NARRATIVES AND VISION the name of a hero of antiquity, a reason which we shall presently discover.

THE BOOK OF DANIEL IS NOT WHAT IS COMMONLY CALLED A PROPHECY; IT IS RATHER AN APOCAL BELONGS TO A CLASS OF LITERATURE WHICH SPRANG UP IN THE LAST DAYS OF THE JEWISH NATIONALITY, OLD PROPHETS HAD DISAPPEARED; IT IS DESIGNED TO COMFORT THE PEOPLE WITH HOPES OF FUTURE REST OF THE NATIONAL POWER; ITS METHOD IS THAT OF VISION AND SYMBOLIC REPRESENTATION. DANIEL IS BOOK OF THIS KIND IN THE OLD TESTAMENT; THE NEW TESTAMENT CANON CLOSES, AS YOU KNOW, SIMILAR BOOK. I SHALL NOT UNDERTAKE TO INTERPRET TO YOU THESE VISIONS OF THE BOOK OF DANIEL CONFESSEDLY OBSCURE AND MYSTERIOUS. BUT THERE IS ONE PORTION OF THE BOOK, THE ELEVENTH WHICH IS ADMITTED TO BE A MINUTE AND REALISTIC DESCRIPTION OF THE COALITIONS AND THE C BETWEEN THE GRÆCO-SYRIAN AND THE GRÆCO-EGYPTIAN KINGS, EVENTS WHICH TOOK PLACE ABC MIDDLE OF THE SECOND CENTURY BEFORE CHRIST. THESE PERSONAGES ARE NOT NAMED, BUT THEY ARI DESCRIBED, AND THE INTRIGUES AND VICISSITUDES OF THAT PORTION OF JEWISH HISTORY IN WHICH THEY CHIEF ACTORS ARE FULLY TOLD. MOREOVER THE RECITAL IS PUT IN THE FUTURE TENSE; "THERE SHALL ST THREE KINGS IN PERSIA; AND THE FOURTH SHALL BE RICHER THAN THEY ALL; AND WHEN HE IS WAXE THROUGH HIS RICHES, HE SHALL STIR UP ALL AGAINST THE REALM OF GREECE." IF, NOW, THE BOOK OF D WRITTEN IN THE EARLY DAYS OF THE EXILE, THIS WAS A VERY CIRCUMSTANTIAL PREDICTION OF WHAT HAP THE SECOND CENTURY,--A PREDICTION UTTERED THREE HUNDRED YEARS BEFORE THE EVENT. AND R THESE PREDICTIONS, IF SUCH THEY ARE, WE MUST SAY THIS, THAT WE HAVE NO OTHERS LIKE THEM. TH PROPHETS NEVER UNDERTAKE TO TELL THE PARTICULARS OF WHAT IS COMING TO PASS; THEY GIVE OUT, VERY LARGE AND GENERAL, THE NATURE OF THE EVENTS WHICH ARE TO COME. NO SUCH CAREFULLY F programme as this is found in any other predictive utterance.

BUT THERE ARE THOSE--AND THEY INCLUDE THE VAST MAJORITY OF THE LEADING CHRISTIAN SCHOL

PRESENT DAY--WHO SAY THAT THESE WORDS WERE NOT WRITTEN IN THE EARLY DAYS OF THE EXILE; THAT T HAVE BEEN WRITTEN ABOUT THE MIDDLE OF THE SECOND CENTURY; THAT THEY WERE THEREFORE AN AC WHAT WAS GOING ON, BY AN ONLOOKER, COUCHED IN THESE PHRASES OF VISION AND PROPHECY. THE PEO ISRAEL WERE PASSING THROUGH A TERRIBLE ORDEAL; THEY NEEDED TO BE HEARTENED AND NERVED FOR AND ENDURANCE. THEIR HEROIC LEADER, JUDAS MACCABEUS, WAS URGING THEM ON TO PRODIGIES OF V THEIR CONFLICT WITH THE VILE ANTIOCHUS; SUCH A RINGING MANIFESTO AS THIS, PUT FORTH IN THE PR THE CONFLICT, MIGHT HAVE A POWERFUL INFLUENCE IN REINFORCING THEIR PATRIOTISM AND CONFIRMI FAITH. IT MIGHT ALSO HAVE APPEARED AT SOME STAGE OF THE CONFLICT WHEN IT WOULD HAVE BEEN IMP AND PERHAPS IMPOSSIBLE TO SECURE CURRENCY FOR THE BOOK IF THE REFERENCE TO EXISTING RULERS I EXPLICIT; SUCH A DEVICE AS THE AUTHOR ADOPTED MAY HAVE BEEN PERFECTLY UNDERSTOOD BY THE I ALTHOUGH SLIGHTLY VEILED IN THE FORM OF ITS DELIVERANCE, IT WAS, PERHAPS, FOR THIS VERY REASO better fitted for its purpose.

IT MIGHT, THEN, HAVE BEEN WRITTEN WHEN THE PTOLEMIES AND THE SELEUCIDÆ WERE WASTI FIELDS OF PALESTINE WITH THEIR CONFLICTS. BUT WAS IT WRITTEN THEN? HOW DO WE KNOW THAT IT V CIRCUMSTANTIAL PREDICTION MADE THREE HUNDRED YEARS BEFORE? WE DO NOT KNOW, WITH A CERTAINTY, WHEN IT WAS WRITTEN; BUT THERE ARE STRONG REASONS FOR BELIEVING THAT THE LATER true date.

1. THE BOOK IS NOT IN THE HEBREW COLLECTION OF THE PROPHETS. THAT COLLECTION WAS MADE A HUNDRED YEARS AFTER THE TIME AT WHICH DANIEL IS HERE SAID TO HAVE LIVED; IF SO GREAT A PROPH BEEN EXISTING THEN, IT IS STRANGE THAT IT SHOULD NOT HAVE BEEN GATHERED WITH THE OTHER PRO NEHEMIAH'S COLLECTION. IT IS FOUND, INSTEAD, AMONG THE KETUBIM,--THE LATER AND SUPPLEM writings of the Hebrew Bible.

2. IT IS STRANGE ALSO, AS I HAVE INTIMATED, THAT NO MENTION OF DANIEL OR OF HIS BOOK IS FO THE HISTORIES OF THE EXILE AND THE RETURN, OR IN ANY OF THE PROPHECIES UTTERED IN ISRAEL RETURN. THAT THERE SHOULD BE NO ALLUSION IN ANY OF THESE BOOKS TO SO DISTINGUISHED A PERSO hardly be explained.

3. JESUS, THE SON OF SIRACH, ONE OF THE WRITERS OF THE APOCRYPHA, WHO LIVED ABOUT B.C. 200 GIVES A FULL CATALOGUE OF ALL THE GREAT WORTHIES OF ISRAEL; HE HAS A LIST OF THE PROPHETS; HI the other prophets; he does not name Daniel.

4. THE NATURE OF THIS PREDICTION, IF IT BE A PREDICTION, IS UNACCOUNTABLE. DANIEL IS SAID T LIVED IN THE BABYLONIAN PERIOD, AND LOOKED FORWARD FROM THAT DAY. HIS PEOPLE WERE IN EXI THERE IS NOT A VISION OF HIS THAT HAS ANY REFERENCE TO THEIR RETURN FROM THE CAPTIVITY, TO THE OF THE TEMPLE, OR TO ANY OF THE EVENTS OF THEIR HISTORY BELONGING TO THE TWO CENTURIES FOLL STRANGE THAT IF, STANDING AT THAT POINT OF TIME, HE WAS INSPIRED TO PREDICT THE FUTURE OF T PEOPLE, HE SHOULD NOT HAVE HAD SOME MESSAGE RESPECTING THOSE GREAT EVENTS IN THEIR HISTOR WERE TO HAPPEN WITHIN THE NEXT CENTURY. INSTEAD OF THIS, HIS VISIONS, SO FAR AS HIS OWN PEOP CONCERNED, OVERLEAP THREE CENTURIES AND LAND IN THE DAYS OF ANTIOCHUS EPIPHANES. HERE THI AT ONCE TO BE VERY SPECIFIC; THEY TELL ALL THE PARTICULARS OF THIS PERIOD, BUT BEYOND THIS PEI GIVE NO PARTICULARS AT ALL; THE VISION OF THE MESSIANIC TRIUMPH WHICH FOLLOWS IS VAGUE AND like the rest of the prophecies. These circumstances strongly support the theory of the later date.

5. WORDS APPEAR IN THIS WRITING WHICH ALMOST CERTAINLY FIX IT AT A LATER DATE THAN THE BA PERIOD. THERE ARE CERTAINLY NINE UNDOUBTED PERSIAN WORDS IN THIS BOOK; THERE ARE NO PERSIA IN EZEKIEL, WHO LIVED AT THE TIME WHEN DANIEL IS PLACED AT THE BABYLONIAN COURT, NOR IN ZECHARIAH, OR MALACHI. THERE ARE SEVERAL GREEK WORDS, NAMES OF MUSICAL INSTRUMENTS, AN ALMOST CERTAIN THAT NO GREEK WORDS WERE IN USE IN BABYLONIA AT THAT EARLY DAY. THIS PHIL ARGUMENT MAY SEEM VERY DUBIOUS AND FAR-FETCHED, BUT IT IS REALLY ONE OF THE MOST CONCLUSIVE THE DATE OF A DOCUMENT. THERE IS NO WITNESS SO COMPETENT AS THE WRITTEN WORD. LET ME GIV HOMELY ILLUSTRATION. SUPPOSE YOU FIND IN SOME LATE HISTORY OF THE UNITED STATES A QUOTED LI TO HAVE BEEN WRITTEN BY PRESIDENT ZACHARY TAYLOR, WHO DIED IN 1850, RESPECTING A CERTAIN P contest. The letter contains the following paragraph:--

"ON RECEIVING THIS INTELLIGENCE, I CALLED UP THE SECRETARY OF STATE BY TELEPHONE, AND A HOW HE EXPLAINED THE DEFEAT. HE TOLD ME THAT, IN HIS OPINION, BOODLE WAS AT THE BOTTOM

DETERMINED TO MAKE AN INVESTIGATION, AND AFTER WIRING TO THE MEMBER OF CONGRESS IN THAT I ORDERED MY SERVANT TO ENGAGE ME A SECTION IN A PULLMAN CAR, AND STARTED THE SAME NIGHT scene of the contest."

NOW OF COURSE YOU KNOW THAT THIS PARAGRAPH COULD NOT HAVE BEEN WRITTEN BY PRESIDENT NOR DURING THE PERIOD OF HIS ADMINISTRATION. THE TELEPHONE WAS NOT THEN IN EXISTENCE; THERE PULLMAN CARS; THE WORDS "BOODLE" AND "WIRE," IN THE SENSE HERE USED, HAD NEVER BEEN HE PRECISELY THE SAME WAY THE TRAINED PHILOLOGIST CAN OFTEN DETERMINE WITH GREAT CERTAINTY TH WRITING. HE KNOWS THE BIOGRAPHY OF WORDS OR WORD-FORMS; AND HE MAY KNOW THAT SOME C WORDS OR THE WORD-FORMS CONTAINED IN A CERTAIN WRITING WERE NOT YET IN THE LANGUAGE AT WHEN IT IS SAID TO HAVE BEEN WRITTEN. IT IS BY EVIDENCE OF THIS NATURE THAT THE CRITICS FIX TH the Book of Daniel at a period long after the close of the Babylonian empire.

THIS VERDICT REDUCES, SOMEWHAT, THE ELEMENT OF THE MARVELOUS CONTAINED IN THE BOOK; NOT IN ANY WISE REDUCE THE MORAL AND SPIRITUAL VALUE OF IT. THE AGE OF THE MACCABEES, WHEN TH APPEARED, WAS ONE OF THE GREAT AGES OF JEWISH HISTORY. JUDAS MACCABEUS IS ONE OF THE FIRST ISRAELITISH HEROES; AND THE STRUGGLE, IN WHICH HE WAS THE LEADER, AGAINST THE DISSOLUTE SYRI BROUGHT OUT SOME OF THE STRONGEST QUALITIES OF THE HEBREW CHARACTER. THE GENUINE HUM FERVID CONSECRATION, THE DAUNTLESS FAITH OF THE JEWS OF THIS GENERATION PUT TO SHAME THE CC THEIR COUNTRYMEN IN MANY AGES MORE CELEBRATED. AND IT CANNOT BE DOUBTED THAT THIS BOOK W THE EFFECT AND THE CAUSE OF THIS LOFTY NATIONAL PURPOSE. "RARELY," SAYS EWALD, "DOES IT HAPPE BOOK APPEARS AS THIS DID, IN THE VERY CRISIS OF THE TIMES, AND IN A FORM MOST SUITED TO SUCH A ARTIFICIALLY RESERVED, CLOSE AND SEVERE, AND YET SHEDDING SO CLEAR A LIGHT THROUGH OBSCURI MARVELOUSLY CAPTIVATING. IT WAS NATURAL THAT IT SHOULD SOON ACHIEVE A SUCCESS ENTIRELY CORRE to its inner truth and glory. And so, for the last time in the literature of the Old Testament, we have IN THIS BOOK AN EXAMPLE OF A WORK WHICH, HAVING SPRUNG FROM THE DEEPEST NECESSITIES OF THE N IMPULSES OF THE AGE, CAN RENDER TO THAT AGE THE PUREST SERVICE; AND WHICH, BY THE DEVELOP EVENTS IMMEDIATELY AFTER, RECEIVES WITH SUCH POWER THE STAMP OF DIVINE WITNESS THAT IT SUBSEC attains imperishable sanctity." [Footnote: Quoted by Stanley, *History of the Jewish Church*, iii. p. 336.]

CHAPTER VII.

THE POETICAL BOOKS.

THE POETICAL BOOKS OF THE OLD TESTAMENT NOW INVITE OUR ATTENTION,--"THE LAMENT "PROVERBS," "ECCLESIASTES," "THE SONG OF SOLOMON," "JOB," AND "THE PSALMS." ECCLESIASTES IS N POETICAL FORM, BUT IT IS A PROSE POEM; THE MOVEMENT OF THE LANGUAGE IS OFTEN LYRICAL, AND THE is all expressed in poetic phrases. The other books are all poetical in form as well as in fact.

LAMENTATIONS, CALLED IN THE HEBREW BIBLE BY THE QUAINT TITLE "AH HOW," THE FIRST TWO OF THE BOOK, AND IN THE GREEK BIBLE "THRENOI," SIGNIFYING MOURNING, IS PLACED IN THE MIDDLE LATEST GROUP OF THE HEBREW WRITINGS. IN THE ENGLISH BIBLE IT FOLLOWS THE PROPHECY OF JEREM CALLED IN OUR VERSION "THE LAMENTATIONS OF JEREMIAH." THIS TITLE PRESERVES THE ANCIENT TRADI THERE IS NO REASON TO DOUBT THAT THE TRADITION EMBODIES THE TRUTH. "IN FAVOR OF THIS OPINI BLEEK, "WE MAY NOTE THE AGREEMENT OF THE SONGS WITH JEREMIAH'S PROPHECIES IN THEIR WHOLE CH AND SPIRIT, IN THEIR PURPORT, AND IN THE TONE OF DISPOSITION SHOWN IN THEM, AS WELL AS LANGUAGE.... AS REGARDS THE OCCASION AND SUBSTANCE OF THESE SONGS, THE TWO FIRST AND THE RELATE TO THE MISERY WHICH HAD BEEN SENT ON THE JEWISH PEOPLE, AND PARTICULARLY ON JERUSA MIDDLE ONE, HOWEVER, CHIEFLY REFERS TO THE PERSONAL SUFFERINGS OF THE AUTHOR." [FOOTNOTE:

102.]

These five parts are not the five chapters of a book; they are five distinct poems, each complete IN ITSELF, THOUGH THEY ARE ALL CONNECTED IN MEANING. YOU NOTICE THE REGULARITY OF THE STRUC IS EVEN EXHIBITED TO SOME EXTENT IN THE OLD VERSION. THE FIRST AND SECOND, THE FOURTH AND FI EACH TWENTY-TWO VERSES OR STANZAS; THE THIRD ONE HAS SIXTY-SIX STANZAS. ALL BUT THE LAST ARE POEMS. THERE ARE TWENTY-TWO LETTERS IN THE HEBREW ALPHABET; EACH OF THESE LETTERS, IN REGU begins a verse in four of these songs; in the third lamentation there are three verses for each letter.

THE TIME AT WHICH THESE ELEGIES WERE WRITTEN WAS UNDOUBTEDLY THE YEAR OF THE CAP JERUSALEM BY THE ARMY OF NEBUCHADNEZZAR, 5B6C.. THE CHALDEAN ARMY HAD BEEN INVESTING T CITY FOR MORE THAN A YEAR; THE WALLS WERE FINALLY BROKEN DOWN, AND THE CHALDEANS RUSHED IN GAINED ENTRANCE ON ONE SIDE, THE WRETCHED KING ZEDEKIAH ESCAPED ON THE OTHER WITH A FEW F AND FLED DOWN THE JERICHO ROAD; HE WAS PURSUED AND OVERTAKEN, HIS SONS AND PRINCES WERE BEFORE HIS FACE, THEN HIS OWN EYES WERE PUT OUT, AND HE WAS LED AWAY IN CHAINS TO BABYLON, WHI AFTERWARD DIED IN CAPTIVITY. AFTER A FEW MONTHS' WORK OF THIS SORT, A PORTION OF THE CHALDEA NEBUZAR-ADAN RETURNED TO THE DISMANTLED AND PILLAGED CITY AND UTTERLY DESTROYED BOTH TH THE TEMPLE. IT IS SUPPOSED THAT JEREMIAH, WHO WAS ALLOWED TO REMAIN IN THE CITY DURING THIS INTERVAL, WROTE THESE ELEGIES IN THE MIDST OF THE DESOLATION AND FEAR THEN IMPENDING. "NEV DEAN MILMAN, "WAS RUINED CITY LAMENTED IN LANGUAGE SO EXQUISITELY PATHETIC. JERUSALEM IS, AS I PERSONIFIED AND BEWAILED WITH THE PASSIONATE SORROW OF PRIVATE AND DOMESTIC ATTACHMENT; WH MORE GENERAL PICTURES OF THE FAMINE, COMMON MISERY OF EVERY RANK AND AGE AND SEX, A DESOLATION, THE CARNAGE, THE VIOLATION, THE DRAGGING AWAY INTO CAPTIVITY, THE REMEMBRANCE O GLORIES, OF THE GORGEOUS CEREMONIES, AND OF THE GLAD FESTIVALS, THE AWFUL SENSE OF THE DIVI HEIGHTENING THE PRESENT CALAMITIES, ARE SUCCESSIVELY DRAWN WITH ALL THE LIFE AND REALITY O witness." [Footnote: *History of the Jews*, i. 446.] THE ETHICAL AND SPIRITUAL QUALITIES OF THE BOOK ARE AND HIGH; THE WRITER DOES NOT FAIL TO ENFORCE THE TRUTH THAT IT IS BECAUSE "JERUSALEM HATH SINNED" THAT "SHE IS BECOME AN UNCLEAN THING." AND IN THE MIDST OF ALL THIS CALAMITY THE rebellion against God; it is only the cry of a desolate but trusting soul to a just and faithful Ruler.

THE PROVERBS, IN THE HEBREW BIBLE, IS CALLED "MISHLE," OR SOMETIMES "MISHLE SHELOMOH." FIRST WORD SIGNIFIES PARABLES OR PROVERBS OR SAYINGS; THE SECOND WORD IS THE SUPPOSED NAME AUTHOR, SOLOMON. BY THE LATER JEWS IT IS SOMETIMES CALLED "SEPHER CHOKMAH,"--THE BO Wisdom,--the same title as that which is borne by one of the apocryphal books.

HERE, DOUBTLESS, WE HAVE AGAIN, IN THE NAME OF THE AUTHOR, WHAT DELITZSCH CALLS A CO DENOMINATOR. ON THIS SUBJECT THE WORDS OF WILLIAM ALDIS WRIGHT, IN SMITH'S "BIBLE DICTIO express a conservative judgment:--

"THE SUPERSCRIPTIONS WHICH ARE AFFIXED TO SEVERAL PORTIONS OF THE BOOK OF PROVERBS IN I. xxv. 1, attribute the authorship of those portions to Solomon, the son of David, king of Israel. With THE EXCEPTION OF THE LAST TWO CHAPTERS, WHICH ARE DISTINCTLY ASSIGNED TO OTHER AUTHORS, IT IS THAT THE STATEMENT OF THE SUPERSCRIPTIONS IS IN THE MAIN CORRECT, AND THAT THE MAJORIT PROVERBS CONTAINED IN THE BOOK WERE UTTERED OR COLLECTED BY SOLOMON. IT WAS NATURAL AND ACCORDANCE WITH THE PRACTICE OF OTHER NATIONS THAT THE HEBREWS SHOULD CONNECT SOLOMO WITH A COLLECTION OF MAXIMS AND PRECEPTS WHICH FORM A PART OF THEIR LITERATURE TO WHICH HE I TO HAVE CONTRIBUTED MOST LARGELY (1 KINGS, IV. 32). IN THE SAME WAY THE GREEKS ATTRIBUTED M THEIR SAYINGS TO PYTHAGORAS; THE ARABS TO LOKMAN, ABU OBEID, AL MOFADDEL, MEIDAN Samakhshari; the Persians to Ferid Attar; and the northern people to Odin.

"BUT THERE CAN BE NO QUESTION THAT THE HEBREWS WERE MUCH MORE JUSTIFIED IN ASSIGNI PROVERBS TO SOLOMON THAN THE NATIONS WHICH HAVE JUST BEEN ENUMERATED WERE IN ATTRIBUT COLLECTIONS OF NATIONAL MAXIMS TO THE TRADITIONAL AUTHORS ABOVE MENTIONED." [FOOTNOTE: A of Proverbs."]

THIS IS, UNDOUBTEDLY, AS MUCH AS CAN BE TRULY SAID RESPECTING THE SOLOMONIAN AUTHORS these sayings. Professor Davidson, writing at a later day, is more guarded.

"IN THE BOOK WHICH NOW EXISTS WE FIND GATHERED TOGETHER THE MOST PRECIOUS FRUITS WISDOM OF ISRAEL DURING MANY HUNDREDS OF YEARS, AND UNDOUBTEDLY THE LATER CENTURIES WER or at all events fuller, in their contributions than the earlier. The tradition, however, whic Solomon with the direction of mind known as 'The Wisdom' cannot be reasonably set a Making allowances for the exaggerations of later times, we should leave history and altogether unexplained if we disallowed the claim of Solomon to have exercised a creative i upon the wisdom in Israel." [Footnote: Art. "Proverbs," *Encyc. Brit.*]

The book is divided into several sections:

1. A general introduction, explaining the character and aim of the book, which occu first six verses.

2. A connected discourse upon wisdom, not in the form of maxims, but rather in the m of a connected essay, fills the first nine chapters.

3. The next thirteen chapters (x.-xxii. 16) contain three hundred and seven miscellaneous proverbs, each consisting of two phrases, the second of which is generally ant to the first, as "A wise son maketh a glad father, but a foolish son is a heaviness to his m There is only one exception (xix. 7), where the couplet is a triplet. Probably one phrase h lost. The heading of this section is "The Proverbs of Solomon;" the section ends with the second chapter.

4. From xxii. 17 to xxiv. 22 is a more connected discussion, though in a brief exhortat listen to "the words of the wise."

5. At xxiv. 23, begins another short section which extends through the chapter, under this title: "These also are sayings of the wise."

6. The next five chapters (xxv.-xxix.) have for their caption this sentence: "These a proverbs of Solomon, which the men of Hezekiah, king of Judah, copied out."

7. Chapter xxx. is said to contain "The words of Agur, the son of Jakeh, the oracli author is wholly unknown.

8. Chapter xxxi. 1-9, contains "The words of King Lemuel, the prophecy that his m taught him." He too stands here upon the sacred page but the shadow of a name.

9. The book closes with an acrostical poem---twenty-two verses beginning with the H letters in the order of the alphabet--upon "The Virtuous Woman." The word "virtue" here in the Roman sense; it signifies rather the vigorous woman, the capable woman.

Of these sections it seems probable that the one here numbered 6 is the oldest, and contains the largest proportion of Solomonian sayings. Professor Davidson thinks that i have taken its present form earlier than the eighth century.

The character of the teaching of the book is not uniform, but on the whole it is best d as prudential rather than prophetic. It embodies what we are in the habit of calling "good sense." There is an occasional maxim whose application to our own time may be doubted, and and then one whose morality has been superseded by the higher standards of the New Tes but, after making all due deductions, we shall doubtless agree that it is a precious legacy of counsel, and shall consent to these words of Professor Conant:--

"The gnomic poetry of the most enlightened of other nations will not bear compariso in the depth and certainty of its foundation principles, or in the comprehensiveness and grandeur of its conceptions of human duty and responsibility." [Footnote: Smith's *Bible Dictionary*, iii. 2616.]

Ecclesiastes, or the Preacher, bears in the Hebrew collection the name, "Koheleth, means the assembler of the people, and therefore, probably, the man who addresses the as Ecclesiastes is the Greek name of the book in the Septuagint; we have simply copied the word in English letters.

The first verse is, "The words of Koheleth (the Preacher), the son of David, K Jerusalem." The only son of David who was ever king in Jerusalem was Solomon; was Solomon author of this book? This is the apparent claim; the question is whether we have not here, as case of Daniel, a book put forth pseudonymously; whether the author does not personate So and speak his message through Solomon's lips. That this is the fact modern scholars unanimously maintain. Their reasons for their opinion may be briefly stated:

1. In the conclusion of the book the author speaks in his own person, laying aside th disguise which he has been wearing. In several other passages the literary veil becomes trans Thus (i. 12), "I Koheleth was king over Israel in Jerusalem." This sounds like the voice o looking backward and trying to put himself in Solomon's place. Again, in this and the fo chapter, he says of himself: "I have gotten me great wisdom above all that were before Jerusalem;" "I was great, and increased more than all that were before me in Jerusalem," e of which," says Bleek, "does not appear very natural as coming from the son of David, wh captured Jerusalem." Nobody had been before him in Jerusalem except his father David.

2. The state of society as described in the book, and particularly the reference to rul better with the theory that it was written during the Persian period, after the Captivity, satraps of the Persian king were ruling with vacillating arbitrariness and fitful violence.

3. The religious condition of the people as here depicted, and the religious ideas of t represent the period following the Captivity, and do not represent the golden age of Israel.

4. More important and indeed perfectly decisive is the fact that the book is full of Ch and that the Hebrew is the later Hebrew, of the days of Ezra, Nehemiah, Daniel, and Es could not have been written by Solomon, any more than the "Idylls of the King" could ha written by Edmund Spenser. There are those, of course, who maintain that the book was wri Solomon; just as there are those who still maintain that the sun revolves around the ea reason for this opinion is found in the first sentence of the book itself. The book announce author, it is said; and to question the truth of this claim is to deny the veracity of Scriptur question we may call, from the array of conservative writers who have given us Smith's Dictionary," such a witness as Professor Plumptre:--

"The hypothesis that every such statement in a canonical book must be received as l true is, in fact, an assumption that inspired writers were debarred from forms of composition were open, without blame, to others. In the literature of every other nation the form of p authorship, when there is no *animus decipiendi*, has been recognized as a legitimate channel fo expression of opinions, or the quasi-dramatic representation of character. Why should we on the assertion that if adopted by the writers of the Old Testament it would make them falsehood?...There is nothing that need startle us in the thought that an inspired writer m liberty which has been granted without hesitation to the teachers of mankind in every country." [Footnote: Art. "Ecclesiastes," vol. i. p. 645.]

That such is the character of the book and that it appeared some time during the Per are well-ascertained results of scholarship.

The doctrine of the book is not so easily summarized. It is a hard book to interpr Ginsberg gives a striking *résumé* of the different theories of its teaching which have promulgated. There is no room here to enter upon the great question. Let it suffice to sa seem to have in these words the soliloquy of a soul struggling with the problem of evil, so borne down by a dismal skepticism, sometimes asserting his faith in the enduring righteou The writer's problem is the one to which Mr. Mallock has given an epigrammatic statement: worth living?" He greatly doubts, yet he strongly hopes. Much of the time it appears to him best thing a man can do is to enjoy the present good and let the world wag. But the outco this struggle is the conviction that there is a life beyond this life and a tribunal at which will be righted, and that to fear God and keep his commandments is the whole duty of man are thus many passages in the book which express a bitter skepticism; to winnow the wheat the chaff and to find out what we ought to think about life is a serious undertaking. It is wise and skillful interpreter who can steer his bark along these tortuous channels of refl not run aground. Yet, properly interpreted, the book is sound for substance of doctrine, experience which it delineates, though sad and depressing, is full of instruction for u Stanley's words about it are as true as they are eloquent; they will throw some light on which lies just before us:--

"As the Book of Job is couched in the form of a dramatic argument between the patria his friends, as the Song of Songs is a dramatic dialogue between the Lover and the Loved

THE BOOK OF ECCLESIASTES IS A DRAMA OF A STILL MORE TRAGIC KIND. IT IS AN INTERCHANGE OF VOICI AND LOWER, MOURNFUL AND JOYFUL, WITHIN A SINGLE HUMAN SOUL. IT IS LIKE THE STRUGGLE BETWEEN PRINCIPLES IN THE EPISTLE TO THE ROMANS. IT IS LIKE THE QUESTION AND ANSWER OF 'THE TWO VOI OUR MODERN POET.... EVERY SPECULATION AND THOUGHT OF THE HUMAN HEART IS HEARD AND EXPRES RECOGNIZED IN TURN. THE CONFLICTS, WHICH IN OTHER PARTS OF THE BIBLE ARE CONFINED TO A SINGLI A SINGLE CHAPTER, ARE HERE EXPANDED INTO A WHOLE BOOK." AND AFTER QUOTING A FEW OF THE DA MORE CYNICAL UTTERANCES, THIS CLEAR-SIGHTED TEACHER GOES ON: "THEIR CRY IS INDEED FULL OF D DESPAIR AND PERPLEXITY; IT IS SUCH AS WE OFTEN HEAR FROM THE MELANCHOLY, SKEPTICAL, INQUIRINC OF OUR OWN AGE; SUCH AS WE OFTEN REFUSE TO HEAR AND REGARD AS UNWORTHY EVEN A GOOD MAN'S OR CARE, BUT THE ADMISSION OF SUCH A CRY INTO THE BOOK OF ECCLESIASTES SHOWS THAT IT IS NOT the notice of the Bible, not beneath the notice of God." [Footnote: *History of the Jewish Church*, ii. 283, 284.]

"THE SONG OF SONGS" IS ANOTHER OF THE BOOKS ASCRIBED TO SOLOMON. IT MAY HAVE BEEN WRI in Solomon's time; that it was composed by Solomon himself is not probable.

IT HAS GENERALLY BEEN REGARDED AS AN ALLEGORICAL POEM; THE JEWS INTERPRETED IT AS SETT THE LOVE OF JEHOVAH FOR ISRAEL; THE CHRISTIAN INTERPRETERS HAVE MADE IT THE REPRESENTATION O OF CHRIST FOR HIS CHURCH. THESE ARE THE TWO PRINCIPAL THEORIES, BUT IT MIGHT BE INSTRUCTIV ARCHDEACON FARRAR RECITE TO US A SHORT LIST OF THE EXPLANATIONS WHICH HAVE BEEN GIVEN OF TH the course of the ages:--

"IT REPRESENTS, SAY THE COMMENTATORS, THE LOVE OF GOD FOR THE CONGREGATION OF ISRAEL; THE HISTORY OF THE JEWS FROM THE EXODUS TO THE MESSIAH; IT IS A CONSOLATION TO AFFLICTED ISRA OCCULT HISTORY; IT REPRESENTS THE UNION OF THE DIVINE SOUL WITH THE EARTHLY BODY, OR OF THI WITH THE ACTIVE INTELLECT; IT IS THE CONVERSATION OF SOLOMON AND WISDOM; IT DESCRIBES THE CHRIST TO HIS CHURCH; IT IS HISTORICO-PROPHETIC; IT IS SOLOMON'S THANKSGIVING FOR A HAPPY REIGN LOVE-SONG UNWORTHY OF ANY PLACE IN THE CANON; IT TREATS OF MAN'S RECONCILIATION TO GOI PROPHECY OF THE CHURCH FROM THE CRUCIFIXION TILL AFTER THE REFORMATION; IT IS AN ANTICIPATI APOCALYPSE; IT IS THE SEVEN DAYS' EPITHALAMIUM ON THE MARRIAGE OF SOLOMON WITH THE DAUGH PHARAOH; IT IS A MAGAZINE FOR DIRECTION AND CONSOLATION UNDER EVERY CONDITION; IT T HIEROGLYPHICS OF THE SEPULCHRE OF THE SAVIOUR, HIS DEATH, AND THE OLD TESTAMENT SAINTS; IT HEZEKIAH AND THE TEN TRIBES; IT IS WRITTEN IN GLORIFICATION OF THE VIRGIN MARY. SUCH W IMPOSSIBLE AND DIVERGING INTERPRETATIONS OF WHAT MANY REGARDED AS THE VERY WORD OF GOD ONLY, TILL THE BEGINNING OF THIS CENTURY, SAW THE TRUTH,--WHICH IS SO OBVIOUS TO ALL WHO G BIBLE WITH THE HUMBLE DESIRE TO KNOW WHAT IT SAYS, AND NOT TO INTERPRET IT INTO THEIR OWN FANCIES,--THAT IT IS THE EXQUISITE CELEBRATION OF A PURE LOVE IN HUMBLE LIFE; OF A LOVE WI splendor can dazzle and no flattery seduce."

THESE LAST SENTENCES OF CANON FARRAR GIVE THE PROBABLE CLEW TO THE INTERPRETATION OF IT IS A DRAMATIC POEM, CELEBRATING THE STORY OF A BEAUTIFUL PEASANT GIRL, A NATIVE OF THE VILLAGE OF SHUNEM, WHO WAS CARRIED AWAY BY SOLOMON'S OFFICERS AND CONFINED IN HIS HARI JERUSALEM. BUT IN THE MIDST OF ALL THIS SPLENDOR HER HEART IS TRUE TO THE PEASANT LOVER WHOM LEFT BEHIND, NOR CAN ANY BLANDISHMENTS OF THE KING DISTURB HER CONSTANCY; HER HONOR UNSTAINED, AND SHE IS CARRIED HOME AT LENGTH, HEART-WHOLE AND HAPPY, BY THE SWAIN WHO HAS C JERUSALEM FOR HER RESCUE. THIS IS THE BEAUTIFUL STORY. THE PHRASES IN WHICH IT IS TOLD ARE, INDI EXPLICIT FOR OCCIDENTAL EARS; THE COLOR AND THE HEAT OF THE TROPICS IS IN THE POETRY, BUT IT IS PURE; IT CELEBRATES THE TRIUMPH OF MAIDEN MODESTY AND INNOCENCE. "THE SONG BREATHES AT TH TIME," SAYS EWALD, "SUCH DEEP MODESTY AND CHASTE INNOCENCE OF HEART, SUCH DETERMINED DEFIA THE OVER-REFINEMENT AND DEGENERACY OF THE COURT-LIFE, SUCH STINGING SCORN OF THE GROWING C OF LIFE IN GREAT CITIES AND PALACES, THAT NO CLEARER OR STRONGER TESTIMONY CAN BE FOUND OF T VIGOR WHICH, IN THIS CENTURY, STILL CHARACTERIZED THE NATION AT LARGE, THAN THE COMBINATION simplicity in the Canticles." [Footnote: *History of Israel*, iv. 43.]

THE BOOK OF JOB HAS BEEN THE SUBJECT OF A GREAT AMOUNT OF CRITICAL STUDY. THE EARLIEST TRADITION IS THAT IT WAS WRITTEN BY MOSES; THIS TRADITION IS PRESERVED IN THE TALMUD, WHICH AF states that it was composed by an Israelite who returned to Palestine from the Babylonian Captivity.

IT IS ALMOST CERTAIN THAT THE FIRST OF THESE TRADITIONS IS BASELESS. THE THEORY THAT IT WAS WR the Captivity is held by many scholars, but it is beset with serious difficulties.

THE BOOK CONTAINS NO ALLUSION WHATEVER TO THE LEVITICAL LAW, NOR TO ANY OF THE RELIG AND CEREMONIES OF THE JEWS. THE INFERENCE HAS THEREFORE BEEN DRAWN THAT IT MUST HAVE BEEN BEFORE THE GIVING OF THE LAW, PROBABLY IN THE PERIOD BETWEEN ABRAHAM AND MOSES. IT INCONCEIVABLE THAT A DEVOUT HEBREW SHOULD HAVE TREATED ALL THE GREAT QUESTIONS DISCUSSE BOOK WITHOUT ANY REFERENCE TO THE RELIGIOUS INSTITUTIONS OF HIS OWN PEOPLE. IT IS EQUALLY DI UNDERSTAND HOW THE DIVINE INTERPOSITION FOR THE PUNISHMENT OF THE WICKED AND THE REWARDIN RIGHTEOUS COULD HAVE BEEN SO FULLY CONSIDERED WITHOUT A GLANCE AT THE LESSONS OF THE EXOI EXODUS HAD TAKEN PLACE BEFORE THE BOOK WAS WRITTEN. BUT THESE ARGUMENTS FOR AN EARLY OI QUITE NEUTRALIZED BY THE DOCTRINE OF THE BOOK. THE VIEW OF DIVINE PROVIDENCE SET FORTH IN I UNLIKE THAT CONTAINED IN THE PENTATEUCH. IT IS NOT NECESSARY TO SAY THAT THERE IS ANY CON BETWEEN THESE TWO VIEWS; BUT THE SUBJECT IS APPROACHED FROM A VERY DIFFERENT DIRECTION, A WHOLE TONE OF THE BOOK INDICATES A STATE OF RELIGIOUS THOUGHT QUITE DIFFERENT FROM THAT WH AMONG THE HEBREWS BEFORE THE EXODUS. "IF WE ARE TO BELIEVE THAT MOSES WROTE IT," SAYS A LAT "THEN WE MUST BELIEVE THAT HE HELD THESE VIEWS AS AN ESOTERIC PHILOSOPHY, AND OMITTED FR RELIGION WHICH HE GAVE TO HIS PEOPLE THE TRUTHS WHICH HAD BEEN REVEALED TO HIM IN THE DESI BOOK ITSELF MUST HAVE BEEN SUPPRESSED UNTIL LONG AFTER HIS DAY. THE IGNORANT ISRAELITES CO HAVE BEEN TRAINED UNDER THE DISCIPLINE OF THE LAW IF THEY HAD HAD AT THE SAME TIME THE FIERY, HALF-SKEPTICAL, AND ENIGMATICAL COMMENTARY WHICH THE BOOK OF JOB FURNISHES. THERE IS N ABNORMAL OR CONTRARY TO THE CONCEPTION OF AN INSPIRED REVELATION IN THE DEVELOPMENT OF WIDER VIEWS AND DEEPER ANALYSIS THROUGH SUCCESSIVE SACRED WRITERS. BUT IT IS REPULSIVE TO CONC INSPIRED TEACHER AS FIRST GAINING THE WIDER VIEW, AND THEN DELIBERATELY HIDING IT, TO UTTER TH CRUDER AND MORE PARTIAL FORMS." [FOOTNOTE: RAYMOND'S *The Book of Job*, P. 18.] THE FACT THAT NEITHI THE PERSON NOR THE BOOK OF JOB IS MENTIONED IN THE HISTORICAL BOOKS OF THE JEWS, AND THAT REFERENCE TO HIM IS IN THE BOOK OF EZEKIEL, WOULD INDICATE THAT THE DATE OF THE BOOK MUST H MUCH LATER THAN THE TIME OF MOSES. THIS ARGUMENT COULD NOT BE PRESSED, HOWEVER, FOR W noted already the silence of the earlier historical books concerning the Mosaic law.

The dilemma of the critics may be summed up as follows:--

1. THE ABSENCE OF ALLUSION TO THE HISTORY OF THE EXODUS AND TO THE MOSAIC SYSTEM SHOWS MUST HAVE BEEN WRITTEN BEFORE THE EXODUS. 2. THE ABSENCE OF ALL REFERENCE TO THE BOOK HEBREW HISTORY, AND MORE ESPECIALLY THE DOCTRINAL CHARACTER OF THE BOOK, SHOWS THAT IT C HAVE BEEN WRITTEN BEFORE THE AGE OF SOLOMON. THE LATTER CONCLUSION IS HELD MUCH MORE FIRM THE FORMER; AND THE SILENCE RESPECTING THE HISTORY AND THE LAW IS EXPLAINED ON THE THEORY BOOK IS A HISTORICAL DRAMA, THE SCENE OF WHICH IS LAID IN THE PERIOD BEFORE MOSES, AND THE I UNITIES OF WHICH HAVE BEEN PERFECTLY OBSERVED BY THE WRITER. *The people of this drama* LIVED BEFORE TH EXODUS AND THE GIVING OF THE LAW, AND THEIR CONVERSATIONS DO NOT, THEREFORE, REFER TO A EVENTS WHICH HAVE HAPPENED SINCE. THE LOCALITY OF THE DRAMA IS THE "LAND OF UZ," AN GEOGRAPHERS AGREE THAT THE DESCRIPTIONS OF THE BOOK APPLY TO THE REGION KNOWN IN THE GEOGRAPHIES AS "ARABIA DESERTA," SOUTHEAST OF PALESTINE. IT IS ADMITTED THAT THE SCENERY AND OF THE BOOK ARE NOT JEWISH; AND THEY AGREE MORE PERFECTLY WITH WHAT IS KNOWN OF THAT COUN WITH ANY OTHER. THAT JOB WAS A REAL PERSONAGE, AND THAT THE DRAMA IS FOUNDED UPON HIS tradition cannot be doubted. It is probable that it was written after the time of Josiah.

I NEED NOT REHEARSE THE STORY. JOB IS OVERTAKEN BY GREAT LOSSES AND SUFFERINGS; IN THE HIS CALAMITIES THREE FRIENDS DRAW NEAR TO CONDOLE WITH HIM, AND ALSO TO ADMINISTER TO HIM WHOLESOME REPROOF AND ADMONITION. THEIR THEORY IS THAT SUFFERING SUCH AS HE IS ENDURING I OF THE DIVINE DISPLEASURE; THAT JOB MUST HAVE BEEN A GREAT SINNER, OR HE COULD NOT BE SUCH A S THIS ARGUMENT JOB INDIGNANTLY REPELS. HE DOES NOT CLAIM TO BE PERFECT, BUT HE KNOWS THAT BEEN AN UPRIGHT MAN, AND HE KNOWS THAT BAD MEN ROUND ABOUT HIM ARE PROSPERING, WHILE SCOURGED AND OVERWHELMED WITH TROUBLE; HE SEES THIS HAPPENING ALL OVER THE EARTH,--TH AFFLICTED, THE EVIL EXALTED; AND HE KNOWS, THEREFORE, THAT THE DOCTRINE OF HIS MISERABLE C CANNOT BE TRUE. SIN DOES BRING SUFFERING, THAT HE ADMITS; BUT THAT ALL SUFFERING IS THE RESULT denies. He cannot understand it; his heart is bitter when he reflects upon it; and the insistence of his visitors awakes in him a fierce indignation, and leads him to charge God with injustice and (They are shocked and scandalized at his almost blasphemous outcries against God; b maintains his righteousness, and drives his critics and censors from the field. Finally] himself is represented as answering Job out of the whirlwind, in one of the most sublime pa in all literature,--silencing the arguments of his friends, sweeping away all the reasonings which have preceded, explaining nothing, but only affirming his own infinite power and wisdom. Befoi august manifestation Job bows with submission; the mystery of evil is not explained; he is convinced that it cannot be explained, and is content to be silent and wait. The teaching of the book is well summarized in these words of Dr. Raymond:--

"The current notion that calamity is always the punishment of crime and prosperity alw reward of piety is not true. Neither is it true that the distress of a righteous man is an indi God's anger. There are other purposes in the Divine mind of which we know nothing. For ins a good man may be afflicted, by permission of God, and through the agency of Satan, to pr genuine character of his goodness. But whether this or some other reason, involved administration of the universe, underlies the dispensation of temporal blessings and afflict thing is certain: the plans of God are not, will not be, cannot be revealed; and the resig faith, not of fatalism, is the only wisdom of man." [Footnote: *The Book of Job*, p. 49.]

I have reserved for the last the most precious of all the Hebrew writings, the *Book of Psalms* The Hebrews called it "Tehillim," praise-book or hymn-book, and the title exactly describ the form in which we have it, it was a hymn-book prepared for the service of the later temple.

If the question "Who wrote the Psalms?" were to be propounded in any meeting of Su school teachers, nine tenths of them would unhesitatingly answer, "David." If the same q were put to an assembly of modern Biblical scholars some would answer that David wrote ve and perhaps not any of the psalms; that they were written during the Maccabean dynasty, (or two hundred years before Christ. Both these views are extreme. We may believe that Da write several of the psalms, but it is more than probable that the great majority of them other writers.

Seventy-three psalms of the book seem to be ascribed to David in their titles. "A Ps David," "Maschil of David," "Michtam of David," or something similar is written over sev three different psalms. Concerning these titles there has been much discussion. It h maintained that they are found in the ancient Hebrew text as constituent parts of the Ps are therefore entitled to full credit. But this theory does not seem to be held by the m modern scholars. "The variations of the inscriptions," says a late conservative writer, ' Septuagint and the other versions sufficiently prove that they were not regarded as fixed portions of the canon, and that they were open to conjectural emendations." [Footnote: *Speaker's Commentary*, iv. 151.] Dr. Moll, the learned author of the monograph on the Psalms in Lange's "Commentar in his introduction: "The assumption that all the inscriptions originated with the authoi Psalms, and are therefore inseparable from the text, cannot be consistently maintained. most be held only of a few.... There is now a disposition to admit that some of them may originated with the authors themselves."

The probability is that most of these inscriptions were added by editors and transcriber Psalms. You open your hymn-book, and find over one hymn the name of Watts, and over an the name of Wesley, and over another the name of Montgomery. Who inserted these nam the authors, of course, but the editor or compiler of the collection. Compilers in these careful and accurate, but they do make mistakes, and you find the same hymn ascribed to di authors in different books, while hymns that are anonymous in one book are credited in a rightly or wrongly, to the name of some author. The men who collected the hymn-book of made similar mistakes, and the old copies do not agree in all their titles.

But while the inscriptions over the psalms do not, generally, belong to the psalms the and are not in all cases accurate, most of them were, no doubt, suffixed to the psalms at a v day. "On the whole," says Dr. Moll, "an opinion favorable to the antiquity and value o superscriptions has again been wrought out, which ascribes them for the most part to traditi indeed a very ancient one."

Even if the titles were rightly translated, then, they would not give us conclusive pr(authorship of the Psalms. But some of the best scholars assert that they are not rightly 1 The late Professor Murray of Johns Hopkins University, whose little book on the Psalms is vouched for as one of the most admirable productions of Biblical scholarship which has yet appeared country, says that "whenever we have an inscription in our version stating that the psal David' it is almost invariably a mistranslation of the original." It should be written "to Dav it signifies that the compilers ascribed the psalm to a more ancient collection to which the David had been appended, not because he wrote all the poems in it, but because he originati collection and wrote many of its songs. This older collection was called "The Psalms oi something as a popular hymn-book of these times is called Robinson's "Laudes Domini," bec Dr. Robinson compiled the book, and wrote some of the hymns. This old Davidic collection in existence, but many of the psalms in our book were taken from it, and the titles in our are attempts to credit to this old book such of them as were thus borrowed.

This method of crediting is not altogether unknown in this critical age. In the variou commentaries on the Sunday-school lessons I often find sentences and paragraphs cred "William Smith" which were taken from Dr. Smith's "Bible Dictionary," the articles from they are taken being signed in all cases by the initials of the men who wrote them. I fi quotations from the "Speaker's Commentary," of which Canon Cook is the editor, ascribed C. Cook," or to "Cook," though the table of contents in the volume from which the quota taken bears in capital letters the name of the writer of the commentary on this particular like manner "Lange" gets the credit of all that is written in his famous "Bibelwerk," th wrote very little of it himself. The power to distinguish between editorship and authorship probably, possessed by ancient compilers in any greater degree than by modern ones; a inscriptions over the psalms must be estimated with this fact in view.

I have spoken of the present collection of the Psalms as one book, but it is in real books. It is so divided in the Revised Version. The concluding verse of the Forty-first Psa follows: "Blessed be the Lord God of Israel, from everlasting to everlasting. Amen and am doxology marks the close of the first hymn-book prepared by the Jews for the worship second temple. It was probably formed soon after the first return from the Exile. All th except the first, the tenth, and the thirty-third are credited to the old Davidic Psalm Boo of the thirty-third has probably been omitted by some copyist; the ninth and tenth in s(Hebrew copies are written as one psalm, and there is an acrostical arrangement which sho they really belong together. The psalm may have been divided for liturgical purposes, or by in copying. The title of the ninth, therefore, covers the tenth. The first and second are, only psalms that are not ascribed to the old book of which this book was simply an abridgment.

At the end of the Seventy-second Psalm is the doxology which marks the close of thi of these hymn-books. After a while the psalms of the first book grew stale and familiar, an book was wanted. "Gospel Hymns No. 1," of the Moody and Sankey psalmody, had to be foll after a year or two by "Gospel Hymns No. 2," and then by "No. 3" and "No. 4" and "No. 5," finally they were all bound up together. I may be pardoned for associating things sacred wi not very sacred, and poetry with something that is not always poetry, but the illustration, f all, shows exactly how these five hymn-books of the Jews first came to be, and how they v length combined in one.

The last verse of the Seventy-second Psalm has puzzled many readers: "The prayers of the son of Jesse are ended." After this you find in our collection several psalms ascribed t some of which he undoubtedly wrote. The probable explanation is that the Seventy-seconi was the last psalm of the old Davidic hymn-book; the compiler made it the last one of this book, and carelessly copied into this psalm the inscription with which the old book ended.

The second of these hymn-books begins, therefore, with Psalm xlii., and ends with Psalm lxxii., a collection of thirty-one songs of praise.

NUMBER THREE OF THE TEMPLE-SERVICE CONTAINS EIGHTEEN PSALMS, AND ENDS WITH PSALM LXXX BOOK, AS WELL AS THE ONE THAT PRECEDES IT, IS ASCRIBED BY A PROBABLE TRADITION TO NEHEMIAI compiler.

THE LAST VERSE OF PSALM CVI. INDICATES THE CLOSE OF THE FOURTH BOOK. IT CONTAINS BUT SI PSALMS, AND IS THE SHORTEST BOOK OF THE FIVE. THE FIFTH BOOK INCLUDES THE REMAINING FO PSALMS, AMONG THEM THE "SONGS OF DAVID," OR PILGRIM SONGS, SUNG BY THE PEOPLE ON THEIR JOU TO JERUSALEM TO KEEP THE SOLEMN FEASTS. IT IS PROBABLE THAT THIS FIFTH BOOK WAS COMPILED AUTHORITIES IN CHARGE OF THE TEMPLE WORSHIP, AND THAT THEY AT THE SAME TIME COLLECTED THE (BOOKS AND PUT THEM ALL TOGETHER, COMPLETING IN THIS WAY THE GREATER BOOK OF SACRED LYRICS W been so precious to many generations not only of Jews, but also of Christians.

VARIOUS UNSUCCESSFUL ATTEMPTS HAVE BEEN MADE TO CLASSIFY THESE BOOKS ACCORDING TC SUBJECT-MATTER. IT IS PLAIN THAT THE FIRST TWO ARE COMPOSED CHIEFLY OF THE OLDEST PSALMS AND ADAPTED TO THE GENERAL PURPOSES OF WORSHIP; THE THIRD BOOK REFLECTS THE GRIEF OF THE NATI CAPTIVITY; THE FOURTH, THE JOY OF THE RETURNING EXILES; THE FIFTH CONTAINS A MORE MISCI collection. THE JEWISH SCHOLARS RECOGNIZE AND SOMETIMES ATTEMPT TO EXPLAIN THIS ARRANGEMENT PSALMS INTO FIVE BOOKS. THE HEBREW MIDRASH ON PSALM I. I., SAYS: "MOSES GAVE THE FIVE BOOKS O LAW TO THE ISRAELITES, AND AS A COUNTERPART OF THEM, DAVID GAVE THE PSALMS CONSISTING OF FIVE THIS IS, OF COURSE, ERRONEOUS; THE PRESENT COLLECTION OF PSALMS WAS MADE LONG AFTER THE DAVID; BUT IT IS NOT UNLIKELY THAT SOME NOTION OF A SYMMETRICAL ARRANGEMENT OF THE PS correspond to the five-fold division of the Law, influenced the compilers of this Praise Book.

OF THE CONTENTS OF THIS BOOK, OF THE PECULIAR STRUCTURE OF HEBREW POETRY, AND OF THE REFERENCES IN MANY OF THE PSALMS, MUCH MIGHT BE SAID, BUT THIS INVESTIGATION WOULD LE somewhat aside from our present purpose.

IT MAY, HOWEVER, BE WELL TO ADD A WORD OR TWO RESPECTING SOME OF THE INSCRIPTION NOTATIONS BORNE BY THE PSALMS IN OUR TRANSLATION. MANY OF THEM ARE COMPOSED OF HEBREW TRANSLITERATED INTO ENGLISH,--SPELLED OUT WITH ENGLISH LETTERS. KING JAMES' TRANSLATORS DID WHAT THEY MEANT, SO THEY REPRODUCED THEM IN THIS WAY. THERE HAS BEEN MUCH DISCUSSION AS MEANING OF SEVERAL OF THEM, AND THE SCHOLARS ARE BY NO MEANS AGREED; THE INTERPRETATION follow are mainly those given by Professor Murray:--

FIRST IS THE FAMOUS "SELAH," WHICH WE USED TO HEAR PRONOUNCED WITH GREAT SOLEMNITY WH PSALMS WERE READ. IT IS A MUSICAL TERM, MEANING, PERHAPS, SOMETHING LIKE OUR "DA CAPO' POSSIBLY, "FORTE"--A MARK OF EXPRESSION LIKE THOSE ITALIAN WORDS WHICH YOU FIND OVER THE S your sheet music.

"MICHTAM" AND "MASCHIL" ARE ALSO MUSICAL NOTES, INDICATING THE TIME OF THE ME METRONOME-MARKS, SO TO SPEAK; AND "GITTITH" AND "SHIGGAION" ARE MARKS THAT INDICATE THE melody to which the psalm is to be sung.

"Negiloth" means stringed instruments; it indicates the kind of accompaniment with which the psalm was to be sung. "Nehiloth" signifies pipes or flutes, perhaps wind instruments in general.

THE INSCRIPTION "TO THE CHIEF MUSICIAN" MEANS, PROBABLY, "FOR THE LEADER OF THE CHOIR INDICATES THAT THE ORIGINAL COPY OF THE PSALM THUS INSERTED IN THE BOOK WAS ONE THAT HAD BEI THE CHORISTER IN THE OLD TEMPLE. "UPON SHEMIMITH" MEANS "SET FOR BASS VOICES;" "UPON ALAM "SET FOR FEMALE VOICES." "UPON MUTHLABBEN," A CURIOUS TRANSLITERATION, MEANS "ARRANGED FOR THE SOPRANO VOICES." PROFESSOR MURRAY SUPPOSES THAT THIS PARTICULAR PSALM WAS USED FOR REHEA the women singers.

SOME OF THESE INSCRIPTIONS DESIGNATE THE AIRS TO WHICH THE PSALMS WERE SET, PART OF WHIC TO BE SACRED, AND PART SECULAR. SUCH IS "SHUSHAN EDUTH," OVER PSALM LX., MEANING "FAIR AS L THY LAW," APPARENTLY THE NAME OF A POPULAR RELIGIOUS AIR. ANOTHER, PROBABLY SECULAR, IS OVEI XXII., "AIJELETH SHAHAR," "THE STAG AT DAWN," AND ANOTHER, OVER PSALM 1VI., "JONATHELEM RECH which is, being interpreted, "O silent dove, what bringest thou us from out the distance?"

THESE INSCRIPTIONS AND MANY OTHER FEATURES OF THIS ANCIENT HEBREW POETRY HAVE FUR PUZZLES FOR THE UNLEARNED AND PROBLEMS FOR THE SCHOLARS, BUT THE MEANING OF THE PSALMS THI IS FOR THE MOST PART CLEAR ENOUGH. THE HUMBLE DISCIPLE PAUSES WITH SOME BEWILDERMENT

"Neginoth" or "Michtam;" he classes them perhaps among the mysteries which the angels de look into; but when he reads a little farther on, "The Lord is my shepherd; I shall not w "God is our refuge and strength, a very present help in trouble;" or "Create in me a clean God, and renew a right spirit within me," he knows full well what these words mean. Ther life so lofty that these psalms do not lift up a standard before it; there is no life so lowly t not find in them words that utter its deepest humility and its faintest trust. Wherever we psalms find us; they search the deep things of our hearts; they bring to us the great things Of how many heroic characters have these old temple songs been the inspiration! Jewish sain patriots chanted them in the synagogue and on the battle-field; apostles and evangelists s among perils of the wilderness, as they traversed the rugged paths of Syria and Gal Macedonia; martyrs in Rome softly hummed them when the lions near at hand were crouch their prey: in German forests, in Highland glens, Lutherans and Covenanters breathed th out through their cadences; in every land penitent souls have found in them words to tell of their sorrow, and victorious souls the voices of their triumph; mothers watching their b night have cheered the vigil by singing them; mourners walking in lonely ways have been lig the great hopes that shine through them, and pilgrims going down into the valley of the sh death have found in their firm assurances a strong staff to lean upon. Lyrics like these, in so much of the divine truth was breathed when they were written, and which a hundred gen of the children of men have saturated with tears and praises, with battle shouts and sobs with all the highest and deepest experiences of the human soul, will live as long as joy lives and long after sorrow ceases; will live beyond this life, and be sung by pure voices in that land from the silent dove, coming from afar, brings us now and then upon her shining wings some glimpses of a glory that eye hath never seen.

Note. The reference on pages 200 and 201 to the Gospel Hymns is not strictly acc "Number Five" has not been bound up with the other numbers.

Chapter VIII.

The Earlier New Testament Writings

The books of the New Testament are now before us. Our task is not without its diffic questions will confront us which have never yet been answered, and probably will nev nevertheless, compared with the Old Testament writings, the books of the New Testament a known documents; we are on firm ground of history when we talk about them; of but few famous books of Greek and Latin authors can we speak so confidently as to their date an authorship as we can concerning most of them.

We have in the New Testament a collection of twenty-seven books, by nine different a Of these books thirteen are ascribed to the Apostle Paul; five to John the son of Zebedee Peter; two to Luke; one each to Matthew, Mark, James, and Jude, and the authorship of unknown.

Of these books it must be first remarked that they were not only written separately there is no trace in any of them of the consciousness on the part of the author that contributing to a collection of sacred writings. Of the various epistles it is especially evi they were written on special occasions, with a certain audience immediately in view; the t that they were to be preserved and gathered into a book, which was to be handed down thro coming centuries as an inspired volume, does not appear to have entered the mind of the

But this fact need not detract from their value; often the highest truth to which a m utterance is truth of whose value he is imperfectly aware.

It must also be remembered that these books of the New Testament were nearly all wr apostles. The only clear exceptions are the Gospel of Mark, the Gospel of Luke, the Act Apostles, and the Epistle to the Hebrews; and the authors of these books, though not apostles, were undoubtedly in the closest relations with apostolic men, and reflected their thoug apostolic men had received a special training and a definite commission to bear witness o Master, to tell the story of his life and death, and to build up his kingdom in the world.

We must admit that they possessed unusual qualifications for this work. Those who ha for three years in constant and loving intercourse with Jesus Christ ought to have been men. And he promised them, before he parted from them, that the Spirit of truth should c them and abide with them to lead them into all truth.

Now although we may find it difficult to give a satisfactory definition of inspiration; we may be utterly unable to express, in any formularies of our own, the influence of the Spirit upon human minds, yet we can easily believe that these apostolic men were excepti qualified to teach religious truth. No prophet of the olden time had any such preparatio mission as that which was vouchsafed to them. No school of the prophets, from the days of S downward, could be compared to that sacred college of apostles,--that group of divine peri who followed their Master through Galilee and Perea, and sat down with him day by day, fo memorable years, on the mountain top and by the lake side, to listen to the words of life lips of One who spake as never man spake.

To say that this training made them infallible is to speak beyond the record. Ther promise of infallibility, and the history makes it plain enough that no such gift was bestow Spirit of all truth was promised; but it was promised for their guidance in all their work, preaching, their administration, their daily conduct of life. There is no hint anywhere special illumination or protection would be given to them when they took the pen into the to write; they were then inspired just as much as they were when they stood up to speak, down to plan their missionary campaigns,--just as much and no more.

Now it is certain that the inspiration vouchsafed them did not make them infallible ordinary teaching, or in their administration of the church. They made mistakes of a very nature. It is beyond question that the majority of the apostles took at the beginning an view of the relation of the Gentiles to the Christian church. They insisted that Gentiles become Jews before they could become Christians; that the only way into the Christian chu through the synagogue and the temple. It was a grievous and radical error; it struc foundations of Christian faith. And this error was entertained by these inspired apostles day of Pentecost; it influenced their teaching; it led them to proclaim a defective gospel. T the assertion of a skeptic, it is the clear testimony of the Apostle Paul. If you will read th chapter of his Epistle to the Galatians you will learn from the mouth of an unimpeachable that the very leaders of the apostolic band, Peter and James and John, were greatly in e respect to a most important subject of the Christian teaching. In his account of that famous at Antioch, Paul says that Peter and James and John were wholly in the wrong, and that P his part, had been acting disingenuously:--

"But when Cephas came to Antioch, I resisted him to the face, because he stood conde For before that certain came from James, he did eat with the Gentiles: but when they came, back and separated himself, fearing them that were of the circumcision. And the rest of t [the Jewish Christians] dissembled likewise with him; insomuch that even Barnabas was ca away with their dissimulation. But when I saw that they walked not uprightly according to t of the gospel, I said unto Cephas before them all, If thou, being a Jew, livest as do the Gent not as do the Jews, how compellest thou the Gentiles to live as do the Jews?"

Now it is evident that one or the other of these opposing parties in the apostolic coll have been in error, if not greatly at fault, with respect to this most vital question of Chris and doctrine. When one apostle resists another to the face because he stands condemned,

HIM THAT HE WALKS NOT UPRIGHTLY, ACCORDING TO THE TRUTH OF THE GOSPEL, IT MUST BE THAT O OTHER OF THEM HAS, FOR THE TIME BEING, CEASED TO BE INFALLIBLE IN HIS ADMINISTRATION OF THE TRU GOSPEL. AND IF THESE APOSTOLIC MEN, SITTING IN THEIR COUNCILS, TEACHING IN THEIR CONGREGAT MAKE SUCH MISTAKES AS THESE, HOW CAN WE BE SURE THAT THEY NEVER MAKE A MISTAKE WHEN TH DOWN TO WRITE, THAT THEN THEIR WORDS ARE ALWAYS THE VERY WORD OF GOD? WE CAN HAVE N ASSURANCE. INDEED WE ARE EXPRESSLY TOLD THAT THEIR WORDS ARE NOT, IN SOME CASES, THE VERY GOD; FOR THE APOSTLE PAUL PLAINLY TELLS US OVER AND OVER, IN HIS EPISTLES TO THE CORINTHIANS VII.; 2 COR. XI.), THAT UPON CERTAIN QUESTIONS HE IS GIVING HIS OWN OPINION,--THAT HE HA COMMANDMENT OF THE LORD. WITH RESPECT TO ONE MATTER HE SAYS THAT HE IS SPEAKING AFTER I JUDGMENT, BUT THAT HE "THINKS" HE HAS THE SPIRIT OF THE LORD; TWO OR THREE TIMES HE D declares that it is he, Paul, and not the Lord, that is speaking.

ALL OF THESE FACTS, AND OTHERS OF THE SAME NATURE CLEARLY BROUGHT BEFORE US BY T TESTAMENT ITSELF, MUST BE HELD FIRMLY IN OUR MINDS WHEN WE MAKE UP OUR THEORY OF WHAT WRITINGS ARE. THAT THESE BOOKS WERE WRITTEN BY INSPIRED MEN IS, INDEED, INDUBITABLE; THAT THE POSSESSED A DEGREE OF INSPIRATION FAR EXCEEDING THAT VOUCHSAFED TO ANY OTHER RELIGIOUS TEAC HAVE LIVED ON THE EARTH IS TO MY MIND PLAIN; THAT THIS DEGREE OF INSPIRATION ENABLED THEM WITNESS CLEARLY TO THE GREAT FACTS OF THE GOSPEL OF CHRIST, AND TO PRESENT TO US WITH SUFFICIE AND WITH SUBSTANTIAL VERITY THE DOCTRINES OF THE KINGDOM OF HEAVEN I AM VERY SURE; BUT TI WERE ABSOLUTELY PROTECTED AGAINST ERROR, NOT ONE WORD IN THE RECORD AFFIRMS, AND THEY T HAVE TAKEN THE UTMOST PAINS TO DISABUSE OUR MINDS OF ANY SUCH IMPRESSION. THAT IS A THEORY A THEM WHICH MEN MADE UP OUT OF THEIR OWN HEADS HUNDREDS OF YEARS AFTER THEY WERE DEAD. W CERTAINLY FIND THAT THEY WERE NOT INFALLIBLE; BUT WE SHALL ALSO FIND THAT, IN ALL THE GREAT MA PERTAIN TO CHRISTIAN FAITH AND PRACTICE, WHEN THEIR FINAL TESTIMONY IS COLLECTED AND DIGES CLEAR, HARMONIOUS, CONSISTENT, CONVINCING; THAT THEY HAVE BEEN GUIDED BY THE SPIRIT OF THE tell us the truth which we need to know respecting the life that now is and that which is to come.

FURTHERMORE, IT IS A MATTER OF REJOICING WHEN WE TAKE UP THESE BOOKS OF THE NEW TESTAM FIND THEIR SUBSTANTIAL INTEGRITY UNIMPEACHED. THERE IS NO REASON TO SUSPECT THAT ANY IM CHANGES HAVE BEEN MADE IN ANY OF THESE BOOKS SINCE THEY CAME FROM THE HANDS OF THEIR W WHATEVER MAY BE SAID ABOUT THE FIRST THREE GOSPELS (AND WE SHALL COME TO THAT QUESTION IN (CHAPTER), THE REMAINING BOOKS OF THE NEW TESTAMENT HAVE COME DOWN TO US, UNALTERED, FRO MEN WHO FIRST WROTE THEM. THERE IS NONE OF THAT PROCESS OF REDACTION, AND ACCRETIC RECONSTRUCTION WHOSE TRACES WE HAVE FOUND IN MANY OF THE OLD TESTAMENT BOOKS. THERE M HERE AND THERE, A WORD OR TWO OR A VERSE OR TWO WHICH HAS BEEN INTERPOLATED BY SOME OI COPYIST, BUT THESE ALTERATIONS ARE VERY SLIGHT. THE BOOKS IN OUR HANDS ARE THE VERY SAME BOOK were in the hands of the contemporaries and successors of the apostles.

I SHALL NOT ATTEMPT ANY ELABORATE DISCUSSION OF THESE TWENTY-SEVEN BOOKS. I ONLY PROPOS RAPIDLY OVER THEM, INDICATING, WITH THE UTMOST BREVITY, THE SALIENT FACTS, SO FAR AS WE KNOW RESPECTING THEIR AUTHORSHIP, THE DATE AND THE PLACE AT WHICH THEY WERE WRITTEN, A circumstances which attended the production of them.

FROM THE FACT THAT THE GOSPELS STAND FIRST IN THE NEW TESTAMENT COLLECTION IT IS (ASSUMED THAT THEY ARE THE EARLIEST OF THE NEW TESTAMENT BOOKS, BUT THIS IS AN ERROR. SEVER EPISTLES WERE CERTAINLY WRITTEN BEFORE ANY OF THE GOSPELS; AND ONE OF THE GOSPELS, THAT OF J written later than any of the Epistles, except the three brief ones by the same author.

THE FIRST OF THESE NEW TESTAMENT BOOKS THAT SAW THE LIGHT WAS, AS IS GENERALLY SUPPOS FIRST EPISTLE TO THE THESSALONIANS. IT WAS IN THE YEAR 48 OF OUR ERA THAT ST. PAUL SET OUT ON MISSIONARY JOURNEY FROM ANTIOCH THROUGH CYPRUS AND EASTERN ASIA MINOR, A JOURNEY OCCUPIED ABOUT A YEAR. TWO YEARS AFTERWARD, HIS SECOND JOURNEY TOOK HIM THROUGH THE EASTE OF ASIA MINOR AND ACROSS THE ÆGEAN SEA TO EUROPE, WHERE HE PREACHED IN TROAS, PHI THESSALONICA, ATHENS, AND CORINTH. HIS STAY IN THESSALONICA WAS INTERRUPTED, AS YOU WILL REM BY THE HOSTILITY OF THE JEWS, AND HE REMAINED BUT A SHORT TIME IN THAT PLACE; LONG ENOUGH, I TO GATHER A VIGOROUS CHURCH. AFTERWARD, WHILE HE WAS IN CORINTH, HE LEARNED FROM ONE OF HIS THAT THE PEOPLE OF THESSALONICA HAD MISUNDERSTOOD PORTIONS OF HIS TEACHING, AND WERE IN

DOUBT ON CERTAIN IMPORTANT SUBJECTS. TO SET THEM RIGHT ON THESE MATTERS HE WROTE HIS FIRS' which was forwarded to them from Corinth, probably about the year 52.

THIS EXPLANATION WAS ALSO MISUNDERSTOOD BY THE THESSALONIANS, AND IT BECAME NEC DURING THE NEXT YEAR TO WRITE TO THEM AGAIN. THESE TWO LETTERS ARE IN ALL PROBABILITY THE F CHRISTIAN WRITINGS THAT WE POSSESS. THEY CONTAIN INSTRUCTION AND COUNSEL OF WHICH THE CHRIS THESSALONICA WERE JUST THEN IN NEED. THE QUESTION WHICH HAD MOST DISTURBED THEM HAD RELA THE SECOND COMING OF CHRIST. THEY EXPECTED HIM TO RETURN VERY SOON; THEY WERE IMPATIENT C THEY THOUGHT THAT THOSE WHO DIED BEFORE HIS COMING WOULD MISS THE GLORIOUS SPECTAC THEREFORE THEY DEPLORED THE HARD FATE OF SOME OF THEIR NUMBER WHO HAD BEEN SNATCHED DEATH BEFORE THIS SUBLIME EVENT. IN HIS FIRST EPISTLE THE APOSTLE ASSURES THEM THAT THE DEAD WOULD BE RAISED TO PARTICIPATE IN THEIR REJOICING. "WE WHO ARE ALIVE WHEN THE LORD RETURNS," "WILL HAVE NO ADVANTAGE OVER THOSE WHO HAVE BEEN CALLED TO THEIR REWARD BEFORE US; FOR THE RAISED FROM THEIR GRAVES TO TAKE PART WITH US IN THIS GREAT TRIUMPH." IT IS MANIFEST THAT PAUL, WROTE THIS, EXPECTED THAT CHRIST WOULD RETURN TO EARTH WHILE HE WAS ALIVE. ALFORD A CONSERVATIVE COMMENTATORS SAY THAT HE HERE DEFINITELY EXPRESSES THAT EXPECTATION; OTHERS THESE WORDS CAN BE SO INTERPRETED, BUT CONCEDE THAT HE DID ENTERTAIN SOME SUCH EXPECTA DOES NOT SEEM IMPROPER TO ADMIT," SAYS BISHOP ELLICOTT, "THAT IN THEIR IGNORANCE OF THE DA LORD THE APOSTLES MIGHT HAVE IMAGINED THAT HE WHO WAS COMING WOULD COME SPEEDILY." [FOO *Com. in loc.*] "IT IS UNMISTAKABLY CLEAR FROM THIS," SAYS OLSHAUSEN, "THAT PAUL DEEMED IT POSSIBL HE AND HIS CONTEMPORARIES MIGHT LIVE TO SEE THE COMING AGAIN OF CHRIST." "THE EARLY CHUR EVEN THE APOSTLES THEMSELVES," SAY CONYBEARE AND HOWSON, "EXPECTED THEIR LORD TO COME A THAT VERY GENERATION. ST. PAUL HIMSELF SHARED IN THAT EXPECTATION, BUT BEING UNDER THE GU THE SPIRIT OF TRUTH, HE DID NOT DEDUCE ANY ERRONEOUS CONCLUSIONS FROM THIS MISTAKEN PI [FOOTNOTE*Life and Epistles of St. Paul*, I. 401.] IT IS EVIDENT, THEN, THAT ST. PAUL AND THE REST O APOSTLES WERE MISTAKEN ON THIS POINT; THIS IS ONE OF THE EVIDENCES WHICH THEY THEMSELVES HAV pains to point out to us of the fact that though they were inspired men they were not infallible.

PAUL'S FIRST LETTER TO THE CHRISTIANS AT THESSALONICA WAS INTERPRETED BY THEM, VERY NAT TEACHING THAT THE RETURN OF THE LORD WAS IMMINENT; AND THEY BEGAN TO NEGLECT THEIR DAILY TO BEHAVE IN THE SAME FOOLISH WAY THAT MEN HAVE BEHAVED IN ALL THE LATER AGES, WHEN THEY H THEIR HEADS FULL OF THIS NOTION. HIS SECOND LETTER WAS WRITTEN CHIEFLY TO REBUKE THIS FANATICI BID THEM GO RIGHT ON WITH THEIR WORK MAKING READY FOR THE LORD'S COMING BY A FAITHFUL DISC THE DUTIES OF THE PRESENT HOUR. ST. PAUL MIGHT HAVE BEEN MISTAKEN IN HIS THEORIES ABOUT THE R HIS MASTER, BUT HIS PRACTICAL WISDOM WAS NOT AT FAULT; IT WAS HIS SPIRIT THAT SURVIVED IN ABF DAVENPORT, THE CONNECTICUT LEGISLATOR, WHO, IN THE "DARK DAY" OF 1780 WHEN HIS COLLEAGUES THAT THE END OF THE WORLD HAD COME, REFUSED TO VOTE FOR THE ADJOURNMENT OF THE HOUSE, BU on calling up the next bill; saying as Whittier has phrased it:--

> "'This well may be
> The Day of Judgment which the world awaits;
> But be it so or not, I only know
> My present duty, and my Lord's command
> To occupy till he come. So at the post
> Where he hath set me in his providence,
> I choose, for one, to meet him face to face,--
> No faithless servant frightened from my task,
> But ready when the Lord of the harvest calls;
> And therefore, with all reverence, I would say,
> Let God do his work, we will see to ours.
> Bring in the candles.' And they brought them in."

THESE TWO LETTERS ARE, THEN, THE EARLIEST OF THE NEW TESTAMENT WRITINGS. LIKE MOST OF EPISTLES OF PAUL THEY BEGIN WITH A SALUTATION. THE COMMON SALUTATION WITH WHICH THE GREEK

THEIR LETTERS WAS "LIVE WELL!" THAT OF THE ROMAN WAS "HEALTH TO YOU!" BUT PAUL ALMOST ALWAY WITH A CHRISTIAN GREETING, "GRACE, MERCY, AND PEACE TO YOU." IN THESE LETTERS HE ASSOCIAT himself in this greeting his two companions, Timothy and Silas.

THE LAST WORDS OF HIS EPISTLES ARE ALMOST ALWAYS PERSONAL MESSAGES TO INDIVIDUALS KNC HIM IN THE SEVERAL CHURCHES,--TO MEN AND WOMEN WHO HAD "LABORED WITH HIM IN THE GOSPEL,"-- YET SIGNIFICANT WORDS, WHICH "SHOW A HEART WITHIN BLOOD-TINCTURED, OF A VEINED HUMANIT LETTERS WERE WRITTEN BY AN AMANUENSIS,--ALL SAVE THESE CONCLUDING WORDS WHICH PAUL ADDEI OWN CHIROGRAPHY. HE SEEMS TO DESIRE TO PUT MORE OF HIMSELF INTO THESE PERSONAL MESSAGES TH THE DIDACTIC AND DOCTRINAL PARTS OF HIS EPISTLES. AT THE END OF THE SECOND OF THE LETTI THESSALONIANS WE FIND THESE WORDS: "THE SALUTATION OF ME PAUL WITH MINE OWN HAND, WHICH TOKEN IN EVERY EPISTLE: SO I WRITE;" BETTER, PERHAPS, "THIS IS MY HANDWRITING." THIS SIGNATURE AI CONCLUDING GREETING ARE TO BE PROOF TO THEM OF THE GENUINENESS OF THE LETTER. IT APPEARS F REFERENCES IN THE SAME EPISTLE (CH. II. 2) THAT SOME BUSYBODY HAD BEEN WRITING A LETTER THESSALONIANS, WHICH PURPORTED TO BE A MESSAGE FROM PAUL; HE PUTS THEM ON THEIR GUARD A THESE SUPPOSITITIOUS DOCUMENTS. AT THE END OF THE LETTER TO THE GALATIANS YOU FIND IN VERSION: "YE SEE HOW LARGE A LETTER I HAVE WRITTEN UNTO YOU WITH MY OWN HAND;" BUT TH RENDERING IS IN THE NEW VERSION: "SEE WITH HOW LARGE LETTERS [WHAT A BOLD CHIROGRAPHY] I HAVE UNTO YOU WITH MY OWN HAND." "THESE LAST COARSE CHARACTERS ARE MY OWN HANDWRITING." IT IS UNIVERSALLY ASSUMED THAT PAUL WAS A SUFFERER FROM SOME AFFECTION OF THE EYES; THE LARGE LI THUS EXPLAINED. MR. CONYBEARE, IN A FOOT-NOTE ON THIS PASSAGE, SPEAKS OF RECEIVING A LETTER F VENERABLE NEANDER A FEW MONTHS BEFORE HIS DEATH, WHICH ILLUSTRATES THIS POINT IN A STRIKING "HIS LETTER," SAYS MR. CONYBEARE, "IS WRITTEN IN THE FAIR AND FLOWING HAND OF AN AMANUENSIS ENDS WITH A FEW IRREGULAR LINES IN LARGE AND RUGGED CHARACTERS, WRITTEN BY HIMSELF AND EXPL CAUSE OF HIS NEEDING THE SERVICES OF AN AMANUENSIS, NAMELY THE WEAKNESS OF HIS EYES (PROBAB VERY MALADY OF ST. PAUL). IT WAS IMPOSSIBLE TO READ THIS AUTOGRAPH WITHOUT THINKING OF THE PASSAGE, AND OBSERVING THAT HE MIGHT HAVE EXPRESSED HIMSELF IN THE VERY WORDS OF ST. PAUL: 'F THE SIZE OF THE CHARACTERS IN WHICH I HAVE WRITTEN TO YOU WITH MY OWN HAND.'" [FOO *Life and Epistles of St. Paul*, ii. 149.]

THERE IS ANOTHER TOUCHING SENTENCE AT THE END OF PAUL'S LETTER TO THE COLOSSIANS W WRITTEN FROM ROME WHEN HE WAS PRISONER THERE: "THE SALUTATION OF ME PAUL WITH MINE OWN REMEMBER MY BONDS. GRACE BE WITH YOU. AMEN." THIS SEEMS TO SAY: "THERE IS A MANACLE, Y REMEMBER, ON MY WRIST. I CANNOT WRITE VERY WELL. GRACE BE WITH YOU." I WILL ONLY ADD TH SUBSCRIPTIONS WHICH FOLLOW THE EPISTLES IN THE OLD VERSION ARE NO PART OF THE EPISTLES, AND IN CASES THEY ARE ERRONEOUS. THEY EMBODY CONJECTURES OF LATER COPYISTS, OR TRADITIONS WHICH ARE FOUNDATION. THESE LETTERS TO THE THESSALONIANS, FOR EXAMPLE, ARE SAID TO HAVE BEEN WRITT ATHENS; BUT WE KNOW THAT THEY WERE WRITTEN FROM CORINTH. FOR PAUL EXPRESSLY SAYS (III. 6) T LETTER WAS WRITTEN IMMEDIATELY AFTER THE RETURN OF TIMOTHY FROM THESSALONICA, AND WE AR ACTS XVIII. 5, THAT SILAS AND TIMOTHY JOINED HIM AT CORINTH AFTER HE HAD LEFT ATHENS AND HAD CORINTH. BESIDES, HE ASSOCIATES SILAS AND TIMOTHY WITH HIMSELF IN HIS GREETINGS, AND THEY W WITH HIM AT ATHENS. THE EVIDENCE IS THEREFORE CONCLUSIVE, THAT THE SUBSCRIPTION IS INCORRE WILL NOT FIND ANY OF THESE SUBSCRIPTIONS IN THE NEW VERSION. SOME OF THEM ARE UNDOUBTEDLY BUT SOME OF THEM ARE NOT; AND IN NO CASE IS THE SUBSCRIPTION AN INTEGRAL PART OF THE EPIST EXCISION OF THESE TRADITIONAL ADDENDA WAS ONE OF THE FIRST RESULTS OF WHAT IS CALLED THI CRITICISM," AND ADMIRABLY ILLUSTRATES THE USES OF THIS KIND OF CRITICISM, WHICH, TO SOME OF OUR BRETHREN, IS SUCH A FRIGHTFUL THING. WHY SHOULD IT BE REGARDED AS A DANGEROUS, ALMOST A D PROCEEDING, TO LET THE BIBLE TELL ITS OWN STORY ABOUT ITS ORIGIN, INSTEAD OF TRUSTING TO traditions and mediæval guesses and *a priori* theories of seventeenth century theologians?

THESE TWO LETTERS WERE, NO DOUBT, READ IN THE ASSEMBLIES OF THE THESSALONIAN CHRISTIA THAN ONCE, AND WERE SACREDLY TREASURED BY THEM. THEY WERE THE ONLY CHRISTIAN DOCUMENTS P BY THEM; AND THERE WAS, AT THIS TIME, NO OTHER CHURCH SO RICH AS THEY WERE. THE GOSPELS, AS W THEM NOW, WERE NOT THEN IN THE POSSESSION OF ANY CHRISTIAN CHURCH. THE STORY OF THE GOS BEEN REPEATED TO THEM BY PAUL AND SILAS AND TIMOTHY, AND HAD BEEN DILIGENTLY IMPRESSED UPO

MEMORIES; BUT IT WAS ONLY AN ORAL GOSPEL THAT HAD BEEN DELIVERED TO THEM; THE WRITTEN RI CHRIST'S LIFE AND SAYINGS WAS NOT IN THEIR HANDS. THEY REMEMBERED, THEREFORE, THE THINGS WH BEEN TOLD THEM CONCERNING THE LIFE AND DEATH OF JESUS CHRIST; THEY REPEATED THEM OVEI ANOTHER, AND THEY EXPLAINED AND SUPPLEMENTED THESE REMEMBERED WORDS BY THE TWO LETTER they had received from the great apostle.

THE NEXT YEAR AFTER PAUL WROTE THESE LETTERS TO THE THESSALONIANS FROM CORINTH, HE RI JERUSALEM AND ANTIOCH (ACTS XVIII. 18-23), AND THE YEAR FOLLOWING, PROBABLY 54, HE SET OUT THIRD MISSIONARY JOURNEY, WHICH TOOK HIM THROUGH GALATIA AND PHRYGIA IN ASIA MINOR TO EI WHERE HIS HOME WAS FOR TWO OR THREE YEARS. WHILE THERE, PERHAPS IN THE YEAR 57, HE WROTE THE HIS LETTERS TO THE CHRISTIANS IN CORINTH. SHORTLY AFTER WRITING IT HE WENT ON TO MACEDON THE SECOND OF HIS LETTERS TO THE CORINTHIANS WAS WRITTEN; PRESENTLY HE FOLLOWED HIS LETTERS AND WHILE THERE, PROBABLY IN 58, HE WROTE HIS LETTER TO THE GALATIANS. GALATIA WAS A PROVINC THAN A CITY; THERE MAY HAVE BEEN SEVERAL CHURCHES, WHICH HAD BEEN ESTABLISHED BY PAUL, PROVINCE; AND THIS MAY HAVE BEEN A CIRCULAR LETTER, TO BE HANDED ABOUT AMONG THEM, COPIES C BE MADE, PERHAPS, FOR THE USE OF EACH OF THE CHURCHES. IT WAS IN THE SPRING OF THE NEXT YEAR, W WAS STILL IN CORINTH, THAT HE WROTE HIS LETTER TO THE ROMANS, THE LONGEST, AND FROM SOME VIEW, THE MOST IMPORTANT OF HIS EPISTLES. HE HAD NEVER, AT THE TIME OF THIS WRITING, BEEN IN (CH. I. 13), BUT HE HAD MET ROMAN CHRISTIANS IN MANY OF THE CITIES OF THE EAST WHERE HE HAI AND TAUGHT; AND, DOUBTLESS, SINCE ALL ROADS LED TO ROME, AND THE METROPOLIS OF THE WC CONSTANTLY DRAWING TO ITSELF MEN OF EVERY NATION AND PROVINCE, MANY OF PAUL'S CONVERTS IN A MACEDONIA AND ACHAIA HAD MADE THEIR WAY TO THE ETERNAL CITY, AND HAD JOINED THEMSELVES THE CHRISTIAN COMMUNITY. THE LONG LIST OF PERSONAL GREETINGS WITH WHICH THE EPISTLE CLOSI how large was his acquaintance in the Roman church, and, doubtless, by his correspondence, he had BECOME FULLY INFORMED CONCERNING THE NEEDS OF THESE DISCIPLES. HE TELLS THE ROMANS, IN TH THAT HE HOPES TO VISIT THEM BY AND BY; HE DID NOT, HOWEVER, AT THAT TIME, EXPECT TO APPEAR THEM AS A PRISONER. THIS WAS THE FATE AWAITING HIM. SHORTLY AFTER WRITING THIS EPISTLE HE R FROM CORINTH TO JERUSALEM, BEARING A COLLECTION WHICH HAD BEEN GATHERED IN EUROPE FOR T CHRISTIANS OF THE MOTHER CHURCH; AT JERUSALEM HE WAS ARRESTED; IN THAT CITY AND IN CÆSARE FOR A LONG TIME IMPRISONED; FINALLY, PROBABLY IN THE SPRING OF 61, HE WAS SENT AS A PRISONER TO BECAUSE HE HAD APPEALED TO THE IMPERIAL COURT; AND HERE, FOR AT LEAST TWO YEARS, HE DWELT A I IN LODGINGS OF HIS OWN, CHAINED BY DAY AND NIGHT TO A ROMAN SOLDIER. DURING THIS IMPRISON PROBABLY IN 62, HE WROTE THE LETTERS TO THE COLOSSIANS, THE EPHESIANS, THE PHILIPPIANS, AND PH FROM THE FIRST IMPRISONMENT HE SEEMS TO HAVE BEEN RELEASED; AND TO HAVE GONE WESTWARD AS SPAIN, AND EASTWARD AS FAR AS ASIA MINOR, PREACHING THE GOSPEL. DURING THIS JOURNEY HE IS SUP TO HAVE WRITTEN THE FIRST LETTER TO TIMOTHY AND THE LETTER TO TITUS. AT LENGTH HE WAS RE-AI BROUGHT TO ROME WHERE, IN THE SPRING OF 68, JUST BEFORE HIS DEATH, HE WROTE THE SECOND L Timothy, the last of his thirteen epistles.

MUCH OF THIS ACCOUNT OF THE LATE YEARS OF PAUL'S LIFE, FOLLOWING THE CLOSE OF HIS FIRST TW ROME, WHERE THE NARRATIVE IN THE ACTS OF THE APOSTLES ABRUPTLY LEAVES HIM, IS TRADITIOI CONJECTURAL; I DO NOT GIVE IT TO YOU AS INDUBITABLE HISTORY; IT FURNISHES THE MOST REA EXPLANATION THAT HAS BEEN SUGGESTED OF THAT PRODUCTIVE ACTIVITY OF HIS WHICH FINDS I expression in the letters that bear his name.

OF THESE LETTERS IT IS IMPOSSIBLE TO GIVE ANY ADEQUATE ACCOUNT IN THIS PLACE. LET IT SUFFIC THAT THE PRINCIPAL THEME OF THE TWO EPISTLES TO THE THESSALONIANS IS THE EXPECTED RETURN OF EARTH; THAT THOSE TO THE CORINTHIANS ARE LARGELY OCCUPIED WITH QUESTIONS OF CHRISTIAN CASU THOSE TO THE GALATIANS AND THE ROMANS ARE THE GREAT DOCTRINAL EPISTLES UNFOLDING THE I CHRISTIANITY TO JUDAISM, AND DISCUSSING THE PHILOSOPHY OF THE NEW CREED; THAT THE EPISTLE PHILIPPIANS IS A LUMINOUS EXPOSITION OF CHRISTIANITY AS A PERSONAL EXPERIENCE; THAT THOSE COLOSSIANS AND THE EPHESIANS ARE THE DEFENSE OF CHRISTIANITY AGAINST THE INSIDIOUS ERROR GNOSTICS, AND A WONDERFUL REVELATION OF THE IMMANENT CHRIST; THAT THE EPISTLE TO PHILE letter of personal friendship, embodying a great principle of practical religion; and that the letters to Timothy and Titus are the counsel of an aged apostle to younger men in the ministry.

"May we go farther," with Archdeacon Farrar, "and attempt, in one or two wo description of each separate epistle, necessarily imperfect from the very brevity, and yet expressive of some one main characteristic. If so we might perhaps say that the First Epistle Thessalonians is the epistle of consolation in the hope of Christ's return; and the secon immediate hindrances to that return, and our duties with regard to it. The First Episti Corinthians is the solution of practical problems in the light of eternal principles; the si impassioned defense of the apostle's impugned authority, *Apologia pro vita sua.* The Epistle to th Galatians is the epistle of freedom from the bondage of the law; that to the Romans of jus by faith. The Epistle to the Philippians is the epistle of Christian gratitude and of Christi sorrow; that to the Colossians the epistle of Christ the universal Lord; that to the Ephesians, so rich and many-sided, is the epistle of the 'heavenlies,' the epistle of grace, the epistle of ascens the ascended Christ, the epistle of Christ in his one and universal church; that to Phili Magna Charta of Emancipation. The First Epistle to Timothy and that to Titus are the manuals of a Christian pastor; the Second Epistle to Timothy is the last message of a Christian ere his [Footnote: *The Life and Work of St. Paul*, chap. xlvi.]

The genuineness of several of these books has been assailed by modern criticism authorship of Paul has been disputed in the cases of nine out of the thirteen epistles. The E the Galatians, that to the Romans, and the two to the Corinthians are undisputed; all the been spoken against. I have attended to these criticisms; but the reasons urged for deny Pauline authorship of these epistles seem to me in many cases far-fetched and fanciful extreme. Respecting the pastoral epistles, those to Timothy and Titus, it may be admitted th are some difficulties. It is not easy for us to understand how there could have been develope churches at that early day so much of an ecclesiasticism as these letters assume; and there is the suggestion that the peculiar errors against which some of these counsels are directed belong to a later day rather than to the apostolic age. To this it may be replied that ecclesiasticism which grows rapidly when once it has taken root, and that the germs of Gnosticism were church from the earliest day. And although the vocabulary of these epistles differs in striking way, as Dr. Harnack has pointed out, [Footnote: *Encyc. Brit.*, art. "Pastoral Epistles."] fro that of Paul's other epistles, I can easily imagine that in familiar letters to his pupils he wo into a different style from that in which he wrote his more elaborate theological trea could find in the letters of Macaulay or Charles Kingsley many words that he would not f history of the one or the sermons of the other. Putting all these objections together, I do not find in them any adequate reason for denying that these epistles were written by St. Paul. Indeed, to me incredible that the Second Epistle of Timothy should have been written by any oth than that which wrote the undoubted letters to the Corinthians and the Romans.

When we come to the other disputed epistles, those to the Thessalonians, the Ephesi Philippians, and the Colossians, I confess that the doubts of their genuineness seem to outcome of a willful dogmatism. What Archdeacon Farrar says of the cavils respecting the to the Philippians applies to much of this theoretic criticism: "The Tübingen school, in its stages, attacked it with the monotonous arguments of their credulous skepticism. With thos if an epistle touches on points which make it accord with the narrative of the Acts it was fo suit them; if it seems to disagree with them the discrepancy shows that it is spurious. If the is Pauline it stands forth as a proved imitation; if it is un-Pauline it could not have proceed the apostle." [Footnote: *Life and Work of St. Paul*, chap, xlvi] One grows weary with this reckless a carping skepticism, much of which springs from a theory of a permanent schism in the church,--a theory which was mainly evolved from the inner consciousness of some mystical G philosopher, and which has been utterly exploded.

We may, then, receive as genuine the thirteen epistles ascribed to St. Paul; and we hav reason for believing that we have them in their integrity, substantially as he wrote them.

The title of one of these epistles, that to the Ephesians, is, however, undoubtedly er As Mr. Conybeare says, the least disputable fact about the letter is that it was not address Ephesians. For it is incredible that Paul should have described a church in whose fellowship

LIVED AND LABORED FOR TWO YEARS AS ONE OF WHOSE RELIGIOUS LIFE HE KNEW ONLY BY REPORT (CH. I. IT IS STRANGE THAT HE SHOULD NOT HAVE A SINGLE WORD OF GREETING TO ANY OF THESE EPHESIAN C SEVERAL OF THE EARLY CHRISTIAN FATHERS TESTIFY THAT THE WORDS "AT EPHESUS" ARE OMITTED FRO VERSE OF THE MANUSCRIPT KNOWN TO THEM. THE TWO OLDEST MANUSCRIPTS NOW IN EXISTENCE, THAT VATICAN AND THAT KNOWN AS THE SINAITIC MANUSCRIPT, BOTH OMIT THESE WORDS. THE DESTINATION epistle is not indicated. The place filled by the words "at Ephesus" is left blank. Thus it reads: "Paul, AN APOSTLE OF CHRIST JESUS THROUGH THE WILL OF GOD, TO THE SAINTS WHICH ARE AND THE FA CHRIST JESUS." SOME OF THE OLD FATHERS EXPATIATE ON THIS TITLE, DRAWING DISTINCTIONS BETWEEN T WHICH *are* AND THE SAINTS WHICH *seem to be*,--AN AMUSING EXAMPLE OF EXEGETICAL THOROUGHN UNDOUBTEDLY THE LETTER WAS DESIGNED AS A CIRCULAR LETTER TO SEVERAL CHURCHES IN WESTE LAODICEA AMONG THE NUMBER; AND A BLANK WAS LEFT IN EACH COPY MADE, IN WHICH THE NAME C CHURCH TO WHICH IT WAS DELIVERED MIGHT BE ENTERED. SOME KNOWING COPYIST AT A LATER DAY WR WORDS "AT EPHESUS" INTO ONE OF THESE COPIES; AND IT IS FROM THIS THAT THE MANUSCRIPT DESC from which our translation was made.

THAT THESE LETTERS OF PAUL WERE HIGHLY PRIZED AND CAREFULLY PRESERVED BY THE CHURCHES THEY WERE WRITTEN WE CANNOT DOUBT; AND AS FROM TIME TO TIME MESSENGERS PASSED BACK AND BETWEEN THE CHURCHES, COPIES WERE MADE OF THE LETTERS FOR EXCHANGE. THE CHURCH AT THES WOULD SEND A COPY OF ITS LETTER TO THE CHURCH AT PHILIPPI AND TO THE CHURCH AT CORINTH AI CHURCH AT EPHESUS, AND WOULD RECEIVE IN RETURN COPIES OF THEIR LETTERS; AND THUS THE WRITING EARLY OBTAINED A CONSIDERABLE DISTRIBUTION. WE HAVE AN ILLUSTRATION OF THESE EXCHANGES IN TH WORDS OF THE EPISTLE TO THE COLOSSIANS (IV. 16): "AND WHEN THIS EPISTLE HATH BEEN READ AMON CAUSE THAT IT BE READ ALSO IN THE CHURCH OF THE LAODICEANS; AND THAT YOU ALSO READ THE EPIS LAODICEA." IT IS PROBABLE THAT THE LAST-NAMED EPISTLE WAS THE ONE OF WHICH WE HAVE JUST speaking, called in our version, the Epistle to the Ephesians.

THE EPISTLE TO THE HEBREWS IS ASCRIBED IN ITS TITLE TO "PAUL THE APOSTLE." BUT THE T added at a late date; the Greek Testaments contain only the brief title "To the Hebrews," leaving the QUESTION OF AUTHORSHIP UNSETTLED. OF ALL THE OTHER EPISTLES ASCRIBED TO PAUL HIS NAME IS WORD; THIS EPISTLE DOES NOT ANNOUNCE ITS AUTHOR. IN THE EARLY CHURCH THERE WAS MUCH CON' ABOUT IT; THE EASTERN CHRISTIANS GENERALLY ASCRIBED IT TO PAUL, WHILE THE WESTERN CHURCH, FOURTH CENTURY, REFUSED TO RECOGNIZE HIS AUTHORSHIP. ONE SENTENCE IN THE EPISTLE (CH. SUPPOSED TO SIGNIFY THAT THE WRITER WAS OF THE NUMBER OF THOSE WHO HAD RECEIVED THE GC SECOND HAND, AND THIS WAS AN ADMISSION THAT PAUL ALWAYS REFUSED TO MAKE; HE STEADILY CON THAT HIS KNOWLEDGE OF THE GOSPEL WAS AS DIRECT AND IMMEDIATE AND COPIOUS AS THAT OF ANY APOSTLES. FOR THESE AND OTHER REASONS IT HAS BEEN CONTENDED THAT THE LETTER WAS WRITTEN BY NOT AN APOSTLE, BUT AN ASSOCIATE AND PUPIL OF APOSTOLIC MEN; THE MOST PLAUSIBLE CONJECTURE ASC TO APOLLOS. THE DATE OF IT IS NOT EASILY FIXED; IT WAS PROBABLY WRITTEN BEFORE THE DESTRU JERUSALEM; SUCH AN ELABORATE DISCUSSION OF THE JEWISH RITUAL WOULD SCARCELY HAVE BEEN MADE A temple was destroyed, without any reference to the fact of its destruction.

FOLLOWING THE LETTER TO THE HEBREWS IN OUR NEW TESTAMENT ARE SEVEN EPISTLES ASCRIBED DIFFERENT AUTHORS, JAMES, PETER, JOHN, AND JUDE. THESE ARE COMMONLY CALLED THE "CATHOLIC EI -CATHOLIC MEANING GENERAL OR UNIVERSAL,--SINCE THEY ARE NOT ADDRESSED TO ANY ONE CONGREG TO THE WHOLE CHURCH, TO CHRISTIANS IN GENERAL. TWO OF THEM, HOWEVER, THE SECOND AND T John, hardly deserve the designation, for they are addressed to individuals.

THE AUTHOR OF THE EPISTLE OF JAMES IS NOT EASILY IDENTIFIED. THERE ARE NUMEROUS JAMESES NEW TESTAMENT HISTORY; WE DO NOT READILY DISTINGUISH THEM. IT WAS NOT JAMES THE SON OF ZI FOR HE WAS PUT TO DEATH BY HEROD ONLY SIX OR SEVEN YEARS AFTER THE DEATH OF OUR LORD (AC PROBABLY THIS WAS THE ONE NAMED JAMES THE LORD'S BROTHER, WHO WAS A NEAR RELATIVE OF BROTHER OR COUSIN, AND WHO WAS THE LEADING MAN--PERHAPS THEY CALLED HIM BISHOP--OF THE CHU JERUSALEM. HE MAY, ALSO, BE IDENTICAL WITH THAT JAMES THE SON OF ALPHEUS, WHO WAS ONE C APOSTLES. THE LETTER WAS ISSUED AT AN EARLY DAY, PROBABLY BEFORE THE YEAR 60. IT WAS ADDRESSE "TWELVE TRIBES WHICH ARE OF THE DISPERSION,"--THAT WAS THE NAME BY WHICH THE JEWS SCA' THROUGH ASIA AND EUROPE WERE GENERALLY KNOWN. TO CHRISTIANS WHO HAD BEEN JEWS, THEREFC

LETTER WAS WRITTEN; IN THIS RESPECT IT IS TO BE CLASSED WITH THE LETTER TO THE HEBREWS; BUT IN OF ITS TEACHING IT IS WHOLLY UNLIKE THAT LETTER; INSTEAD OF PUTTING EMPHASIS ON THE R SYMBOLICAL ELEMENTS OF RELIGION, IT LEAVES THESE WHOLLY ON ONE SIDE, AND MAKES THE ETHICAL CO THE CHRISTIAN TEACHING THE MATTER OF SUPREME CONCERN. THERE IS MORE OF APPLIED CHRISTIANIT THAN IN ANY OTHER OF THE EPISTLES; AND BOTH IN STYLE AND IN SUBSTANCE WE ARE REMINDED BY I teaching of our Lord more strongly than by any other portion of the New Testament.

THE FIRST EPISTLE OF PETER IS ADDRESSED TO THE SAME CLASS OF PERSONS,--TO "THE ELECT ' SOJOURNERS OF THE DISPERSION" IN VARIOUS PROVINCES OF ASIA MINOR. THE ONLY INTIMATION C LOCALITY OF THE WRITING IS CONTAINED IN ONE OF THE CONCLUDING VERSES: "SHE THAT IS IN BABY TOGETHER WITH YOU, SALUTETH YOU." WHAT BABYLON IS THIS? IS IT THE FAMOUS CAPITAL OF THE EU SO SOME HAVE SUPPOSED, FOR THERE IS A TRADITION THAT PETER JOURNEYED TO THE DISTANT E FOUNDED CHRISTIAN CHURCHES AMONG THE JEWS, WHO, IN LARGE NUMBERS, WERE DWELLING THERE. TAKE IT TO BE THE MYSTICAL BABYLON,--ROME UPON HER SEVEN HILLS. THIS THEORY HELPS TO SUPP(CONTENTION, FOR WHICH THERE IS SMALL EVIDENCE, THAT PETER WAS THE FIRST BISHOP OF ROME. T CONJECTURE HAS A FIRMER BASIS. BUT WHO IS "SHE" THAT SENDS HER SALUTATIONS TO THESE ASIAN SAIN IT THE CHURCH OR THE WIFE OF THE APOSTLE? EITHER INTERPRETATION IS DIFFICULT; I CANNOT CHOOS THEM. OF THE ORIGIN OF THIS LETTER WE KNOW LITTLE; BUT THERE IS NOTHING IN IT INCONSISTEN UNBROKEN TRADITION WHICH ASCRIBES IT TO THE IMPETUOUS LEADER OF THE APOSTOLIC BAND. LIKE THI OF JAMES IT IS FULL OF A STRENUOUS MORALITY; WHILE IT DOES NOT DISREGARD THE ESSENTIALS OF doctrine it puts the emphasis on Christian conduct.

THE SECOND EPISTLE OF PETER IS THE ONE BOOK OF THE NEW TESTAMENT CONCERNING GENUINENESS THERE IS MOST DOUBT. FROM THE EARLIEST DAYS THE CANONICITY OF THIS BOOK H DISPUTED. IT IS NOT MENTIONED BY ANY EARLY CHRISTIAN WRITER BEFORE THE THIRD CENTURY; AND WHO IS THE FIRST TO ALLUDE TO THE BOOK, TESTIFIES THAT ITS GENUINENESS HAS BEEN DOUBTED. VERSIONS DO NOT CONTAIN IT; EUSEBIUS MARKS IT DOUBTFUL; ERASMUS AND CALVIN, IN LATER TIMES, RE IT AS A DUBIOUS DOCUMENT. IT SEEMS ALMOST INCREDIBLE, WITH SUCH WITNESSES AGAINST IT, THAT TH SHOULD BE GENUINE; BUT IF IT IS NOT THE WORK OF ST. PETER IT IS A FRAUDULENT WRITING, FOR I ANNOUNCES HIM AS ITS AUTHOR AND REFERS TO HIS FIRST EPISTLE. THERE IS A REMARKABLE SIMILARITY THIS LETTER AND THE SHORT EPISTLE OF JUDE; IT WOULD APPEAR THAT THIS MUST BE AN IMITAT ENLARGEMENT OF THAT, OR THAT A CONDENSATION OF THIS. THERE ARE SOME PASSAGES IN THIS BC WHICH WE COULD ILL AFFORD TO PART,--WITH WHICH, INDEED, WE NEVER SHALL PART; FOR WHETHER TI WRITTEN BY PETER OR BY ANOTHER THEY EXPRESS CLEAR AND INDUBITABLE VERITIES; AND EVEN TH(AUTHOR, LIKE THAT BALAAM WHOM HE QUOTES, MAY HAVE BEEN NO TRUE PROPHET, HE WAS CONSTRAINEI as Balaam was, to utter some wholesome and stimulating truth.

THE THREE EPISTLES OF JOHN ARE THE LAST WORDS OF THE DISCIPLE THAT JESUS LOVED. THE EVII THEIR GENUINENESS, PARTICULARLY OF THE FIRST OF THEM, IS ABUNDANT AND CONVINCING; POLYCARP, JOHN'S PUPIL AND FRIEND, QUOTES FROM THIS BOOK, AND THERE IS AN UNBROKEN CHAIN OF TESTIMON THE EARLY FATHERS RESPECTING IT. OF COURSE THOSE WHO HAVE DETERMINED, FOR DOGMATIC REASONS, THE FOURTH GOSPEL, ARE BOUND TO REJECT THESE EPISTLES ALSO; BUT THAT PROCEDURE IS unwarranted, as we shall see in the next chapter. These epistles were probably written from Ephesus DURING THE LAST YEARS OF THE FIRST CENTURY. THE FIRST IS A MEDITATION ON THE GREAT FA INCARNATION AND ITS MYSTIC RELATION TO THE LIFE OF MEN; IT SOUNDS THE VERY DEPTHS OF THAT V REVELATION WHICH WAS MADE TO THE WORLD IN THE PERSON AND WORK OF JESUS CHRIST. THE OTHER PERSONAL LETTERS, WHEREIN THE FRAGRANCE OF A GRACIOUS FRIENDSHIP STILL LINGERS, AND IN WHI(HOW THE SPIRIT OF CHRIST WAS BEGINNING, EVEN THEN, TO TRANSFIGURE WITH ITS BENIGNANT GENTL courtesies of life.

THE BOOK OF JUDE, THE LAST OF THE EPISTLES, IS ONE OF WHOSE AUTHOR WE HAVE LITTLE KNOWLE STYLES HIMSELF "THE BROTHER OF JAMES," BUT THAT, AS WE HAVE SEEN, IS A VAGUE DESCRIPTION. OF TH RELATION BETWEEN THIS LETTER AND SECOND PETER I HAVE SPOKEN. IT IS NOT IN THE EARLY SYRIA(EUSEBIUS AND ORIGEN QUESTION IT, AND CHRYSOSTOM DOES NOT MENTION IT; WE MAY FAIRLY I WHETHER IT CAME FROM THE HAND OF ANY APOSTOLIC WITNESS. ONE FEATURE OF THIS SHORT LETTEF MENTION; THE WRITER QUOTES FROM ONE OF THE OLD APOCRYPHAL BOOKS, THE BOOK OF ENOCH, TREA'

SCRIPTURE. IF A NEW TESTAMENT CITATION AUTHENTICATES AN ANCIENT WRITING, ENOCH MUST BE REG AN INSPIRED BOOK. WE MUST EITHER REJECT JUDE OR ACCEPT ENOCH, OR ABANDON THE RULE THAT N New Testament citation the proof of Old Testament canonicity. The abandonment of the rule is the simplest and the most rational solution of the difficulty.

I HAVE NOW RUN RAPIDLY OVER THE HISTORY OF TWENTY-ONE OF THE TWENTY-SEVEN BOOKS OF T TESTAMENT,--ALL OF THE EPISTLES OF THE INSPIRED BOOK. THE END OF THE FIRST CENTURY FOUND THI SCATTERED THROUGH EUROPE AND ASIA, EACH PROBABLY IN POSSESSION OF THE CHURCH TO WHICH IT H/ SENT; THOSE ADDRESSED TO INDIVIDUALS PROBABLY IN THE HANDS OF THEIR CHILDREN OR CHILDREN'S SOME EXCHANGES, SUCH AS I HAVE SUGGESTED, HAD TAKEN PLACE; AND SOME CHURCHES MIGHT POSSESSED SEVERAL OF THESE APOSTOLIC LETTERS, BUT THERE WAS YET NO COLLECTION OF THEM BEGINNING OF THIS COLLECTION OF THE NEW TESTAMENT WRITINGS I SHALL SPEAK IN THE CHAPTER U canon.

I SAID AT THE BEGINNING THAT THESE WRITERS PROBABLY HAD NO THOUGHT WHEN THEY COMPOSI LETTERS THAT THEY WERE CONTRIBUTING TO A VOLUME THAT WOULD OUTLAST EMPIRES, AND BE A M STUDY AND A GUIDE OF CONDUCT IN LANDS TO THE WORLD THEN UNKNOWN, AND IN GENERATIONS FART THEM THAN THEY WERE FROM ABRAHAM. BUT EACH OF THEM UTTERED IN SINCERITY THE WORD THAT SEEMED THE WORD OF THE HOUR; AND GOD WHO GIVES LIFE TO THE SEED GAVE VITALITY TO THESE TRU SO THAT THEY ARE AS FULL OF DIVINE ENERGY TO-DAY AS EVER THEY WERE. IT IS EASY TO CAVIL AT A SENT AND THERE, OR TO PICK FLAWS IN THEIR LOGIC; BUT THE QUESTION ALWAYS RETURNS, WHAT KIND OF F THEY BORNE? "BY THEIR FRUITS YE SHALL KNOW THEM." ONE OF THE MOST PRECIOUS GIFTS OF GOD TO CONTAINED IN THESE TWENTY-ONE BRIEF LETTERS. IT IS NOT IN EQUAL MEASURE IN ALL OF THEM, BUT NONE AMONG THEM THAT DOES NOT CONTAIN SOME PORTION OF IT. THE TREASURE IS IN EARTHEN VESSE SO WHEN THE APOSTLES WERE ALIVE AND SPEAKING; IT IS SO NOW; IT ALWAYS WAS AND ALWAYS WILL BE SO THE TREASURE IS THERE, AND HE WHO WITH OPEN MIND AND REVERENT SPIRIT SEEKS FOR IT WILL FIND and will know that the excellency of the power is of God, and not of men.

CHAPTER IX.

THE ORIGIN OF THE GOSPELS

WE HAVE ARRIVED IN OUR STUDY OF THE SACRED SCRIPTURES AT THE THRESHOLD OF THE MOST IN AND THE MOST MOMENTOUS TOPIC WHICH IS PRESENTED TO THE STUDENT OF THE BIBLICAL LITERAT QUESTION OF THE ORIGIN OF THE GOSPELS. THESE GOSPELS CONTAIN THE RECORD OF THE LIFE AND THI JESUS CHRIST, THAT MARVELOUS PERSONALITY IN WHOM THE HISTORIES, THE PROPHECIES, THE LITURGIE OLD TESTAMENT ARE FULFILLED, AND FROM WHOM THE GROWING LIGHT AND FREEDOM AND HAPPI EIGHTEEN CHRISTIAN CENTURIES ARE SEEN TO FLOW. MOST CERTAIN IT IS THAT THE HISTORY OF ENLIGHTENED LANDS OF EARTH DURING THESE CHRISTIAN CENTURIES COULD NOT BE UNDERSTOOI CONSTANT REFERENCE TO THE POWER WHICH CAME INTO THE WORLD WHEN JESUS CHRIST WAS BORN TREMENDOUS SOCIAL FORCE MADE ITS APPEARANCE JUST THEN BY WHICH THE WHOLE LIFE OF MANKIND H AFFECTED EVER SINCE THAT DAY. THE MOST POWERFUL INSTITUTIONS, THE MOST BENIGN INFLUENCES W AT WORK IN THE WORLD TO-DAY, CAN BE FOLLOWED BACK TO THAT PERIOD AS SURELY AS ANY GREAT RIVI FOLLOWED UP TO THE SPRINGS FROM WHICH IT TAKES ITS RISE. IF WE HAD NOT THESE FOUR GOSPELS WE BE COMPELLED TO SEEK FOR AN EXPLANATION OF THE CHIEF PHENOMENA OF MODERN HISTORY. "WE SAYS MR. HORTON, "THIS ASTONISHING INFLUENCE BACK TO THAT LIFE, AND IF WE KNEW NOTHING AT ALI BUT HAD TO CONSTRUCT IT OUT OF THE CREATIVE IMAGINATION, WE SHOULD HAVE TO FIGURE TO OURSEI SAYINGS, AND IMPRESSIONS WHICH WOULD ACCOUNT FOR WHAT HAS FLOWED FROM IT. THUS, IF THE PLACE

THIS BIOGRAPHY COMES WERE ACTUALLY A BLANK, WE SHOULD BE ABLE TO SURMISE SOMETHING OF WHAT TO BE THERE, JUST AS ASTRONOMERS SURMISED THE EXISTENCE OF A NEW PLANET, AND KNEW IN WHAT QU THE HEAVENS TO LOOK FOR IT BY OBSERVING AND REGISTERING THE INFLUENCES WHICH RETARDED OR the movements of the other planets." [Footnote: *Inspiration and the Bible,* p. 65.]

THAT PLACE IS NOT A BLANK; IT IS FILLED WITH THE FOURFOLD RECORD OF THE LIFE FROM WHICH MIGHTY INFLUENCES HAVE FLOWED. MUST NOT THIS RECORD PROVE TO BE THE MOST INSPIRING THEME (HUMAN INVESTIGATION? IS IT ANY WONDER THAT MORE STUDY HAS BEEN EXPENDED UPON THIS THEM upon any other which has ever claimed the attention of men?

WHAT DO WE KNOW OF THE ORIGIN OF THIS FOUR-FOLD RECORD? ORIGIN IT MUST HAVE HAD LIK OTHER BOOK, AN ORIGIN IN TIME AND SPACE. THAT THERE ARE DIVINE ELEMENTS IN IT THE MOST OF US BUT THE FORM IN WHICH WE HAVE IT IS A PURELY HUMAN FORM, AND IT WOULD BE WORTHLESS TO US IF I' NOT IN PURELY HUMAN FORM. THE SENTENCES OF WHICH IT IS COMPOSED WERE CONSTRUCTED BY H MINDS, AND WERE WRITTEN DOWN BY HUMAN HANDS ON PARCHMENT OR PAPYRUS LEAVES. WHEN, AND WH and by whom? These are the questions now before us.

LET US GO BACK TO THE LAST HALF OF THE SECOND CENTURY AND SEE WHAT TRACES OF THESE BOOI find.

IRENÆUS, BISHOP OF LYONS, IN FRANCE, WHO DIED ABOUT 200, SPEAKS DISTINCTLY OF THESE GOSPELS, WHICH, HE DECLARES, ARE EQUAL IN AUTHORITY TO THE OLD TESTAMENT SCRIPTURES, AND W ASCRIBES TO THE FOUR AUTHORS WHOSE NAMES THEY NOW BEAR. WITH THE FANCIFUL REASONING THEN (AMONG CHRISTIAN WRITERS, HE FINDS A REASON IN THE FOUR QUARTERS OF THE GLOBE WHY THERE SHC been four Gospels and no more.

CLEMENT OF ALEXANDRIA WAS LIVING AT THE SAMQ TIME. HE ALSO QUOTES LIBERALLY IN HIS V FROM ALL THESE FOUR BOOKS, OF WHICH HE SPEAKS AS "THE FOUR GOSPELS THAT HAVE BEEN HANDED D us."

TERTULLIAN, WHO WAS BORN IN CARTHAGE ABOUT 160, ALSO QUOTES ALL THESE GOSPELS AS AUTHC Christian writings.

IT IS CLEAR, THEREFORE, THAT IN THE WEST, THE EAST, AND THE SOUTH,--IN ALL QUARTE CHRISTIANITY WAS THEN ESTABLISHED,--THE FOUR GOSPELS WERE RECOGNIZED AND READ IN THE CHU the latter half of the second century. Let us go back a little farther.

Justin Martyr was born at Rome about the year 100, and was writing most abundantly from his FORTIETH TO HIS FORTY-FIFTH YEAR. IN ONE OF THE BOOKS WHICH HE HAS LEFT US, IN DESCRIBING THE C THE CHRISTIANS, HE USES THE FOLLOWING LANGUAGE: "ON THE DAY WHICH IS CALLED SUNDAY THE ASSEMBLY IN THE SAME PLACE OF ALL WHO LIVE IN CITIES OR IN COUNTRY DISTRICTS, AND THE RECORD APOSTLES OR THE WRITINGS OF THE PROPHETS ARE READ AS LONG AS WE HAVE TIME. THEN THE CONCLUDES, AND THE PRESIDENT VERBALLY INSTRUCTS AND EXHORTS US TO THE IMITATION OF THESE THINGS. THEN WE ALL RISE UP TOGETHER AND OFFER OUR PRAYERS." IN ANOTHER PLACE HE SPEAKS OF SO COMMANDED BY "THE APOSTLES IN THE RECORDS WHICH THEY MADE, AND WHICH ARE CALLED GOSPELS." DOES NOT SAY HOW MANY OF THESE GOSPELS THE CHURCH IN HIS DAY POSSESSED, BUT WE FIND IN HIS WRI UNMISTAKABLE QUOTATIONS FROM AT LEAST THREE OF THEM. DR. EDWIN ABBOTT, OF LONDON, WHO HUMPHRY WARD REFERS TO AS MASTER OF ALL THE GERMAN LEARNING ON THIS SUBJECT, SAYS THAT IT W POSSIBLE "TO RECONSTRUCT FROM HIS (JUSTIN'S) QUOTATIONS A FAIRLY CONNECTED NARRATIVE INCARNATION, BIRTH, TEACHING, CRUCIFIXION, RESURRECTION, AND ASCENSION OF THE LORD;" THAT THIS IS ALL FOUND IN THE THREE SYNOPTIC GOSPELS, AND THAT JUSTIN QUOTES NO WORDS OF CHRIST AND no incidents that are not found in these Gospels. [Footnote: *Encyc. Brit.,* vol. x. p. 817.]

WE MAY FULLY ACCEPT DR. ABBOTT'S TESTIMONY SO FAR AS THE QUOTATIONS OF JUSTIN FROM T THREE GOSPELS ARE CONCERNED; BUT HIS ARGUMENTS, WHICH ARE INTENDED TO PROVE THAT THEI CERTAIN REFERENCE TO THE FOURTH GOSPEL IN JUSTIN'S WORKS, APPEAR TO ME INCONCLUSIVE. WHEI SAYS: "FOR INDEED CHRIST ALSO SAID, 'EXCEPT YE BE BORN AGAIN, YE SHALL NOT ENTER INTO THE KIN(HEAVEN,' BUT THAT IT IS IMPOSSIBLE FOR THOSE WHO WERE ONCE BORN TO ENTER INTO THEIR MOTHER' IS PLAIN TO ALL," HE IS QUOTING WORDS THAT ARE FOUND IN THE FOURTH GOSPEL, AND NOT IN ANY OF THREE. THE ATTEMPT TO SHOW THAT HE FOUND THESE AND SIMILAR CITATIONS IN THE SAME SOURC which the author of the fourth Gospel derived them is not successful.

Several indirect lines of evidence tend to confirm the belief that Justin possessed al our Gospels. This, then, carries us back to the first half of the second century. Between 100 Papias of Hierapolis, Clement of Rome, and Polycarp of Smyrna were writing. Papias, who v about 130-140 A. D., composed five books or commentaries on what he calls "The Oracles o Lord." He gives us some account of the origin of at least two of these Gospels. "Mark," i "was the interpreter of Peter;" "Matthew wrote his scriptlogia) in Hebrew, and each man interpreted them as best he could." "Interpreted" here evidently means translated. Else repeats a tradition of "the elder," by which word he apparently means the Apostle John, wi may have known, in these words: "Mark, having become Peter's interpreter, wrote down accu all that he remembered,--not, however, in order,--both the words and the deeds of Christ never heard the Lord, nor attached himself to him, but later on, as I said, attached himself who used to adapt his lessons to the needs of the occasion, but not as though he was comp connected treatise of the discourses of our Lord; so that Mark committed no error in writ some matters just as he remembered them. For one object was in his thoughts, to mak omissions and no false statements in what he heard." [Footnote: Quoted by Abbott, as above is a perfect description of the Gospel of Mark as we have it in our hands to-day. And the tes of Papias to its authorship, and to the spirit and purpose of the author, is significan memorable. Evidence of this nature would be regarded as decisive in any other case of criticism.

Polycarp, who was the friend and pupil of John the Apostle, was born about the year 6 suffered martyrdom about 155. In his writings we find no express mention of the Gospels, b do find verbally accurate quotations from them. It is clear that he was acquainted with th Polycarp was the teacher of Irenæus of Lyons whom I first quoted, and he was the pupil and of St. John and the other apostles; and Irenæus, who quotes all these Gospels so freely, b testimony respecting Polycarp, in a letter which he wrote to Florinus.

"I saw you, when I was yet a boy, in Lower Asia with Polycarp.... I could even point out t the place where the blessed Polycarp sat and spoke, and describe his going out and coming manner of life, his personal appearance, the addresses he delivered to the multitude, how h of his intercourse with John, and with the others who had seen the Lord, and how he recal words, and everything that he had heard about the Lord, about his miracles and his t Polycarp told us, as one who had received it from those who had seen the Word of Life wi own eyes, and all this in complete harmony with the Scriptures. To this I then listened, thro mercy of God vouchsafed to me, with all eagerness, and wrote it not on paper, but in my hea still by the grace of God I ever bring it into fresh remembrance."

These living witnesses give us solid ground for our statement that the Gospels--the fi of them at any rate--were in existence during the last years of the first century. Indee prolong this search for the origin of the books, it is now freely admitted, by many of t radical critics, that the first three Gospels were written before the year 80, and that Mark been written before 70.

It is interesting to contrast the course of New Testament criticism with that engaged Old Testament. In the study of the origin of the Pentateuch the gravitation of opinion steadily downward, toward a later date, so that the great majority of scholars are now ce the books must have been put into their present form long after the time of Moses. In the s the origin of the Gospels the date has been steadily pushed upward, to the very age of the . The earlier critics, Strauss and Baur, insisted that they must have appeared much later, far c second century; but the more recent and more scientific criticism has demolished or discredited their theories, and has carried the Gospels back to the last part of the first century.

Are we entitled, then, to say that these Gospels were written by Matthew, Mark, Lu John? We should be cautious, no doubt, in making such a statement. The Gospels themselv not so explicit on this point as we could desire. Their titles do not warrant this assertion. "The Gospel of St. Matthew" or "The Gospel of St. Mark;" it is the "Gospel according Matthew" or St. Mark. The import of the title would be fully satisfied with the explanation is the story as Matthew or Mark was wont to tell it, put into form by some person or frienI in his last days, or even after his death. But the testimony of Papias, to which I have referr my own mind good evidence that these Gospels were written by the men who bear their nan the case of Luke, as we shall presently see, the evidence is much stronger. And after going evidence as carefully as I am able, the theory that the four Gospels were written by the mi names they bear, all of whom were the contemporaries of our Lord, and two of whom wi apostles, seems to me, on the whole, the best supported by the whole volume of evidence. Ti is not absolutely clear; perhaps it was left somewhat obscure for the very purpose of stim study. At all events, the study which has been given to the subject has confirmed rati weakened the belief that the Gospels are contemporary records of the life of Christ. Mr. I distinguished Unitarian scholar, sums up the evidence as follows: "It consists in the indisi fact that throughout a community of millions of individuals, scattered over Europe, A Africa, the Gospels were regarded with the highest reverence, as the works of those to wi are ascribed, at so early a period that there could be no difficulty in determining whether genuine or not, and when every intelligent Christian must have been deeply interested to the truth.... This fact is itself a phenomenon admitting of no explanation except that ' Gospels had all been handed down as genuine from the apostolic age, and had every accompanied our religion as it spread throughout the world."

When we turn from the external or historical evidence for the genuineness of the G study their internal structure and their relations to one another, we come upon some curi These Gospels, in the form in which we possess them, are written in the Greek language. B Greek language was not the vernacular of the Jews in Palestine when our Lord was on the e. language which was then spoken by them, as I have before explained, was the Aramaic. It is that Palestine was, to some extent, a bilingual country,--like Wales, one writer suggests, w English and the Welsh languages are now freely spoken,--that Aramaic and Greek wei indifferently. I can hardly imagine that a people as tenacious of their own institutions as could have adopted Greek as generally as the Welsh have adopted the English tongue. Wales, if a Welshman were speaking to a congregation of his countrymen on any importan he would be likely to speak the Welsh language. And much more probable does it seem to m the discourses and the common conversation of Jesus must have been spoken in the verna The discourses and sayings of our Lord, as reported for us in these Gospels, are not therefo us in the words that he used. We have a translation of his words from the Aramaic into thi made either by the writers of the Gospels, or by some one in their day. We have quoti testimony of Papias, that the Gospel of Matthew was originally written in Hebrew (by wi undoubtedly means Aramaic), and that each one interpreted it as best he could; and if this then that copy first made by Matthew did contain many of our Lord's very words. But that copy has never been seen since that day; we have no manuscript of any New Testament book e in the Greek language. There are a few cases in which the writers of the Gospels have preser us the very words used by Christ. Thus in the healing of the deaf man in the neighborh Decapolis, of which Mark tells us (vii. 34), Jesus touched his ears, and said unto him, "Ephpha that is, "Be opened." The Evangelist gives us the Aramaic word which Jesus used, and transl for his readers into Greek. Likewise in the healing of the ruler's daughter (Mark v. 41) he ' by the hand, and said unto her, "Talitha cumi, which is, being interpreted," the Evangelist e "Damsel, I say unto thee, Arise." Doubtless most readers get the impression that our Lor here some cabalistic words in a foreign tongue; the fact is that these are the words of the speech of the people; only the Evangelist seems to have thought them especially memorable, has given us not merely, as he generally does, a translation into the Greek of our Lord's w the Aramaic words themselves, with their meaning appended in a Greek phrase. The same is ti our Lord's words on the cross: "Eli, Eli, lama sabachthani?" These are Aramaic words, th words that Jesus uttered. The Roman soldiers who stood near might not know what he mea every Jew who distinctly heard him must have understood him, for he was speaking in no fc tongue, but in the language of his own people.

When we speak, therefore, of the Greek as the original language of the Gospels, we speak with entire accuracy. The Greek does not give us our Lord's original words. These w not, except in the cases I have named, and a few others less important. No man on earth kn ever will know what were the precise words that our Lord used in his Sermon on the Mount conversation with the woman at the well, in his last discourses with his disciples. We havi reason to believe that the substance of what he said is faithfully preserved for us; the record, so marvelously accordant in its report of his teachings, makes this perfectly clear very words we have not, and this fact itself is the most convincing dis-proof of the dogma o inspiration. If our Lord had thought it important that we should have his very words he have seen to it that his very words were preserved and recorded for us, instead of tha' translation of his words, made by his followers, which we now possess. These evangelists have written Aramaic, doubtless did write Aramaic; and they would certainly have kept our discourses and sayings in the Aramaic original if they had been instructed to do so. The f they were not instructed to do so, but were permitted to give his teachings to the world words than those in which they were spoken, shows how little there was of modern liter Christ's conception of the work of revelation.

The first three of these Gospels exhibit many striking similarities; they appear to giv somewhat different standpoints, a condensed and complete synopsis of the events of our Lo therefore they are called the Synoptic Gospels. The fourth Gospel differs widely from matter and form. It will be more convenient, therefore, to speak first of the Synoptic Matthew, Mark, and Luke.

The singular fact respecting these Gospels is the combination in them of likene difference. A considerable portion of each one of them is to be found, word for word, in both of the others; other considerable portions of each are not found in either of the ot passages are nearly alike, but slightly different in two or in all of them. Did these thre write independently each of the other? If so, how does it happen that their phraseology is identical? Did they copy one from another? If so, why did they copy so little? Why, for exam each one of them omit so much that the others had written? And why are there so man differences in passages that are nearly identical? If we accepted the theory of verbal inspir might offer some sort of explanation of this phenomenon. We might say that the Holy dictated these words, and that that is the end of it; since no explanation can be offered of why the Holy Ghost chose one form of expression rather than another. But the Gospels th contain abundant proof that the Holy Ghost did not dictate the words employed by these writers.

The two genealogies of our Lord, one in Matthew and the other in Luke, are widely d From Abraham to David they substantially agree; from David to Christ, Matthew makes t eight generations, and Luke thirty-eight; only two of the intermediate names in the one found in the other; the one list makes Jacob the father of Joseph, and the other declare name of Joseph's father was Heli. All sorts of explanations, some plausible and others prepos have been offered of this difficulty; the one explanation that cannot be allowed is that th were dictated by Omniscience. In the story of the healing of the blind near Jericho, Matt Mark expressly say that the healing took place as Christ was departing from the city; Luk was before he entered it. Matthew says that there were two blind men; Mark and Luke th was but one. About these details of the transaction there is some mistake,--that is the only be said about it. The various explanations offered are weak and inadmissible. But what diff does it make to anybody whether the healing took place before or after Jesus entered th whether there was one man healed or two? The moral and spiritual lessons of the story ar distinct in the one case as in the other; and it is these moral and spiritual values o inspiration is intended to secure.

Similarly, Luke (iv. 38-39) expressly tells us that the healing of Peter's wife's mother to before the calling of Simon and Andrew; while Matthew and Mark tell us with equal exp that the calling took place before the healing. No reconciliation is possible here; eithe Matthew and Mark must have misplaced these events.

So in Matthew xxvii. 9, certain words are said to have been spoken by Jeremiah the prc These words are not in Jeremiah; they are in Zechariah xi. 13. It is simply a slip of the Evan(memory.

So in the record of the inscription on the cross when Jesus was crucified. Each of tı Evangelists copies it for us in a different form. The meaning is the same in all the cases, copy was not exactly made by some of them, perhaps not by any of them. If the Holy Ghos dictated the words, they must, in a case like this, have been exactly alike in all the Evangei substance is given, but the inexactness of the copy shows that the words could not hav dictated by Omniscience. It is sometimes explained that this inscription was in three lan(Greek, Latin, and Hebrew, and that we may have the exact translations of the different ins(This might account for three of them, but not for four.

From these and many other similar facts, we know that the theory of verbal inspiratio true; but that these Evangelists were allowed to state each in his own language the facts ı him concerning our Lord, and that nothing like infallible accuracy was so much as attempt only inspiration that can be claimed for them is that which brought the important facts remembrance, and guarded them against serious errors of history or doctrine.

But now the question returns, if they wrote these Gospels in their own langua(independently of one another, how happens it that they use so often the very same woi phrases and sentences? Take, for example, the following verses from parallel narratives in and in Mark, concerning the calling of the first apostles:--

Matthew iv. 18-22.

And walking by the sea of Galilee, he saw two brethren, Simon who is called Pete Andrew his brother, casting a net into the sea; for they were fishers. And he saith unto the ye after me, and I will make you fishers of men. And they straightway left the nets, and ı him. And going on from thence he saw two other brethren, James the son of Zebedee, and J(brother, in the boat with Zebedee their father, mending their nets; and he called them. straightway left the boat and their father, and followed him.

Mark i. 16-20.

And passing along by the sea of Galilee, he saw Simon and Andrew the brother of casting a net in the sea: for they were fishers. And Jesus said unto them, Come ye after mi will make you to become fishers of men. And straightway they left the nets, and followed h going on a little further, he saw James the son of Zebedee, and John his brother, who also the boat mending the nets. And straightway he called them: and they left their father Zebe boat with the hired servants, and went after him.

There are slight verbal variations, but in general the words are the same, a corresponding sentences are in precisely the same order in both narratives. Now, as Arch Thomson says, in Smith's "Bible Dictionary," "The verbal and material agreement of the firs Evangelists is such as does not occur in any other authors who have written independently other."

Besides many such passages which are substantially alike but verbally or syntactically d there are quite a number which are identical, word for word, and phrase for phrase. These agreements occur most frequently, as is natural, in the reports of our Lord's discourses and but they also occur in the descriptive and narrative portions of the gospel. This is the fact so difficult to reconcile with

Suppose three competent and truthful reporters are employed by you to write an ex unvarnished report of some single transaction which has occurred, and which each of th witnessed. Each is required to do his work without any conference with the others. Whe reports are brought to you, if they are very faithful and accurate for substance, you wi surprised to find some circumstances mentioned by each that are not mentioned by either others, and it will be strange if there are not some important discrepancies. But if on readi you find that the reports, taken sentence by sentence, are almost identical,--that there occasional difference in a word or in the order of a phrase,--then you at once say, "These r

MUST HAVE BEEN COPYING FROM SOME OTHER REPORTER'S NOTE-BOOK, OR ELSE THEY MUST HAVE COMPARING NOTES; THEY COULD NOT HAVE WRITTEN WITH SUCH VERBAL AGREEMENT IF THEY HAD INDEPENDENTLY." SUPPOSE, FOR EXAMPLE, THAT EACH OF THE THREE REPORTS BEGAN IN JUST THESE "THE FIRST OBJECT THAT ATTRACTED MY NOTICE ON ENTERING THE DOOR WAS A CHAIR." NOW IT IS E IMPROBABLE THAT ALL THESE WRITERS, WRITING INDEPENDENT REPORTS OF A TRANSACTION, SHOULD BEC SAME WAY BY MENTIONING THE FIRST OBJECT THAT ATTRACTED THE ATTENTION OF EACH. AND EVE SHOULD SO BEGIN, IT IS WHOLLY BEYOND THE RANGE OF POSSIBILITIES THAT THEY SHOULD ALL SELECT FR MULTITUDE OF THE WORDS IN THE ENGLISH LANGUAGE THE VERY SAME WORDS IN WHICH TO MAI STATEMENT; AND SHOULD PUT THESE WORDS IN THE VERY SAME ORDER, OUT OF THE MULTITUDE OF I ORDERS INTO WHICH THEY COULD GRAMMATICALLY BE PUT. THERE IS NOT ONE CHANCE IN A MILLION TH COINCIDENCE WOULD OCCUR. BUT SUCH COINCIDENCES OCCUR VERY OFTEN IN THE FIRST THREE GOSPE CAN WE ACCOUNT FOR IT? WE SAY THAT THEY WROTE INDEPENDENTLY, THAT THEIR WORDS WERE NOT D them; how does it happen that there is so much verbal agreement?

WE MAY GET SOME HINT OF THE MANNER IN WHICH THESE BIOGRAPHIES WERE PRODUCED IF WE TU the beginning of Luke's Gospel:--

"FORASMUCH AS MANY HAVE TAKEN IN HAND TO DRAW UP A NARRATIVE CONCERNING THOSE M WHICH HAVE BEEN FULFILLED AMONG US, EVEN AS THEY DELIVERED THEM UNTO US, WHICH FROM THE BEC WERE EYEWITNESSES AND MINISTERS OF THE WORD, IT SEEMED GOOD TO ME ALSO, HAVING TRACED THE CC ALL THINGS ACCURATELY FROM THE FIRST, TO WRITE UNTO THEE IN ORDER, MOST EXCELLENT THEOPHILUS MIGHTEST KNOW THE CERTAINTY CONCERNING THE THINGS WHEREIN THOU WAST INSTRUCTED." THE READING OF THIS LAST PHRASE IS, "WHICH THOU WAST TAUGHT BY WORD OF MOUTH." THIS IS THE MOR meaning of the Greek. The passage contains these statements:--

1. Theophilus had been orally taught the Gospels.

2. MANY PERSONS, NOT APOSTLES, HAD UNDERTAKEN TO WRITE OUT PARTS OF THE GOSPEL STORY, had heard it from eyewitnesses and ministers of the word.

3. LUKE ALSO, AS ONE WHO HAD FULL AND ACCURATE INFORMATION, HAD DETERMINED TO RED knowledge to an orderly written narrative, for the benefit of his friend Theophilus.

It appears from this clear statement that written memoranda of the discourses of our Lord and OF THE INCIDENTS OF HIS LIFE HAD BEEN MADE BY MANY PERSONS. NUMBERS OF THESE HAD UNDERTA COMBINE THEIR MEMORANDA WITH THEIR RECOLLECTIONS IN AN ORDERLY STATEMENT. THIS FACT ITSE HOW POWERFUL AN IMPRESSION HAD BEEN MADE BY OUR LORD'S LIFE AND DEATH UPON THE PEOPI PALESTINE. EVERYTHING RELATING TO HIM WAS TREASURED WITH THE UTMOST CARE; LUKE, FOR I BELIEVING THAT HE HAD GAINED BY CAREFUL INVESTIGATION SUFFICIENT KNOWLEDGE TO WAR UNDERTAKING, SETS OUT TO COLLECT THE FACTS AND PRESENT THEM IN A CONSECUTIVE AND INTELLIGI FORM. YET LUKE, IN THIS ANNOUNCEMENT OF HIS PURPOSE, BETRAYS NO CONSCIOUSNESS THAT HE IS USIN DIFFERENT POWERS FROM THOSE EMPLOYED BY THE MANY OTHERS OF WHOM HE SPEAKS. RATHER DOES HI CLEARLY RANK HIMSELF WITH THEM, AS ONE OF MANY GLEANERS IN THIS FRUITFUL FIELD. HE DO thoroughness and painstaking accuracy; I believe that every honest man will concede his claim.

THIS, THEN, WAS THE WAY IN WHICH LUKE WENT TO WORK TO WRITE HIS GOSPEL. THIS IS GUESSWORK; IT IS THE EXPLICIT STATEMENT OF THE AUTHOR HIMSELF. HAVE WE NOT GOOD REASON FOR I that the Gospels of Matthew and Mark were composed in much the same way?

IN ADDITION TO THE WRITTEN MEMORANDA OF CHRIST'S LIFE WHICH WERE IN THE HANDS OF THE A AND OF MANY OTHERS, THERE WAS ANOTHER SOURCE FROM WHICH THE EVANGELISTS MUST HAVE DRAWN ALLUDES TO IT WHEN HE SPEAKS OF THE FACT THAT THEOPHILUS HAD RECEIVED MUCH OF HIS NARRA WORD OF MOUTH." THERE WAS, UNQUESTIONABLY, AN ORAL GOSPEL, COVERING THE LARGER PART OF TH AND THE WORDS OF JESUS, WHICH HAD BEEN WIDELY CIRCULATED IN PALESTINE AND IN THE WHOLE MIS FIELD. WHEN IT IS SAID (ACTS VIII. 1-4; XI. 19) THAT THEY WHICH WERE SCATTERED ABROAD BY TH PERSECUTIONS WENT EVERYWHERE PREACHING THE WORD, IT MUST BE UNDERSTOOD THAT THEY WENT SIMPLY TELLING THE STORY OF JESUS, HIS BIRTH, HIS LIFE, HIS DEEDS, HIS WORDS, HIS DEATH UPON THE SOMETIMES, WHEN PREACHING TO JEWS, THEY WOULD SHOW THE CORRESPONDENCE BETWEEN HIS LIFE AN OLD TESTAMENT PROPHECIES, TO PROVE THAT HE WAS THE MESSIAH; BUT THE SUBSTANCE OF THEIR PRE WAS THE TELLING OVER AND OVER AGAIN OF THE STORY OF JESUS. IT WAS UPON THIS ORAL GOSPEL

APOSTLES AND THE FIRST MISSIONARIES MAINLY RELIED. WHAT THEY DESIRED TO DO WAS TO MAKE KN SPEEDILY AND AS RAPIDLY AS POSSIBLE THE WORDS OF HIS LIPS AND THE FACTS OF HIS LIFE. AND IT IS PROBABLE THAT BEFORE THEY SET OUT ON THESE MISSIONARY TOURS, THEY TOOK GREAT PAINS TO REHEAI ANOTHER THE STORY WHICH THEY WERE GOING FORTH TO TELL. "THE APOSTLES," SAYS PROFESSOR "GUIDED BY THE PROMISED SPIRIT OF TRUTH, REMAINED TOGETHER IN JERUSALEM IN CLOSE COMMUNIO period long enough to shape a common narrative, and to fix it with requisite surroundings."

IT WAS THESE CONCERTED RECOLLECTIONS AND REHEARSALS THAT GAVE TO SO MANY PASSAGES OF TI ITS IDENTITY IN FORM. SOME OF THE SENTENCES OFTEN AND DEVOUTLY REPEATED WERE REMEMBEREI WORD FOR WORD; IN SOME OF THEM THERE WERE VERBAL DIFFERENCES AND DISCREPANCIES, AS THE REPEATED BY ONE AND ANOTHER. THE VERBAL RESEMBLANCES AS WELL AS THE VERBAL DIFFERENCES EXPLAINED BY THIS THEORY OF AN ORAL GOSPEL, PREPARED AT FIRST FOR PREACHING BY THE APOSTLES, only in their memory.

THE PRESERVATION OF SO MANY PASSAGES IN WORDS AND SENTENCES NEARLY OR EXACTLY SIM NOTHING MIRACULOUS. EVEN IN OUR OWN TIME THERE ARE, AS WE ARE TOLD, SECRET SOCIETIES WHOSE RI NEVER BEEN WRITTEN, BUT HAS BEEN HANDED DOWN WITH NEARLY VERBAL ACCURACY, FROM GENERA GENERATION. FOR THE HEBREWS, WHO WERE A PEOPLE AT THIS TIME GREATLY DISINCLINED TO WR THOROUGHLY PRACTICED IN REMEMBERING AND REPEATING THE SAYINGS OF THEIR WISE MEN, THIS TASI not be difficult.

THE APOSTLES AND THE EARLY EVANGELISTS, AS WESTCOTT SUGGESTS, WERE PREACHERS, NOT HISTOI PAMPHLETEERS. THEY BELIEVED IN LIVING WITNESSES MORE THAN IN TRANSMITTED DOCUMENTS. THEY I WRITE OUT THE RECORD AT FIRST, PARTLY BECAUSE THEY WERE NATURALLY DISINCLINED TO WRITE, AND DOUBT, BECAUSE THEY EXPECTED THE IMMEDIATE RETURN OF OUR LORD TO EARTH. THEIR GOSPEL WAS TI FOR MANY YEARS A SPOKEN AND NOT A WRITTEN WORD. AS THEY WENT ON REPEATING IT, CHANGES WOUI IN THE REPETITION OF THE WORDS; TO THE REMEMBRANCE OF ONE AND ANOTHER OF THEM THE SPIRIT WOULD BRING FACTS AND CIRCUMSTANCES THAT THEY DID NOT THINK OF AT FIRST; WORDS, PHRASES, GE OUR LORD WOULD REAPPEAR IN THE MEMORY OF EACH, AND THUS THE NARRATIVE BECAME VARIED AND with the personal peculiarities of the several writers.

YEARS PASSED, AND THE EXPECTED RETURN OF THE LORD TO EARTH DID NOT TAKE PLACE. THE WERE SPREADING OVER ASIA AND EUROPE, AND THE APOSTLES WERE UNABLE PERSONALLY TO INSTRUC WHO WERE PREACHING THE GOSPEL IN OTHER LANDS. THUS THE NEED OF A WRITTEN RECORD BEGAN ITSELF FELT; AND THE APOSTLES THEMSELVES WROTE OUT THE STORY WHICH THEY HAD BEEN TELLING, WRITTEN FOR THEM BY THEIR COMPANIONS AND FELLOW-HELPERS IN THE GOSPEL. THE ORAL GOSPEL AS IT THEIR MEMORIES WOULD FORM, NO DOUBT, THE SUBSTANCE OF IT, AND THE WRITTEN MEMORANDA DISCOURSES AND INCIDENTS, TO WHICH LUKE REFERS, WOULD BE DRAWN UPON IN COMPLETING THE BIOG THE ORAL GOSPEL THUS CAREFULLY PREPARED AND TRANSMITTED BY MEMORY WOULD BE SUBSTANTI SAME, YET MANY DIFFERENCES IN ARRANGEMENT OF WORDS AND PHRASES WOULD NATURALLY HAVE CREP WRITTEN MEMORANDA WOULD IN MANY CASES BE VERBALLY IDENTICAL. AND EACH EVANGELIST, GLEANIN this wide field, would collect some facts and sayings omitted by the others.

THERE ARE OTHER EXPLANATIONS OF THE ORIGIN OF THE SYNOPTIC GOSPELS, SOME OF WH ingenious and plausible, but I shall not burden your minds with them, since the theory which I have presented appears to me the simplest, the most natural, and the most comprehensive of them all.

THE FOURTH GOSPEL, IT IS EVIDENT, MUST HAVE HAD A DIFFERENT ORIGIN. BEYOND QUESTION CONSECUTIVE NARRATIVE, COMPOSED BY A SINGLE WRITER, AND NOT, LIKE THE SYNOPTICS, A COMPILA MEMORANDA, ORAL OR WRITTEN. IT APPEARS TO BE, IN PART AT LEAST, A SUPPLEMENTARY NARRATIVE, C MUCH THAT IS CONTAINED IN THE OTHER GOSPELS, SUPPLYING SOME OMISSIONS, AND CORRECTING, PC CERTAIN UNIMPORTANT ERRORS. MR. HORTON ILLUSTRATES THE SUPPLEMENTARY WORK OF THIS EVAN SEVERAL INSTANCES. "THE COMMUNION OF THE LORD'S SUPPER," HE SAYS, "WAS SO UNIVERSALLY KNOWN OBSERVED WHEN HE WROTE THAT HE ACTUALLY DOES NOT MENTION ITS INSTITUTION, BUT HE RE WONDERFUL DISCOURSE CONCERNING THE BREAD OF LIFE WHICH IS AN INDISPENSABLE COMMENTARY UNNAMED INSTITUTION, AND BY FILLING IN WITH GREAT DETAIL THE CIRCUMSTANCES OF THE LAST EV FURNISHED A FRAMEWORK FOR THE ORDINANCE WHICH IS AMONG OUR MOST PRECIOUS POSSESSIONS. O OTHER HAND, BECAUSE THE COMMON TRADITION WAS VERY VAGUE IN ITS DATE HE GAVE PRECISION TO THI

WHICH THEY HAD RECORDED BY FIXING THE TIME OF ITS OCCURRENCE.... IN MATT, IV. 12 AND MARK I. TEMPTATION, IMMEDIATELY FOLLOWING CHRIST'S BAPTISM, IS IMMEDIATELY FOLLOWED BY THE STAT 'WHEN HE HEARD THAT JOHN WAS DELIVERED UP, HE WITHDREW INTO GALILEE; AND LEAVING NAZA CAME AND DWELT IN CAPERNAUM.' BUT THIS SUMMARY NARRATIVE HAD EXCLUDED ONE OF THE INTERESTING FEATURES OF THE EARLY MINISTRY OF JESUS. ACCORDINGLY THE FOURTH GOSPEL ENLARGE AND EMPHASIZES THE MARKS OF TIME. AFTER THE BAPTISM, ACCORDING TO THIS AUTHORITY, JESUS 'WEN TO CAPERNAUM, HE AND HIS MOTHER AND HIS BRETHREN AND HIS DISCIPLES, AND THERE THEY ABODE NC DAYS' (II. 12). THEN HE WENT UP TO THE PASSOVER AT JERUSALEM, WHERE HE HAD THE INTERVIEW NICODEMUS. AFTER THAT HE WENT INTO THE COUNTRY DISTRICTS OF JUDEA, WHERE JOHN WAS BAPTI ÆNON, AND THEN THE WRITER ADDS, AS IF HIS EYE WERE ON THE CONDENSED AND MISLEADING NARRATI COMMON TRADITION, 'FOR JOHN WAS NOT YET CAST INTO PRISON.' THE TWO GREAT TEACHERS, THE FOR AND THE GREATER-THAN-HE, WERE ACTUALLY BAPTIZING SIDE BY SIDE, AND IT WAS BECAUSE JESUS S REPUTATION OVERSHADOWING JOHN'S THAT HE VOLUNTARILY WITHDREW INTO GALILEE, PASSING Samaria. So that while there had been two journeys to Galilee before John was imprisoned, and that EARLY PERIOD OF THE LIFE WAS FULL OF UNIQUE AND WONDERFUL INTEREST, ALL HAD BEEN COMPRE CRUSHED INTO THE BRIEF STATEMENT OF MATT. IV. 12 AND MARK I. 14. IN THIS CASE WE SEEM TO EVANGELIST DELIBERATELY LOOSENING AND BREAKING UP THE CURRENT HISTORY IN ORDER THAT HE MI INTO THE CRAMPED AND LIFELESS FRAMEWORK SOME OF THE MOST VALUABLE EPISODES OF THE LORD'S THE FOURTH EVANGELIST HAD TREATED THE TRIPLE NARRATIVE IN THE WAY THAT MANY OF US HAVE REGARDING IT AS A SIN AGAINST THE HOLY SPIRIT TO SUGGEST THAT THERE WAS ANY INCOMPLETENE MISLEADING ABBREVIATIONS IN IT, WE SHOULD HAVE LOST THE WONDERFUL ACCOUNTS OF THE CONVERSAT Nicodemus and with the woman at the well." [Footnote: *Inspiration and the Bible,* pp. 95-99.]

IF SUCH IS THE RELATION OF THE FOURTH GOSPEL TO THE SYNOPTICS, IT FOLLOWS THAT IT MUST F THE WORK OF ONE WHO WAS THOROUGHLY FAMILIAR WITH THE EVENTS RECORDED. THAT THE NARRAT EVIDENCE OF HAVING BEEN WRITTEN BY AN EYEWITNESS IS TO MY OWN MIND CLEAR. THAT THE WRITER I TO CONVEY THE IMPRESSION THAT HE IS THE BELOVED DISCIPLE IS ALSO MANIFEST. EITHER IT WAS WRI JOHN THE APOSTLE, OR ELSE THE WRITER WAS A DELIBERATE DECEIVER. THERE CAN BE NO SUCH EXPLAN HIS PERSONATION OF JOHN AS THAT WHICH SATISFIES OUR MINDS IN THE CASE OF DANIEL AND ECCLESIA book is either the work of John, or it is a cunning and conscienceless fraud. And it seems to me that ANY ONE WHO WILL READ THE BOOK WILL FIND IT IMPOSSIBLE TO BELIEVE THAT IT IS AN IMPOSTURE. IF AN OF THE AGES BEARS IN ITSELF THE WITNESS TO THE TRUTH IT IS THE FOURTH GOSPEL. IT SHINES BY ITS C ANY OF US COULD TELL THE DIFFERENCE BETWEEN THE SUN IN THE HEAVENS AND A BRASS DISK SUSPENDE SKY REFLECTING THE SUN'S RAYS; AND IN MUCH THE SAME WAY THE FACT IS APPARENT THAT THE BOOK counterfeit gospel.

IT IS TRUE THAT HISTORICAL CRITICISM HAS RAISED DIFFICULTIES ABOUT IT; THE BATTLE OF THE BEEN RAGING AROUND IT FOR HALF A CENTURY; BUT ONE AFTER ANOTHER OF THE POSITIONS TAKEN BY STRAUSS AND BAUR HAVE BEEN SHOWN TO BE UNTENABLE; AND IT CAN TRUTHFULLY BE SAID, IN THE W PROFESSOR LADD, "THAT THE VIGOROUS AND DETERMINED ATTACKS UPON THE GENUINENESS OF THI GOSPEL HAVE GREATLY INCREASED INSTEAD OF IMPAIRING OUR CONFIDENCE IN THE TRADITIONA [Footnote: *What is the Bible?* P. 327.] AND I AM READY TO GO FARTHER WITH THE SAME BRAVE BUT REVE SCHOLAR, AND SAY, "HAVING THUS GROUNDED IN HISTORICAL AND CRITICAL RESEARCHES THE GENUINENI FOURTH GOSPEL, WE HAVE NO HESITATION IN AFFIRMING WHAT POSITION IT MUST TAKE IN SACRED SCRIP IS THE HEART OF JESUS CHRIST WITH WHICH WE HERE COME IN CONTACT. INSPIRATION AND REFLECTION UPON THE CHOICEST AND MOST UNDOUBTED MATERIAL OF HISTORY, AND FUSING ALL THE MATERIAL WITH CHARACTERISTICS OF REVELATION, ARE NOWHERE ELSE SO APPARENT AS IN THE GOSPEL OF THE APOSTI [Footnote: *Doctrine of Sacred Scripture*, i. 573]

SUCH, THEN, IS THE FOURFOLD BIOGRAPHY OF JESUS THE CHRIST PRESERVED FOR US IN TH TESTAMENT. IF THIS STUDY HAS REMOVED SOMETHING OF THE MYSTERY WITH WHICH THE ORIGIN O WRITINGS HAS BEEN SHROUDED, IT HAS, I TRUST, AT THE SAME TIME, MADE THEM APPEAR MORE REAL ANI HUMAN; AND IT HAS SHOWN THE PROVIDENTIAL OVERSIGHT BY WHICH THEIR ARTLESS RECORD, MAN MANIFOLD, YET SIMPLE AND CLEAR AS THE DAYLIGHT, HAS BEEN PRESERVED FOR US. OF THESE FOUR GOS ARE CERTAINLY ENTITLED TO SAY AS MUCH AS THIS, THAT WHATEVER VERBAL DISCREPANCIES MAY BE DE them, and however difficult it may be satisfactorily to explain all the phenomena of their s and relations, in one thing they marvelously agree, and that is in the picture which they c the life and character of Jesus Christ. In this each one of them is self-consistent, and th consistent with one another. And this, if we will reflect upon it, is a marvelous, not 1 miraculous fact. That four such men as these Evangelists incontestably were should have suc in giving us four portraitures of the Divine Man, without contradicting themselves, and contradicting one another,--four distinct views of this wonderful Person, which show us i sides of his character, and which we yet instantly recognize as the same person, is a ver wonder. No such task was ever laid on any other human biographer as that which confronte men; no character so difficult to comprehend and describe ever existed; for one man to pres the unities of art in describing him would be notable; for four men to give us, independent narratives, from the simple pages of which the same lineaments shine out, so that no on thinks of saying that the Jesus of Matthew is a different person from the Jesus of Mark or John,--this, I say, is marvelous.

And it is this character, majestic in its simplicity, glorious in its humility, the Id Humanity, the Mystery of Godliness, that these Gospels are meant to show us. If they onl him clearly before us, make his personality real and familiar and vivid before our eyes, so ' may know him and love him, that is all we want of them. Infallibility in details would be wo if this were wanting; any small discrepancies are beneath notice if this is here. And this is her for yourselves. From the page of Matthew, illuminated with the words of prophecy that te Messiah's coming; from the vivid and rapid record of Mark, in which the Wonder-worker d his power; from the tender story of Luke, speaking the word of grace to those that are lowi and farthest off; from the mystical Gospel of the beloved disciple opening to us the deep things that only love can see, the same divine form appears, the same divine face shines, the same divine is speaking. Behold the man!

Chapter X.

New Testament History and Prophecy

The Acts of the Apostles contains the history of the Christian church from the tim ascension of our Lord to the end of the second year of Paul's first imprisonment at Ro period covered by the history is therefore only about thirty years. The principal events rec it are the great Pentecostal Revival, the Martyrdom of Stephen, the first persecution of t and the dispersion of the disciples, the conversion and the missionary work of Paul, wi circumstances of his arrest at Jerusalem, his journey as a prisoner to Rome, and a brief acc his residence in that city. In the first part of the book Peter, the leader of the apostolic b central figure; the last part is occupied with the life and work of Paul.

Who is the writer? Irenæus, about 182, names Luke as the author of the book, and spe though the fact were undisputed. He calls him "a follower and disciple of apostles," and i that "he was inseparable from Paul and was his fellow-helper in the gospel." This is the f distinct reference to the book in any ancient Christian writing. After this, Clement of A Tertullian, Origen, and Eusebius bear the same testimony. But these are late witnesses. The of them testified a hundred years after the death of Luke. The direct testimony to the ex this book in the first two cenuries is not, therefore, altogether satisfactory. The indirect is, however, clear and strong.

That the Acts was written by the author of the Third Gospel is scarcely doubted by any critical scholar. The fact of the identity of authorship is stated with the utmost explicitnes introduction of the Acts. "The former treatise I made, O Theophilus, concerning all tl began both to do and to teach" (Luke i. I, 2). The author of the Acts of the Apostles c intends to say that he is the writer of the Third Gospel. If he is not the author of the Thir he is an artful and shameless deceiver. But the whole atmosphere of the book forbids thi that it is a cunning imposition. And the internal evidence that the two books were writte same author is ample and convincing. The style and the method of the treatment of the tw are unmistakably identical. Every page bears witness to the fact that the author of the Thir and the author of the Acts are one and the same person. Now we know, beyond all reas doubt, that the Gospel of Luke was written certainly as early as the year 80 A. D. And th good reason, as we have seen already, for accepting the ancient and universal tradition of the church that Luke was its author. If Luke wrote the two books, the date of both of them is carried the last part of the first century. But the concluding portion of the Acts of the Apostles seems to fix the date of that book much more precisely. The author, after narrating Paul's journey to R arrival there, and his first unsatisfactory interview with the Jewish leaders, closes his book compendious statement:--

"And he abode two whole years in his own hired dwelling, and received all that went him, preaching the kingdom of God, and teaching all things concerning the Lord Jesus Chr all boldness, none forbidding him."

This is the last word in the New Testament history respecting the Apostle Paul. Nc evident that this writer was Paul's friend and traveling companion. It is true that he keeps out of sight in the history. We only know when he joined Paul by the fact that the narrativ from the third person singular to the first person plural; he ceases to say "he," and begin "we." Thus we are made aware that he joined Paul at Troas on his second missionary journey went with him as far as Philippi; rejoined him at the same place on his third missionary tour accompanied him to Jerusalem; was his fellow-voyager on that memorable journey to Rome there abode with him for two years. The Epistle to the Colossians and the Epistle to Philemon were written during this imprisonment at Rome, and in both of these Epistles Paul speaks of t that Luke is near him. In the second letter to Timothy, which is supposed to have been w during the second imprisonment at Rome, and near the close of his life, he says again, "Onl is with me. Take Mark, and bring him unto me, for he is useful to me for ministering." I common opinion concerning the date of this letter is correct, then Luke must have remain Paul at Rome until the close of his life. But the narrative in Luke does not give any accou closing years of Paul's life. It breaks off abruptly at the end of his two years' residence i Why is this? Evidently because there is no more to tell at this time. The writer continues th up to the date of his writing and stops there. If he had been writing after the death of would certainly have told us of the circumstances of his death. There is no rational expla this abrupt ending, except that the book was written at about the time when the story clo was certainly about 63 A. D. And if the Book of Acts was written as early as this, the Go Luke, the "former treatise" by the same author, must have been written earlier than this. T Book of Acts not only furnishes strong evidence of its own early date, but helps to esta early date of the third Gospel.

These conclusions, to my own mind, are irresistible. No theory which consists wit common honesty of the writer can bring these books down to a later date. And I cannot do honesty of the writer. His writings prove him to be a careful, painstaking, veracious histo many slight matters this accuracy appears. The political structure of the Roman Empire at t was somewhat complicated. The provinces were divided between the Emperor and the Se those heads of provinces who were directly responsible to the Emperor and the military aut were called proprætors; those who were under the jurisdiction of the Senate were called pr In mentioning these officers Luke never makes a mistake; he gets the precise title every tim indeed, the critics thought they had caught him in an error. Sergius Paulus, the Roman

Cyprus, he calls proconsul. "Wrong!" said the critics, "Cyprus was an imperial province; the t this officer must have been proprætor." But when the critics studied a little more, they fc that Augustus put this province back under the Senate, so that Luke's title is exactly right clinch the matter, old coins of this very date have been found in Cyprus, giving to th magistrate of the island the title of proconsul. Such evidences of the accuracy of the writ wanting. It is needless to insist that he never makes a mistake; doubtless he does, in somi matters, and we have learned to take such a view of the inspiration of the Scriptures t discovery of some small error does not trouble us in the least; but the admission that h infallible is perfectly consistent with the belief that he is an honest, competent, faithful wi is all that he claims for himself, this is all that we claim for him, but this we do claim. We believe that he was a conscienceless impostor. We do not believe that the man who told the Ananias and Sapphira was himself a monumental liar. We believe that he meant to tell th and the whole truth, and nothing but the truth. Therefore, we believe that he lived in th the apostles, and received from them, as he says that he did, the facts that he recorde Gospel; that he was the traveling companion and missionary helper of Paul, as he intimates t was, and that he has given us a true account of the life and work of that great apostle.

The constant and undesigned coincidences between the Acts of the Apostles and the of Paul--the many ways in which the personal and historical references of the latter sup statements of the former--are also strong evidence of the genuineness of the Acts. Puttin indirect and incidental proofs together the historical verity of the Acts seems to me vi established. That there are critical difficulties may be admitted; some passages of this writing are not easily explained; there are discrepancies, for example, between the story resurrection and ascension of Christ as told in Luke and the same story as related in t possibly the writer obtained fuller information in the interval between the publication of t books by which he corrected the earlier narrative. In the different accounts of the conv Paul there are also disagreements which we cannot reconcile; nevertheless, in the word Donaldson, "Even these very accounts contain evidence in them that they were written by t writer, and they do not destroy the force of the rest of the evidence." [Footnote: *Encyc. Brit.*, i. 124.]

The theory of Baur that this book was written in the last part of the second centi disciple of St. Paul, and that it is mainly a work of fiction, intended to bring about a recon between two bitterly hostile parties in the church, the Pauline and the Petrine sects, need n us long. Baur contends that the church in the first two centuries was split in twain, the fol Peter insisting that no man could become a Christian without first becoming a Jew, the foll Paul maintaining that the Jewish ritual was abolished, and that the Gentiles ought immediate access to the Christian fellowship. Their antagonism was so radical and far-reachi at the end of the apostolic age the two parties had no dealings with each other. "Then words of Professor Fisher, who is here summarizing the theory of Baur, "followed attem reconcile the difference, and to bridge the gulf that separated Gentile from Jewish, Pau Petrine Christianity. To this end various irenical and compromising books were written in th of the apostles and their helpers. The most important monument of this pacifying effort is the Book of Acts, written in the earlier part of the second century by a Pauline Christian who, by Paul something of a Judaizer, and then representing Peter as agreeing with him in the rec of the rights of the Gentiles, hoped, not in vain, to produce a mutual friendliness betw respective partisans of the rival apostles. The Acts is a fiction founded on facts, and writt specific doctrinal purpose. The narrative of the council or conference of the Apostles, for (Acts xx.), is pronounced a pure invention of the writer, and such a representation of the co of things as is inconsistent with Paul's own statements, and for this and other reasons plai The same ground is taken in respect to the conversion of Cornelius, and the vision o concerning it." [Footnote: *The Supernatural Origin of Christianity,* pp. 211,212.]

For this theory there is, of course, some slight historical basis. It is true, as we have se Peter and Paul did have a sharp disagreement on this very question at Antioch. It is also t both these great apostles behaved quite inconsistently, Peter at Antioch, and Paul afte

Jerusalem, when he consented to the propositions of the Judaizers, and burdened himsel certain Jewish observances in a vain attempt to conciliate some of the weaker brethren. T story of the Acts unflinchingly shows us the weaknesses and errors of the great apostle evidence of its veracity. But the notion that it is a work of fiction fabricated for such pu are outlined above is utterly incredible. Those Epistles of Paul which Baur admits to be (contain abundant disproof of his theory. There never was any such schism as he fancies spends a good part of his time in his last missionary journey in collecting funds for the i those poor "saints," for so he calls them, at Jerusalem; and every reference that he makes t(of the most affectionate character. Paul recognizes in the most emphatic way the authori' other apostles, and the fellowship of labor and suffering by which he is united to them. All much more of the same import we find in those epistles which Baur admits to be the ge writings of Paul. In short, it may be said that after the thorough discussion to which his th been subjected for the last twenty-five years, it has scarcely a sound leg left to stand on. admitted to be one of the most brilliant works of the historical imagination which the ce produced. It is supported by vast learning, and it has thrown much light on certain movemi the early church; but, taken as a whole it is unscientific and contradictory; it raises two di where it disposes of one, and it ignores more facts than it includes.

We return from this excursion through the fields of destructive criticism with / conviction that this narrative of the Acts of the Apostles was written by Luke the Evang companion and fellow-worker of Paul, and that it gives us a veracious history of the earliest the Christian church.

The last of the New Testament books does not belong chronologically at the en collection. There was a tradition, to which Irenæus gives currency, that it was written du reign of Domitian, about 97 or 98 A. D. But this tradition is now almost universally discr Critics of all classes date the book as early as 75-79 A. D., while the best authorities put it ni years earlier, in the autumn of 68 or the spring of 69. As Archdeacon Farrar suggests, it w vastly better if these books of the New Testament were arranged in true chronological o could be more easily understood. The fact that this weird production stands at the en collection has made upon many minds a wrong impression as to its meaning, and has given it / of significance to which it is not entitled.

The authorship of the book is quite generally ascribed to John the son of Zebedee, bro James, and one of the apostles of our Lord. Even the destructive critics agree to this; somi them say that there is less doubt about the date and the authorship of this book than abou any other New Testament writing. In making this concession they intend, however, to discr Johannine authorship of the Fourth Gospel. The more certain we are that John wro Revelation, they argue, the more certain are we that he did not write the Gospel which name; for the style of the two writings is so glaringly contrasted that it is simply imposs both could have come from the same writer. This does not seem nearly so clear to me as it i some of these learned and perspicacious critics. A great contrast there is, indeed, between of the Revelation and that of the Gospel; but this contrast may be explained. It is said, in place, that the Greek of the Apocalypse is very bad Greek, full of ungrammatical se abounding in Hebraisms, while that of the Gospel is good Greek, accurate and rhetoric structure. But this is by no means an unaccountable phenomenon. The first book was written by the apostle very soon, probably, after his removal to Ephesus. He had never, I suppose, i accustomed to use the Greek familiarly in his own country; had never written in it at all, not strange that he should express himself awkwardly when he first began to write Greek; Aramaic idioms should constantly reproduce themselves in his Greek sentences. After he h living for twenty-five years in the cultivated Greek city of Ephesus, using the Greek i continually, it is probable that he would write it more elegantly.

But it is said that the rhetorical style of the one book differs radically from that of Doubtless. The one book is an apocalypse, the other is a biography. John may not have b practiced *litterateur,* but he certainly had literary sense and feeling enough to know how to pu

DIFFERENT COLOR AND ATMOSPHERE INTO AN APOCALYPTICAL WRITING FROM THAT WHICH HE WOULD EM REPORT OF THE LIFE AND WORDS OF JESUS. WITHOUT ANY REFLECTION, INDEED, HE WOULD INSTINCTIVEL APOCALYPTIC IMAGERY; HIS PAGES WOULD FLARE AND RESOUND WITH THE LURID SYMBOLISM PECULIAR APOCALYPSES. HOW DEFINITE A TYPE OF LITERATURE THIS WAS WE SHALL PRESENTLY SEE; NO WRITER, WHI IT, WOULD CLEARLY MANIFEST HIS OWN PERSONALITY. AND IF THROUGH ALL THIS DISGUISE WE DO SYMPTOMS OF A TEMPER MORE FERVID AND A SPIRIT MORE JUDAIC THAN THAT WHICH FINDS EXPRESSION I FOURTH GOSPEL, LET US REMEMBER THAT THE RIPENED WISDOM OF THE OLD MAN SPEAKS IN THE LATT THE INTENSE ENTHUSIASM OF CONSCIOUS STRENGTH IN THE FORMER. THIS JOHN, LET US NOT FORGET, W HIS YOUTH A PARAGON OF MILDNESS; IT WAS HE AND HIS BROTHER JAMES WHO EARNED THE SOBRIQU BOANERGES, "SONS OF THUNDER;" IT WAS THEY WHO WANTED TO CALL DOWN FIRE FROM HEAVEN TO CONS INHOSPITABLE SAMARITAN VILLAGE. MOREOVER, WE SHALL SEE AS WE GO ON THAT THE TIMES IN WHI APOCALYPSE WAS WRITTEN WERE TIMES IN WHICH THE MILDEST, MANNERED MEN WOULD BE APT TO FORGE DECORUM, AND SPEAK WITH UNWONTED INTENSITY. A MAN WITH ANY BLOOD IN HIM, WHO UNDERTO WRITE IN THE YEAR 68 OF THE THEMES WITH WHICH THE SOUL OF THIS APOSTLE WAS THEN ON FIRE, W LIKELY TO SHOW, NO MATTER IN WHAT VEHICLE OF SPEECH HIS THOUGHT MIGHT BE CONVEYED, SOME SIGI tumult then raging within him.

ALL THESE CIRCUMSTANCES, TAKEN TOGETHER, ENABLE ME TO EXPLAIN THE DIFFERENCE BETW LITERARY FORM OF THE REVELATION AND THAT OF THE GOSPEL. BUT WHEN WE COME TO LOOK A LI DEEPLY INTO THE MEANING OF THE TWO BOOKS, WE SHALL FIND THAT BENEATH ALL THIS DISSIMILARITY SOME REMARKABLE POINTS OF AGREEMENT. QUITE A NUMBER OF THE LEADING IDEAS AND CONCEPTIONS ONE BOOK REAPPEAR IN THE OTHER; THE IDEA OF CHRIST AS *Word* OR *Logos* OF GOD, THE REPRESENTATIO OF CHRIST AS THE LAMB, AS THE GOOD SHEPHERD, AS THE LIGHT, ARE PECULIAR TO JOHN; WE FINI EMPHASIZED IN THE GOSPEL AND IN THE REVELATION. THE UNITY OF THE TWO BOOKS IN FUNDAM CONCEPTIONS HAS BEEN ADMIRABLY BROUGHT OUT BY DR. SEARS, IN HIS VOLUME ENTITLED "THE HI CHRIST." AND AFTER WEIGHING THE EVIDENCE, I FIND NEITHER HISTORICAL NOR PSYCHOLOGICAL SUFFICIENT TO OVERTHROW MY BELIEF THAT THE FOURTH GOSPEL, AS WELL AS THE REVELATION, WAS W John the Apostle.

THE GREEK NAME OF THE BOOK MEANS AN UNCOVERING OR UNVEILING, AND IS FAIRLY INTERI THEREFORE, BY OUR WORD REVELATION. IT BELONGS TO A CLASS OF BOOKS WHICH WERE PRODUCED NUMBERS DURING THE TWO CENTURIES PRECEDING THE BIRTH OF CHRIST AND THE TWO CENTURIES FO AND NO ONE CAN UNDERSTAND IT OR INTERPRET IT WHO DOES NOT KNOW SOMETHING OF THIS SPI LITERATURE, OF THE FORMS OF EXPRESSION PECULIAR TO IT, AND OF THE PURPOSES WHICH IT WAS INTE serve.

WE HAVE IN THE OLD TESTAMENT ONE APOCALYPTIC BOOK, THAT OF DANIEL, AND THE apocalyptical elements in two or three of the prophecies. The fact that the Book of Daniel bears this CHARACTER IS A STRONG ARGUMENT FOR THE LATENESS OF ITS ORIGIN; FOR IT WAS IN THE LAST YEARS OF NATIONALITY THAT THIS KIND OF WRITING BECAME POPULAR. WE HAVE SIX OR SEVEN BOOKS OF THIS KIND ARE WRITTEN MAINLY FROM THE STANDPOINT OF THE OLD DISPENSATION, PART OF WHICH APPEARED JUST AND PART SHORTLY AFTER THE BEGINNING OF OUR ERA; AND THERE ARE NEARLY A DOZEN VOLUMES OF APOCALYPSES, ALL OF WHICH EMPLOY SIMILAR FORMS OF EXPRESSION, AND ARE DIRECTED TOWARDS SIMILA DOUBTLESS THESE ARE ONLY A FEW OF THE GREAT NUMBER OF APOCALYPTICAL BOOKS WHICH THO produced. Their characteristics are well set forth by Dr. Davidson:--

"THIS BRANCH OF LATER JEWISH LITERATURE TOOK ITS RISE AFTER THE OLDER PROPHECY HAD CEAS ISRAEL SUFFERED SORELY FROM SYRIAN AND ROMAN OPPRESSION. ITS OBJECT WAS TO ENCOURAGE AND C THE PEOPLE BY HOLDING FORTH THE SPEEDY RESTORATION OF THE DAVIDIC KINGDOM OF MESSIAH. AT ITSELF TO THE NATIONAL HOPE, IT PROCLAIMED THE IMPENDING OF A GLORIOUS FUTURE, IN WHICH ISR FROM HER ENEMIES SHOULD ENJOY A PEACEFUL AND PROSPEROUS LIFE UNDER HER LONG-WISHED-FOR DE THE OLD PROPHETS BECAME THE VEHICLE OF THESE UTTERANCES. REVELATIONS, SKETCHING THE HISTORY AND OF HEATHENISM, ARE PUT INTO THEIR MOUTHS. THE PROPHECIES TAKE THE FORM OF SYMBOLICAL AND MARVELOUS VISIONS.... WORKING IN THIS FASHION UPON THE BASIS OF WELL-KNOWN WRITINGS, IMIT THEIR STYLE, AND ARTIFICIALLY REPRODUCING THEIR SUBSTANCE, THE AUTHORS NATURALLY AD ANONYMOUS. THE DIFFICULTY WAS INCREASED BY THEIR HAVING TO PAINT AS FUTURE, EVENTS ACTUALLY N

TO FIT THE MANIFESTATION OF A PERSONAL MESSIAH INTO THE HISTORY OF THE TIMES. MANY APOC EMPLOYED OBSCURE SYMBOLS AND MYSTERIOUS PICTURES, VEILING THE MEANING THAT IT MIGHT NOT BE seen. [Footnote: *Encyc. Brit.*, i. 174.]

"EVERY TIME," SAYS DR. HARNACK, "THE POLITICAL SITUATION CULMINATED IN A CRISIS FOR THE PE GOD, THE APOCALYPSES APPEARED STIRRING UP THE BELIEVERS; IN SPIRIT, FORM, PLAN, AND EXECUTIO CLOSELY RESEMBLED EACH OTHER.... THEY ALL SPOKE IN RIDDLES; THAT IS, BY MEANS OF IMAGES, SY MYSTIC NUMBERS, FORMS OF ANIMALS, ETC., THEY HALF CONCEALED WHAT THEY MEANT TO REVEAL. THE FOR THIS PROCEDURE ARE NOT FAR TO SEEK: (1.) CLEARNESS AND DISTINCTNESS WOULD HAVE BEEN TOO ONLY THE MYSTERIOUS APPEARS DIVINE. (2.) IT WAS OFTEN DANGEROUS TO BE TOO DISTINCT." [Footnote: *Encyc. Brit.*, xx. 496.]

THAT THESE WRITINGS APPEARED IN TROUBLOUS TIMES, AND THAT THEY DEALT WITH AFFAIRS OF TH AND OF THE IMMEDIATE FUTURE, MUST ALWAYS BE BORNE IN MIND. CERTAIN SYMBOLICAL CONCEPTIO COMMON TO THEM; EARTHQUAKES DENOTE REVOLUTIONS; STARS FALLING FROM HEAVEN TYPIFY THE DO kings and dynasties; a beast is often the emblem of a tyrant; the turning of the sun into darkness and THE MOON INTO BLOOD SIGNIFY CARNAGE AND DESTRUCTION UPON THE EARTH. WE HAVE THESE SYMBO SEVERAL OF THE OLD TESTAMENT WRITINGS AS WELL AS IN MANY OF THE APOCALYPTICAL BOOKS WHICH IN OUR CANON; AND THE INTERPRETATION OF SUCH PASSAGES IS NOT AT ALL DIFFICULT WHEN WE UNDERS usage of the writers.

OF THESE APOCALYPTIC BOOKS ONE OF THE MOST REMARKABLE IS THE BOOK OF ENOCH, WHICH A TO HAVE BEEN WRITTEN A CENTURY OR TWO BEFORE CHRIST. IT PURPORTS TO BE A REVELATION MADE THROUGH THE PATRIARCH ENOCH; IT CONTAINS AN ACCOUNT OF THE FALL OF THE ANGELS, AND OF A R GIANTS THAT SPRUNG FROM THE UNION OF THESE EXILED CELESTIALS WITH THE DAUGHTERS OF MEN ENOCH ON A TOUR OF OBSERVATION THROUGH HEAVEN AND EARTH UNDER THE GUIDANCE OF ANGE EXPLAIN TO HIM MANY THINGS SUPERNAL AND MUNDANE; IT DEALS IN ASTRONOMICAL AND METEORO MYSTERIES OF VARIOUS SORTS, AND IN A SERIES OF SYMBOLICAL VISIONS SEEKS TO DISCLOSE THE EVENTS FUTURE. IT IS A GROTESQUE PRODUCTION; ONE DOES NOT FIND MUCH SPIRITUAL NUTRIMENT IN IT, BU makes a quotation from it, in his epistle, as if he considered it Holy Scripture.

"THE FOURTH BOOK OF ESDRAS" IS ANOTHER JEWISH BOOK OF THE SAME KIND, WHICH MAY HAVE WRITTEN ABOUT THE HUNDREDTH YEAR OF OUR ERA. IT PURPORTS TO BE THE WORK OF EZRA, WHOM IT M CHRONOLOGICALLY, PUTTING HIM IN THE THIRTIETH YEAR OF THE CAPTIVITY. THE PROBLEM OF THE WR restoration of the nation, destroyed and scattered by the Roman power. He makes the ancient scribe AND LAW-GIVER OF ISRAEL HIS MOUTHPIECE, BUT HE IS DEALING WITH THE EVENTS OF HIS OWN NEVERTHELESS, HIS ALLUSIONS ARE VEILED AND OBSCURE; HE SPEAKS IN RIDDLES, YET HE SPEAKS TO A WHO UNDERSTAND HIS RIDDLES, AND KNOW HOW TO TAKE HIS SYMBOLIC VISIONS. THIS BOOK IS IN OUR EN Apocrypha, under the title 2 Esdras.

"THE BOOK OF JUBILEES," WHICH ASSUMES TO BE A REVELATION MADE TO MOSES ON MOUNT S "THE ASCENSION OF MOSES," "THE APOCALYPSE OF MOSES," AND THE "APOCALYPSE OF BARUCH," ARE similar books of the Jewish literature.

Of apocalyptical Christian writings, I may mention "The Sibylline Books," "The Apocalypse of PAUL," "THE APOCALYPSE OF PETER," "THE REVELATION OF BARTHOLOMEW," AND "THE ASCENSI ISAIAH," AND THERE IS ALSO ANOTHER "APOCALYPSE OF JOHN," A FEEBLE IMITATION OF THE ONE WITH OUR CANON CLOSES. THESE BOOKS APPEARED IN THE SECOND, THIRD, AND FOURTH CENTURIES OF OUR E GENERALLY LOOK FORWARD TO THE SECOND COMING OF CHRIST, AND SET FORTH IN VARIOUS FIGURES AND THE CONFLICTS AND PERSECUTIONS WHICH HIS SAINTS MUST ENCOUNTER, THE DESTRUCTION OF HIS FOES establishment of his kingdom.

IT WILL BE SEEN, THEREFORE, THAT THE REVELATION OF ST. JOHN IS NOT UNIQUE; AND THE INFER NOT BE RASH THAT MUCH LIGHT MAY BE THROWN UPON ITS DARK SAYINGS BY A CAREFUL STUDY OF K books.

IT MAY BE ANSWERED THAT THE WRITER OF THIS BOOK IS INSPIRED, AND THAT NOTHING CAN BE LEA THE MEANING OF AN INSPIRED BOOK BY STUDYING UNINSPIRED BOOKS. I REPLY THAT NO INSPIRED BOOK C UNDERSTOOD AT ALL WITHOUT A CAREFUL STUDY OF UNINSPIRED BOOKS. THE GREEK GRAMMAR AND TH LEXICON ARE UNINSPIRED BOOKS, AND NO MAN CAN UNDERSTAND A SINGLE ONE OF THE BOOKS OF TH

Testament without carefully studying both of them, or else availing himself of the labor one else who has diligently studied them. An inspired writer uses language,--the same langu uninspired writers use; the meaning of language is fixed not by inspiration, but by usage; you study the grammar and the lexicon to learn about the usage. And the case is precisely simil an inspired writer uses a peculiar form of literature like the apocalyptical writings. He kno he uses symbolisms of this class that they will be interpreted according to the common us expects and desires that they shall be so understood; and, therefore, in order to underst we must know what the usage is.

When our Lord, speaking of the calamities which were about to fall upon the Jewish r said, "Immediately after the tribulation of those days, the sun shall be darkened, and the mo not give her light, and the stars shall fall from heaven, and the powers of the heavens shaken," he was speaking to people who were perfectly familiar with language of this sort, i the same expressions occur over and over again in their prophets, and are there distinctly i to mean great political overturnings. He used the apocalyptic phraseology, and he expected give it the apocalyptic signification. If we wish to understand the Scripture, we must underst language of Scripture, and this means not only the grammatical forms, but also the symboli of the language.

We have seen that the apocalypses are apt to appear in times of great calamity, and w accepted the verdict of later scholarship, that this Apocalypse of St. John appeared about A.D. Was this a time of trouble in that Eastern world? Verily it was; the most appallin perhaps in the world's history. The unspeakable Nero was either still upon the throne of the Roman Empire, or had just reeled from that eminence to the doom of a craven suicide. The last year life were gorged with horror. The murder of his brother, the burning of Rome, probably connivance, if not by his command, in order that he might sate his appetite for sensations upo horrid spectacle; following this the fiendish scheme to charge this incendiarism upon the Christians, and slaughter them by tens of thousands in all the cities of the Empire,--these are only ins a career which words are too feeble to portray. Those who succeeded him in this supreme were not much less ferocious; the very name of pity seemed to have been blotted from the speech; the whole Empire reeked with cruelty and perfidy. While such men ruled at Rome it not be supposed that the imperial representatives in the provinces would be temperate an Some of them, at any rate, had learned the lesson of the hour, and were as perfidious, as th as base as their master could have wished. Such a one was that Gessius Floras who was procurator of Judea, and who seemed to have exhausted the ingenuity of a malignant na stirring up the Jews to insurrection. By every species of indignity and cruelty he finally s long-suffering people into a perfect fury, and the rebellion which broke out in Palestine in 66 was one of the most fearful eruptions of human nature that the world has ever seen. Flo raised the demon; now the legions of Rome must be called in to exorcise it. It was a t struggle. All the energies of Jewish fanaticisms were enlisted; the Zealots, the fiercest par them, not content with slaughtering their Roman enemies, turned their hands against ever their own nation who ventured to question the wisdom of their desperate resistance. In Je itself a reign of terror raged which makes the French Revolution seem in comparison a ca orderly procedure.

At the beginning of the outbreak Nero had sent one of his trusted generals, Vespas Vespasian's son Titus, to put down the insurrection. Neither of these soldiers was a sentime both believed as heartily as did Wentworth in later years that the word of the hour was T They started with their armies from Antioch in March, 67, resolved on sweeping Palestine v besom of destruction. Cities and villages, one by one, were besieged, captured, destroyed women, and children were indiscriminately massacred. The Jewish army fought every inch ground like tigers; but they were overpowered and beaten in detail, and steadily forced sc Blackened walls, pools of blood, and putrefying corpses were all that the Romans left in t ruthlessly they drove the doomed people before them toward their stronghold of Jerusale autumn of that year Vespasian withdrew his army into winter-quarters, and left the Ze

Jerusalem to their orgy of brigandage and butchery. He could well afford to rest and let them do his deadly work.

In the spring of the following year, the siege of Jerusalem began. The Christians of the city had fled to Pella, east of the Jordan; the remnant of the Jews held their sacred heights with t of despair.

It is at this very juncture that this book of the Revelation was written. John testifies t written on Patmos, a desolate islet of the Ægean Sea, west of Asia Minor, to which he ha been banished by some tool of Nero, or else had betaken himself for solitude and reflec him, in this retreat, the awful tidings had come of the scourge that had fallen on the l fathers; added to this, the conflagration at Rome, the Neronian persecution, all the horr past decade were fresh in his memory. May we not say that the time was ripe for an apoca message?

It is in these events, then, that we must find the explanation of much of this sym language. Such is the law of the apocalypse, and this apocalypse may be expected to conform law. St. John is instructed by the angel to write "the things which thou sawest, and the thin are, and the things which shall come to pass hereafter,"--"the things which must *shortly* come to pass," the first verse more explicitly states. It is the past which he has seen, the present, immediate future with which his visions are concerned. It is not any attempt to outline th course of human history; it is the picture, in mystic symbols, of the present crisis and deliverance which is to follow it. There is no room here for a commentary on the Apocalyps only indicate, in a rapid glance, the outline of the book.

The first three chapters are occupied with the epistles to the seven churches which are administering reproof, exhortation, comfort, and counsel to the Christians in these ch faithful, stirring, persuasive appeals, whose meaning can be easily understood, and whose t often sorely needed by the churches of our own time.

Then begins the proper Apocalypse, with the first vision of the throne in heaven, and thereon the Lamb that was slain, who is also the Lion of the tribe of Judah. The book seal seven seals is given to him to open, and the opening of each seal discloses a new vision. Th seal opened shows a white horse bearing a rider who carries a bow and wears a crown, and goes forth conquering and to conquer. This is the emblem of the Messiah whose conquest world is represented as beginning. But the Messiah once said, "I came not to bring peace, sword," and the consequences of his coming must often be strife and sorrow because malignity of men. And therefore the three seals which are opened next disclose a fiery h symbol of War, a black horse, whose rider is Famine, a pale horse in whose saddle is Death opening of the fifth seal shows the martyred multitude before the throne of God. T discloses the desolation and the ruin taking place upon the earth. Thus the mighty panoram constantly before our eyes; the confusion, the devastation, the woes, the scourges of through which Messiah's Kingdom is advancing to its triumph. The seals, the trumpets, th bring before us representations of the retributions and calamities which are falling upon m Sometimes we seem to be able to fix upon a historical event which the vision clearly symb sometimes the meaning to us is vague; perhaps if we had lived in that day the allusion woul been more intelligible.

There is, however, one great central group of these visions round about which the oth to be arrayed as scenic accessories, whose interpretation the writer has taken great pains to These are the visions found in chapters xii., xiii., xvi., and xvii. The woman, sun-clad, with the moon under her feet and a crown of twelve stars upon her head (chap, xii.), is beyond all quest ancient Jewish church; the child which is born to the woman is the Christian church; the g dragon that seeks to devour the child is the Satanic power, the Prince of this world. The D here on the earth because he has been expelled from heaven. The war of the Dragon agai woman indicates the persecutions of the church; the flight of the woman to the wilder symbolize the recent escape of the mother church from Jerusalem to Pella.

The next vision shows a Beast, coming up out of the sea, with seven heads and ten horn on his horns ten diadems, and on his heads names of blasphemy. Here we have an instance o confounding of symbols, the merging of one in another, which is very common in the apoc writings. The beast is, primarily, Nero, or the Roman Empire, as represented by--Nero. Th horns are the ten chief provinces; the seven heads are seven emperors. "It is a symbol," sa Farrar, "interchangeably of the Roman Empire and of the Emperor. In fact, to a greater degree than at any period of history, the two were one. Roman history had dwindled down into a pe drama. The Roman Emperor could say with literal truth, '*L'Etat c'est moi'*. And a wild beast was a Jew's natural symbol either for a Pagan Kingdom or for its autocrat." [Footnote: *The Early Days of Christianity*, p. 463.] I can do no better than to repeat to you a small part of Dr. Farrar's i comment upon this vision.

"This wild beast of Heathen Rome has ten horns, which represent the ten main provin Imperial Rome. It has the power of the Dragon, that is, it possesses the Satanic dominion 'Prince of the power of the air.'

"On each of its heads is the name of blasphemy. Every one of the seven Kings, hov counted, had borne the (to Jewish ears) blasphemous surname of Augustus (Sebastos, one adored); had received apotheosis, and been spoken of as *Divine* after his death; had been crown with statues, adorned with divine attributes, had been saluted with divine titles, and, instances, had been absolutely worshiped, and that in his lifetime....

"The diadems are on the horns, because the Roman *Proconsuls*, as delegates of the Emperc enjoy no little share of the Cæsarean autocracy and splendor, but the name of blasphemy is the heads, because the Emperor alone receives divine honors and alone bears the daring Augustus." [Footnote: *Ibid*., p. 464.]

One of the heads of this Beast was wounded to death, but the deadly wound was hea was the universal belief among Pagans and Christians that the world had not yet seen th Nero. Either his suicide was feigned and ineffectual, and he was in hiding, or else he would c life and resume his savage splendors and his gilded villainies. To make it certain that the wri refers to this expectation, we find, in chapter xvii., another reference to the Beast, which first a riddle, but which is easily interpreted. "The five are fallen, the one is, the other i come"; "The Beast that thou sawest was and is not, and is about to come out of the abyss.' Beast that was and is not, even he is an eighth, and is of the seven." The head and the Beast identified. The meaning is that five Roman Emperors are dead, Augustus, Tiberius, Cal Claudius, Nero; "one is,"--Galba is now reigning; "the other" (Otho) "is not yet come;" but hi come soon for Galba is an old man and cannot long survive, and "the Beast that was and is Nero,--who is "about to come out of the abyss,"--to return to life,--"even he is an eighth, a the seven." He is one of the seven, for he was the fifth, and he will be the eighth. It universal Christian belief that Nero, raised from the dead, would be the future Antichrist this belief which the vision reflects. To make the case still clearer the writer gives us, by th Hebrew Kabbalistic method, the number of the Beast, that is to say, the numerical value name. Each letter of the old alphabets has a numerical value. Thus the writer of the S points out the Greek name of Jesus--ΙΗΣΟΥΣ,--by saying that its whole number is equivalent to units, eight tens, and eight hundreds. This is the exact numerical value of the six Greei composing the Saviour's name, 10+8+200+70+400+200=888. Precisely so John here tells us v is the numerical value of the letters in the name of the Beast. If we tried the Latin or t names of Nero the clue would not be found; but John was writing mainly for Hebrews, a Hebrew letters of *Kesar Neron*, the name by which every Jew knew this Emperor, amount to exac 666.

Many other of the features of this veiled description tally perfectly with the charac infamous ruler; and when the evidence is all brought together it seems as though the apos scarcely have made his meaning more obvious if he had written Nero's name in capital letters.

This is the central vision of the Apocalypse, as I have said; round about this the cyclorama revolves; and it has been the standing enigma of the interpreters in all the ages. church generally divined its meaning; but in later years the high-soaring exegesis which ha

THIS APOCALYPSE ALL OVER THE CENTURIES AND FOUND IN IT PROPHETIC SYMBOLS OF ALMOST ALL TH THAT HAVE HAPPENED IN MEDIÆVAL AND MODERN HISTORY, HAS IDENTIFIED THE BEAST WITH COU CHARACTERS, AMONG THEM GENSERIC, KING OF THE VANDALS, BENEDICT, TRAJAN, PAUL V., CALVIN, I MOHAMMED, NAPOLEON. ALL THIS WILD GUESSING ARISES FROM IGNORANCE OF THE ESSENTIAL CHARAC purpose of the apocalyptical writings.

I CAN FOLLOW THIS ENTICING THEME NO FURTHER. LET IT SUFFICE TO CALL THE ATTENTION OF ALL TO REACH SOME SOBER CONCLUSIONS UPON THE MEANING OF THE BOOK TO ARCHDEACON FARRAR'S DAYS OF CHRISTIANITY," IN WHICH THE WHOLE SUBJECT IS TREATED WITH THE AMPLEST LEARNING soundest literary judgment.

THE BOOK OF REVELATION HAS BEEN, AS I HAVE INTIMATED, THE FAVORITE TRAMPING GROUND OF HOSTS OF THEOLOGICAL VISIONARIES; MEN WHO POSSESSED NOT THE SLIGHTEST KNOWLEDGE OF THE H THE NATURE OF APOCALYPTIC LITERATURE, AND WHOSE APPETITE FOR THE MYSTERIOUS AND THE MONST INSATIABLE, HAVE EXPATIATED HERE WITH BOUNDLESS LICENSE. TO FIND IN THESE VISIONS DESCRIPTI EVENTS NOW PASSING AND CHARACTERS NOW UPON THE STAGE IS A SORE TEMPTATION. TO USE THESE WORDS, THE BEAST, THE DRAGON, THE FALSE PROPHET, AS MISSILES WHEREWITH TO ASSAIL THOSE WHO TO A SCHOOL OR A PARTY WITH WHICH YOU ARE AT VARIANCE, IS A CHANCE THAT NO PROPERLY CON PARTISAN COULD WILLINGLY FORE-GO. THUS WE HAVE SEEN THIS BOOK DRAGGED INTO THE CONTROVER APPLIED TO THE EVENTS OF ALL THE CENTURIES, AND THE HISTORY OF ITS INTERPRETATION IS, AS C INTERPRETERS CONFESSES, THE OPPROBRIUM OF EXEGESIS. BUT IF ONE CEASES TO LOOK AMONG THESE S FOR A PREDICTIVE OUTLINE OF MODERN HISTORY, "A SORT OF ANTICIPATED GIBBON," AND BEGINS TO RE THE LIGHT OF THE APOCALYPTIC METHOD, IT MAY HAVE RICH AND LARGE MEANINGS FOR HIM. HE WILL ABLE, INDEED, TO EXPLAIN IT ALL; TO SOME OF THESE RIDDLES THE CLUE HAS BEEN LOST; BUT, IN THE DR. FARRAR, "HE WILL FIND THAT THE APOCALYPSE IS WHAT IT PROFESSES TO BE,--AN INSPIRED OUT CONTEMPORARY HISTORY, AND OF THE EVENTS TO WHICH THE SIXTH DECADE OF THE FIRST CENT IMMEDIATE RISE. HE WILL READ IN IT THE TREMENDOUS MANIFESTO OF A CHRISTIAN SEER AGAINST THE STAINED TRIUMPH OF IMPERIAL HEATHENISM; A PÆAN AND A PROPHECY OVER THE ASHES OF THE MARTY THUNDERING REVERBERATIONS OF A MIGHTY SPIRIT STRUCK BY THE FIERCE PLECTRUM OF THE N PERSECUTION, AND ANSWERING IN IMPASSIONED MUSIC WHICH, LIKE MANY OF DAVID'S PSALMS, DIES AV into the language of rapturous hope." [Footnote: *Early Days of Christianity*, p. 429.]

FOR WE MUST NOT FORGET THAT THIS IS A SONG OF TRIUMPH. THIS SEER IS NO PESSIMIST. THE ST HOT, THE CARNAGE IS FEARFUL, THEY THAT RISE UP AGAINST OUR LORD AND HIS MESSIAH ARE MANY AND BUT THERE IS NO MISGIVING AS TO THE EVENT. FOR ALL THESE WOES THERE IS SOLACE, AFTER ALL THESE PEACE. EVEN IN THE MIDST OF THE RAGING WARS AND PERSECUTIONS, THE DOOR IS OPENED NOW AND INTO THE UPPER REALM OF ENDLESS JOY AND UNFADING LIGHT. AND HE "WHOSE NAME IS CALLED THE W GOD," UPON WHOSE GARMENT AND WHOSE THIGH THE NAME IS WRITTEN, "KING OF KINGS AND LO LORDS," WILL PREVAIL AT LAST OVER ALL HIS FOES. THE BEAST AND THE DRAGON, AND THE FALSE PRO THE SCARLET WOMAN (THE HARLOT CITY UPON HER SEVEN HILLS WHOSE MYSTIC NAME IS BABYLON) WI CAST INTO THE LAKE OF FIRE; THEN TO THE PURIFIED EARTH THE NEW JERUSALEM SHALL COME DOW HEAVEN FROM GOD. THIS IS THE EMBLEM AND THE PROPHECY, NOT OF THE CITY BEYOND THE STARS, BUT PURIFIED SOCIETY WHICH SHALL YET EXIST UPON THE EARTH,--THE FRUITION OF HIS WORK WHO CAME JUDGE THE WORLD, BUT TO SAVE THE WORLD. IT IS ON THESE PLAINS, ALONG THESE RIVERS, BY THESE FA THAT THE NEW JERUSALEM IS TO STAND; IT IS NOT HEAVEN; IT IS A CITY THAT COMES DOWN OUT OF HEAV GOD. NO STATEMENT COULD BE MORE EXPLICIT. THE GLORIOUS VISIONS WHICH FILL THE LAST CHAPTER WONDERFUL BOOK ARE THE PROMISE OF THAT "ALL HAIL HEREAFTER," FOR WHICH EVERY CHRISTIAN EVERY LOVER OF MANKIND, IS ALWAYS LOOKING AND LONGING AND FIGHTING AND WAITING. AND HE WHO MOUTH OF THIS SEER, TESTIFIETH THE WORDS OF THE PROPHECY OF THIS BOOK SAITH, "YEA, I COME (Even so, come, Lord Jesus."

CHAPTER XI.

THE CANON

WE HAVE STUDIED WITH WHAT CARE WE WERE ABLE TEE HISTORICAL PROBLEM OF THE ORIG AUTHORSHIP OF THE SEVERAL BOOKS OF THE OLD AND NEW TESTAMENT; WE NOW COME TO A I interesting question,--the question of the canon.

THIS WORD, AS USED IN THIS CONNECTION, MEANS SIMPLY AN AUTHORITATIVE LIST OR CATALOGU CANON OF THE BIBLE IS THE DETERMINED AND OFFICIAL TABLE OF CONTENTS. THE SETTLEMENT OF TH THE PROCESS OF DETERMINING WHAT AND HOW MANY BOOKS THE BIBLE SHALL CONTAIN. IN TH Testament are thirty-nine books, in the New Testament twenty-seven; and it is a fixed principle with PROTESTANTS THAT THESE BOOKS AND NO OTHERS CONSTITUTE THE SACRED SCRIPTURES,--THAT NO MC added and none taken away.

THE POPULAR BELIEF RESPECTING THIS MATTER HAS BEEN LARGELY FOUNDED UPON THE WORDS WIT the Book of Revelation concludes:--

"FOR I TESTIFY UNTO EVERY MAN THAT HEARETH THE WORDS OF THE PROPHECY OF THIS BOOK, IF SHALL ADD UNTO THEM, GOD SHALL ADD UNTO HIM THE PLAGUES WHICH ARE WRITTEN IN THIS BOOK: AN MAN SHALL TAKE AWAY FROM THE WORDS OF THE BOOK OF THIS PROPHECY, GOD SHALL TAKE AWAY H from the tree of life, and out of the holy city, which are written in this book."

THE COMMON NOTION IS THAT THE "BOOK" HERE REFERRED TO IS THE BIBLE; AND THAT THESE SE THEREFORE, ARE THE DIVINE AUTHORIZATION OF THE PRESENT CONTENTS OF THE BIBLE, A SOLEMN FROM THE LORD HIMSELF TO THE INTEGRITY OF THE CANON. BUT THIS IS A MISAPPREHENSION. TH REFERRED TO IS THE REVELATION OF ST. JOHN,--NOT THE BIBLE, NOT EVEN THE NEW TESTAMENT. WH WORDS WERE WRITTEN, SAYS DR. BARNES IN HIS "COMMENTARY," "THE BOOKS THAT NOW CONSTITUTE W CALL THE BIBLE WERE NOT COLLECTED INTO A SINGLE VOLUME. THAT PASSAGE, THEREFORE, SHOUL ADDUCED AS REFERRING TO THE WHOLE OF THE SACRED SCRIPTURES." IN FACT, WHEN THESE WORD REVELATION WERE WRITTEN, SEVERAL OF THE BOOKS OF THE NEW TESTAMENT WERE NOT YET IN EXIST THIS IS BY NO MEANS THE LAST OF THE NEW TESTAMENT WRITINGS, THOUGH IT STANDS AT THE EN COLLECTION. THE GOSPEL AND THE EPISTLES OF JOHN WERE ADDED AFTER THIS; AND WE MAY TRUST plagues were "added" to the beloved disciple for writing them.

NEVERTHELESS, AS I SAID, IT IS ASSUMED THAT THE CONTENTS OF THE BIBLE ARE FIXED; THAT THE C IS AND FOR A LONG TIME HAS BEEN COMPLETE AND PERFECT; THAT IT ADMITS NEITHER OF SUBTRACTION ADDITIONS; THAT NOTHING IS IN THE BOOK WHICH OUGHT NOT TO BE THERE, AND THAT THERE IS NOTHI OF ITS COVERS WHICH OUGHT TO BE WITHIN THEM; THAT THE CANON IS SETTLED, INFLEXIBLY AND INFA finally.

THE QUESTIONS NOW TO BE CONSIDERED ARE THESE: WHO SETTLED IT? WHEN WAS IT SETTLED? C GROUNDS WAS IT DETERMINED? WAS ANY QUESTION EVER RAISED CONCERNING THE SACREDNESS OR AUTH ANY OF THE BOOKS NOW INCLUDED IN THE CANON? DID ANY OTHER BOOKS, NOT NOW INCLUDED IN THE ever claim a place in it? If so, why were these rejected and those retained?

THIS IS, AS WILL BE SEEN, A SIMPLE QUESTION OF HISTORY. WE CAN TRACE WITH TOLERABLE CERTA STEPS BY WHICH THIS COLLECTION OF SACRED WRITINGS WAS MADE; WE KNOW PRETTY WELL WHO DID WHEN AND HOW IT WAS DONE. AND THERE IS NOTHING PROFANE OR IRREVERENT IN THIS INQUIRY, FOR T OF COLLECTING THESE WRITINGS AND FIXING THIS CANON HAS BEEN DONE MAINLY, IF NOT WHOLLY, BY WERE NOT INSPIRED AND DID NOT CLAIM TO BE. THERE IS NOTHING MYSTERIOUS OR MIRACULOUS ABOU DOINGS ANY MORE THAN THERE IS ABOUT THE ACTS OF THE FRAMERS OF THE WESTMINSTER CONFESSIO AMERICAN CONSTITUTION. THEY WERE DEALING WITH SACRED MATTERS, NO DOUBT, WHEN THEY WERE T DETERMINE WHAT BOOKS SHOULD BE RECEIVED AND USED AS SCRIPTURES, BUT THEY WERE DEALING WIT in exactly the same way that we do, by using the best lights they had.

AS WE HAVE LEARNED IN PREVIOUS CHAPTERS, THE BEGINNING OF OUR CANON WAS MADE BY EZR scribe, who, in the fifth century before Christ, newly published and consecrated the Penta Five Books of Moses, as the Holy Book of the Jewish people.

After Ezra came Nehemiah, to whom the beginning of the second collection of Scriptures, called the Prophets, is ascribed in one of the apocryphal books. But this collec not apparently finished and closed by Nehemiah. The histories of Joshua and Judges, of Samu Kings, and the principal books of the Prophets were undoubtedly gathered by him; but it seem that the collection was left open for future prophecies.

About the same time the third group of the Old Testament Scriptures, "The Hagiograp "Writings," began to be collected. No book of the Bible contains any information concer making of these two later collections, the Prophets and the Hagiographa; and we are oblig wholly upon Jewish tradition, and upon references which we find in Jewish writers. Pro Westcott, who is one of the most conservative of Biblical scholars, says that "the cc evidence of tradition and of the general course of Jewish history leads to the conclusio canon in its present shape was formed gradually during a lengthened interval, beginning w and extending through a part, or even the whole of the Persian period," circa B.C. 458 to 332. Without adopting this conclusion, we may remark that this last date, 332, was nearly a cent Nehemiah and Malachi, the last of the prophets; so that if the canon was closed at a date s this, it must have been closed by men who were certainly not known to have been inspired. If forming, through all this period, then it must have been formed in part by men in behalf of no claim of inspiration has ever been set up.

According to Jewish tradition the work of collecting, editing, and authorizing th writings was done by a certain "Great Synagogue," founded by Ezra, presided over by Nehi after him, and continuing in existence down to about the year B.C. 200. This is wholly a traditio and has been proved to be baseless. There never was such a synagogue; the Scriptures know nothing about it; the apocryphal writers, so numerous and widely dispersed, have never heard of it and Josephus are ignorant concerning it. None of the Jewish authors of the period wh discuss the Scriptures and their authority makes mention of this Great Synagogue. The sto existence is first heard from some Jewish rabbin hundreds of years after Christ.

We have proof enough in the New Testament that the Jews had certain Sacred Scriptu New Testament writers often quote them and refer to them; but there is no conclusive pr they had been gathered at this time into a complete collection. Jesus tells the Jews that t the Scriptures, but he does not say how many of these Scriptures there were in his day reminds Timothy that from a child he had known the Holy Scriptures, but he gives no list titles. If we found all the books of the Old Testament quoted or referred to by the New writers, then we should know that they possessed the same books that we have. Most of thes are thus referred to; but there are seven Old Testament books whose names the New Te never quotes, and at least five to which it makes no reference whatever: Ecclesiastes, Solomon, Esther, Ezra, and Nehemiah. To Judges, Chronicles, and Ezekiel it refers only same way that it refers to a number of the apocryphal books. Some of these omissions appear significant. The New Testament gives us therefore no definite information by which determine whether the Old Testament canon was closed at the time of Christ, nor does it what books it was composed.

We have seen already that two different collections of Old Testament writings existence, one in Hebrew, and the other a translation into the Greek, made by Jews in Ale and called the Septuagint. The latter collection was the one most used by our Lord and the much the greater number of quotations from the Old Testament found in the Gospels Epistles are taken from the Septuagint. This Greek Bible contained quite a number of book are not in the Hebrew Bible: they were later in their origin than any of the Old Testame most of them were originally written in Greek; and while they were regarded by some of t conservative of the Jews in Egypt as inferior to the Law and the Prophets, they were g ranked with the books of the Hagiographa as sacred writings. This is evident from the fact t were mingled indiscriminately with these books of the older Scriptures. You know tha

speaking now of the apocryphal books which you find in some of your old Bibles, between th
and New Testaments. These were the later books contained in the Septuagint, and not
Hebrew Bible. But they were not sorted out by themselves in the Septuagint; they were inte
through the other books, as of equal value. Thus in the Vatican Bible, of which we shall lea
by and by, Esdras First and Second succeed the Chronicles; Tobit and Judith are be
Nehemiah and Esther; the Wisdom of Solomon and Sirach follow Solomon's Song; Baruch i
to Jeremiah; Daniel is followed by Susanna and Bel and the Dragon, and the collection cl
the three books of Maccabees.

All the old manuscripts of the Bible which we possess--those which are regarded as ab
others sacred and authoritative--contain these apocryphal writings thus intermingled with the books
of our own canon. It is clear, therefore, that to the Alexandrian Jews these later books we
Scriptures; and it is certain also that our Lord and his apostles used the collection which c
these books. It is said that they do not refer to them, and it is true that they do not men
by name; but they do use them occasionally. Let me read you a few passages which will illu
their familiarity with the apocryphal books.

James i.19: "Let every man be swift to hear, slow to speak." Sirach v. 11; iv. 29: "Be swif
hear." "Be not hasty in thy tongue."

Hebrews i. 3: "Who being the effulgence of his glory, and the very image of his substan
upholding all things by the word of his power." Wisdom vii. 26: "For she (Wisdom) is
brightness of the everlasting light, the unspotted mirror of the power of God, and the im
goodness."

Rom. ix. 21: "Hath not the potter a right over the clay, from the same lump to make one
vessel unto honor, and another unto dishonor?" Wisdom xv. 7: "For the potter, temperi
earth, fashioneth every vessel with much labor for our service; yea, of the same clay he make
the vessels that serve for clean uses, and likewise also such as serve to the contrary: but wh
use of either sort, the potter himself is the judge."

I Cor. ii. 10, 11: "The Spirit searcheth all things, yea, the deep things of God. For who
men knoweth the things of a man, save the spirit of the man, which is in him? even so the thi
God none knoweth save the Spirit of God." Judith viii. 14: "For ye cannot find the depth
heart of man, neither can ye perceive the things that he thinketh: then how can ye search
that hath made all these things, and know his mind, or comprehend his purpose?"

Several similar indications of the familiarity of the New Testament writers with
apocryphal books might be pointed out. These are not express citations, but they are
appropriations of the thought and the language of the apocryphal writers. We have, then,
indubitable proof that the apocryphal books were in the hands of the New Testament writ
so far as New Testament use authenticates an Old Testament writing, several of the apo
books stand on much better footing than do five of our Old Testament books.

It is true that the Hebrew or Palestinian canon differed from the Greek or Alexandri
the books which were written in Greek had never been translated into the Hebrew, and co
of course, be incorporated into the Hebrew canon; and there was undoubtedly a strong
among the stricter Jews against recognizing any of these later books as Sacred Sc
nevertheless, the Greek Bible, with all its additions, had large currency among the Jews
Palestine, and the assertion that our Lord and his apostles measured the Alexandrian Bib
Palestinian canon, and accepted all the books of the latter while declining to recognize
additions of the former, is sheer assumption, for which there is not a particle of eviden
against which the facts already adduced bear convincingly. Paul, in his letter to Timothy,
the "Scriptures" as having been in the hands of Timothy from his childhood; and we have
reason to believe that the Scriptures to which he refers was this Greek collection conta
Apocrypha. Whatever Paul says about the inspiration of the Scriptures must be interprete
this fact in mind. To find in these words of Paul the guarantee of the inspiration and infall
the books of the collection which are translated from the Hebrew, and not those which a
in Greek, is a freak of exegesis not more violent than fantastic. We know that Paul read

SOME OF THESE APOCRYPHAL BOOKS, AND THERE ARE SEVERAL OF THE BOOKS IN OUR HEBREW BIBLE NEVER QUOTES OR REFERS TO IN THE REMOTEST WAY. THE ATTEMPT WHICH IS OFTEN MADE TO SHOW NEW TESTAMENT WRITERS HAVE ESTABLISHED, BY THEIR TESTIMONY, THE OLD TESTAMENT CAN CONTAINING JUST THOSE BOOKS WHICH ARE IN OUR OLD TESTAMENT, AND NO MORE, IS A MOST UNWARR distortion of the facts.

IT IS TRUE THAT AT THE TIME OF CHRIST THE PALESTINIAN JEWS HAD NOT, FOR A CENTURY OR SO, NEW BOOKS TO THEIR COLLECTION, AND WERE NOT INCLINED TO ADD ANY MORE. THEIR CANON WAS PR CLOSED TO THIS EXTENT, THAT NO NEW BOOKS WERE LIKELY TO GET IN. BUT IT WAS NOT YET SETTLED LATER BOOKS, WHICH HAD BEEN TRYING TO MAINTAIN A FOOTING IN THE CANON, SHOULD NOT BE ESTHER, ECCLESIASTES, AND SOLOMON'S SONG WERE REGARDED BY SOME OF THE PALESTINIAN JEWS AS BOOKS, BUT THEIR RIGHT TO THIS DISTINCTION WAS HOTLY DISPUTED BY OTHERS. THIS QUESTION WAS NO at the time of our Lord.

"THE CANON," SAYS DAVIDSON, "WAS NOT CONSIDERED TO BE CLOSED IN THE FIRST CENTURY BEFO THE FIRST AFTER CHRIST. THERE WERE DOUBTS ABOUT SOME PORTIONS. THE BOOK OF EZEKIEL GAVE BECAUSE SOME OF ITS STATEMENTS SEEMED TO CONTRADICT THE LAW. DOUBTS ABOUT SOME OF THE WERE OF A MORE SERIOUS NATURE--ABOUT ECCLESIASTES, THE CANTICLES, ESTHER, AND THE PROVERBS. WAS IMPUGNED BECAUSE IT HAD CONTRADICTORY PASSAGES AND A HERETICAL TENDENCY; THE SECOND BEC ITS WORLDLY AND SENSUAL TONE; ESTHER FOR ITS WANT OF RELIGIOUSNESS; AND PROVERBS ON ACC INCONSISTENCIES. THIS SKEPTICISM WENT FAR TO PROCURE THE EXCLUSION OF THE SUSPECTED WORKS FR CANON AND THEIR RELEGATION TO THE CLASS OF *genuzim*. BUT IT DID NOT PREVAIL. HANANIAH, SON Hezekiah, son of Garon, about 32 B.C.., IS SAID TO HAVE RECONCILED THE CONTRADICTIONS AND ALLAYI DOUBTS. BUT THESE TRACES OF RESISTANCE TO THE FIXITY OF THE CANON WERE NOT THE LAST. THEY R ABOUT 65 A. D., AS WE LEARN FROM THE TALMUD, WHEN THE CONTROVERSY TURNED MAINLY UPC CANONICITY OF ECCLESIASTES, WHICH THE SCHOOL OF SCHAMMAI, WHICH HAD THE MAJORITY, OPPOSED; THAT BOOK WAS PROBABLY EXCLUDED. THE QUESTION EMERGED AGAIN AT A LATER SYNOD IN JABNEH OR WHEN R. ELEASER BEN ASARIA WAS CHOSEN PATRIARCH, AND GAMALIEL THE SECOND, DEPOSED. HERE DECIDED, NOT UNANIMOUSLY, HOWEVER, BUT BY A MAJORITY OF HILLELITES, THAT ECCLESIASTES AND T OF SONGS 'POLLUTE THE HANDS,' *i.e.*, BELONG PROPERLY TO THE HAGIOGRAPHA. THIS WAS ABOUT 90 A. THUS THE QUESTION OF THE CANONICITY OF CERTAIN BOOKS WAS DISCUSSED BY TWO SYNODS." [Foc *Encyc. Brit.*, v. 3.]

BY SUCH A PLAIN TALE DO WE PUT DOWN THE FICTION, SO WIDELY DISSEMINATED, THAT THE CANON OLD TESTAMENT WAS "FIXED" LONG BEFORE THE TIME OF CHRIST, AND, PRESUMABLY, BY INSPIRED MEN. NOT "FIXED," EVEN IN PALESTINE, UNTIL SIXTY YEARS AFTER OUR LORD'S DEATH; SEVERAL OF THE BOOK DISPUTE DURING THE WHOLE APOSTOLIC PERIOD, AND THESE ARE THE VERY BOOKS WHICH ARE NOT REFER THE NEW TESTAMENT. WHETHER THE MEN WHO FINALLY "FIXED" IT WERE EXCEPTIONALLY QUALIFIED TO THE ETHICAL AND SPIRITUAL VALUES OF THE WRITINGS IN QUESTION MAY BE DOUBTED. THEY WERE THE MEN WHO SLEW OUR LORD AND PERSECUTED HIS FOLLOWERS. WHEN WE ARE ASKED WHAT ARE OUR HIS REASONS FOR BELIEVING THAT ESTHER AND ECCLESIASTES AND SOLOMON'S SONG ARE SACRED BOOKS AN TO BE IN THE OLD TESTAMENT CANON, LET US ANSWER: IT IS NOT BECAUSE ANY PROPHET OR INSPIRED ADJUDGED THEM TO BE SACRED, FOR NO SUCH PERSON HAD ANYTHING TO SAY ABOUT THEM; IT IS NOT OUR LORD AND HIS APOSTLES INDORSED THEM, FOR THEY DO NOT EVEN MENTION THEM; IT IS NOT BECA HELD A PLACE IN A COLLECTION OF SACRED SCRIPTURES USED BY OUR LORD AND HIS APOSTLES, FO POSITION IN THAT COLLECTION WAS IN DISPUTE AT THAT TIME; IT IS BECAUSE THE CHIEF PRIESTS AND SCRI REJECTED CHRIST PRONOUNCED THEM SACRED. THE EXTERNAL AUTHORITY FOR THESE BOOKS REDUCES THIS. THOSE WHO INSIST THAT ALL PARTS OF THE OLD TESTAMENT ARE OF EQUAL VALUE AND AUTHORITY A QUESTIONING OF THE SACREDNESS OF ONE BOOK CASTS DOUBTS UPON THE WHOLE COLLECTION, OUGH THESE FACTS IN THE FACE AND SEE ON WHAT A SLENDER THREAD THEY SUSPEND THE BIBLE WHICH THEY VALUE. THESE LATER BOOKS, SAYS ONE, "HAVE BEEN DELIVERED TO US; THEY HAVE THEIR USE AND VALUE, IS TO BE ASCERTAINED BY A FRANK AND REVERENT STUDY OF THE TEXTS THEMSELVES; BUT THOSE WHO PLACING THEM ON THE SAME FOOTING OF UNDISPUTED AUTHORITY WITH THE LAW, THE PROPHETS, PSALMS, TO WHICH OUR LORD BEARS DIRECT TESTIMONY, AND SO MAKE THE WHOLE DOCTRINE OF TH DEPEND ON ITS WEAKEST PART, SACRIFICE THE TRUE STRENGTH OF THE EVIDENCE ON WHICH THE OLD T is received by Christians." [Footnote: *The Old Testament in the Jewish Church*, p. 175.]

SUCH, THEN, IS THE STATEMENT WITH RESPECT TO THE OLD TESTAMENT CANON IN THE APOSTOLIC PALESTINIAN CANON, WHICH WAS IDENTICAL WITH OUR OLD TESTAMENT, WAS PRACTICALLY SETTLED AT T OF JAMNIA ABOUT 90 A. D., THOUGH DOUBTS WERE STILL ENTERTAINED BY DEVOUT JEWS CONCERNING THE ALEXANDRIAN COLLECTION, CONTAINING OUR APOCRYPHAL BOOKS, WAS, HOWEVER, WIDELY CIRCULA AS IT WAS THE GREEK VERSION WHICH HAD BEEN MOST USED BY THE APOSTLES, SO IT WAS THE GREEK V WHICH THE EARLY CHRISTIAN FATHERS UNIVERSALLY STUDIED AND QUOTED. VERY FEW IF ANY OF THESE FATHERS OF THE FIRST TWO CENTURIES UNDERSTOOD THE HEBREW; THEY COULD NOT, THEREFORI PALESTINIAN MANUSCRIPTS; THE GREEK BIBLE WAS THEIR ONLY TREASURY OF INSPIRED TRUTH, AND TH BIBLE CONTAINED THE APOCRYPHA. ACCORDINGLY WE FIND THEM QUOTING FREELY AS SACRED SCRIPTUR APOCRYPHAL BOOKS. WESTCOTT GIVES US A TABLE, IN SMITH'S "BIBLE DICTIONARY," OF CITATIONS MAD THESE APOCRYPHAL BOOKS BY FIFTEEN OF THE GREEK FATHERS, BEGINNING WITH CLEMENT OF RO ENDING WITH CHRYSOSTOM, AND BY EIGHT LATIN WRITERS, BEGINNING WITH TERTULLIAN AND ENDI AUGUSTINE. EVERY ONE OF THESE APOCRYPHAL BOOKS IS THUS QUOTED WITH SOME SUCH FORMULA AS SCRIPTURE SAITH," OR "IT IS WRITTEN," BY ONE OR MORE OF THESE WRITERS; THE BOOK OF WISDOM IS BY ALL OF THEM EXCEPT POLYCARP AND CYRIL; BARUCH AND THE ADDITIONS TO DANIEL ARE QUOTE GREAT MAJORITY OF THEM; ORIGEN QUOTES THEM ALL, CLEMENT OF ALEXANDRIA ALL BUT ONE, CYPRIA TWO. IT WILL THEREFORE BE SEEN THAT THESE BOOKS MUST HAVE HAD WIDE ACCEPTANCE AS SACRED SC DURING THE FIRST CENTURIES OF THE CHRISTIAN CHURCH. IN THE FACE OF THESE FACTS, WHICH MAY BE SOURCES AS UNASSAILABLE AS SMITH'S "BIBLE DICTIONARY," WE HAVE SUCH STATEMENTS AS THE FOLLOWI forth by teachers of the people, and indorsed by eminent theological professors:--

"WE MAY SAY OF THE APOCRYPHAL BOOKS OF THE OLD TESTAMENT THAT, WHILE SOME WHO WEF JEWS AND WHO WERE UNACQUAINTED WITH HEBREW USED THEM TO SOME EXTENT, YET THEY NEVER wide acceptance, and soon dropped out altogether."

"CERTAIN APOCRYPHAL WRITINGS HAVE SINCE BEEN BOUND UP WITH THE SEPTUAGINT, BUT *there is no reason to think that they made any part of it in the days of our Saviour*"!

"THESE BOOKS WERE NOT RECEIVED AS CANONICAL BY THE CHRISTIAN FATHERS, BUT WERE EX declared to be apocryphal"!

THE LAST STATEMENTS ARE COPIED FROM A VOLUME ON THE BIBLE, PREPARED FOR POPULAR CIRCU by the president of a theological seminary!

IT IS TRUE THAT SOME OF THE MOST INQUISITIVE AND CRITICAL OF THE CHRISTIAN FATHERS EN DOUBTS ABOUT THESE APOCRYPHAL BOOKS; MELITO OF SARDIS TRAVELED TO PALESTINE ON PURPOSE TO INTO THE MATTER, AND CAME BACK, OF COURSE, WITH THE PALESTINIAN CANON TO WHICH, HOWEVER, HE ADHERE. ORIGEN MADE A SIMILAR INVESTIGATION, AND SEEMS TO HAVE BEEN CONVINCED THAT THE LATI OUGHT TO BE REGARDED AS UNCANONICAL; NEVERTHELESS, HE KEEPS ON QUOTING THEM; JEROME WAS STRENUOUSLY TO CHALLENGE THE CANONICITY OF THESE LATER GREEK BOOKS AND TO MAINTAIN A CONSISTENT OPPOSITION TO THEM. WHILE, THEREFORE, SEVERAL OF THESE EARLY FATHERS WERE LED INVESTIGATIONS IN PALESTINE TO BELIEVE THAT THE NARROWER CANON WAS THE MORE CORRECT C OPINIONS HAD BUT LITTLE WEIGHT WITH THE PEOPLE AT LARGE; AND EVEN THESE FATHERS THEMSELVES F constantly quoted as Sacred Scripture the questionable writings.

IN 393 THE AFRICAN BISHOPS HELD A COUNCIL AT HIPPO, IN WHICH THE CANON WAS DISCUSSED. TH AGREED UPON INCLUDES ALL THE OLD TESTAMENT SCRIPTURES OF OUR CANON, AND, IN ADDITION T WISDOM, ECCLESIASTICUS, TOBIT, JUDITH, AND THE TWO BOOKS OF MACCABEES. IN 397 ANOTHER COU Carthage reaffirmed the list of its predecessor. Augustine was the leader of both councils.

IN SPITE OF THE PROTESTS OF JEROME AND OF OTHER SCHOLARS IN ALL THE CENTURIES, THIS SUBSTANCE, WAS REGARDED AS AUTHORITATIVE, UNTIL THE COUNCIL OF TRENT, IN 1546, WHEN THE LON WAS FINALLY SETTLED, SO FAR AS THE ROMAN CATHOLIC CHURCH IS CONCERNED, BY THE ADOPTIO AUGUSTINIAN CANON, EMBRACING THE APOCRYPHAL BOOKS, THE LIST CONCLUDING WITH THE FO ANATHEMA. "IF ANY ONE WILL NOT RECEIVE AS SACRED AND AUTHORITATIVE THE WHOLE BOOKS WITH PARTS, LET HIM BE ACCURSED." THIS DETERMINES THE MATTER FOR ALL GOOD CATHOLICS. SINCE 1546, TI KNOWN EXACTLY HOW MANY BOOKS THEIR BIBLE CONTAINS. AND IF USAGE AND TRADITION ARE AND OUG AUTHORITATIVE, THEY HAVE THE STRONGEST REASONS FOR RECEIVING AS SACRED THE BOOKS OF THEIR B is beyond question that the books which they accept and which we reject have been receiv used as Sacred Scriptures in all the ages of the church. Most of us who do not accept us tradition as authoritative will continue, no doubt, to think our own thoughts about the matter.

The Council of Trent marks the definite separation of the Roman Catholic Church fi Protestant reformers. Up to this time there had been among the reformers some differ opinion respecting the Old Testament books; when they were excluded from the Holy Chu were compelled to fall back upon the authority of the Bible, the present limits of the cano became an important question. They did not settle it all at once. Luther, in making his version of the Bible, translated Judith, Wisdom, Tobit, Sirach, Baruch, 1 and 2 Maccabe Greek additions to Esther and Daniel, with the Prayer of Manasseh. Each of these bo prefaces with comments of his own. First Maccabees he regards as almost equal to the othe of Holy Scripture, and not unworthy to be reckoned among them. He had doubted long Wisdom should not be admitted to the canon, and he truly says of Sirach that it is a rig book, the work of a wise man. Baruch and 2 Maccabees he finds fault with; but of none of apocryphal books does he speak so severely as of Esther, which he is more than willing to c of the canon. The fact that Luther translated these apocryphal books is good evidenc thought them of value to the church; nevertheless, he considered the books of the Hebre with the exception of Esther, as occupying a higher plane than those of the Apocrypha. G this opinion gained acceptance among the Protestants; the apocryphal books were separat the rest, and although by some of the Reformed churches, as by the Anglican church, t commended to be read "for example of life and instruction of manners," they ceased to be r as authoritative sources of Christian doctrine. Since the sixteenth century, there has b question among Protestants as to the extent of the canon. The books which now compose c Testament, and no others, have been found in the Bible of the Protestants for the pa hundred years. The apocryphal books have sometimes been printed between the Old and th Testaments, but they have not been used in the churches, [Footnote: The English Church uses some portions of them.] nor have they been regarded as part of the Sacred Scripture.

The history of the New Testament canon is much less obscure, and may be more b treated. The Bible of the early Christians was the Old Testament. They relied wholly upo religious instruction; they had no thought of any other Sacred Scripture.

I have explained in a former chapter how the Epistles and the Gospels originated; bu these writings first came into the hands of the disciples there was not, it is probable, any co in their minds that these were sacred writings, to be ranked along with the books of Testament. They read them for instruction and suggestion; they did not at first think o holy. But their conviction of the value and sacredness of these writings soon began to st we find them quoting Gospels and Epistles with the same formula that they apply to t Testament books; and thus they began to feel the need of making a collection of this literature for use in the churches. It is not until the second half of the second century th collection comes into view. It consisted at first of two parts, The Gospel and The Apostle; part contained the four Gospels, and the second the Acts, thirteen Epistles of Paul, one one of John, and the Revelation. It will be seen that this twofold Testament omitted seve books,--the Epistle to the Hebrews, two of John's Epistles, one of Peter's, and the Epistles o and Jude.

About this time there was also in circulation certain writings which are not now in ou but which were sometimes included by the authorities of that time among the apostolic w and were quoted as Scripture by the early fathers. There was a book called "The Gospel ac to the Egyptians," and another entitled "The Preaching of Peter," and another called "T Paul," and another called "The Shepherd of Hermas," and an epistle attributed to Barna several others, all claiming to be sacred and apostolic writings. It became, therefore, a de important question for these early Christians to decide which of these writings were sac which were not; and they began to make lists of those which they regarded as canonical. Th of these lists is a fragmentary anonymous canon, which was made about 170. It mentions books in our New Testament but four,--Hebrews, First and Second Peter, and James.

Irenæus, who died about 200, had a canon which included all the books of our Testament except Hebrews, Jude, James, Second Peter, and Third John. First Peter, Second and "The Shepherd of Hermas" he put by themselves in a second class of writings, whic thought excellent but not inspired.

Clement of Alexandria (180) puts into his list most of our canonical books, but regards of them as of inferior value, among them Hebrews, Second John, and Jude. In the same l inferior writings he includes "The Shepherd of Hermas," the "Epistle of Barnabas," an "Apocalypse of Peter."

Tertullian (200) omits entirely James, Second Peter, and Third John, but includes useful though not inspired books, Hebrews, Jude, "The Shepherd of Hermas," Second John Second Peter.

These are the greatest authorities of the first two centuries. No Christian teachers o were better informed or more trustworthy than these, and it will be seen that they were agreeing with one another or with our canon; that each one of them received as sacred som which we do not possess, and rejected some which we receive.

Coming down into the third century, we find Origen (250), one of the great scholars, wrestling with the problem. He seems to have made three classes of the New Testament writing authentic, the non-authentic, and the doubtful. The authentic books are the Gospels, the thirteen Epistles of Paul, and the Apocalypse; the non-authentic ones are "The Sheph Hermas," "The Epistle of Barnabas," and several other books not in our canon; and the do ones are James, Jude, Second and Third John, and Second Peter. It will be seen that Origen none that are not in our collection, but that he is in doubt respecting some that are in it.

Facts like these are writ large over every page of the history of the early church. An have eminent theological professors asserting that the canon of the New Testament wa settled "during the first half of the second century, within fifty years after the death of John." A more baseless statement could not be fabricated. It is from teachers of this class hear the most vehement outcries against the "Higher Criticism."

Eusebius, who died in 340, has a list agreeing substantially with that of Origen.

Cyril of Jerusalem (386) includes all of our books except the Apocalypse, and no others.

Athanasius (365) and Augustine (430) have lists identical with ours. This indicates a s progress toward unanimity, and when the two great councils of Hippo and Carthage confirm judgment of the two great fathers last named, the question of the New Testament ca practically settled. [Footnote: It is noted, however, that the reception of the doubtful boo canon does not imply a recognition of their equality with the other books. The distinct a of their inferiority was made by all the ecclesiastical authorities of that period. None of fathers believed that all these writings were equally inspired and equally autho Nevertheless, considerable independent judgment on the subject still seems to have been to and writings which we do not now receive were long included in the New Testament col The three oldest manuscripts of the Bible now in existence are the Sinaitic, the Vatican, Alexandrian Bibles, dating from the fourth and the fifth centuries. Of these the Sinaiti Alexandrian Bibles both include some of these doubtful books in the New Testament col the Sinai Bible has "The Epistle of Barnabas" and "The Shepherd of Hermas;" the Alexan Bible the Epistle of Clement and one of Athanasius. These old Bibles are clear witnesses to that the contents of the New Testament were not clearly defined even so late as the fif Indeed, there was always some freedom of opinion concerning this matter until the Refor era. Then, of course, the Council of Trent fixed the canon of the New Testament as well Old for all good Catholics; and the New Testament of the Catholics, unlike their Old Tes identical with our own.

The Protestants of that time were still in doubt about certain of the New Testamen Luther, as every one knows, was inclined to reject the Epistle of James; he called it "a righ epistle." The letter to the Hebrews was a good book, but not apostolic; he put it in a subo

CLASS. JUDE WAS A POOR TRANSCRIPT OF SECOND PETER, AND HE ASSIGNED THAT ALSO TO A LOWER PLA APOCALYPSE," SAYS DAVIDSON, "HE CONSIDERED NEITHER APOSTOLIC NOR PROPHETIC, BUT PUT IT ALMOS LEVEL WITH THE FOURTH BOOK OF ESDRAS, WHICH HE SPOKE ELSEWHERE OF TOSSING INTO THE ELBE." PRINCIPLE OF JUDGMENT IN MANY OF THESE CASES WAS QUITE TOO SUBJECTIVE; HE CARRIED THE PRO PRINCIPLE OF PRIVATE JUDGMENT TO AN EXTREME; I ONLY QUOTE HIS OPINIONS TO SHOW WITH WHAT FR the strong men of the Reformation handled these questions of Biblical criticism.

ZWINGLI REJECTED THE APOCALYPSE. ŒCOLAMPADIUS PLACED JAMES, JUDE, SECOND PETER, SE AND THIRD JOHN AND THE APOCALYPSE ALONG WITH THE APOCRYPHAL BOOKS, ON A LOWER LEVEL T other New Testament Scriptures.

THE GREAT MAJORITY OF THE REFORMERS, HOWEVER, SPEEDILY FIXED UPON THAT CANON WHICH V receive, and their decision has not been seriously called in question since the sixteenth century.

I HAVE NOW ANSWERED MOST OF THE QUESTIONS PROPOSED AT THE BEGINNING OF THIS CHAPTE HAVE SEEN THAT WHILE THE GREAT MAJORITY OF THE BOOKS IN BOTH TESTAMENTS HAVE BEEN UNI RECEIVED, QUESTIONS HAVE BEEN RAISED AT VARIOUS TIMES CONCERNING THE CANONICITY OF SEVERAI BOOKS IN EITHER TESTAMENT; THAT MANY GOOD MEN, FROM THE SECOND CENTURY BEFORE CHRIST U SIXTEENTH CENTURY AFTER CHRIST, HAVE DISPUTED THE AUTHORITY OF SOME OF THESE BOOKS. WE H ALSO THAT QUITE A NUMBER OF OTHER BOOKS HAVE AT ONE TIME AND ANOTHER BEEN REGARDED AS SA NUMBERED AMONG THE HOLY SCRIPTURES; WE HAVE SEEN THAT THE FINAL JUDGMENT RESPECTIN DOUBTFUL BOOKS IS DIFFERENT IN DIFFERENT BRANCHES OF THE CHURCH, THE ROMAN CATHOLIC CH THE GREEK CATHOLIC CHURCH ADMITTING INTO THEIR CANONS SEVERAL BOOKS THAT THE REFORMED exclude from theirs.

WE HAVE SEEN THAT THE DECISION WHICH HAS BEEN REACHED BY THE SEVERAL BRANCHES OF THE RESPECTING THIS MATTER HAS BEEN REACHED AS THE RESULT OF DISCUSSION AND ARGUMENT; THAT THE C OF THE DISPUTED BOOKS WAS FREELY CANVASSED BY THE CHURCH FATHERS IN THEIR WRITINGS, BY THE COUNCILS IN THEIR ASSEMBLIES, BY THE REFORMERS IN THEIR INQUIRIES; THAT NO SUPERNATURAL METHO BEEN EMPLOYED TO DETERMINE THE CANONICITY OF THESE SEVERAL BOOKS; BUT THAT THE ENLIGHTEN of the church has been the arbiter of the whole matter.

THE GROUNDS UPON WHICH THE JEWS ACTED IN ADMITTING OR REJECTING BOOKS INTO THEIR SCR IT MIGHT BE DIFFICULT FOR US TO DETERMINE. IN SOME CASES WE KNOW THAT THEY WERE FANCIFUL AND But the grounds on which the Christians proceeded in making up their canon we know pretty well.

THE FIRST QUESTION RESPECTING EACH ONE OF THE CHRISTIAN WRITINGS SEEMS TO HAVE BEEN: ' WRITTEN BY AN APOSTLE?" IF THIS QUESTION COULD BE ANSWERED IN THE AFFIRMATIVE, THE BO ADMITTED. AND IN DECIDING THIS QUESTION, THE CHRISTIANS OF LATER TIMES MADE APPEAL TO THE (OF THOSE OF EARLIER TIMES; AUTHORITY AND TRADITION HAD MUCH TO DO IN DETERMINING IT. "W GENERAL OPINION OF THE EARLY CHURCH THAT THIS BOOK WAS WRITTEN BY AN APOSTLE?" THEY ASKE THIS SEEMED TO BE THE CASE, THEY WERE INCLINED TO ADMIT IT. BESIDES, THEY COMPARED SCRIPTU SCRIPTURE: CERTAIN BOOKS WERE UNQUESTIONABLY WRITTEN BY PAUL OR LUKE OR JOHN; OTHER BOOK WERE DOUBTED WERE ALSO ASCRIBED TO THEM; IF THEY FOUND THE LANGUAGE OF THE DISPUTE CORRESPONDING TO THAT OF THE UNDISPUTED BOOK, IN STYLE AND IN FORMS OF EXPRESSION, THEY JUD IT MUST HAVE BEEN WRITTEN BY THE SAME MAN. UPON SUCH GROUNDS OF EXTERNAL AND INTERNAL EVID FINALLY CAME TO BE BELIEVED THAT ALL OF THE NEW TESTAMENT BOOKS EXCEPT FOUR WERE WR APOSTLES, AND THAT THESE FOUR, MARK, LUKE, THE ACTS OF THE APOSTLES, AND THE EPISTLE TO THE were written by men under the immediate direction of apostles.

BUT, IT MAY BE SAID, THERE HAVE BEEN GREAT DIFFERENCES OF OPINION ON THIS MATTER THROUG AGES, DOWN TO THE SIXTEENTH CENTURY; HOW DO WE KNOW BUT THAT THOSE GOOD AND HOLY M IGNATIUS AND CLEMENT AND TERTULLIAN AND ORIGEN IN THE EARLY CHURCH, AND LUTHER AND ZW ŒCOLAMPADIUS IN THE REFORMED CHURCH, WERE RIGHT IN REJECTING SOME BOOKS THAT WE RECEIVE receiving some that we reject?

IF YOU WERE A GOOD CATHOLIC, THAT QUESTION WOULD NOT TROUBLE YOU. FOR THE FUNDAMENT OF YOUR CREED WOULD THEN BE, THE HOLY CATHOLIC CHURCH, WHEN SHE IS REPRESENTED BY HER BIS A GENERAL COUNCIL, CAN NEVER MAKE A MISTAKE. AND THE HOLY CATHOLIC CHURCH IN A GENERAL C TRENT, IN 1546, SAID THAT SUCH AND SUCH BOOKS BELONGED TO THE BIBLE, AND THAT NO OTHERS DO;

COUNCIL OF THE VATICAN, IN 1870, SAID THE SAME THING OVER AGAIN, MAKING IT DOUBLY SURE; SO, TH good Catholic, you would have no right to any doubts or questions about it.

BUT, BEING A PROTESTANT, YOU CANNOT HELP KNOWING THAT ALL GENERAL COUNCILS HAVE MA AND TERRIBLE MISTAKES; THAT NO ONE OF THEM EVER WAS INFALLIBLE; AND SO YOU COULD NOT REST WITH THE DECISIONS OF TRENT AND THE VATICAN, EVEN IF THEY GAVE YOU THE SAME BIBLE THAT Y POSSESS, WHICH, OF COURSE, THEY DO NOT. WHAT CERTAINTY HAS THE PROTESTANT, THEN, THAT HIS CA CORRECT ONE? HE HAS NO ABSOLUTE CERTAINTY. THERE IS NO SUCH THING AS ABSOLUTE CERTAINTY WI TO HISTORICAL RELIGIOUS TRUTH. BUT THIS DISCUSSION HAS MADE ONE OR TWO THINGS PLAIN TO TH apprehension.

THE FIRST IS THAT THE BOOKS OF THIS BIBLE ARE NOT ALL OF EQUAL RANK AND SACREDNESS. IF TH TRUTH WHICH ALL THE AGES, WITH ALL THEIR VOICES, JOIN TO DECLARE, IT IS THAT THE BIBLE IS MADE U DIFFERENT KINDS OF BOOKS, WITH VERY DIFFERENT DEGREES OF SACREDNESS AND AUTHORITY. FOR ONE, WISH TO PART WITH ANY OF THEM; I FIND INSTRUCTION IN ALL OF THEM, THOUGH IN SOME OF THEM ESTHER AND ECCLESIASTES, IT IS RATHER AS RECORDS OF SAVAGERY AND OF SKEPTICISM, FROM WHICH CHRISTIAN OUGHT TO RECOIL, THAT I CAN SEE ANY VALUE IN THEM. AS POWERFUL DELINEATIONS OF TH SENTIMENTS THAT THE CHRISTIAN OUGHT NOT TO CHERISH, AND THE KIND OF DOUBTS THAT HE CANNOT WITHOUT IMPERILLING HIS SOUL, THEY MAY BE USEFUL. IT IS NOT, THEREFORE, AT ALL DESIRABLE TI ANCIENT RECORDS SHOULD BE TORN ASUNDER AND PORTIONS OF THEM FLUNG AWAY. THAT PRO MUTILATION NONE OF US IS WISE ENOUGH TO ATTEMPT. LET THE BIBLE STAND; THERE ARE GOOD USES F PART OF IT. BUT LET US REMEMBER THE LESSON WHICH THIS SURVEY HAS BROUGHT HOME TO US, THA BOOKS ARE NOT ALL ALIKE, AND THAT THE MESSAGE OF DIVINE WISDOM IS SPOKEN TO US IN SOME OF TH more clearly than in others,

RICHARD BAXTER IS AN AUTHORITY IN RELIGION FOR WHOSE OPINION ALL CONSERVATIVE PEOPLE O ENTERTAIN RESPECT. HE CANNOT BE SUSPECTED OF BEING A "NEW DEPARTURE" MAN; HE WAS A S Presbyterian, and he passed to the "Saints' Rest" nearly two hundred years ago. With a few words of his upon the question now before us, this chapter may fitly close:--

"AND HERE I MUST TELL YOU A GREAT AND NEEDFUL TRUTH, WHICH CHRISTIANS, FEARING TO CO OVERDOING, TEMPT MEN TO INFIDELITY. THE SCRIPTURE IS LIKE A MAN'S BODY, WHERE SOME PARTS ARE B THE PRESERVATION OF THE REST, AND MAY BE MAIMED WITHOUT DEATH. THE SENSE IS THE SOUL SCRIPTURE, AND THE LETTERS BUT THE BODY OR VEHICLE. THE DOCTRINE OF THE CREED, LORD'S PR DECALOGUE, BAPTISM AND THE LORD'S SUPPER, IS THE VITAL PART AND CHRISTIANITY ITSELF. TH TESTAMENT LETTER (WRITTEN AS WE HAVE IT ABOUT EZRA'S TIME) IS THAT VEHICLE WHICH IS AS IMPERFEC REVELATION OF THOSE TIMES WAS. BUT AS, AFTER CHRIST'S INCARNATION AND ASCENSION, THE SPIRIT W ABUNDANTLY GIVEN, AND THE REVELATION MORE PERFECT AND SEALED, SO THE DOCTRINE IS MORE FULI VEHICLE OR BODY, THAT IS THE WORDS, ARE LESS IMPERFECT AND MORE SURE TO US; SO THAT HE WHICH D OF THE TRUTH OF SOME WORDS IN THE OLD TESTAMENT OR OF SOME CIRCUMSTANCES IN THE NEW, H REASON THEREFORE TO DOUBT OF THE CHRISTIAN RELIGION OF WHICH THESE WRITINGS ARE BUT THE BODY, SUFFICIENT TO ASCERTAIN US OF THE TRUTH OF THE HISTORY AND DOCTRINE." [FOOTNOTE: *The Catechizing of Christian Families*, p. 36.]

CHAPTER XII.

HOW THE BOOKS WERE WRITTEN.

THE BOOKS OF THE OLD TESTAMENT WERE ORIGINALLY WRITTEN UPON SKINS OF SOME SORT. THE PROVIDED THAT THE LAW MIGHT BE INSCRIBED ON THE SKINS OF CLEAN ANIMALS, TAME OR WILD, OR I

CLEAN BIRDS. THESE SKINS WERE USUALLY CUT INTO STRIPS, THE ENDS OF WHICH WERE NEATLY JOINED T MAKING A CONTINUOUS BELT OF PARCHMENT OR VELLUM WHICH WAS ROLLED UPON TWO STICKS AND FASTE A THREAD. THEY WERE COMMONLY WRITTEN ON ONE SIDE ONLY, WITH AN IRON PEN WHICH WAS DIPPED composed of lampblack dissolved in gall juice.

THE HEBREW IS A LANGUAGE QUITE UNLIKE OUR OWN IN FORM AND APPEARANCE. NOT ONLY DO WI IT FROM RIGHT TO LEFT, INSTEAD OF FROM LEFT TO RIGHT, BUT THE CONSONANTS ONLY OF THE SEVERA WRITTEN IN DISTINCT CHARACTERS ON THE LINE; THE VOWELS BEING LITTLE DOTS OR DASHES STANDING CONSONANTS, OR WITHIN THEIR CURVES. THESE VOWEL POINTS WERE NOT USED IN THE ORIGINAL HEBRE ARE A MODERN INVENTION, ORIGINATING SOME CENTURIES AFTER CHRIST. IT IS TRUE THAT IT WAS THE THE JEWS IN FORMER TIMES THAT THESE VOWEL POINTS WERE AN ORIGINAL PART OF THE LANGUAG SCHOLARS MADE THIS CLAIM WITH GREAT CONFIDENCE, WHICH SHOWS HOW LITTLE RELIANCE IS TO BE PL JEWISH TRADITION. THE EVIDENCE IS ABUNDANT THAT THE HEBREW WAS ORIGINALLY WRITTEN WITHOUT PRECISELY AS STENOGRAPHERS OFTEN WRITE IN THESE DAYS. WE KNOW FROM THE TESTIMONY OF OLD S AND INTERPRETERS OF THE HEBREW THAT THEY CONSTANTLY ENCOUNTERED THIS DIFFICULTY IN RI LANGUAGE. WRITE A PARAGRAPH OF OUR OWN LANGUAGE WITHOUT VOWELS AND LOOK AT IT. OR, BET SOME ONE ELSE TO TREAT FOR YOU IN THE SAME WAY A PARAGRAPH WITH WHICH YOU ARE NOT FAMILIAR, A IF YOU CAN DECIPHER IT. UNDOUBTEDLY, YOU COULD WITH SOME DIFFICULTY MAKE OUT THE SENSE C PASSAGES. IT WOULD PUZZLE YOU AT FIRST, BUT AFTER YOU HAD HAD SOME PRACTICE IN SUPPLYING THE V YOU WOULD LEARN TO READ QUITE READILY. STENOGRAPHERS, AS I HAVE SAID, HAVE A SOMEWHAT SIMIL NEVERTHELESS, YOU WOULD SOMETIMES BE IN UNCERTAINTY AS TO THE WORDS. SUPPOSE YOU HAVE THE CONSONANTS *brd*, HOW WOULD YOU KNOW WHETHER THE WORD WAS BARD, OR BIRD, OR BREAD, OR BOARI BRAD, OR BROAD, OR BRIDE, OR BRAID, OR BROOD, OR BREED? IT MIGHT BE ANY ONE OF THEM. YOU USUALLY TELL WHAT IT WAS BY A GLANCE AT THE CONNECTION, BUT YOU COULD NOT TELL INFALLIBLY MIGHT BE SENTENCES IN WHICH MORE THAN ONE OF THESE WORDS WOULD MAKE SENSE, AND IT WOU IMPOSSIBLE TO DETERMINE WHICH THE WRITER MEANT TO USE. NOW THE OLD HEBREW AS IT CAME FRO HANDS OF THE ORIGINAL WRITERS WAS ALL IN THIS FORM; WHILE, THEREFORE, THE MEANING OF THE W GENERALLY BE GAINED WITH SUFFICIENT ACCURACY, YOU SEE AT A GLANCE THAT ABSOLUTE CERTAINTY IS QUESTION; THAT THE JEWISH SCHOLARS WHO SUPPLIED THESE VOWEL POINTS A THOUSAND YEARS OR MOI the original manuscripts were written may sometimes have got the wrong word.

JEROME GIVES NUMEROUS ILLUSTRATIONS OF THIS UNCERTAINTY. IN JER. IX. 21, "DEATH IS COME U OUR WINDOWS," HE SAYS THAT WE HAVE FOR THE FIRST WORD THE THREE HEBREW CONSONANTS CORRESI to our *dbr*; THE WORD MAY BE *dabar*, SIGNIFYING DEATH, OR *deber*, SIGNIFYING PESTILENCE; IT IS IMPOSSIBLE TELL WHICH IT IS. IN HABAKKUK III. 5, WE HAVE THE SAME CONSONANTS, AND THERE THE WORD IS W PESTILENCE. EITHER WORD WILL MADE GOOD SENSE IN EITHER PLACE; AND WE ARE PERFECTLY HELPLES CHOICE BETWEEN THEM. AGAIN, IN ISAIAH XXVI. 14, WE HAVE A PREDICTION CONCERNING THE WI "THEREFORE HAST THOU VISITED AND DESTROYED THEM AND MADE ALL THEIR MEMORY TO PERISI HEBREW WORD HERE TRANSLATED "MEMORY" CONSISTS OF THREE CONSONANTS REPRESENTED BY OUR *zkr*; IT MAY BE THE WORD *zeker*, WHICH SIGNIFIES MEMORY, OR THE WORD *zakar*, WHICH SIGNIFIES A MALE PERSON. AND JEROME SAYS THAT IT IS BELIEVED THAT SAUL WAS DECEIVED, PERHAPS WILLINGLY, I DIFFERENCE IN THESE WORDS (I SAM. XV.); HAVING BEEN COMMANDED TO CUT OFF EVERY-MEMORIAL OR VESTIGE--OF AMAIEK, HE TOOK THE WORD TO *zakar*, INSTEAD OF ZEKER, AND CONTENTED HIMSELF W DESTROYING THE MALES OF THE ARMY AND KEEPING FOR HIMSELF THE SPOIL. JEROME'S CONJECTURE IN T IS SUFFICIENTLY FANCIFUL; NEVERTHELESS HE ILLUSTRATES THE IMPOSSIBILITY OF DETERMINING THE EXAC OF MANY HEBREW SENTENCES. THIS IMPOSSIBILITY IS ABUNDANTLY DEMONSTRATED BY THE SEPTUAGINT, I FIND MANY UNDOUBTED ERRORS IN THAT TRANSLATION FROM THE HEBREW INTO THE GREEK, WHICH HA from this lack of precision in the Hebrew language.

WHEN, THEREFORE, WE KNOW THAT THE BIBLE WAS WRITTEN IN SUCH A LANGUAGE--A LANGUAGE VOWELS--AND THAT IT WAS NOT UNTIL SIX HUNDRED YEARS AFTER CHRIST THAT THE VOWEL POINTS WERE AND THE WORDS WERE WRITTEN OUT IN FULL, THE THEORY OF THE VERBAL INERRANCY OF THE TEXT AS WI IT BECOMES INCREDIBLE. UNLESS THE MEN WHO SUPPLIED THE VOWEL POINTS WERE GIFTED WITH SUPERN KNOWLEDGE THEY MUST HAVE MADE MISTAKES IN SPELLING OUT SOME OF THESE WORDS. I DO NOT BELIE THESE MISTAKES WERE SERIOUS, OR THAT THEY AFFECT IN ANY IMPORTANT WAY THE MEANING OF THE S

BUT THE ASSUMPTION THAT IN THIS STUPENDOUS GAME OF GUESS-WORK NO WRONG GUESSES WERE MADI THE HIGHEST DEGREE GRATUITOUS. THE SUBSTANTIAL TRUTHFULNESS OF THE RECORD IS NOT IMPEACHI DISCOVERY, BUT THE VERBAL INERRANCY OF THE DOCUMENT CAN NEVER BE MAINTAINED BY ANY HONI who knows these facts.

IT IS UNSAFE AND MISCHIEVOUS TO INDULGE *a priori* REASONINGS ABOUT INSPIRATION; WE HAVE H TOO MUCH OF THAT; BUT THE FOLLOWING PROPOSITION IS UNASSAILABLE: IF THE DIVINE WISDO PROPOSED TO DELIVER TO MAN AN INFALLIBLE BOOK, HE WOULD NOT HAVE HAD IT RECORDED IN A L WHOSE WRITTEN WORDS CONSIST ONLY OF CONSONANTS, LEAVING READERS A THOUSAND YEARS AFTER TO VOWELS BY CONJECTURE. THE VERY FACT THAT SUCH A LANGUAGE WAS CHOSEN IS THE CONCLUSI unanswerable evidence that God never designed to give us an infallible book.

WE ARE FAMILIAR WITH THE FACT THAT THE OLD TESTAMENT WRITINGS IN GENERAL USE AMONG CHURCHES WERE THOSE OF THE SEPTUAGINT. THE CHRISTIANS FROM THE SECOND TO THE SIXTEENTH KNEW VERY LITTLE HEBREW. BUT DURING ALL THESE AGES THE PALESTINIAN JEWS AND THEIR SUCCESSORS LANDS WERE PRESERVING THEIR OWN SCRIPTURES; IT WAS THEY WHO ADDED AT A LATE DAY--PROBABLY AS THE SIXTH CENTURY--THE VOWEL POINTS, WHICH WERE INVENTED IN SYRIA; AND WHEN, AT LENGTH, UN IMPULSE OF BIBLICAL STUDY WHICH LED TO THE REFORMATION, CHRISTIAN SCHOLARS BEGAN TO THINK BACK TO THE ORIGINAL HEBREW, THEY WERE OBLIGED TO OBTAIN FROM THE JEWS THE COPIES WHIC STUDIED. IT IS SOMEWHAT REMARKABLE THAT THE JEWS, WHO WERE THE EXCLUSIVE CUSTODIANS OF THE WRITINGS UP TO THE SIXTEENTH CENTURY, HAD NOT BEEN CAREFUL TO PRESERVE THEIR OLD MANUSCRIF THE VOWEL POINTS HAD BEEN INTRODUCED INTO THE TEXT, THEY SEEM TO HAVE BEEN WILLING THAT C WRITTEN IN THIS MANNER SHOULD PASS OUT OF EXISTENCE. ACCORDINGLY WE HAVE FEW HEBREW MANU THAT ARE EVEN SUPPOSED TO BE MORE THAN SIX OR SEVEN HUNDRED YEARS OLD. THERE IS ONE COPY PENTATEUCH WHICH MAY HAVE BEEN MADE AS EARLY AS 580 A. D., BUT THIS IS EXTREMELY DOUBTFUL; FROM THIS I DO NOT KNOW THAT THERE ARE ANY HEBREW BIBLES WHICH CLAIM TO BE OLDER THAN T CENTURY. OF THESE HEBREW MANUSCRIPTS NEARLY SIX HUNDRED ARE NOW KNOWN TO BE IN EXISTEN THE GREATER PART OF THESE ARE ONLY FRAGMENTARY COPIES OF THE PENTATEUCH OR OF SINGLE BOOKS. TWO CLASSES OF THESE--SYNAGOGUE ROLLS, PREPARED FOR READING IN THE WAY THAT I HAVE DESCRIF manuscripts in the book form, some on parchment and some on paper.

THE VARIATIONS IN THESE MANUSCRIPTS ARE FEW. COMPARED WITH THE GREEK MANUSCRIPTS O NEW TESTAMENT, THE ACCURACY OF THESE HEBREW CODICES IS REMARKABLE. IT IS EVIDENT THAT THE THE SCRIBES TO GUARD THEIR SCRIPTURES AGAINST ERROR HAS BEEN SCRUPULOUS AND VIGILANT. DOUBT INTENSE DEVOTION TO THE VERY LETTER OF THE SACRED BOOKS HAS BEEN EXERCISED FOR MANY CENT KNOW THAT IN THE EARLIEST DAYS THIS PRECISION WAS NOT SOUGHT; FOR THE SEPTUAGINT TRANSLATI DURING THE SECOND AND THIRD CENTURIES BEFORE CHRIST, GIVES US INDUBITABLE PROOF, WHEN WE C IT WITH THE HEBREW TEXT, THAT CHANGES, SOME OF THEM RADICAL AND SWEEPING, HAVE BEEN MADE TEXT OF THE HEBREW BOOKS SINCE THAT TRANSLATION WAS FINISHED. BUT IT IS EVIDENT THAT THE SCR EARLY DAY, CERTAINLY AS EARLY AS THE BEGINNING OF THE CHRISTIAN ERA, DETERMINED TO HAVE A UNI AN UNCHANGEABLE TEXT. FOR THIS PURPOSE THEY CHOSE SOME MANUSCRIPT COPY OF THE SCRIF DOUBTLESS THE ONE WHICH SEEMED TO THEM MOST ACCURATE, AND MADE THAT THE STANDARD; ALL TH MADE SINCE THAT TIME HAVE BEEN RELIGIOUSLY CONFORMED TO THAT. CONSEQUENTLY, ALL THE MANUSCRIPTS NOW IN EXISTENCE ARE REMARKABLY UNIFORM. THE OLD TESTAMENT CONTAINS MORE THREE TIMES AS MANY PAGES AS THE NEW TESTAMENT; BUT WHILE WE HAVE MORE THAN ONE HUNDRE FIFTY THOUSAND "VARIOUS READINGS" IN THE GREEK MANUSCRIPTS AND VERSIONS OF THE NEW TESTAM HAVE LESS THAN TEN THOUSAND SUCH VARIATIONS IN THOSE OF THE OLD TESTAMENT. IT MUST BE REME HOWEVER, THAT THIS UNIFORMITY HAS ITS SOURCE IN SOME COPY CHOSEN TO BE THE STANDARD HUND YEARS AFTER MOST OF THE OLD TESTAMENT BOOKS WERE WRITTEN; AND IT DOES NOT GUARANTEE CORRESPONDENCE BETWEEN THIS COPY AND THE AUTOGRAPHS OF THE ORIGINAL WRITERS. [FOOTNOTE INTERESTING DISCUSSION OF THE PRESERVATION AND TRANSMISSION OF THE HEBREW TEXT, THE R referred to Mr. Robertson Smith's *The Old Testament in the Jewish Church*, Lectures ii. and iii.]

OUR CHIEF INTEREST CENTRES, HOWEVER, IN THE GREEK MANUSCRIPTS OF THE BIBLE PRESERV TRANSMITTED BY CHRISTIANS, AND INCLUDING BOTH TESTAMENTS. ALL THE OLDEST AND MOST I documents that we possess belong to this class.

THE ORIGINAL NEW TESTAMENT WRITINGS WHICH CAME FROM THE HANDS OF THE APOSTLES AN AMANUENSES WE DO NOT POSSESS. THESE WERE PROBABLY WRITTEN, NOT ON SKINS, BUT UPON THE PAI PAPER COMMONLY USED AT THAT DAY, WHICH WAS A FRAIL AND FLIMSY FABRIC, AND UNDER ORI CIRCUMSTANCES WOULD SOON PERISH. FRAGMENTS OF THIS PAPYRUS HAVE COME DOWN TO US, BUT ONLY WHICH WERE PRESERVED WITH EXCEPTIONAL CARE. JEROME TELLS US OF A LIBRARY IN CASSAREA THAT WA DESTROYED, OWING TO THE CRUMBLING OF ITS PAPER, THOUGH IT WAS ONLY A HUNDRED YEARS OLD. PAI WAS SOMETIMES USED BY THE APOSTLES; PAUL REQUESTS TIMOTHY, IN HIS SECOND LETTER, TO BRING WI when he comes, certain parchments that belong to him. But these materials were costly, and it is not LIKELY THAT THE APOSTLES USED THEM TO ANY EXTENT IN THE PREPARATION OF THE BOOKS OF TESTAMENT. AT ANY RATE THE AUTOGRAPHIC COPIES OF THESE BOOKS DISAPPEARED AT AN EARLY DA SEEMS STRANGE TO US. PLACING THE ESTIMATE THAT WE DO UPON THESE WRITINGS, WE SHOULD HAVE TA GREATEST CARE TO PRESERVE THEM. IT IS CLEAR THAT THE CHRISTIANS INTO WHOSE HANDS THEY FE VALUE THEM AS HIGHLY AS WE DO. AS WESTCOTT SAYS, "THEY WERE GIVEN AS A HERITAGE TO MAN, AND some time before men felt the full value of the gift."

AT THE CLOSE OF THE SECOND CENTURY THERE WERE DISPUTES CONCERNING THE CORRECT RI CERTAIN PASSAGES, BUT NEITHER PARTY APPEALS TO THE APOSTOLIC ORIGINALS,--SHOWING THAT THEY MUS THAT TIME HAVE PERISHED. IN AFTER YEARS LEGENDS WERE TOLD ABOUT THE PRESERVATION OF THESE but these are contradictory and incredible.

NO MANUSCRIPT IS NOW IN EXISTENCE WHICH WAS WRITTEN DURING THE FIRST THREE CENTURIES. HAVE ONE OR TWO THAT DATE BACK TO THE FOURTH CENTURY; AND FROM THAT TIME THROUGH ALL THE INVENTION OF PRINTING MANY COPIES WERE MADE OF THE SACRED SCRIPTURES, IN WHOLE OR IN PART, ARE STILL IN THE HANDS OF SCHOLARS. IT IS FROM THESE OLD GREEK MANUSCRIPTS THAT OUR RECEIVE THE NEW TESTAMENT IS DERIVED; BY A COMPARISON OF THEM THE SCHOLARS OF THE SEVENTEENTH made up a Greek New Testament which they regarded as approximately accurate, and from that our English version was made.

THE NUMBER OF THESE OLD MANUSCRIPTS IS LARGE, AND THE FIRST GENERAL DIVISION OF THEM "UNCIALS" OR "CURSIVES," AS THEY ARE CALLED; THE UNCIAL MANUSCRIPTS BEING WRITTEN IN CAPITAL LE CURSIVES IN SMALL LETTERS MORE OR LESS CONNECTED, AS IN OUR WRITTEN HAND. THE UNCIALS ARE TH AS THEY ARE THE FEWEST; THERE ARE ONLY ONE HUNDRED AND TWENTY-SEVEN OF THEM IN ALL; WH cursives there are about fifteen hundred.

YET MOST OF THESE MANUSCRIPTS ARE FRAGMENTARY. SOME OF THEM CONTAIN ONLY THE GOS PORTIONS OF THEM; SOME OF THEM CONTAIN THE ACTS AND THE CATHOLIC EPISTLES; SOME OF TH EPISTLES OF PAUL OR A SINGLE EPISTLE; SOME ARE SELECTIONS FROM THE GOSPELS OR THE EPISTLES, P to be read in church, and called lectionaries.

PROFESSOR EZRA ABBOT GIVES US A CLASSIFICATION OF THESE MANUSCRIPTS WHICH WILL BE instructive.

"FOR THE NEW TESTAMENT,...WE HAVE MANUSCRIPTS MORE OR LESS COMPLETE, WRITTEN IN UNC CAPITAL LETTERS, AND RANGING FROM THE FOURTH TO THE TENTH CENTURY; OF THE GOSPELS TWI BESIDES THIRTY SMALL FRAGMENTS; OF THE ACTS AND CATHOLIC EPISTLES TEN, BESIDES SIX SMALL FRAG THE PAULINE EPISTLES ELEVEN, BESIDES NINE SMALL FRAGMENTS, AND OF THE REVELATION FIVE. ALL HAVE BEEN MOST THOROUGHLY COLLATED, AND THE TEXT OF THE MOST IMPORTANT OF THEM PUBLISHED. ONE OF THESE MANUSCRIPTS, THE SINAITIC, CONTAINING THE WHOLE OF THE NEW TESTAME ANOTHER, THE VATICAN, CONTAINING MUCH THE LARGER PART OF IT, WERE WRITTEN PROBABLY AS EAI MIDDLE OF THE FOURTH CENTURY; TWO OTHERS, THE ALEXANDRIAN AND THE EPHRAEM, BELONG TO MIDDLE OF THE FIFTH, OF WHICH DATE ARE TWO MORE, CONTAINING CONSIDERABLE PORTIONS OF THE G VERY REMARKABLE MANUSCRIPT OF THE GOSPELS AND ACTS--THE CAMBRIDGE MANUSCRIPT, OR CODEX BELONGS TO THE SIXTH CENTURY.... I PASS BY A NUMBER OF SMALL BUT VALUABLE FRAGMENTS OF THE FI SIXTH CENTURIES. AS TO THE CURSIVE MANUSCRIPTS RANGING FROM THE TENTH CENTURY TO THE SIXTI HAVE OF THE GOSPELS MORE THAN SIX HUNDRED; OF THE ACTS OVER TWO HUNDRED; OF THE PAULINE NEARLY THREE HUNDRED; OF THE REVELATION ABOUT ONE HUNDRED,--NOT RECKONING THE LECTIC MANUSCRIPTS CONTAINING THE LESSONS FROM THE GOSPELS, ACTS, AND EPISTLES, READ IN THE SERVICI church, of which there are more than four hundred." [Footnote: *Anglo-American Bible Revision*, p. 95.]

Out of all this vast mass of extant manuscripts, only twenty-seven contain the New Te entire.

The three oldest and most valuable manuscripts among those named by Professor Abb the passage above, are the Sinaitic, the Vatican, and the Alexandrian manuscripts.

Of these old Bibles perhaps the oldest is the one in the Vatican Library at Rome. enrolled in that library as late as the year 1475; what its history was before that time is unk whose hands or at what place it was written, no one can tell. Some have supposed that brought from Constantinople to Rome, in the fifteenth century, by John Bessarion, a patriarch; some that it was written in Alexandria, when that city was the metropolis of th culture; some that it was produced in Southern Italy when that region was celebrated learning. The signs favor the latter theory. The form of the letters is like those found o Herculaneum; and other manuscripts of the Bible found in southern Italy agree remarka this one in many peculiar readings. But this is all guess-work. Nobody knows where the ol came from or who brought it to Rome.

Some things, however, the old book plainly tells us about its own history. It be unmistakable marks of great antiquity. The scholar who is familiar with old Greek manusc judge by looking at a document something about its probable age. By the form of the lette presence or absence of certain marks of punctuation, by the general style of the manuscrip determine within a century or so the date at which it was written.

This old Bible is written in the uncial or capital letters; this would make it tolerab that it must be older than the tenth century. We have scarcely any uncial manuscripts late tenth century. But other unmistakable marks take it back much farther than this. The w written continuously, with no breaks or spaces between them; there are no accents, no r smooth breathings, no punctuation marks of any sort. These are signs of great age. A peculiarity is the manner of the division of the books into sections. I cannot stop to describ the various methods of division adopted in antiquity. The present separation into chapte verses was, as you know, a quite modern device. But the divisions of this old Bible follow a m that we know to have been in use at a very early day; and the conclusion of all the scholars must have been written as early as the year 350, possibly as early as 300.

It is not, however, a roll, but a book in form like those we handle every day. Before t manuscripts were generally prepared in this way. Martial, the Latin poet, who died abou mentions as a novelty in his day books with square leaves, bound together at the edges.

The Vatican Bible is a heavy quarto, the covers are red morocco discolored with a leaves, of which there are 759, are of fine and delicate vellum. It contains the Septuagint tr of the Old Testament, except the first forty-five chapters in Genesis and a few of the Psal have been torn out and lost. Of the New Testament writings, the last five chapters of H First and Second Timothy, Titus, Philemon, and the Apocalypse are wanting. Otherwise Testaments are complete.

We may recall another fact, to which allusion has been made, that this old Bible c among the Old Testament books those books which we now call apocryphal, and that apocryphal books, instead of being divided from the rest in a separate group, are mingle them, the *order* of the books being quite unlike that of our Bibles or of the Hebrew cano apocryphal First Book of Esdr *precedes* our Book of Ezra; while our Book of Ezra is united w Nehemiah, forming the Second Book of Esdras. Judith and Tobit follow Esther, and next the twelve minor prophets, and so on.

The same thing is true of all these oldest Bibles; they all contain the apocryphal bo these books are mingled with the other books, either promiscuously, or by some syst classification which accepts them as equal in value with the other Old Testament writings. no indication in these old Bibles that the apocryphal books are any less sacred or authorita the others.

Another manuscript Bible, scarcely less venerable and no less precious than the Vatica is the one known as the Sinaitic manuscript This was discovered by Constantine Tischend

German scholar, in an ancient convent at the base of Mount Sinai. The first journey of Tisc to the Sinaitic peninsula was undertaken in 1844, for the express purpose of searching in t monasteries of this neighborhood for ancient copies of the Scriptures that might be presi them. The monks of this old convent admitted him to their ancient library,--a place not frequented by them,--and there in the middle of the room he found a waste basket, filled with leaves and torn pieces of old parchment gathered to be burned. In looking them over he discove hundred and twenty leaves of a Bible that seemed to him of great antiquity. He asked f leaves, but when they found that he wanted them, the monks began to suspect their vali permitted him to take only forty-three of them. In 1853 he returned again, but this time c find the rest of the precious manuscript. He feared that it had been destroyed long before was not the case. Stimulated by his desire to possess the loose leaves, the monks had made for the rest of the volume, and, using as samples the leaves they had refused to give him, t found them all and secreted them. Upon his second visit they did not show him the book, hc nor reveal to him in any way its existence.

Six years later, in 1859, he returned again, this time fortified with a letter from the Em Russia, the head of the Greek Church; and this mighty document made the monks open treasures for his inspection. He obtained permission, first, to carry the old Bible to Cair copied, and finally, under the imperial influence, the monks surrendered it, and suffered removed to St. Petersburg, where since 1859 it has been sacredly kept.

"The Sinai Bible," says Dr. F. P. Woodbury, "contains the New Testament, the Epistl Barnabas, a portion of the Shepherd of Hennas, and twenty-two books of the Old Testame whole is written on fine vellum made from antelope skins into the largest pages known ancient manuscripts. While most of the oldest manuscripts have only three columns to th and the Vatican Bible has three, the Sinai Bible alone shows four. The letters are somewh than those of the Vatican and much more roughly written. The book contains many blun copying, and there are a few cases of willful omission. Its remote age is attested by many same proofs that have been mentioned in the description of the Vatican Bible." [Footnote: F interesting sketch of "Three Old Bibles," in *Sunday Afternoon*, vol. i pp. 65-71.]

It is known that the Emperor Constantine, in the year 331, authorized the preparation costly and beautiful copies of the Holy Scriptures under the care of Eusebius of C Tischendorf himself thinks--and his conjecture is accepted by other scholars--that this is those fifty Bibles, and that it was sent from Byzantium to the monks of this convent Emperor Justinian, who was its founder. At all events, it is incontestably a manuscript of gr certainly of the fourth century, and probably of the first half of that century.

The other great Bible is the one known as the Alexandrian, which was presented, in 1 King Charles I of England by Cyril Lucar, patriarch of Constantinople, who had brought Alexandria. It was transferred in 1753 from the king's private library to the British Museum it is now preserved. It is bound in four folio volumes, three of which contain the text of and one of the New Testament. The portion which contains the Old Testament is more than that which contains the New, quite a number of leaves having been lost from the latt material of which this volume is composed is thin vellum, the page being about thirteen inchi by ten broad, containing from fifty to fifty-two lines on each page, each line consisting (twenty letters. The number of pages is 773, of which 640 are occupied with the text of tl Testament and 133 with the New. The characters are uncial, but larger than the Vatican ma There are no accents or breathings, no spaces between the letters or words save at the paragraph, and the contractions, which are not numerous, are only such as are found in th manuscripts. The punctuation consists of a point placed at the end of a sentence, usually on with the top of the preceding letter." [Footnote: *Encyc. Brit.*, i. p. 496.] The general verdict (scholars is that this manuscript belongs to about the middle of the fifth century.

The contents of this old Bible are curious, and they are curiously arranged. The firs contains the Pentateuch, Joshua, Judges, Ruth, the two books of Samuel, the two books of and the two books of Chronicles. The second contains, first, the twelve minor prophet

Hosea to Malachi), then Isaiah, Jeremiah, *Baruch*, Lamentations, *The Epistle of Jeremiah*, Ezekiel, Daniel, Esther, *Tobit*, *Judith*, *Esdras I.* (the apocryphal Esdras), Esdras II. (including our Nehem and part of our Ezra), and *the four books of the Maccabees.* The third volume contains An Epistle Athanasius to Marcellenus on the Psalms; The Hypothesis of Eusebius on the Psalms; th Book of the Psalms, of which there are one hundred and fifty-one, and fifteen Hymns; t Proverbs, Ecclesiastes, Canticles, Wisdom of Solomon, and Ecclesiasticus, or Sirach. The volume contains the four Gospels, the Acts, the seven Catholic Epistles (one of James, Peter, three of John, and one of Jude), fourteen Epistles of Paul (including the one to the Hebrews), The Revelation of John, two Epistles of Clement to the Corinthians, and eight Psalms of Solomon.

This, it will be admitted, is a generous Bible. It contains most of the apocryphal boo several others that we do not find in the other collections. It is probable that the Athanasius and Eusebius on the Psalms were admitted rather as introduction or commenta as text; but the rest, judging from the positions in which they stand, must have been rega Sacred Scriptures.

These, then, are the three oldest, most complete, and most trustworthy copies of th Scriptures now in existence. By all scholars they are regarded as precious beyond price; reading in which they agree would probably be regarded as the right reading, if all t manuscripts in the world were against them.

I have suggested that these old manuscripts do not always agree. The fact is that no them are exactly alike, and that there are a great many slight differences between those most closely assimilated. Of these differences Professor Westcott says that "there cann than 120,000,--though of these a very large proportion consists of differences of spel isolated aberrations of scribes." It is not generally difficult for the student on comparin tell which is the right reading. A word may be misspelled, for example, in several different w student knows the right way to spell it, and is not in doubt concerning the word. "Probab Mr. Westcott, "there are not more than from sixteen hundred to two thousand places in w true reading is a matter of uncertainty, even if we include in this questions of order, infle orthography; the doubtful readings by which the sense is in any way affected are very muc and those of dogmatic importance can be easily numbered."

The ways in which these errors and variations arose are easily explained. The men who c these manuscripts were careful men, many of them, but all of them were fallible. Sometim would mistake a letter for another letter much like it, and change the form of a word in sometimes there would be two clauses of a sentence ending with the same word, and the ey copyist, glancing back to the manuscript after writing the first of these words, would ali the second one, and go on from that; so that the clause preceding it would be omitted. So in copying the continuous writing of the uncial manuscripts, mistakes would be made in di words. For example, if a number of English words, written in close order, with no spaces be them, were given you to copy, and you found "infancy," you might make two words of it o and if you were a little careless you might write it "in fancy" when it should be "infancy," *vice versa.* A case might arise in which it would be difficult for you to tell whether it should be "in fancy" or "infancy." Such uncertainties the copyists encountered, and such mistakes they sometimes made.

Mistakes of memory they also made in copying, just as I sometimes do when I underta copy a passage from Mr. Westcott or Mr. Davidson into one of these chapters. I look up book, and take a sentence in my mind, but perhaps while I am writing it down I will change s the order of the words, or it may be put a word of my own in the place of another tha resembles it, as "but" for "though," or "from" for "out of," or "doubtless" for "without d try to copy very exactly, but there are, unquestionably, now and then such slips as thes quotations. And such mistakes were made by the copyists of the Old Scriptures.

There are some instances of intentional changes. Sometimes a copyist evidently substi word that he thought was plainer for one that was more obscure; a more elegant word for elegant; a grammatical construction for one that was not grammatical.

Other differences have arisen from the habit of some of the copyists or owners of manu of writing glosses, or brief explanatory notes, on the margin. Some of these marginalia wer by subsequent scribes into the text, where, in our version, they still remain. Some of them, h were removed in the late revision.

The great majority of these errors are, however, as I have said, extremely unimporta nearly all of them seem to have arisen in the ways I have suggested--through simple carel and not with any intent of corrupting the text.

The translations of the Bible which were made in early days into other languages than our own must be dismissed with the briefest mention. The most important version of the Old Test was the Septuagint, of which nothing more needs to be said.

You will remember that the Hebrew was a dead language while our Lord was on the ear Jews of Palestine speaking the Aramaic. For their use, translations of the Hebrew into the called Targums, were made. There is a great variety of these, and there are many opinion their age; but it is not likely that the oldest of them was committed to writing before t century A. D. They are curious specimens of the translator's work, combining text and comm in a remarkable manner. Additions and changes are freely made; the simple sentences of record are greatly expanded; not only is a spade generally called a useful ligneous and f agricultural implement, but many things are said concerning the aforesaid spade which M David or Isaiah never dreamed of saying.

For example, in Judges v. 10, the Hebrew is literally translated in our English Bib "Speak, ye that ride on white asses, ye that sit in judgment and walk by the way." The Tar Jonathan expatiates thereon as follows: "Those who had interrupted their occupations are r asses covered with many colored caparisons, and they ride about freely in all the territory and congregate to sit in judgment. They walk in their old ways, and are speaking of the pow hast shown in the land of Israel," etc. This may be pronounced a remarkably free translat the Targums generally evince a similar liberality of sentiment and phraseology.

Besides these, the ancient translations of the Bible, which must be mentioned, are t Latin, made in the second century, out of which, by many revisions, grew that Latin Vulgat is now used in the Catholic ritual; an ancient Syriac version of about the same age; two E versions, in different dialects, made in the third century; the Peshito-Syriac, the Gothic Ethiopic in the fourth, and the Armenian in the fifth; besides several later translations, the Arabic and the Slavonic. These ancient translations are all of value to modern sc helping them to reach more certain conclusions respecting the nature of the Sacred Script the right reading in disputed passages.

The ages which we have been traversing in this chapter--when the Bible was a manusc were ages of great darkness. The copies of the book were few, and the common people neither possess them nor read them. It is hard for us who have had the book in our hands fr infancy, who have gone to it so freely for light in darkness, for comfort in sorrow, for w work with, for weapons to fight with, to understand how men could have lived the life without it; how a godly seed could have been nourished in the earth without the sincere mi word for them to feed on.

It was indeed a great privation that they suffered, but we must not suppose that they w without witness. For there is another and even a clearer revelation than the written word is a godly life. Godly lives there were in all these dark times; and it was at their fires that of gospel truth was kindled and kept burning. There may be reason for a question whether not come to trust in these times too much in a word that is written, and to undervalue th revelation which God is making of his truth and love in the characters of his children. For in the light that Christ is constantly manifesting to the world in the lives of men that we meaning in the words of the book. "The Christian," says Dr. Christlieb, "is the world's Bible is the word that is known and read of men. Let it be our care to make it, not an infallib clear, an adequate, and a safe revelation of the truth and love of God to men.

Chapter XIII.

How Much Is the Bible Worth?

Of the Bible as a book among books, of the human elements which enter into its compo: some account has been given in the preceding chapters. But in these studies the whole stor' Bible has not been told. There is need, therefore, that we should enlarge our view somew take more directly into account certain elements with which we have not hitherto bee concernedOur study has, indeed, made a few things plain. Among them is the certainty th Bible is not an infallible Book, in the sense in which it is popularly supposed to be infallible we study the history of the several books, the history of the canon, the history of the di: and reproduction of the manuscript copies, and the history of the versions,--when we discov the "various readings" of the differing manuscripts amount to one hundred and fifty thous impossibility of maintaining the verbal inerrancy of the Bible becomes evident. We see how i ignorance and error have been suffered to mingle with this stream of living water through course; if our assurance of salvation were made to depend upon our knowledge that every v the Bible was of divine origin, our hopes of eternal life would be altogether insecure.

The book is not infallible historically. It is a veracious record; we may depend upc truthfulness of the outline which it gives us of the history of the Jewish people; discrepancies and contradictions which appear here and there upon its pages show that its ' were not miraculously protected from mistakes in dates and numbers and the order of events.

It is not infallible scientifically. It is idle to try to force the narrative of Genesis int correspondence with geological science. It is a hymn of creation, wonderfully beautiful a the central truths of monotheistic religion and of modern science are involved in it; but intended to give us the scientific history of creation, and the attempt to make it f construction is highly injudicious.

It is not infallible morally. By this I mean that portions of this revelation involve an i morality. Many things are here commanded which it would be wrong for us to do. This saying that these commands were not divinely wise for the people to whom they were given it denying that the morality of the New Testament, which is the fulfillment and consumm the moral progress which the book records, is a perfect morality; it is simply asserting t stages of this progress from a lower to a higher morality are here clearly marked; that the of the earlier time are therefore inadequate and misleading in these later times; and tha' who accepts the Bible as a code of moral rules, all of which are equally binding, will be led gravest errors. It is no more true that the ceremonial legislation of the Old Testament i than that large portions of the moral legislation are obsolete. The notions of the write books concerning their duties to God were dim and imperfect; so were their notions con their duties to man. All the truth that they could receive was given to them; but there w truths which they could not receive, which to us are as plain as the daylight.

Not to recognize the partialness and imperfection of this record in all these respect: guilty of a grave disloyalty to the kingdom of the truth. With all these facts staring him i the attempt of any intelligent man to maintain the theoretical and ideal infallibility of these writings is a criminal blunder. Nor is there any use in loudly asserting the inerrancy books, with vehement denunciations of all who call it in question, and then in a breath a that there may be some errors and discrepancies and interpolations. Perfection is perfect stoutly affirm that a thing is perfect, and then admit that it may be in some respects imperfi insensate procedure. Infallibility is infallibility. The Scriptures are, or they are not, infal admission that there may be a few errors gives every man the right, nay it lays upon him the i finding what those errors are. Our friends who so sturdily assert the traditional theory

BE AWARE OF THE EXTENT TO WHICH THEY STULTIFY THEMSELVES WHEN THEIR SWEEPING AND RE ASSERTION THAT THE BIBLE *never* CONTAIN A MISTAKE IS FOLLOWED, AS IT ALWAYS MUST BE, BY THEIR TI AND DEPRECATORY, "HARDLY EVER." THE OLD RABBINICAL THEORY, AS ADOPTED AND EXTENDED BY SOM POST-REFORMATION THEOLOGIANS, THAT THE BIBLE WAS VERBALLY DICTATED BY GOD AND IS AB ACCURATE IN EVERY WORD, LETTER, AND VOWEL-POINT, AND THAT IT IS THEREFORE BLASPHEMY TC QUESTION CONCERNING ANY PART OF IT, IS A CONSISTENT THEORY. BETWEEN THIS AND A FREE BUT INQUIRY INTO THE BIBLE ITSELF, TO DISCOVER WHAT HUMAN ELEMENTS IT CONTAINS AND HOW IT IS AFF THEM, THERE IS NO MIDDLE GROUND. THAT IT IS USELESS AND MISCHIEVOUS TO MAKE FOR THE BIBLE THAT IT NOWHERE MAKES FOR ITSELF,--TO HOLD AND TEACH A THEORY CONCERNING IT WHICH AT ON DOWN WHEN AN INTELLIGENT MAN BEGINS TO STUDY IT WITH OPEN MIND--IS BEGINNING TO BE VERY PLAI QUIBBLING, THE CONCEALMENT, THE DISINGENUOUSNESS WHICH THIS METHOD OF USING THE BIBLE INVO NOT CONDUCIVE TO CHRISTIAN INTEGRITY. THIS KIND OF "LYING FOR GOD" HAS DRIVEN HUND thousands already into irreconcilable alienation from the Christian church. It is time to stop it.

HOW DID THIS THEORY OF THE INFALLIBILITY OF THE BIBLE ARISE? THOSE WHO HAVE FOLLOWE DISCUSSIONS TO THIS POINT KNOW THAT IT HAS NOT ALWAYS BEEN HELD BY THE CHRISTIAN CHURCH. THE OF THE CANON, TOLD WITH ANY MEASURE OF TRUTHFULNESS, WILL MAKE THIS PLAIN. THE HISTORY VARIATIONS BETWEEN THE SEPTUAGINT AND THE HEBREW SHOWS, BEYOND THE SHADOW OF A DOUBT, TH THEORY OF THE UNCHANGEABLE AND ABSOLUTE DIVINITY OF THE WORDS OF THE SCRIPTURE HAD NO HOLD UPON TRANSCRIBERS AND COPYISTS IN THE EARLY JEWISH CHURCH. THE NEW TESTAMENT WRITER NOT HAVE CONSISTENTLY HELD SUCH A THEORY RESPECTING THE OLD TESTAMENT BOOKS, ELSE THEY W HAVE QUOTED THEM, AS THEY DID, WITH SMALL CARE FOR VERBAL ACCURACY. THEY BELIEVED THEM SUBSTANTIALLY TRUE, AND THEREFORE THEY GIVE THE SUBSTANCE OF THEM IN THEIR QUOTATIONS; BUT T SUCH SLAVISH ATTENTION TO THE LETTER AS THERE MUST HAVE BEEN IF THEY HAD REGARDED THEM A DICTATED BY GOD HIMSELF. THE CHRISTIAN FATHERS WERE INCLINED, NO DOUBT, TO ACCEPT THE RA THEORIES OF INSPIRATION RESPECTING THE OLD TESTAMENT; BUT THEY SOMETIMES AVOID THE DIFI GROWING OUT OF MANIFEST ERRORS IN THE TEXT BY A THEORY OF AN INNER SENSE WHICH IS FAULTLES ADMITTING THAT THE NATURAL MEANING CANNOT ALWAYS BE DEFENDED. AS TO THE EARLY REFORMERS SEEN HOW FREELY THEY HANDLED THE SACRED WRITINGS, SUBMITTING THEM TO A SCRUTINY WHICH THI NOT HAVE VENTURED UPON IF THEY HAD BELIEVED CONCERNING THEM WHAT WE HAVE BEEN TAUGHT. IT UNTIL THE PERIOD SUCCEEDING THE REFORMATION THAT THIS DOGMA OF BIBLICAL INFALLIBILITY W FORMULATED AND IMPOSED UPON THE PROTESTANT CHURCHES. AS TAUGHT BY QUENSTEDT AND VOET CALOVIUS, THE DOGMA ASSERTS THAT "NOT ONLY THE SUBSTANCE OF TRUTH AND THE VIEWS PROPOSED MINUTEST DETAIL, BUT EVEN THE IDENTICAL WORDS, ALL AND IN PARTICULAR, WERE SUPPLIED AND DICTAT HOLY GHOST. NOT A WORD IS CONTAINED IN THE HOLY SCRIPTURES WHICH IS NOT IN THE STRICTE INSPIRED, THE VERY INTERPUNCTUATION NOT EXCEPTED.... ERRORS OF ANY SORT WHATEVER, EVEN VI GRAMMATICAL, AS WELL AS ALL INELEGANCIES OF STYLE, ARE TO BE DENIED AS UNWORTHY OF THE DIV WHO IS THROUGHOUT THE PRIMARY AUTHOR OF THE BIBLE." [FOOTNOTE: *The Doctrine of Sacred Scripture*, II. P. 209.] THIS VIEW WAS LONG MAINTAINED WITH ALL STRICTNESS, AND MANY A MAN HAS BEEN MADE A HERET DENYING IT. WITHIN THE LAST CENTURY THE FORM OF THE DOCTRINE HAS BEEN SOMEWHAT MOD theologians, yet the substance of it is still regarded as essential orthodoxy. Dr. Charles Hodge, in his "THEOLOGY," VOL. I. P. 152, SAYS, "PROTESTANTS HOLD THAT THE SCRIPTURES OF THE OLD AN TESTAMENTS ARE THE WORD OF GOD, WRITTEN UNDER THE INSPIRATION OF GOD THE HOLY GHOST, THEREFORE INFALLIBLE, AND CONSEQUENTLY FREE FROM ALL ERROR, WHETHER OF DOCTRINE, OF PRECEPT." AND AGAIN (P. 163), "ALL THE BOOKS OF SCRIPTURE ARE EQUALLY INSPIRED. ALL ALIKE ARE IN IN WHAT THEY TEACH." SUCH IS THE DOCTRINE NOW HELD BY THE GREAT MAJORITY OF CHRISTIANS. IN pastors do not hold it, but the body of the laity have no other conception.

WHENCE IS IT DERIVED? WHERE DO THE TEACHERS QUOTED ABOVE GET THEIR AUTHORITY F affirmations?

NOT, AS WE HAVE SEEN, FROM ANY STATEMENTS OF THE BIBLE ITSELF. THERE IS NOT ONE WORD BIBLE WHICH AFFIRMS OR IMPLIES THAT THIS CHARACTER OF INERRANCY ATTACHES TO THE ENTIRE COL writings, or to any one of them.

THE DOCTRINE AROSE, AS I HAVE SAID, IN THE SEVENTEENTH CENTURY, AND IT WAS IN PART, NO D

REFLECTION OF THE TEACHING OF THE LATER RABBINS, WHOSE FANTASTIC NOTIONS ABOUT THE ORIGI SACRED BOOKS I HAVE BEFORE ALLUDED TO. IT WAS ALSO DEVELOPED, AS A POLEMICAL NECESSITY, EXIGENCIES OF THAT CONFLICT WITH THE ROMAN CATHOLIC THEOLOGIANS WHICH FOLLOWED THE REF THE EMINENT GERMAN SCHOLAR AND SAINT, PROFESSOR THOLUCK, GIVES THE FOLLOWING ACCOUN origin:

"IN PROPORTION AS CONTROVERSY, SHARPENED BY JESUITISM, MADE THE PROTESTANT PARTY SENS AN EXTERNALLY FORTIFIED GROUND OF COMBAT, IN THAT SAME PROPORTION DID PROTESTANTISM SEE EXALTATION OF THE OUTWARD AUTHORITATIVE CHARACTER OF THE SACRED WRITINGS, TO RECOVER TH AUTHORITY WHICH IT HAD LOST THROUGH ITS REJECTION OF INFALLIBLE COUNCILS AND THE INFALLIBLE A THE POPE. IN THIS MANNER AROSE *not earlier than the seventeenth century*, THOSE SENTIMENTS WHICH REGARD THE HOLY SCRIPTURE AS THE INFALLIBLE PRODUCTION OF THE DIVINE SPIRIT--IN ITS ENTIRE CONTENT VERY FORM--SO THAT NOT ONLY THE SENSE BUT ALSO THE WORDS, THE LETTERS, THE HEBREW VOWEL PC THE VERY PUNCTUATION WERE REGARDED AS PROCEEDING FROM THE SPIRIT OF GOD." [FO *Theological Essays*, COLLECTED BY GEORGE R. NOYES.] THE FACT THAT THE DOCTRINE HAD THIS ORIGIN IS ITSELF SU A THEORY WHICH IS FRAMED IN THE HEAT OF A GREAT CONTROVERSY, BY ONE PARTY IN THE CHURCH, IS somewhat extreme.

THE STRENGTH OF THE DOCTRINE LIES, HOWEVER, IN THE FACT THAT IT IS A THEOLOGICAL INFERENC DOCTRINE OF GOD. "GOD IS THE AUTHOR OF THE BIBLE," MEN HAVE SAID; "GOD IS OMNISCIENT; HE CAN NO MISTAKES; THEREFORE THE BOOK MUST BE INFALLIBLE. TO DENY THAT IT IS INFALLIBLE IS TO DENY GOD'S BOOK; IF IT IS NOT HIS BOOK IT IS WORTHLESS." OR, PUTTING IT IN ANOTHER FORM, THEY HAV "THE BIBLE IS AN INSPIRED BOOK. GOD IS THE SOURCE OF INSPIRATION. HE CANNOT INSPIRE MEN TO ERROR. THEREFORE EVERY WORD OF THE INSPIRED BOOK MUST BE TRUE." THIS IS WHAT THE LOGICIANS *a* C *priori* ARGUMENT. THE VIEW OF WHAT INSPIRATION IS, AND OF WHAT THE BIBLE IS, ARE DEDUCED FRO THEORY OF GOD. IT AMOUNTS TO JUST THIS: IF GOD IS WHAT WE THINK HIM TO BE, HE MUST DO WHAT WISE TO US. THIS IS HARDLY A SAFE ARGUMENT. DOUBTLESS WE WOULD HAVE SAID BEFOREHAND THAT I WHO IS ALL-WISE AND ALL-POWERFUL, SHOULD CREATE A WORLD, HE WOULD MAKE ONE FREE FROM SUFFE EVERY FORM OF EVIL. WE FIND, HOWEVER, THAT HE HAS NOT MADE SUCH A WORLD. AND IT MAY BE WIS US, INSTEAD OF MAKING UP OUR MINDS BEFOREHAND WHAT GOD MUST DO, TO TRY AND FIND OUT WHAT DONE. IT MIGHT SEEM TO US, DOUBTLESS, THAT IF HE HAS GIVEN US A REVELATION, IT MUST BE A F REVELATION. BUT HAS HE? THAT IS THE QUESTION. WE CAN ONLY KNOW BY STUDYING THE REVELATION I HAVE NO RIGHT TO DETERMINE BEFOREHAND WHAT IT MUST BE. WE MIGHT HAVE SAID WITH EQUAL CONF THAT IF GOD WISHED TO HAVE HIS TRUTH TAUGHT IN THE WORLD, HE WOULD CERTAINLY SEND INFALLIBL HE HAS NOT DONE SO. THE TREASURE OF HIS TRUTH IS IN EARTHEN VESSELS, TO-DAY. HAS IT NOT ALW SO?

THE TROUBLE IN THIS WHOLE MATTER ARISES FROM THE FACT THAT MEN HAVE MADE UP THEIR THE THE BIBLE OUT OF THEIR IDEAS ABOUT GOD, AND HAVE THEN GONE TO WORK TO FIT THE FACTS OF THI THEIR PRECONCEIVED THEORIES. THIS HAS REQUIRED A GREAT DEAL OF STRETCHING AND TWISTING AN OFF HERE AND THERE; THE TRUTH HAS BEEN BADLY DISTORTED, SOMETIMES MUTILATED. THE CHANGE THE BIBLE, WHICH GREATLY ALARMS SOME GOOD PEOPLE, ARISES FROM THE FACT THAT CERTAIN HONEST M DETERMINED TO GO DIRECTLY TO THE BIBLE ITSELF AND FIND OUT BY STUDYING IT WHAT MANNER OF I THEY HAVE DISCOVERED THAT IT IS NOT PRECISELY SUCH A BOOK AS IT HAS BEEN BELIEVED TO BE, A ANSWER THAT THEY MAKE TO THOSE WHO HOLD THE OLD THEORY ABOUT IT IS SIMPLY THIS: "WE CANNO WHAT YOU HAVE TOLD US ABOUT THE BIBLE, BECAUSE THE BIBLE CONTRADICTS YOU. IT IS BECAUSE WE I THE BIBLE ITSELF THAT WE REJECT YOUR THEORY. WE BELIEVE THAT THE BIBLE IS AN INSPIRED BOOK, NA IS BY EMINENCE THE INSPIRED BOOK; BUT WHEN YOU ASK US 'WHAT IS AN INSPIRED BOOK?' INSTEA MAKING UP A DEFINITION OF INSPIRATION OUT OF OUR OWN HEADS, WE ONLY SAY, 'IT IS SUCH A BOOK BIBLE IS,' AND THEN WE PROCEED TO FRAME OUR DEFINITION OF INSPIRATION BY THE STUDY OF THI THEREFORE, WHEN YOU SAY THAT INSPIRATION MUST IMPLY INFALLIBILITY, WE ANSWER, NO; IT DOES N here is The Inspired Book and it is not infallible."

IN WHAT SENSE THE BOOK IS INSPIRED WE MAY BE ABLE, AFTER A LITTLE, TO SEE MORE CLEARLY. PRESENT I ONLY DESIRE TO POINT OUT THE SOURCES OF THE TRADITIONAL DOCTRINE OF THE BIBL SOURCES OF THE NEW DOCTRINE. THE ONE IS THE RESULT OF THE SPECULATIONS OF MEN ABOUT WHAT T must be; the other is the result of a careful and reverent study of the Bible itself.

What, then, do we find the Bible to be?

I. It is the book of righteousness. No other book in the world fixes our thoughts so upon the great interest of character. Whatever else the Bible may show us or may fail to sh does keep always before us the fact that the one great concern of every man is to be right and in life. Righteousness tendeth to life; righteousness is salvation; Jehovah is He who righteousness and hateth iniquity, and in his favor is life; these are the truths which form substance of this revelation. It is quite true that in the application of this principle to the every day, the early records show us much confusion and uncertainty; the definiti righteousness which sufficed for the people of that time would not suffice for us at all; bu remains that the only interest of this Book in the individuals and the races which it brings i is in their loyalty or disloyalty to that ideal of conduct which it always lifts up be Righteousness is life; righteousness is salvation; this is the one message of the Bible to men are rites and ceremonies, but these are not the principal thing; "To obey is better than sacri to hearken than the fat of rams." "He hath showed thee, O man, what is good; and what d Lord require of thee, but to do justly, and to love mercy, and to walk humbly with thy Go great truth of the Bible has been but imperfectly apprehended, even among modern Chi there is always a tendency to make the belief in sound dogma, or the performance of decor or the experience of emotional raptures the principal thing; but the testimony of the Bib supremacy of character and conduct is clear and convincing, and the world is coming to uni it.

Now for any man who cares for the right, to whom character is more precious than an else in the world, this book is worth more than any other book can be. Even the Old Te narratives, indistinctly as they reveal the real nature of true conduct to us in this day plainly the fact that nothing else in the world is to be compared with it; and the struc temptations of the heroes of that old book are full of instruction for us; their failures and sins admonish and warn us; their steadfastness and fidelity inspire and hearten us.

II. The Bible is the record of the development of the kingdom of righteousness in the Man knows intuitively that he ought to do right; his notion of what is right is continua purified and enlarged. The Bible is the record of this moral progress in the one nation of to which morality has been the great concern. We have seen, clearly enough, the imperfecti ethical standards to which the early Hebrew legislation was made to conform; we have a that this legislation was always a little in advance of the popular morality, leading it on conceptions and better practices. The legislation concerning divorce, the legislation blood-vengeance, recognizes the evils with which it deals and accommodates itself to th always with the purpose and the result of giving to men a larger thought and a better Laws which conformed to our moral ideal would have been powerless to control such a barbarous people as the Hebrews were when they came out of Egypt. The higher morality m imparted little by little; one principle after another must be drilled into their apprehen could not well be learning more than one or two simple lessons at a time, and while th learning these, other coarse and cruel and savage practices of theirs must be "winked at," says. Against any rule more strict at this early time the Hebrews would have revolted; th wisdom of this legislation is seen in this method which takes men as they are, and does for t thing that is feasible, patiently leading them on and up to higher ground. If you woul running horse by the rein and stop him, you had better run with him for a little. This parable illustrates much of the Old Testament legislation which we find so defective, whe by our standards.

It is in this larger sense that we see the signs of divinity in this old Book. It is a inspiration because it is the record of an inspired or divinely guided development; because th shows as unfolding is divine; because the goal to which we see the people steadily conducte vivid chapters is the goal which God has marked for human progress; because it gives us the and growth of the kingdom of God in the world.

"WHENCE CAME," ASKS ONE, "AND OF WHAT MANNER OF SPIRIT IS THIS *anti-historic* POWER IN ISRAEL ANE THE BIBLE? SOME INNER PRINCIPLE OF DEVELOPMENT STRUGGLES AGAINST THE OUTWARD HIS environment, and will not rest until it prevails. What was it which selected Israel, and in one narrow LAND, WHILE ALL THE SURROUNDING COUNTRY WAS SINKING, LIFTED MAN UP IN SPITE OF HIMSELF? WHIC THE COURSE OF ONE NATIONAL HISTORY CARRIED ON A PROGRESSIVE DEVELOPMENT OF RELIGIOUS LIFE A WHILE OTHER PEOPLES, THOUGH TAUGHT BY MANY WISE MEN AND SEERS, AND NOT WITHOUT THEIR TRU can show no one connected and progressive revelation like this?" [Footnote: *Old Faiths in New Light*, p. 81.]

WHAT IS THE POWER THAT HAS WROUGHT ALL THIS BUT THE DIVINE POWER? IF YOU ASK FOR A PROO EXISTENCE OF GOD, I POINT YOU TO THE LIFE OF THE JEWISH PEOPLE AS THE BIBLE RECORDS *That history is the revelation of God.* IN THE RECORD OF THIS NATION'S LIFE, IN ITS PRIVILEGES AND ITS VICISSITUE CAPTIVITIES AND ITS RESTORATIONS, ITS BLESSINGS AND ITS CHASTENINGS, ITS INSTITUTIONS AND ITS TEACHERS AND ITS LEGISLATORS, ITS SEERS AND ITS LAWGIVERS, IN ALL THE FORCES THAT COMBINE TO MA GREAT MOVEMENT OF THE NATIONAL LIFE, I SEE GOD PRESENT ALL THE WHILE, SHAPING THE ENDS OF TH NO MATTER HOW PERVERSELY IT MAY ROUGH-HEW THEM, TILL AT LAST IT STANDS ON AN ELEVATION FAR A OTHER NATIONS, BREATHING A BETTER ATMOSPHERE, THINKING WORTHIER AND MORE SPIRITUAL THO GOD, OBEYING A FAR PURER MORAL LAW, HOLDING FAST A NOBLER IDEAL OF RIGHTEOUSNESS,--POL GRADUALLY AND FINALLY ROOTED OUT OF THE NATIONAL CONSCIOUSNESS; THE FAMILY ESTABLISHED AN AS IN NO OTHER NATION; WOMAN LIFTED UP TO A DIGNITY AND PURITY KNOWN NOWHERE ELSE IN THE WC SABBATH OF REST SANCTIFIED; THE PRINCIPLES OF THE DECALOGUE FASTENED IN THE CONVICTIONS OF TH the sure foundations laid of the kingdom of God in the world.

WE ARE QUITE TOO APT UNDULY TO DISPARAGE JUDAISM. DOUBTLESS THE FORMALISM THAT OU FOUND IN IT NEEDED REBUKE; ITS WORSHIP AND ITS MORALITY WERE YET FAR AWAY FROM THE IDEAL WHE CAME TO EARTH; NEVERTHELESS, COMPARED WITH ALL THE PEOPLES ROUND ABOUT THEM EVEN THEN--CC WITH CLASSIC GREEKS AND NOBLE ROMANS--THE ETHICAL AND SPIRITUAL DEVELOPMENT OF THE JE REACHED A HIGHER STAGE. IT IS NOT EXTRAVAGANT TO CLAIM FOR THIS RACE THE MORAL LEADERSHIP OF T HEAR ERNEST RENAN, NO CHAMPION OF ORTHODOXY, AS YOU KNOW: "I AM EAGER, GENTLEMEN,"--I FROM A LECTURE OF HIS ON "THE SHARE OF THE SEMITIC PEOPLE IN THE HISTORY OF CIVILIZATION,"--" AT THE PRIME SERVICE WHICH THE SEMITIC RACE HAS RENDERED TO THE WORLD; ITS PECULIAR WC PROVIDENTIAL MISSION, IF I MAY SO EXPRESS MYSELF. WE OWE TO THE SEMITIC RACE NEITHER POLITICA ART, POETRY, PHILOSOPHY, NOR SCIENCE. *We owe to them religion.* THE WHOLE WORLD--WE EXCEPT INDI CHINA, JAPAN, AND TRIBES ALTOGETHER SAVAGE--*has adopted the Semitic religions."* SPEAKING THEN OF TH GRADUAL DECAY OF THE VARIOUS PAGAN FAITHS OF THE ARYAN RACES, RENAN CONTINUES: "IT IS PRECISEL EPOCH THAT THE CIVILIZED WORLD FINDS ITSELF FACE TO FACE WITH THE JEWISH FAITH. BASED UPON T AND SIMPLE DOGMA OF THE DIVINE UNITY, DISCARDING NATURALISM AND PANTHEISM BY THE MARVE TERSE PHRASE, 'IN THE BEGINNING GOD CREATED THE HEAVENS AND THE EARTH,' POSSESSING A LAW, A BC DEPOSITORY OF GRAND MORAL PRECEPTS AND OF AN ELEVATED RELIGIOUS POETRY, JUDAISM H INCONTESTABLE SUPERIORITY, AND IT MIGHT HAVE BEEN FORESEEN THEN THAT SOME DAY THE WORLI BECOME JEWISH, THAT IS TO SAY, WOULD FORSAKE THE OLD MYTHOLOGY FOR MONOTHEISM." [FOC *Religious History and Criticism,* pp. 159, 160.]

HERE IS THE TESTIMONY OF A MAN WHO CAN BE SUSPECTED OF NO UNDUE LEANINGS TOWARD THE R OF THE BIBLE, TO THE FACT THAT THE WORLD IS INDEBTED FOR ITS GREAT THOUGHTS OF RELIGION TO RACES, AND CHIEFLY TO THE HEBREW RACE; THAT THE RELIGION OF JUDAISM, BROUGHT INTO COMPARIS THE OTHER RELIGIONS, IS INCONTESTABLY SUPERIOR. NOW ANY MAN WHO BELIEVES IN RELIGION AND must believe that the people to whom such a task was committed must have been trained by God to PERFORM IT. THE HISTORY OF THIS NATION WILL THEN BE THE HISTORY OF THIS TRAINING. THAT IS EXA THE OLD TESTAMENT IS. NO DISPUTES OVER THE NATURE OF INSPIRATION MUST BE SUFFERED TO OBSCU GREAT FACT. THE OLD TESTAMENT SCRIPTURES DO CONTAIN IN BIOGRAPHY AND HISTORY, IN STATUTE A AND SONG AND SERMON, THE RECORDS OF THE LIFE OF THE NATION TO WHICH GOD AT SUNDRY TIME DIVERS MANNERS WAS REVEALING HIMSELF; WHICH HE WAS PREPARING TO BE THE BEARER OF THE TORCH OWN TRUTH INTO ALL THE WORLD. AND NOW I ASK WHETHER ANYBODY NEEDS TO BE TOLD THAT THES ARE PRECIOUS, PRECIOUS ABOVE ALL PRICE? ARE THERE ANY AUTHENTIC PORTIONS OF THEM THAT ANY M

AFFORD TO DESPISE? IS NOT EVERY STEP IN THE PROGRESS OF THIS PEOPLE OUT OF SAVAGERY INTO A SI FAITH, MATTER OF THE PROFOUNDEST INTEREST TO EVERY HUMAN SOUL? EVEN THE DULLNESS AND IGNOI CRUDITY OF THIS PEOPLE,--EVEN THE CROOKEDNESS AND BLINDNESS OF THEIR LEADERS AND TEACHERS, A INSTRUCTION FOR US; THEY SHOW US WITH WHAT MATERIALS AND WHAT INSTRUMENTS THE DIVINE WISD(PATIENCE WROUGHT OUT THIS GREAT RESULT. WHAT OTHER BOOK IS THERE THAT CAN COMPARE IN VALUE BOOK, WHICH TELLS US THE WAY OF GOD WITH THE PEOPLE WHOM HE CHOSE, AS RENAN DECLARES, TC THE WORLD RELIGION? AND WHEN ONE HAS FIRMLY GRASPED THIS GREAT FACT, THAT THE BIBLE CON HISTORY OF THE RELIGIOUS DEVELOPMENT OF THE JEWISH PEOPLE UNDER PROVIDENTIAL CARE AND TUITI LITTLE IS HE TROUBLED BY THE SMALL DIFFICULTIES WHICH GROW OUT OF THEORIES OF INSPIRATION! LISTEN," SAYS DR. NEWMAN SMYTH, "WITH INCURIOUS COMPLACENCY WHILE SMALL DISPUTANTS DI: VEHEMENTLY THE STORY OF THE ARK OR JONAH'S STRANGE ADVENTURE.... AFTER ALL THE WORK OF THE BIBLE STILL REMAINS, THE GREAT, SUBLIME, ENDURING WORK OF THE ETERNAL WHO LOVES RIGHTEOUS hates iniquity." [Footnote: *Old Faiths in New Light*, pp. 60, 61.]

BUT WHAT HAVE I BEEN VINDICATING? THE BIBLE? NAY, I HAVE CAREFULLY RESTRICTED MY ARGUM THE OLD TESTAMENT. IT IS IN BEHALF OF THE OLD TESTAMENT WRITINGS ALONE THAT I HAVE SC ESTABLISH THIS EXALTED CLAIM. WHAT I HAVE SHOWN YOU IS ONLY THE PEDESTAL ON WHICH THE BEAU STRENGTH OF THE BIBLE RESTS, THE ENDURING PORTALS WHICH OPEN INTO THE GLORY THAT EXCELLET TESTAMENT SHOWS US THE PROGRESSIVE REVELATION OF GOD TO THE JEWISH PEOPLE; THE NEW TEST GIVES US THE CONSUMMATION OF THAT WORK, THE PERFECT FLOWER OF THAT GROWTH OF CENTURI SHADOWS AND HINTS AND REFRACTED LIGHTS OF PROPHECY, BREAKS AT LAST UPON THE WORLD THE LI LIGHTETH EVERY MAN! WHEN THE FULLNESS OF TIME HAD COME, GOD SENT FORTH HIS SON. IT WAS FOR THE AGE-LONG DISCIPLINE OF THIS PEOPLE HAD BEEN PREPARING THEM. TRUE, "HE CAME TO HIS OWN THEY RECEIVED HIM NOT," BUT WHERE ELSE IN THE WORLD WOULD THE SEED OF HIS KINGDOM HAVE FOU LODGMENT AT ALL? THE MULTITUDE REJECTED HIM, BUT THERE WAS A REMNANT WHO DID RECEIVE HIM, WHOM HE GAVE POWER TO BECOME THE SONS OF GOD. SO THE WORD OF GOD, THAT HAD BEEN PAINFULI DIMLY COMMUNICATED TO THE ANCIENT PEOPLE IN LAWS AND ORDINANCES AND PROPHECIES, IN PROVID MERCIES AND CHASTENINGS, IN LIVES OF SAINTS AND PROPHETS AND MARTYRS, WAS NOW MADE FLESH, AND among men full of grace and truth, and they beheld his glory.

IT IS HERE THAT WE FIND THE REAL MEANING OF THE BIBLE. "THE END," AS CANON MOZLEY STRONGLY SHOWN, "IS THE TEST OF A PROGRESSIVE REVELATION." JESUS CHRIST, WHO IS HIMSELF THE TOWARD WHOM THESE LAWS AND PROPHECIES POINT, AND IN WHOM THEY CULMINATE, IS INDEED THE PI REVELATION OF GOD. FROM HIS JUDGMENT THERE IS NO APPEAL; AT HIS FEET THE WISEST OF US MUST LEARN THE WAY OF LIFE. WITH HIS WORDS ALL THESE OLD SCRIPTURES MUST BE COMPARED; SO FAR AS TH WITH HIS TEACHINGS WE MAY TAKE THEM AS ETERNAL TRUTH; THOSE PORTIONS OF THEM WHICH FALL BE STANDARD, WE MAY PASS BY AS A PARTIAL REVELATION UPON US NO LONGER BINDING. HE HIMSELF HAS GIV IN THE SERMON ON THE MOUNT, THE METHOD BY WHICH WE ARE TO TEST THE OLDER SCRIPTURES. W refuse to apply his method and go on to declare every portion of those old records authoritative, we ARE NOT HONORING HIM. THE MISCHIEF AND BANE OF THE TRADITIONAL THEORY IS THAT IT EQUALIZ WHICH ARE UTTERLY UNLIKE. WHEN IT SAYS THAT "ALL THE BOOKS OF THE SCRIPTURE ARE EQUALLY IN ALIKE ARE INFALLIBLE IN WHAT THEY TEACH," IT PUTS THE GOSPELS ON THE SAME LEVEL WITH DEUTERON ECCLESIASTES AND ESTHER. THE EFFECT OF THIS IS NOT TO LIFT THE LATTER UP, BUT TO DRAG THE FOF THEY ARE NOT ON THE SAME LEVEL; IT IS TREASON TO OUR MASTER CHRIST TO SAY THAT THEY ARE ALIK is as much higher than the other as the heavens are higher than the earth.

IT IS HERE, THEN, IN THE SIMPLE VERACIOUS RECORDS THAT BRING BEFORE US THE LIFE OF CHRIST, HAVE THE VERY WORD OF GOD. WHATEVER ELSE THE FOUR GOSPELS MAY OR MAY NOT BE, THEY CERTA CONTAIN THE STORY OF THE LIFE THAT HAS BEEN FOR MANY CENTURIES THE LIGHT AND THE HOPE OF TH is the same unique Person who stands before us in every one of these narratives,--

"So meek, forgiving, godlike, high,
So glorious in humility."

WHAT FAULT HAS CRITICISM TO FIND WITH THIS LIFE? WHAT WORD OR DEED IS HERE ASCRIBED TO H

IS NOT WORTHY OF HIM, THAT IS NOT LIKE HIM? IS IT ANY WONDER TO US WHEN WE READ THIS RECORD T THAT THE GUILELESS NATHANAEL CRIED OUT AS HE COMMUNED WITH HIM, "RABBI, THOU ART THE SON thou art the King of Israel."

IF, THEN, THE NEW TESTAMENT GIVES US THE ARTLESS RECORD OF THE LIFE AND WORDS OF TH PERSON, THE SON OF GOD AND THE SAVIOUR OF THE WORLD; IF IT BRINGS HIM BEFORE US AND MANIF US, SO FAR AS WORDS CAN DO IT, HIS POWER AND HIS GLORY; IF IT SHOWS US HOW, BY BEARING WITNESS T TRUTH IN HIS LIFE AND IN HIS DEATH, HE ESTABLISHED IN THE WORLD THE KINGDOM WHICH FOR LONG BEEN PREPARING; IF IT MAKES KNOWN TO US THE MESSAGES HE BROUGHT OF PARDON AND SALVATION; IF I US THE RECORD OF THE PLANTING AND TRAINING OF HIS CHURCH IN THE EARLY AGES, IS THERE ANY N SHOULD GO ABOUT TO PRAISE AND MAGNIFY ITS WORTH TO THE CHILDREN OF MEN? IF LIGHT IS WORTH TO THOSE WHO SIT IN DARKNESS, OR HOPE TO THOSE WHO ARE OPPRESSED WITH TORMENTING DOUBT; IF V IS TO BE DESIRED BY THOSE WHO ARE IN PERPLEXITY, AND COMFORT BY THOSE WHO ARE IN TROUBLE, AN BY THOSE WHOSE HEARTS ARE FULL OF STRIFE, AND FORGIVENESS BY THOSE WHO BEAR THE BURDEN (STRENGTH IS A GOOD GIFT TO THE WEAK, AND REST TO THE WEARY, AND HEAVEN TO THE DYING, AND T LIFE OF GOD TO THE FAINTING SOUL OF MAN, THEN THE BOOK THAT TELLS US OF JESUS CHRIST AND HIS IS NOT TO BE COMPARED WITH ANY OTHER BOOK ON EARTH FOR PRECIOUSNESS; IT IS THE ONE BOOK TH one of us ought to know by heart.

THE VALUE OF THE BIBLE, THE GREATNESS OF THE BIBLE, ARE IN THIS LIFE THAT IT DISCLOSES TO UPON JESUS," SAYS A MODERN RATIONALIST, "THAT THE WHOLE BIBLE TURNS. IN THIS LIES THE VALUE, NOT THE NEW TESTAMENT, A GREAT PART OF WHICH REFERS TO HIM DIRECTLY, BUT OF THE OLD TESTAMENT RATIONALIST THOUGH HE IS, NO MAN COULD HAVE STATED THE TRUTH MORE CLEARLY. "IT IS UPON JESUS WHOLE BIBLE TURNS." THE OLD TESTAMENT SHOWS US THE WAY PREPARING BY WHICH THE SWIFT FEET MESSENGERS APPROACH THAT TELL US OF HIS COMING; THE NEW TESTAMENT LIFTS THE VEIL AND I BEHOLD THE MAN! THE BIBLE IS OF VALUE TO US, JUST IN PROPORTION AS IT HELPS US TO SEE HIM, TO HIM, TO TRUST HIM. YOU MAY HAVE A CAST-IRON THEORY OF INSPIRATION WITH EVERY JOINT RIVETED; YC BELIEVE IN THE INFALLIBLE ACCURACY OF EVERY VOWEL POINT AND EVERY PUNCTUATION MARK; BUT IF TH DOES NOT BRING YOU INTO A VITAL UNION WITH JESUS CHRIST, SO THAT YOU HAVE HIS MIND AND FOLLOV FOOTSTEPS, IT PROFITETH YOU NOTHING. AND IF, BY YOUR STUDY OF IT, YOU ARE BROUGHT INTO TH fellowship, your theories of inspiration will take care of themselves.

I FEAR THAT WE DO NOT ALWAYS COMPREHEND THE FACT THAT IT IS THIS DIVINE LIFE SHINING OU PAGES THAT MAKES THE BIBLE GLORIOUS. WE STRAIN OUR EYES SO MUCH IN VERIFYING COMMAS, AND IN TO PROVE THAT THE DOT OF A CERTAIN I IS NOT A FLY-SPECK, THAT WE FAIL TO GET MUCH IMPRESSIO MEANING OR THE BEAUTY OF THE SAVIOUR'S LIFE. SEE THOSE TWO CRITICS, WITH THEIR EYES CLOSE WONDERFUL "ECCE HOMO" OF CORREGGIO, DISPUTING WHETHER THERE IS OR IS NOT A VISIBLE STITCI GARMENT OF CHRIST THAT OUGHT TO BE SEAMLESS. HOW RED THEIR FACES; HOW HOT THEIR WORDS! STA A LITTLE, BROTHERS! LOOK AWAY, FOR A MOMENT, FROM THE GARMENT'S SEAM; LET THE INFINITE PAIN INFINITE PITY AND THE INFINITE YEARNING OF THAT FACE DAWN ON YOU FOR A MOMENT, AND YOU WI YOUR QUARRELING. SO, NOT SELDOM, DO THE IDOLATERS OF THE LETTER WHOLLY MISS THE MEANING OF book, and remain in mournful ignorance of him who himself is the Word.

THERE ARE THOSE TO WHOM THE VIEW OF THE BIBLE PRESENTED IN THESE CHAPTERS SEEMS NC INADEQUATE BUT DESTRUCTIVE. "IF THE BIBLE IS NOT INFALLIBLE," THEY SAY, "IT IS NO MORE THAN AI BOOK; WE HAVE NO FURTHER USE FOR IT." IN ONE OF THE LEADING CHURCH REVIEWS I FIND THESE WO JOINT UTTERANCE OF TWO EMINENT AMERICAN THEOLOGIANS: "A PROVED ERROR IN SCRIPTURE CONTRA ONLY OUR DOCTRINE BUT THE SCRIPTURE'S CLAIMS, AND THEREFORE ITS INSPIRATION IN MAKING THOSE [FOOTNOTE*Presbyterian Review*, VOL. II. P. 245.] A PROVED ERROR IN SCRIPTURE STAMPS THE BOOK FRAUDULENT AND WORTHLESS! WORTHLESS IT IS THEN! PROVED ERRORS THERE ARE, SCORES OF THEM. IT IT IS IMBECILITY, TO DENY IT. AND EVERY MAN WHO CAN FIND AN ERROR IN THESE OLD WRITINGS WARRANT OF THESE TEACHERS FOR THROWING THE BOOK AWAY. TENS OF THOUSANDS OF INGENUOUS A MINDED MEN HAVE TAKEN THE WORD OF SUCH TEACHERS, AND HAVE THROWN THE BOOK AWAY. MAY forgive the folly of these blind guides!

BUT WHAT STUPID REASONING IS THIS! "IF THE BIBLE IS NOT INFALLIBLE, IT IS WORTHLESS." YOUR V NOT INFALLIBLE; IS IT THEREFORE WORTHLESS? YOUR PHYSICIAN IS NOT INFALLIBLE; ARE HIS SERVICES

WORTHLESS? YOUR FATHER IS NOT INFALLIBLE; ARE HIS COUNSELS WORTHLESS? WILL YOU SAY THAT THI YOU DISCOVER IN HIM AN ERROR CONCERNING ANY SUBJECT IN HEAVEN OR ON EARTH, THAT MOMENT Y REFUSE TO LISTEN TO HIS COUNSEL? THE CHURCH OF GOD IS NOT INFALLIBLE, AND NEVER WAS, W INFATUATED ECCLESIASTICS MAY HAVE CLAIMED FOR IT; ARE ITS SOLEMN SERVICES AND ITS INSPIRING LAB its uplifting fellowships worthless?

"A SHIP ON A LEE SHORE," SAYS ONE, "IN THE MIDST OF A DRIVING STORM, THROWS UP SIGNAL ROCK FIRES A GUN FOR A PILOT. A WHITE SAIL EMERGES FROM THE MIST; IT IS THE PILOT BOAT. A MAN CLI BOARD, AND THE CAPTAIN GIVES TO HIM THE COMMAND OF THE SHIP. ALL HIS ORDERS ARE OBEYED IMP THE SHIP, LADEN WITH A PRECIOUS CARGO AND HUNDREDS OF HUMAN LIVES, IS CONFIDED TO A ROUGH-L MAN WHOM NO ONE EVER SAW BEFORE, WHO IS TO GUIDE THEM THROUGH A NARROW CHANNEL, WHERE T A FEW FATHOMS TO THE RIGHT OR LEFT WILL BE UTTER DESTRUCTION. THE PILOT IS INVESTED WITH AUTHORITY AS REGARDS BRINGING THE VESSEL INTO PORT." [FOOTNOTE: *Orthodoxy; its Truths and Errors*, BY JAMES FREEMAN CLARKE, P. 114.] IS THIS BECAUSE THE MAN IS INFALLIBLE, BECAUSE HE HAS NEVER DETECTED IN HOLDING AN ERRONEOUS OPINION? DOUBTLESS ANY OF THESE INTELLIGENT PASSENGERS C OUT, BY HALF AN HOUR'S CONVERSATION WITH HIM, THAT HIS MIND WAS FULL OF CRASS IGNORAN MISCONCEPTION. AND NOBODY SUPPOSES THAT HE IS INFALLIBLE, EVEN AS A PILOT. HE MAY MAKE A MIS WHAT THEN? WILL THESE PASSENGERS GATHER AROUND THE CAPTAIN, AND DEMAND THAT HE BE ORDER FROM THE BRIDGE AND THROWN OVERBOARD IF HE DISOBEYS? WILL THEY SAY, "A PILOT WHO IS NOT SUBJECTS INFALLIBLE IS ONE WHOM WE WILL NOT TRUST?" NO; THEY BELIEVE HIM TO BE, NOT OMNISCIE COMPETENT AND TRUSTWORTHY, AND A GREAT BURDEN IS LIFTED FROM THEIR HEARTS WHEN THEY SEE COMMAND OF THE SHIP. ON ALL OTHER SUBJECTS BESIDES RELIGION, PEOPLE ARE ABLE TO EXERCIS COMMON SENSE; WHY CAN THEY NOT USE A MODICUM OF THE SAME COMMON SENSE WHEN THEY COM deal with religious truth?

IT IS NOT TRUE, AS A MATTER OF FACT, THAT THE BIBLE NO LONGER HAS ANY VALUE FOR THOSE CEASED TO HOLD THE TRADITIONAL VIEW OF IT. NOT SELDOM, INDEED, THOSE WHO HAVE BEEN COMPI OVERWHELMING EVIDENCE TO RELINQUISH THE TRADITIONAL VIEW HAVE BEEN DRIVEN BY THE NATURAL AGAINST IT TO UNDERVALUE THE BIBLE, AND EVEN TO TREAT IT WITH CONTEMPT AND BITTERNESS; BUT E OF THESE HAVE COME BACK TO IT AGAIN AND HAVE FOUND IN IT, WHEN THEY STUDIED IT WITH OPEN MORE TRUTH THAN THEY EVER BEFORE HAD KNOWN. LET ME CITE AN EXTREME CASE. I COULD TAKE SOCIETY OF FREE-THINKERS, CONSISTING OF PEOPLE WHO HAVE LONG BEEN OUTSPOKEN IN THEIR REJECTI THE DOCTRINES OF HISTORICAL CHRISTIANITY, MANY OF WHOM FORMERLY FLOUTED THE BIBLE AS A FABLES, BUT WHO ARE NOW STUDYING IT DILIGENTLY WEEK BY WEEK, IN THE MOST SYMPATHETIC SPIRIT. T NOT NOW ACCEPT ITS SUPERNATURALISM; BUT THEY BELIEVE THAT AS A MANUAL OF CONDUCT, AS A GUIDE IT EXCELS ALL OTHER BOOKS. THE YOUNG PEOPLE OF THEIR SUNDAY-SCHOOL ARE TOLD THAT THE BIBLE OTHER BOOKS; THAT THE MEN WHO WROTE IT KNEW MORE ABOUT THE HUMAN SOUL AND ITS STRUGGLE ASPIRATIONS AFTER GOOD THAN ANY OTHER MEN WHO EVER LIVED; AND THEY ARE BESOUGHT TO ATTE CAREFULLY, TO THE LESSONS OF LIFE WHICH THIS ANCIENT BOOK TEACHES. I SHOULD LIKE TO TAKE SO ULTRA ORTHODOX FRIENDS, WHO ARE PETTISHLY CRYING OUT THAT THE BIBLE, IF NOT INFALLIBLE, IS NOTHING, AND SET THEM DOWN FOR A SUNDAY OR TWO IN THE MIDST OF THIS FREE-THINKING SUNDAY they might learn some things about its value that they never knew before.

THIS INCIDENT OUGHT TO BE OF SERVICE, ALSO, TO THOSE WHO, HAVING DISCOVERED THAT TH CONTAINS HUMAN ELEMENTS, HAVE RUSHED TO THE CONCLUSION THAT IT IS NO MORE THAN ANY OTH AND WHO, ALTHOUGH THEY DO NOT CAST IT FROM THEM, HOLD IT OFF, AT ARM'S LENGTH, AS IT W MAINTAIN TOWARD IT AN ATTITUDE OF CRITICAL SUPERIORITY. EVEN THESE FREE-THINKERS TREAT IT M THEY ARE LEARNING TO APPROACH IT WITH OPEN MIND; THEY SIT DOWN BEFORE IT WITH REVERENT EXPI THE BIBLE HAS A RIGHT TO THIS SYMPATHETIC TREATMENT. IT IS NOT JUST LIKE OTHER BOOKS. DO NOT WORD FOR THIS; LISTEN RATHER TO THE TESTIMONY OF ONE WHO WAS KNOWN, WHILE HE WAS ALIVE, AS T heretic of New England:--

"THIS COLLECTION OF BOOKS HAS TAKEN SUCH A HOLD ON THE WORLD AS NO OTHER. THE LITEI GREECE, WHICH GOES UP LIKE INCENSE FROM THAT LAND OF TEMPLES AND HEROIC DEEDS, HAS NOT I INFLUENCE OF THIS BOOK, FROM A NATION ALIKE DESPISED IN ANCIENT AND IN MODERN TIMES. IT IS RE SABBATH IN ALL THE TEN THOUSAND PULPITS OF OUR LAND. IN ALL THE TEMPLES OF RELIGION IS ITS VC up week by week. The sun never sets on its gleaming page. It goes equally to the cottage of t man and the palace of the king. It is woven into the literature of the scholar, and colors t the street. The bark of the merchant cannot sail the sea without it; no ships of war g conflict, but the Bible is there. It enters men's closets; mingles in all their grief and cheef life. The affianced maiden prays God in Scripture for strength in her new duties; men are by Scripture. The Bible attends them in their sickness, when the fever of the world is on th aching head finds a softer pillow when the Bible lies underneath. The mariner escapin shipwreck clutches this first of his treasures and keeps it sacred to God. It goes with the pe his crowded pack; cheers him at eventide when he sits down dusty and fatigued; brighte freshness of his morning face. It blesses us when we are born, gives names to half Christe rejoices with us; has sympathy for our mourning; tempers our grief to finer issues. It is the part of our sermons. It lifts man above himself; our best of uttered prayers are in its storied wherewith our fathers and the patriarchs prayed. The timid man, about awaking from this dr life, looks through the glass of Scripture and his eye grows bright; he does not fear to st to tread the way unknown and distant, to take the death angel by the hand and bid farewe and babes and home. Men rest on this their dearest hopes; it tells them of God and of his Son, of earthly duties and of heavenly rest." [Footnote: Theodore Parker, *Discourses on Religion*.]

This is not mere rhetoric; it is simplest truth of human experience. How is it possible fo man to treat this book just as he would any other book? He ought to come to its perusal expectation of finding in it wisdom and light and life. He must not stultify his reason and moral sense when he reads it; he must keep his mind awake and his conscience active; but th treasure here if he will search for it; search he must, yet the only right attitude before i reverence and trust. Any man of ripe wisdom and high character, who has been known to your life, whose judgment you have verified, whose goodness you have witnessed and experie commands your respectful attention the moment he begins to speak. You do not believe him infallible, but you listen to what he says with trustfulness; you expect to find it true. To say listen to him as you do to every other man is not the fact; the posture of your mind in his p is different from that in which you stand before most other men. It ought to be. He has ga his probity, the power to speak to you with authority. The Bible has gained the same power. You do not use it fairly when you use it as you do every other book. There is the nation's flag proudly fly from the summit of the Capitol. It may be a banner that was borne upon the battlefield, de now with well-mended rents, and with stains of carnage. "Behold it!" cries the idolate absolutely faultless in perfection and beauty! There is not a blemish on its folds, there i imperfection in its web; every thread in warp and woof is flawless; every seam is absolutely st every star is geometrically accurate; every proportion is exact; the man who denies it is a traitor!"

"Absurd!" replies the iconoclast. "See the holes and the stains; there is not one straig there is not a star that is in perfect form; ravel it, and you will find no thread in warp or w is flawless; nay, you may even discover shreds of shoddy mixed with the fine fibre. Your f nothing more than any other old piece of bunting, and if you think it is, you are a fool."

Nay, good friends, you are both wrong. The blemishes are there; it would be fanatic deny them; and he who says that no man can be loyal to the nation who will not profess t banner is immaculate is setting up a fantastic standard of patriotism. But, on the other ha flag is something more than any other old piece of bunting, and he who thinks it something not a fool. It is the symbol of liberty; it is the emblem of sovereignty; it is the pledge of pr it is the sign and guarantee of justice and order and peace. What memories cluster roun dauntless heroism, and holy sacrifice, and noble consecration! What hopes are gleaming f stars and fluttering in its shining folds--hopes of a day when wars shall be no more and all shall be one brotherhood! The man to whom the flag of his country is no more than any other piece of weather-beaten bunting is a man without a country.

Is not my parable already interpreted? Are not the idolaters who make it treason to d a single word of the Bible, and the iconoclasts who treat it as nothing better than any o equally far from the truth? Is it not the part of wisdom to use the book rationally, but revi

REFRAIN FROM WORSHIPING THE LETTER, BUT TO REJOICE IN THE GIFTS OF THE SPIRIT WHICH IT PROF
SAME DIVINE INFLUENCE WHICH ILLUMINES AND SANCTIFIES ITS PAGES IS WAITING TO ENLIGHTEN OUR MIN
WE MAY COMPREHEND ITS WORDS, AND TO PREPARE OUR HEARTS THAT WE MAY RECEIVE ITS MESSAGES. S
THINGS HARD TO UNDERSTAND ARE HERE, BUT THE SPIRIT OF TRUTH CAN MAKE PLAIN TO US ALL THAT W
KNOW. NO MAN WISELY OPENS THE BOOK WHO DOES NOT FIRST LIFT UP HIS HEART FOR HELP TO FIND IN
way of life, and to him who studies it in this spirit it will show the salvation of God.

Lightning Source UK Ltd.
Milton Keynes UK
UKHW030635210219
337759UK00004B/558/P